ELVIS

Word for Word

ELVIS

Word for Word

Jerry Osborne

Harmony Books
New York

Published by Harmony Books, New York, New York
Member of the Crown Publishing Group
Random House, Inc. New York, Toronto, London, Sydney, Auckland
www.randomhouse.com

Originally published, in different form, by Osborne Enterprises Publishing in 1999.

HARMONY BOOKS is a registered trademark and Harmony Books' colophon is a trademark of Random House, Inc.

Printed in the United States of America

Design by Kay Schuckhart/Blond on Pond

Library of Congress Cataloging-in-Publication Data
Osborne, Jerry.
Elvis: word for word / by Jerry Osborne.
Includes index.
1. Presley, Elvis, 1935–1977—Interviews. 2. Presley, Elvis,
1935–1977—Correspondence. 3. Rock musicians—United States—Biography. I. Title.
ML420.P96 O83 2000
782.42166'092—dc21
[B]   00-038479

ISBN 0-609-60803-7

10 9 8 7 6 5 4 3 2 1

First Revised Edition

Acknowledgments

Between the moment of conception and actual printing of *Elvis—Word for Word,* many a helpful hand has been involved.

Among our associates and contributors on this project are a few who deserve an extra-special thank-you. They are: Jean-Marc Gargiulo, for analyzing dozens of concerts and interviews and supplying audiotapes of them, as well as for providing many of our photographs; Bill E. Burk, for excellent research assistance on numerous Memphis-related questions; Bob Williams, for the 1956 photo on our front cover; Mary Hancock Hinds, for ceaseless communications support; Judith M. Ihnken Ebner, for invaluable editorial and trivia assistance; and of course, Tim Robinson, for the original idea.

In addition, information and effort supplied by the people whose names appear below was also of great importance. To these good folks, our deepest gratitude is extended. Their contributions varied, but without each and every one of them this book would have been far less worthy.

Here then, alphabetically listed, are the contributors to *Elvis—Word for Word.*

Bob Alaniz
Carol Alaniz
Patsy Andersen
Pam Arveson
Gord Atkinson
Steven Banas
Howard F. Banney
Luca Barbonaglia
Tina Barbonaglia
Kelly Bart
Randy Bart
Jocelyne Bellanger
Steve Binder
Carlyle Bishop
Karine Blanc
Jean Blankenship
Ed Bonja
Bobbie Burchfield Briggs
Denise Brown
Jack Brown
Pat Brown
Bill E. Burk
James Burton

Shirley Bustos
Carol F. Butler
Sebastiano Cecere
Knox Christie
Lorena Christie
Howard Cockburn
Arlene Cogan
Rich Consola
Lee Cotton
Perry Cox
Rabia Cros
Judy Davis
Chuck Dawson
Devon Dawson
Pat Doan
Lauren Dong
Judith M. Ihnken Ebner
Joe Esposito
Eddie Fadal
Lou Faulkner
Larry Flusser
D. J. Fontana
Alan Fortas

Lynn Free
Arnie Ganem
Jean-Marc Gargiulo
Phil Gelormine
Jim Gibbons
Randy Ladenheim-Gil
Nöel Giulini
Bob Grow
Janice Grow
Debbie Hall
Eddie Hammer
Sherif Hanna
Betty Harper
Andrew Hearn
Kelly C. Hill
Charlotte Boyd Hilliard
Mary Hancock Hinds
Charlie Hodge
Larry Holloway
Pauline Hubbard
Keith Huotari
Ginger Jacobson
Paul Jacobson

Sheila James
Terry Mike Jeffrey
Craig Johnson
Teryn Johnson
Jackie Kahane
Diane Ketchem
Tony Kolodziej
Tracy Kolodziej
Marty Lacker
Darwin Lamm
Rich Little
René Lucas
Dan Martin
Fred Martin
Jeanne Martin
Sandra Martindale
Wink Martindale
Mark McCauslin
Mike McGregor
Nick Molina
Scotty Moore
Todd Morgan
Andrzej Mrozowski

Julie Mundy
Linda Natali
Diana Nartowicz
Linda Ann Osborne
Rodger Osborne
Laura Paczosa
Sam Phillips
Stephen Pounder
Chester Prudhomme
Augusta Pumilia

Reidling, Andy
Eileen Robinson
Tim Robinson
Mike Rosa
Robin Rosaaen
Pam Ross
Pam Ruffner
Kay Schuckhart
Tom Schultheiss
Billy Smith

Jeff Stark
Maria Stark
Carlo Steven
Jeffrey L. Stolper
Mary Stonebraker
Brenda Tall
John Tefteller
Carrie D. Thornton
Alex Ward
Jan Warner

Jim Warner
Red West
Sonny West
Kathy Westmoreland
Joel Whitburn
Marjorie Wilkinson
Anita Wood Brewer
Carole Eversole Yates
Stephen Yates
Sally Yeagley

Jerry Osborne wishes to thank Elvis's longtime girlfriend Anita Wood, pictured here in August 2000 with the author in Memphis, Tennessee. Her help in the creation of this book is greatly appreciated.

Introduction

Maybe someday I will write a book...
—*Elvis Presley, March 1960*

Elvis Presley spoke these seven words in response to a reporter's question about his two-year Army hitch. Unfortunately, during his mere seventeen years of life following that comment, Elvis never did get around to writing a book—whether about Army experiences, or one of an autobiographical nature.

Fortunately, Elvis spent a great deal of his career in front of a microphone, willingly discussing countless topics. Thanks to those recorded interviews, along with many of his writings, his dream book now exists.

Elvis' own words provide the only material necessary for us to observe his life and career like never before—viewed from his distinctive perspective.

Elvis—Word for Word now stands unparalleled in the world of Presley literature. It is the closest anyone will ever get to reading the personal thoughts and feelings of Elvis Presley.

For this project, verification of the material became our prime directive. Except for a few interview transcripts, provided by reliable sources (identified as "Document transcript"), if we could not verify the words attributed to Elvis, they do not appear in this book.

Taking this mandate one level higher, there are, for example, things Elvis said to me during our visits that need no verification as far as I am concerned. Likewise, we know that Sam Phillips, Joe Esposito, D. J. Fontana, Scotty Moore, Charlie Hodge, and others who worked with Elvis have excellent recall of many of his comments. Technically, though, any "he told me" or "he once said" claims not supported by some type of audio, video, or printed backup is hearsay.

Since *Elvis—Word for Word* is not a collection of anyone's personal memoirs and recollections, and in keeping with our steadfast rule against hearsay, we use no citations of what someone—even including this writer—claims Elvis once said.

For each of the more than three hundred entries in *Elvis—Word for Word,* a source is given. Many are records and CDs commercially available. Others, especially of 1970s concerts, are audiotapes made by people in the audience. To ensure gathering as many interesting comments from the concert years as possible, our team listened to recordings of over one hundred Presley shows.

Knowingly altering Elvis' words or intent has been expressly forbidden. The only editing acceptable in *Elvis—Word for Word* is of a very minor nature, such as the deletion of stuttering and other meaningless incidents of spoken debris.

Occasionally, reading Elvis' own words can settle a dispute and set the record straight. Compare the supposed transcript, printed in *Elvis, What Happened?,* of a 1976 phone conversation with Red West, with the actual conversation printed here. In this egregious example, Elvis' words—or ones wrongfully attributed to him—are shamelessly presented to cast Elvis in an unfavorable light. Ironically, it is *Elvis, What Happened?* co-collaborator, Red West, who made the actual audiotape of that call available, for which we thank him.

Some lucky individuals who own letters "from Elvis" that are signed "Elvis Presley" may be dispirited to suddenly learn that someone other than Elvis did the writing and the signing. As you will see in this book, Elvis personally wrote very, very few of the countless letters bearing his name. His handwriting is markedly different from what is found on most fan response mail, nearly all of which is clearly written by a woman.

This should surprise no one, for during his life he received millions of letters. To reply personally to even a fraction of them would have been impossible, given the demands of his career. In some of his early interviews, he even refers to a team of people whose job it was to do nothing but answer fan mail.

As with many a businessperson, it is *possible* that he asked an employee to respond on his behalf, perhaps even dictating the essence of a letter now and then. However, it is more likely that mail of this type was handled by a staff person as a matter of routine.

We have tried to identify and differentiate between his writing and that of others; however, we make no guarantees in this regard. We are not in the field of grapho analysis, nor did we consult with anyone in that practice. On the other hand, we probably do have more examples of his writing, with which to compare, than anyone.

When stating a document is "written and signed by a member of the Presley staff" (including those on Colonel Parker's team), we are not declaring in absolute terms that Elvis had absolutely nothing to do with said document. Whether he did or not will, in most cases, never be known for certain.

For that reason, documents not actually written by him, but bearing his name, qualify as legitimate Elvis memorabilia, and rightfully so. They are traded regularly in the collectibles marketplace, and are always described as "a letter from Elvis Presley." In fact, until publication of *Elvis—Word for Word,* most people had no way of knowing the actual writer of their correspondence and had no basis for comparing writing styles.

Obviously, those letters determined to be written personally by Elvis are considerably more sought-after.

Now some *Elvis—Word for Word* format tips:

The layout of events and interviews is strictly chronological. When available, other details about the event are given, such as location and the names of other people involved.

Text attributed to Elvis Presley is always shown in italics.

Questions or comments by the media are in boldface type. In every case where known, the identity of those speaking with Elvis is given.

We have tried to limit editorial comments; however, when a helpful note or explanatory comment is appropriate, it appears in brackets. Also found in brackets is any supplemental information, such as the last name of someone about whom Elvis refers to only by first name.

To quickly locate anything in *Elvis—Word for Word* by name or subject, simply refer to the index, which we are proud to say is very comprehensive.

And so it is that Elvis Presley never wrote a book—though many, many others certainly have. As of this writing there are more than 1,500 Elvis books, magazines, and major literary pieces known to us, and many others we have yet to discover.

Seemingly every imaginable Presley topic has been investigated, contemplated, and gathered together in print. His life story has been told numerous times, each version a little different.

All those books, but not once has Elvis really had his say.

Now he does and you will read it here, exactly as he shared it…word for word.

—*Jerry Osborne*

ELVIS

Word for Word

LOCATION: *Shreveport, Louisiana. "Louisiana Hayride" Stage Show (and broadcast on KWKH radio).*
EMCEE: *Frank Page.*
SOURCE: *"Elvis on the Louisiana Hayride" (45).*

[Frank Page] He's only nineteen years old. He has a new, distinctive style—Elvis Presley. Let's give him a nice hand. We've been singing your songs around here for weeks and weeks and weeks. Elvis, how are you this evening?
Just fine. How're you, sir?

[F.P.] You all geared-up with your band there...
We're all geared-up.

[F.P.]...to let us hear your songs?
Well I'd like to say how happy we are to be down here. It's a real honor for us to get a chance to appear on the Louisiana Hayride. We're gonna do a song for ya...you got anything else to say, sir?

[F.P.] No, I'm ready.
We're gonna do a song for ya, we got on Sun record, it goes somethin' like this [sings "That's All Right"].

[F.P.] I'd like to know just how you derived that style; how you came about with that rhythm and blues style? That's all it is, that's all you can say.
Well sir, to be honest with you, we just stumbled upon it. I mean we were...

[F.P.] Just stumbled upon it.
Stumbled upon it.

[F.P.] Well you're mighty lucky.
Thank you.

[F.P.] They've been looking for something new in the folk music field for a long time, and I think you've got it.
We hope so.

[F.P.] Alright, how about flippin' the record over there, that Sun recording, and doing the other side for us?
[Sings "Blue Moon of Kentucky."]

With Texas Bill Strength, 1955.

ITEM: *Telegram from Elvis Presley (Houston, Texas) to Vernon Presley (Memphis, Tennessee).*
SOURCE: *Original document.*

Hi Babies.
Here's the money to pay the bills. Don't tell no one how much I sent. I will send more next week. There's a card in the mail.
Love,
Elvis

1955

LOCATION: *Jacksonville, Florida.*
INTERVIEWER: *Mae Axton.*
SOURCE: Elvis Answers Back, Vol. 1 *(CD).*

[Mae Axton] Elvis, you are a sort of a bebop artist more than anything else, aren't ya? Is that what they'd call you?
Well I never have given myself a name but a lot of the disc jockeys call me Boppin' Hillbilly and Be-Bop...I don't know what all.

[M.A.] Sort of a combination of things. You've covered a lot of territory in the last few months, I believe?
Yes ma'am, I've covered a lot, mostly in west Texas is where my records are hottest.

[M.A.] Uh-huh.
Down in San Angelo, and Lubbock, and Midland, Amarillo.

[M.A.] They tell me that they almost mob you there, the teenagers, they like you so much. But do you know I happen to know that you have toured all down in the eastern part of the coun-try too. Down through Florida and around, and that the people went for you there about as well as out in west Texas. Isn't that right?
Well I wasn't very well known down here, I mean, I was with a small company and my records don't have the distribution that they should have, but...

[M.A.] Oh, of course, that's coming. You know it takes a little bit of time for that. And I noticed that the older people got about as big a kick out of you as the teenagers. I thought that was an amazing thing.
(Laughs.) Well I imagine it's the way we...all three of us move on stage. We act like we just...

[M.A.] Yes, and we mustn't leave out Scotty [Moore] and Bill [Black] who really do a terrific job in backin' you up.
Well they sure do. I really am lucky to have those two boys 'cause they really good. Each one of 'em has an individual style of his own and...

[M.A.] You started back in high school didn't you?
Ah.

[M.A.] Singing for public performances for school and things of that sort?
Well, no ma'am. I never did sing anywhere in public anywhere in my life 'til I made this first record.

[M.A.] Is that right? And then you just went right on and into their hearts and you're doing a wonderful job and I want to congratulate you on that. And I wanted to say, too, Elvis, it's been very nice having you in the studio today.
Well, thank you very much, Mae, and I'd like to personally thank you for really promoting my records down here because you really have done a wonderful job and I really do appreciate it, because if you don't have people backin' you, people pushin' you, well you might as well quit.

With Mae Axton, co-writer of "Heartbreak Hotel," 1956.

LOCATION: *WMPS radio, Memphis, Tennessee.*
INTERVIEWER: *Bob Neal.*
SOURCE: Eternal Elvis *(LP).*

[Bob Neal] Scotty Moore, come over here and say howdy to all your friends in Texarkana, will ya?

[Scotty Moore] Howdy! Say hello to all the fine folks down in Texarkana.

[B.N.] I said that before. Now you go ahead and say somethin' new.

[S.M.] Well, we wanna invite everybody out to the show Friday night. And we're gonna have two shows, at seven and nine. And they've all been askin' about the drummer that we had up there last time, D. J. Fontana. And he's gonna be with us. He's a regular member of our band now and he'll be there with us Friday night, along with Floyd Cramer and Jimmy Day, and the Louisiana Hayride band. And, of course, all of us.

[B.N.] Yeah, that'll provide a whole lot o' pickin' and all those numbers that folks like to hear so well, like "Baby, Let's Play House" and "I Forgot to Remember [To Forget]." Might even find "Maybellene" along the line there someplace. Tell you what, before we call over some other folks here to talk…Elvis Presley, how're you doing?
Fine, Bobert. How're you getting' along?

[B.N.] Oh, doin' grand. I know all the folks down in Texarkana been raisin' such a hoop and a holler for you to come down and hoop and holler at 'em. And we got this great big double show scheduled for Friday night [September 2] at the auditorium down there. What'dya think about it?
Well Bob, I been just as anxious to come back as I could be. We've been…I think this makes about the fourth or fifth time we've been to Texarkana. And we've been lucky, every time we've gone back the crowd has increased a little bit, and we really been proud of that 'cause it's kinda unusual, you know.

With Col. Parker, Gladys and Vernon Presley, Colman Tilly, Bob Neal, 1956.

With Johnny
Cash,
Nashville,
1957.

[B.N.] Well it's been about four months now since the last time you were in Texarkana [April 1955]. And aside from that, we've got some extra fine entertainers to take along. I'd like to mention this boy, Johnny Cash, from Memphis, who wrote and recorded "Cry Cry Cry" and "Hey Porter." Johnny is a swell young fellow and I know everybody is going to want to watch him work and see him on the big show. And you worked with Charlene Arthur, from the Big "D," haven't you?

I've worked with Charlene quite a bit, and she's one of the finest entertainers on stage I've ever seen.

[B.N.] Her new record of "Kiss the Baby Goodnight" is sure a hot one too.

Well, I don't know about "Kiss the Baby Goodnight," but uh…

[B.N.] (Laughs.)

In all seriousness, Bob, I think this is 'bout the best one that we've brought to Texarkana, so far. 'Cause I don't know if any of these people ever been up that way or not. Charlene Arthur and uh…and uh…what's it…Johnny Cash.

Radio station
interview,
Memphis,
1955.

[B.N.] None of them have ever appeared in Texarkana.

I don't think they've ever appeared in Texarkana. And we're gonna look forward… we got two shows, one at seven and one at nine, right?

[B.N.] Cor-rect. I guess one of the noisest guys in all this outfit is Bill Black, who thumps on the bass and occasionally tells a story or two, and just in general messes things up. Bill, come over and say howdy to your fans in Texarkana (laughs).

[Bill Black] Bob, I just wanted to say one thing, that Friday night we be down there, and I'll have a brand, spankin' new pose of Elvis for a picture. And they'll be sellin' the same ol' price of only a quarter. And I'll have about four or five million of 'em, but if anybody'd like to have just one, why I'll have plenty of 'em. Before the show, durin' the intermission, after the show, and fact is I might sell 'em out there all night long if [there's anyone] anywhere around. That's all I got to say.

[B.N.] (Laughs.) That's all you got to say. You're gonna save the rest of it for Friday night, huh. Well neighbors, like we mentioned, we're all excited about the big double show in Texarkana Friday night. And I'm gonna be there too, and you can look out for me, and get ready to buy me a hot dog or somethin' like that. We're gonna have such a big time though, with stars like Charlene Arthur, Johnny Cash…Johnny may be kinda new to the folks down around Texarkana, but after you see him and hear him I know you're gonna like him. And of course, the King of Western Bop, Elvis Presley, will be there doin' all of those numbers with the big Louisiana Hayride gang. So, Elvis, before we wind up this little session of talkin' and so forth, why don'cha greet the friends down in Texarkana once more and invite 'em to the show.

Candid, 1955.

Bob, I think you've just about covered everything, exceptin' we've got lots of friends in Texarkana. The few times we've down there we've really made a lot of friends. But I would like to invite everybody out Friday night to see our big show, 'cause I don't know when we'll be comin' back that way. We're goin' on tour out on the West Coast, and Canada, and a lot of places, and probably it's gonna be a pretty long while before we can come back to Texarkana. We'll be lookin' forward to a good crowd.

[B.N.] Yes sir, I doubt frankly whether we'll be able to get back to Texarkana this year, but we wanna see everybody at the big shows Friday night. Remember now, there are two shows, seven and nine o'clock at the Arkansas Municipal Auditorium. If you can't get there for the first one, well, come for the second one. And, if you want to, stay and see 'em both. I

1956

know that you'll see a real terrific show, with Charlene Arthur, Johnny Cash, Elvis Presley, Scotty and Bill, all the gang.

[B.N.] This is Bob Neal, who's been talkin' with Scotty Moore, Bill Black, and Elvis Presley. We want to thank you for lettin' us do a little speakin', and we'll see you for the big one, Friday night.

With J. D. Sumner, Blackwood Brothers, Memphis, 1955.

JANUARY 1956

INTERVIEWER: *Don Davis.*
SOURCE: *Gruen Watch Company "Time Hill Frolic" sponsored radio feature (LP).*
  [Exact date of this recording not known, though it may have been late December 1955 or very early '56. Either way, it actually aired in early January 1956.]

Opening Music: "Blue Moon of Kentucky."

[Don Davis] Who's that man singin' there? Who is that man? Why, of course, it's Elvis Presley and that was the beginning. Elvis Presley, welcome to the show.
Thank you very much, Don. It's really a pleasure to be here.

[D.D.] Elvis, that was the beginning of this great career that you're building for yourself, wasn't it?
That's right. It all started out real quick like, just like that.

[D.D.] Uh-huh. Just shooting right up into stardom. Well c'mon, right into the microphone, buddy, and tell us just where that session was held.
Well, it was held in Memphis, Tennessee, about three blocks from my home, in a recording studio, and I just walked in just by accident and oh, boom!

[D.D.] And there you were huh? Who were the boys on the session with you?
Scotty Moore and Bill Black.

[D.D.] Just a trio makin' all that music?
That's right. Well, actually there's only two. See, I'm just singin', I'm not…I play the guitar but they don't record it.

[D.D.] Elvis, I understand that this sound that you get on record was really a mistake, or at least was kind of a gimmick thing at first. Is that true?
That's right. We just more or less landed upon it accidentally.

[D.D.] Uh-huh.
Nobody knew what they were doin' until we had already done it.

Don Davis interviews Elvis, 1956.

In concert, with Bill Black on bass, 1956.

[D.D.] And the folks all over the country are talking about that sound, and you haven't changed it of course, now have you?
No, I'm still staying with the same pattern.

[D.D.] Uh-huh. Then didn't [RCA Victor's] Mr. Steve Sholes and Mr. Chuck Crumbacker come along and hear some of your singing and have you switch over to one of the big record companies?
That's right. I met Mr. Chuck Crumbacker down in Meridian, Mississippi, at Jimmy Rodgers Memorial Day [May 25, 1955].

[D.D.] Isn't it true that Chuck Crumbacker saw you in a very, uh, sort of conservative outfit down there and told you you're just gonna have to wear louder clothes? Is that true?
Yes sir. He, uh, I was wearing a pink suit.

[D.D.] A pink suit? Very conservative.
Very conservative, pink suit. And he told me I was goin' to have to get something a little louder. He said "you can't see that thing."

[D.D.] What happened when you wore that pink suit in Jacksonville, Florida [May 13, 1955]…as if I didn't know?

[D.D.] Just got in there and had yourself a really good time and the folks took to it.
Just had a ball. And it kind of…it surprised me 'cause it went over very well.

With Steve Sholes and a goateed Col. Parker, 1956.

Well, it was kind of eliminated from me.

[D.D.] I know. Well I'll just tell the folks in case you're a little too modest about it. The folks just went so crazy over Elvis' singing that as soon as he tried to get down off the stage they disrobed the lad, cut it up into two-inch squares and everybody took home a sample. And he no longer has a pink suit. So you had to substitute something pink in your wardrobe… and then you got a car.

Well you can't put the car in a wardrobe, but I had the car even before I got the suit.

[D.D.] Oh you did? So you bought the suit to match the car?

That's right. I kinda thought that would be a gimmick and really, it drew a lot of attention in the trade papers, about the pink suit and the pink car. But I've kinda slacked off on the pink now because I think the color is changing to purple or something.

[D.D.] Well, you certainly live it up on those personal appearances and I know that the folks listening in to the program will want to get out and see Elvis Presley and the grand show, whenever it comes around to their neighborhood. In fact, go on out and see all these live country music entertainers because there's nothing like a live show. I keep sayin' that.
Yeah.

[D.D.] I know that the response has been so tremendous that there's just not gonna be any stoppin' this Elvis Presley boy, and all the folks are going to be hearing a lot more information from him. And of course they're going to be hearing, right here on the show, all of your latest recordings as they come out. Elvis, I want to thank you very much for dropping by the show.
Don, it was really a pleasure and I sure appreciated your spins on my records.

[D.D.] Thanks again, Elvis, and drop around real soon.

Thank you very much.

[D.D.] This young fellow, Elvis Presley, is proof of the old saying that if you've got something different, something good, folks will buy it. And man, he's got it! On stage, he's six-foot of spring steel who really knows how to sell a song. I know lots of fellows say "oh nothing like that'll ever happen to me." Well buddy boy, you just keep a tryin'. It's happening every year. Thank you very much, Elvis Presley, for droppin' by.

JANUARY 17, 1956

ITEM: *Handwritten letter. From Elvis Presley (Memphis, Tennessee) to Sarah Anglin (Hermaville, Mississippi).*
SOURCE: *Document photocopy.*

> *[Envelope has a January 25 Memphis postmark. Letterhead reads "Elvis Presley Fan Club, National Headquarters, 160 Union St.," then the location of WMPS radio where Bob Neal deejayed.]*

> *Dear Sarah,*
> *Glad you like my singing. I don't [know] for sure [if] I'll be on the [Louisiana] Hayride the 21st but I'll try to make it. Sorry I can't send you a free picture but I have to charge 25¢ apiece or get stuck with the cost of the pictures. When we get some in I'll tell Bob [Neal] to keep an eye out for your quarter and put a picture aside so I can personally autograph and mail it to you.*
> *Have loads and loads of mail to answer so… bye for now.*
>
> *Elvis Presley*

JANUARY 18, 1956

ITEM: *Handwritten letter. From Elvis Presley (Memphis, Tennessee) to "Caroline" (Chattanooga, Tennessee).*
SOURCE: *Document photocopy.*

ELVIS PRESLEY FAN CLUB

NATIONAL HEADQUARTERS

60 UNION, MEMPHIS, TENN.

January 17, 1956.

Dear Sarah

Glad you like my singing I don't for sure I'll be on the Hayride the 27st but I'll try to make it Sorry I can't send a free picture but I have to charge 25¢ apiece or get stuck with the cost of the pictures When we get some in I'll tell Bob to keep an eye out for your quarter and put a picture aside so I can personally autograph and mail it to you. Have loads and loads mail to answer so bye for now

Elvis Presley

Letter to a fan, 1956.

[Letterhead reads "Elvis Presley Fan Club, National Headquarters, 160 Union St.," then the location of WMPS radio where Bob Neal deejayed.]

Hello Caroline,
Thanks loads for your flattering letter. I've just come back from cutting my next record in Nashville [January 10]. It will be released Jan. 30th [actually issued January 27th] after my first appearance on Jackie Gleason's TV show, the 28th. I'll probably sing one side of the new release then. I don't think Bob has me booked for Grand Ole Opry for a long time yet. If you'll send 25¢ I'll be glad to autograph and mail you a picture as soon as a fresh supply arrives. Have lots of mail to answer so—bye for now.

Elvis Presley

MARCH 17, 1956

LOCATION: *CBS Studios, New York, New York.*
EVENT: *"Stage Show, Starring Those Fabulous Dorseys, Tommy and Jimmy, with Special Guest, Elvis O'Presley."*
SOURCE: *Videotape.*
  [Billing Elvis as "O'Presley," is, of course, a bit of St. Patrick's Day tomfoolery.]

Thank you very much ladies and gentlemen, that ["Blue Suede Shoes"] was my latest RCA

**"Get well"
telegram to Carl
Perkins, 1956.**

escape…er, release. We have another one here…
we have another song here, friends, that we
hope you like. It's called "Heartbreak Hotel."
   [In this performance, Elvis modifies "so lonely
they could die" to "so lonely they pray to die."]

MARCH 23, 1956

ITEM: *Telegram from Elvis Presley (Richmond,
Virginia) to Carl Perkins (General Hospital,
Dover, Delaware).*
SOURCE: *Document photocopy.*

*We were all shocked and very sorry to hear of
the accident. I know what it is for I had a
few bad ones myself. If I can help you in
any way please call me. I will be at the
Warwick Hotel in New York City.
Our wishes are for a speedy recovery for you
and for the other boys.*

Sincerely,
Alvis [sic] Presley, Bill Black,
Scotty Moore and D. J. Fontana.
[Presley's first name is indeed shown as "Alvis."]

MARCH 24, 1956

LOCATION: *Warwick Hotel, New York, New
York.*
INTERVIEWER: *Robert Carlton Brown.*
SOURCE: Personally Elvis *(LP).*

**[Robert Carlton Brown] Elvis, how do you
feel?**
Well I feel real good.

**[R.C.B.] Well, how about that recording you
went to make for your mother? Is that the way
it happened?**
Yes, that's exactly the way it all started.

**[R.C.B.] What was it gonna be of? What
record were you gonna make?**
*Oh I made the record. In fact, we still got the
record at home. It's so thin we can't play it. But
the record I made was "My Happiness," and
then one of the Ink Spots numbers ["That's
When Your Heartaches Begin"].*

**[R.C.B.] Was this for a birthday present for
your mother?**

I just made one…I did it…you see I worked five days a week, Monday through Friday, and then on Saturday I called this recording company [Memphis Recording Service] up and I asked if they could make me a record. You know, they make personal dubs for people, for weddings and things like that.

[R.C.B.] I mean, was it for any special occasion?
Nah, nah, nothing. I just made it. I just recorded it.

[R.C.B.] Well, when was it your mother found out?
Well I made it to surprise her. When she played it, it was me singing, and she didn't…

[R.C.B.] Well, had you done much singing around before that?
No, I never did sing that much in my life. The only time I ever sung maybe was in a little variety show at school…maybe once every couple of years.

[R.C.B.] Did you have your guitar with you on this record?
Yes, I had an old twenty-dollar guitar, sounded like somebody beatin' on a bucket maybe, or something.

[R.C.B.] Did you do anything more with electricity?
No, I don't. I give it up completely. In fact, during the time I was workin' for the [Crown] electric company, I was in doubts whether I would ever make it or not, because you have to…you have to keep your mind, you know, right on what you're doin', and you have to… you can't be the least bit absentminded or you're liable to blow somebody's house up. I didn't think I was the type for it anyway, but I was gonna give it a try, you know. I was gonna devote all the time I could to learnin' it.

[R.C.B.] What kind of truck were you driving?
Most generally a Dodge pickup.

[R.C.B.] What sort of business was it in?
Well, it was electric. You see, what I was doin' was drivin' a truck, and every once in a while they'd be short of help on one of the jobs. I would deliver material to the different locations where they were wiring houses or building something. And sometimes they would let me help wire or something.

[R.C.B.] How much did you earn at that?
Dollar an hour.

[R.C.B.] And you were at that how long?
I was there about six months. Of course you know, electricians make much more money than that, but that's what I started out making.

[R.C.B.] What kind of hobbies have you got, outside of ridin' motorcycles?
(Laughs.) Well, ah…

[R.C.B.] And girls.
Well I wouldn't call them a hobby (laughs). It's a pastime. I like motorcycle riding. I like water-skiing.

Telephone interview, 1956.

Time to relax and reflect, 1956.

[R.C.B.] Do you get to do much waterskiing?
I do during the summer, I do quite a bit.

[R.C.B.] Is there a lake there?
Yes. [McKellar Lake]

[R.C.B.] You don't fool around with the hi-fi rig at home or anything?
No, that was a year ago.

[R.C.B.] You don't have time for it now, I expect. How about your motorcycle, do you do any racing on it?
No, I don't do any racing on it. We're not at home when it's kinda warm, and a motorcycle's not made for wintertime at all (laughs). But I usually go out and just ride.

[R.C.B.] You just go out by yourself, you don't go in a group?
Nah, I don't go in a group. I'm not home enough for that. I just take my friends ridin' sometimes.

[R.C.B.] You don't wear a black leather jacket, do you?
Yeah, I do, because that's part of it, you know.

[R.C.B.] What else is part of it…a big thick belt?

No, not that. I usually wear a black jacket and a black cap, and a…

[R.C.B.] Do you like that song…"Black Leather Jacket"?
"Black Denim Trousers"…yeah, I like it.

[R.C.B.] Who do you think's the greatest country-and-western singer that's alive today?
I like Sonny James…oh, I couldn't mention all of 'em, I mean.
> *[One wonders on what basis Elvis chooses Sonny James, who at this time had no big hits and had not yet recorded "Young Love," as the "greatest country-and-western singer alive." A possible connection is that he and Sonny had done concerts together. Seemingly more likely choices then might have been Webb Pierce, Eddy Arnold, Hank Snow, Carl Smith, Red Foley, Ernest Tubb, Hank Thompson, Ray Price, Marty Robbins, or Lefty Frizzell—just to name a few.]*

[R.C.B.] Like 'em all, uh?
Yes. In other words, I admire anybody that's good, regardless of what kind of singer they are. Whether they're religious rhythm and blues, hill-

billy or anything else. If they're great, I mean I like 'em. From Roy Acuff on up to Mario Lanza. I just admire 'em if they're really great. They have really built a name for themselves.

[R.C.B.] Um-mmm. How about religious singing yourself, do you do some of that on your personal appearances?
Not on my personal appearances, I don't, because I have out so many records and usually, as a rule, our show is timed so that I don't even get to do half my records.

[R.C.B.] Um-mmm. You think you might do a religious album sometime?
Ah… well.

[R.C.B.] Or don't think you have that type of following?
Well, we have talked about it… [with] Victor… in other words, I think I might get a completely different following if I did.

[R.C.B.] Um-mmm.
Get some new followers maybe.

[R.C.B.] What kind of music do you listen to, outside of country and western, and blues?
Pop.

[R.C.B.] Who do you think is your favorite singer?
In any field?

[R.C.B.] Yeah. One you most admire?
It's a pretty hard question to answer… I've never really… oh yeah, Frank Sinatra, I like.

[R.C.B.] Did you ever listen to any opera or concert soloists perform?
No, [but] I like Mario Lanza.

[R.C.B.] Um-mmm.
I like the way… I like anything he records.

[R.C.B.] Is that serenade [whoever is on stage at this time] over yet?
I don't know whether it's over yet or not.

[R.C.B.] What's your favorite of your own songs?
"I Was the One."

[R.C.B.] "I Was the One"?
Yes.

[R.C.B.] Is that on the album [*Elvis Presley*]?
No, it's not on an album yet.

[R.C.B.] How do you like the album?
I like the way it's selling (laughs).

[R.C.B.] Yeah.
But there's three or four pretty good numbers in it.

[R.C.B.] Which do you like best?
On the album, you mean?

[R.C.B.] Yeah.
There's one called "One-Sided Love Affair."

[R.C.B.] Is that one of the fast ones?
Yeah, it's fast.

[R.C.B.] You like the fast ones better than the ballads, usually?
With me singing 'em I do.

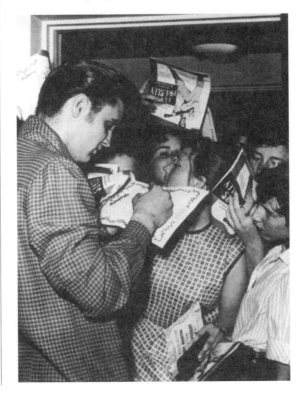

Backstage, signing autographs for fans, 1956.

Meeting fans in downtown Memphis, 1956.

[R.C.B.] That's what I mean.

But as far as my own listening pleasure, I'd rather listen to somebody else sing a ballad…a very beautiful ballad, somethin' like "I'll Be Home," like Pat Boone sings. But me singin' that? I couldn't really.

[R.C.B.] Well your fans seem to like it best… fast tunes you do.

Any audience, as a rule, they go for a fast number. I mean when we're on the stage. In fact, I don't know 'bout other people but me, I've gotten up on stage and I'll do two or three fast ones and I'll have 'em all hopped up, then I'll stop and do a real slow one and I lost 'em for a while. They go to sleep on me.

[R.C.B.] Yeah. How do you feel about your fans…the kids?

Aww, man. I just wish there was some way to go 'round to every one of 'em and really show that you appreciate their liking you and all. But that's impossible, really. I mean lots of times if I'm in a crowd at the door, and the people who hired us are wanting the crowd to leave. Maybe the people want to close up the auditorium. It makes me feel real bad because I can't get to all of 'em.

[R.C.B.] Do the kids of all ages come?

All ages.

[R.C.B.] Mostly girls?

Yeah.

[R.C.B.] Though I heard a middle-aged woman say that she wanted somebody to say hello to you for her son who was in the military.

Yeah.

[R.C.B.] Do you have any real close friends from your childhood that you still see?

Yes sir, I have quite a few. A lot of 'em I haven't seen in years. I have quite a few friends in Tupelo, where I was born and raised. And then there's some people in Memphis now that are real close to me.

[R.C.B.] How do they feel about your success?

Well, they all seem to be backin' me up, you know.

[R.C.B.] There's one of the stories that said you were a little afraid of what they'd think when you first came along.

Yes I was. When my first record came out it was a little eerie, I mean… I thought people would laugh.

[R.C.B.] Did you study any dramatics in high school, or get acting experience?

No I didn't. Except when I was maybe in the fifth, sixth grade, I was in a few Christmas plays.

[R.C.B.] You think a lot of your folks, I've heard from everybody.

Yeah, I do.

[R.C.B.] You call 'em? Call 'em often?

Every day.

[R.C.B.] You talk a long time?

Well, my mother…especially my mother…she is always worried about a wreck, or somethin'…me gettin' sick…so I have to let her know, 'cause she's not in real good health anyway. And if she worries too much it might not be good for her. So I make it a habit of callin' every day or so.

[R.C.B.] Yeah. You've just gotten a new house in Memphis?
Yes sir. They move in Tuesday.

[R.C.B.] What kind of house is it?
It's just a ranch type, seven-room house [1034 Audubon Drive].

[R.C.B.] Uh-huh.
Three bedrooms, a den, playroom. It's a pretty nice place.

[R.C.B.] Yeah, I imagine. Are you gettin' a lot of new furniture too?
Yes. We have to have it. To fill seven rooms you need quite a bit of furniture.

[R.C.B.] What does your father do now?
He doesn't do anything (laughs). Nah, he takes care of all my business. In other words, he's much more important to me at home than he is on a job, because I have so much stuff piled up on me when I'm gone.

[R.C.B.] Um-mmm.
And if he wasn't there to help me, when I got home I wouldn't get a bit o' rest. He takes care of everything…any business that pops up…any insurance, just oodles of things I could mention, well my daddy takes care of 'em for me.

[R.C.B.] What's the Elvis Presley Productions?
Enterprises.

[R.C.B.] Enterprises.
Well that's not anymore. Last year, fifty-five, my manager was Bob Neal, who was a disc jockey in Memphis, and we organized Elvis Presley Enterprises, and had an office [in Memphis]. But when I signed up with Colonel Tom Parker, in Nashville, we didn't figure we needed the office anymore, so he's handling everything out of Nashville.

[R.C.B.] Saving any money?
Yes sir.

[R.C.B.] A lot? I mean you earned more this year than you ever have before. You got any special plans of what you're gonna do with it… sock some away, or what?
Well sir, I'm gonna save every penny that I don't have to have. Course I have to spend a lot because I got lots of overhead. But I'm not doin' unnecessary things.

[R.C.B.] I heard that Colonel Tom Parker has given you a lot of advice and help. What kind?
Everything. In other words, he's the one guy that really gave me my big break. In other words, I don't think…I don't know for sure…I don't think I'd have ever been very big if it wasn't for him. He's a very smart man.

[R.C.B.] You got a lot of sports jackets and suits, and a lot of clothes?
I had quite a few (laughs).

[R.C.B.] You had. What happened?
Well, actually, in the past year I've outgrown most of the things I had.

[R.C.B.] You have, really? Still growing?
When I started singing…well, I was gainin' more weight. When I started singing, I weighed a hundred fifty-three pounds. I weigh a hundred eighty-four now.

[R.C.B.] Oh, you haven't grown *up*?
No, I haven't gotten any taller, but I mean puttin' on a little more weight. In fact I was playin' football when I was in school, and I didn't weigh enough to bump against the big boys.

[R.C.B.] What's your favorite food?
I like pork chops and country ham, cream potatos, stuff like that.

[R.C.B.] That's the stuff you had when you were a kid, I imagine.

Yeah, I was raised up on that stuff. And red-eyed gravy.

[R.C.B.] What's red-eye...that's red-eye peas...green?
No, red-eye gravy...it comes from ham, bacon, stuff like that. It's the grease that you fry it in actually, but they call it red-eye gravy.

[R.C.B.] What kind of dessert?
Well now I eat a lot of Jello, fruit Jello. I like [that] for dessert.

[R.C.B.] Do you drink any, Elvis?
No I don't.

[R.C.B.] Not at all?
Not at all. Never have.

[R.C.B.] You don't smoke.
I never have the taste for that.

[R.C.B.] What kind of clothes do you like the best? Sports?
Well, on the streets, out in public, I like real conservative clothes. Somethin' that's not too flashy. But on stage I like 'em as flashy as you can get 'em.

Radio
interview,
1956.

[R.C.B.] Yeah.
Because on stage your clothes play a very important part in it.

[R.C.B.] Uh-huh.
The way you dress.

[R.C.B.] How many pairs of shoes have you got?
Maybe about twenty.

[R.C.B.] You have any blue suede ones?
No. I have some white suede. Then I have some blue suede boots.

[R.C.B.] What about the blue suede boots... do you wear those on stage?
Never wear 'em...I just got 'em more or less as a trophy (laughs).

[R.C.B.] What other jewels have you got? You got a couple of diamond rings, I see.
Well, that's about all I got.

[R.C.B.] What'd those cost you, Elvis?
Well now, let's see. I don't remember, really. I've had the horseshoe ring for about four or five months. I got this one last week, with my initials on it.

[R.C.B.] Any special presents you got for your parents, besides the house and furniture and cars?
Well...

[R.C.B.] Any things they've always wanted but couldn't afford before?
Well, yes sir. We've gotten quite a bit of stuff. A lot of it is...I mean nothin' real big.

[R.C.B.] I mean little personal things you might have gotten for your mother and father.
Oh sure. I've gotten 'em anything that I think of that I think they might want.

[R.C.B.] Yeah. I mean, can you think of anything extra personal that you knew your mother always wanted.
I've gotten Daddy some suits that he never had

before (laughs). And Mother goes to town now and she buys anything she wants. Which makes me feel real good.

[R.C.B.] You have a happy time when you were a kid?

All my life, I've always had a pretty nice time. We didn't have any money or nothing, but I always managed. We never had any luxuries but we never went hungry.

[R.C.B.] Yeah.

Of course that's somethin' to be thankful for… even if you don't have all the luxuries, because there's so many people who don't.

[R.C.B.] Any other special things you bought yourself?

Well, I bought the motion picture equipment, the lighting, the camera, the projector.

[R.C.B.] What do you use it for?

Oh, I play around with it when I'm home (laughs).

[R.C.B.] Standing stuff, or you don't take it on the road with you.

Yeah. I don't take it on the road. I use it…cartoons and everything I show it on.

[R.C.B.] What kind of audience do you like the best?

Well, what do you mean?

[R.C.B.] Well, your big auditorium full, or television. Does it make any difference to you as far as your feeling goes and how you feel?

Well, audiences are funny. Sometimes you play for an audience that's jam-packed—five or six thousand people—and they're not as responsive as a real smaller audience.

[R.C.B.] I mean, do you find it makes a big difference in your feeling whether you've got an audience that's big or not?

It's according to whether we workin' on a percentage of the show (laughs).

[R.C.B.] Well how 'bout it… can you go into a recording studio cold and start singing?

I have to warm up. I have to get the feeling of what I'm doing.

[R.C.B.] Well, how do you feel when you feel your best?

I'm just…I can't be still. I can tell if I…

[R.C.B.] Are you out of yourself as well, or are you, I mean…like I did a story about Mahalia Jackson not long ago. When she's singing in church, she really loses herself. She closes her eyes and she doesn't…she forgets where she is. When she's singing on television, or something like that, it's a different kind of thing. Is there any difference like that in your singing, that you feel?

Well I'll tell ya, in a place where I feel that I'm gonna have to do my best, I'm not as much at ease as I am at a place where I know there's no critics.

[R.C.B.] Some little place where there's a gang you know are friendly, to do your best, uh?

That's right.

[R.C.B.] Are there any special spots like that you can think of?

No. There's quite a few of 'em, but I couldn't mention any.

[R.C.B.] Elvis, do you think you'll get married one of these days? Or do you get around to thinking about that?

Well, I've been approached with the question, "when you do get married, what kind of girl do you want?"

[R.C.B.] Well, what kind?

That's a question I've never been able to answer. A blonde, or a brunette, or a redhead, or a technicolor.

[R.C.B.] Probably several of these.

I haven't got a dream girl in my mind right now.

[R.C.B.] Well, how about her general character and personality?

Well, I would like to…I don't want anybody that is more or less a snob or put-on.

[R.C.B.] Uh-huh.
I'd want somebody to just be themself.

[R.C.B.] Probably a Southern girl…or that doesn't make any difference?
That wouldn't matter because the girls, most of 'em, are the same everywhere. I mean, there's different varieties in every part of the country.

[R.C.B.] You didn't have any long-term girl-friends when you were younger? In high school?
I had a lot of puppy loves.

[R.C.B.] Yeah.
The longest I ever went with one girl was about a year and a half.

[R.C.B.] Do you still see her?
I see her every once in a while. In fact, I only broke up with her when I started singing. I was away from her so much.

[R.C.B.] How'd she feel about it?
Well it's all over now. It was over a year ago.

[R.C.B.] I meant, is she miserable about it, or has she adjusted?
I don't know. I get a few letters from her every once in a while.

[R.C.B.] Is she cryin' her heart out in them, or has she calmed down?
She may be givin' me a snow job, but she makes like she is. She makes like it's all over, for her.

[R.C.B.] But it's all over as far as you're concerned, uh?
Yes.

[R.C.B.] Who's your favorite actress, in movies or television?
My favorite actress would be the girl that played opposite [Marlon] Brando in On the Waterfront.

[R.C.B.] Saint?
[Eva] Marie Saint.

[R.C.B.] Any others?
There's many others. Oh yeah, the girl who played opposite Frank Sinatra in The Man with the Golden Arm—*Kim Novak. I like Kim Novak.*

[R.C.B.] Do you think you might study acting at some place like the school that Brando went to?
I'd like to. I sure would like to.

[R.C.B.] Why don't you? Too busy, uh?
Well I'm too busy right now, but if it'd come to the point where the people wanted me to, I would.

[R.C.B.] What studio are you testing for?
Paramount. And Hal Wallis.

[R.C.B.] How many hours sleep do you get a night?
Three or four.

[R.C.B.] Three or four?
Yes.

[R.C.B.] Can you get by on that?
I have been (laughs). It's beginnin' to catch up with me right now.

[R.C.B.] It is just since you been travelin' around on the road, or is it a general thing? How much do you usually get?
Well, before I started singin' (yawns), when I was in high school I never did get too much sleep. I mean, I was runnin' around, but I got more than I do now. In other words, when you're on the road the biggest part of the time, you leave a performance and you're en route to somewhere else.

[R.C.B.] Doesn't it kind of get you down after awhile?
Well, it does. But I haven't been in it long yet for it to really show up on me.

[R.C.B.] You don't get much exercise these days, do you?

Not too much. All the exercise I get is on the stage.

[R.C.B.] Yeah.

Probably, if I didn't get that, I would get a little round around the tummy, you know.

[R.C.B.] Yeah.

As much as I eat.

[R.C.B.] You still get to church?

I haven't since I been singing. Because usually... Saturday night is usually our biggest night, regardless of where we are, and on Sunday we always... almost every Sunday we have a matinee at two o'clock somewhere...when we're on the road.

[R.C.B.] What do you do, about six shows a week?

We do seven shows a week. Actually, we do a bit more than that, 'cause as a rule, we do two or three a day. Two or three shows a day...and we have done as many as four...startin' at two o'clock and ending at ten.

[R.C.B.] I see Scotty and Bill have been with you since you started.

Yes sir.

[R.C.B.] You didn't know them before that?

I never did.

[R.C.B.] What do you think of teenage kids, and kids your own age these days? Are they too loud?

[At the time of this question, Elvis was twenty-one years of age.]
No. They're okay. They're just havin' fun, that's all.

[R.C.B.] What do they...

Just havin' a ball.

[R.C.B.] What do they need, if anything? From their parents, or from other people?

I mean you hear so much about...
Juvenile delinquency.

[R.C.B.] Yeah, how wild the kids are...your fans, and kids like that. I don't feel that way, I'm just asking you what you think they need, or what do you think?

Well I'll tell ya, I've never given it too much thought, because, ah...

[R.C.B.] You can tell that they're having a good time.

Yes well, after all...they are the people, mostly, that buy your records, and they're the ones that goes and asks their dad for the money to buy a record.

[R.C.B.] No, I don't mean that so much. I mean, what do you think about kids your own age, generally, aside from your audiences? What do you think about them? Do you think they're gonna be all right?

That's kind of a hard question to answer. I haven't...

[R.C.B.] You haven't given it that much thought.

No I haven't. All I know is that wherever I go, I meet 'em by the hundreds and they're just as nice as they could be.

[R.C.B.] Your parents don't have any great worries about what's going to happen to you, do they...on the road?

The only thing they worry about is wrecks and stuff like that. As far as gettin' in any kind of trouble, I know they don't worry about it. The only kind of trouble I ever been in is...I was stealin' eggs when I was real little (laughs).

[R.C.B.] Well, you could get into worse trouble than that (laughs).

I could if I didn't have any better sense.

[R.C.B.] Do you?

I think I do. I think I know right from wrong. In other words, you have to be careful out

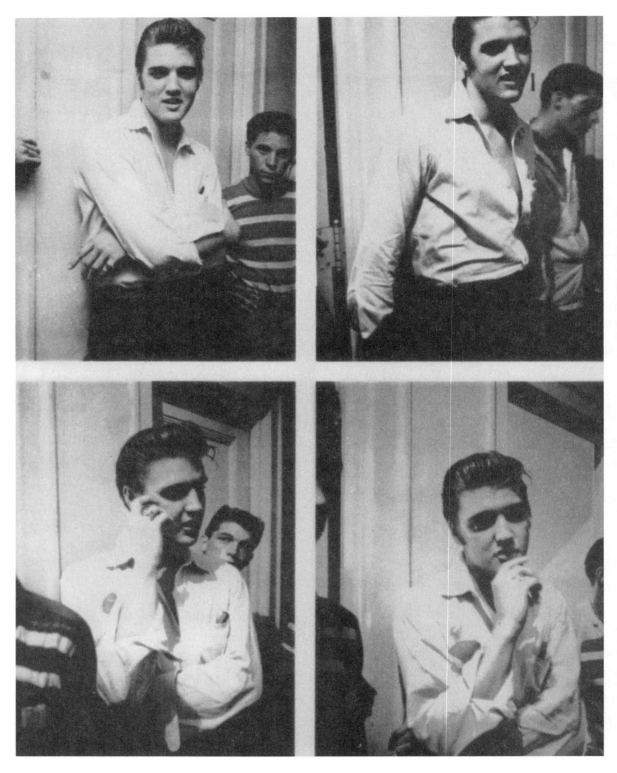

Backstage visit with curious fans, 1956.

there…everywhere…it's so easy to get into trouble. You can get trapped into somethin' maybe you didn't think to do…it's so easy.

[R.C.B.] Well, I heard somebody say that you weren't takin' very good care of yourself. That you were carousing around and didn't know where you were going, and that kind of thing. How do you feel about that?
Well, it's about the truth. It really is. I mean I can't deny it, because half the time I don't know from one day to the next where I'm going, 'cause I have so much on my mind and I'm tryin' to keep up with everything, and trying to keep a level head.

[R.C.B.] Yeah.
And there's so much out there for me to do.

[R.C.B.] Long range, do you feel you got your eye on some objective in the future that you're headed for, or don't'cha think about that?
Yeah, I do. I think about it. Right now, actually I would like to learn how to act in the movies. I really would. Of course, I guess that's, I guess, the right ambition for any young person. I think if he really tried, and he's such a hit, he'd probably do it.

[R.C.B.] Do you have some sort of contract in Shreveport that you got that's holdin' you down there?
I got a contract on the Louisiana Hayride that's tryin' to keep me from gettin' some meals where I can get other ones.

[R.C.B.] How's your time now? Am I holding you too long?
Well I have about ten more minutes.

[R.C.B.] What is the happiest thing to you about being so successful?
The happiest thing?

[R.C.B.] Besides the money. I mean, well, the money obviously, but what do you feel about it?
Well, I would say the money in a way. I mean

that goes…I'd have to, like you say, is the biggest part. Actually, the thing I like about it better is to know that the people…you got so many friends. You got so many people you can go to if you need help. In other words, ah…

[R.C.B.] The difference between… you don't mean admirers, you mean you got a lot of real close friends.
Real close friends I have made since I been in the business.

[R.C.B.] Who are some of them? Do you want to name 'em?
Well, I'd rather not because I'm liable to leave somebody out.

[R.C.B.] What's your biggest kick? I mean, what's been your really highest point of excitement? The one peak?
Probably my biggest thrill, if that's what you're talkin' about.

[R.C.B.] Yeah.
Was when I went with Victor…from the little company I was with [Sun Records]. Second was when I found out I had a screen test coming.

[R.C.B.] Now those are a couple of business things. I'm thinking of one night that really made you feel…
Well, one particular night was in Richmond, Virginia, and in Norfolk, Virginia, too, who-ever it was booked me at the Lion's Club or something, and they came up on stage in the middle of my act and they gave me this scroll with all these hundreds of names on it, that I had drawn the largest crowd that'd ever been to Richmond before…in that particular audito-rium. It was the biggest crowd that'd ever been in the auditorium before.

[R.C.B.] Have you been back home to Tuleepo [Tupelo] is it?
No, I haven't.

[R.C.B.] They don't have any fairs there

where you can perform, or auditoriums?

Well, they have one but I don't work it very often because I don't think it's very good to work your hometown very much.

[R.C.B.] Do you hear anything about what they think of you back home? Do the papers have anything about you?

The papers are always writin' something. Every time I get a speeding ticket they build it up real big, like it's really something. Like last week I got one…ticket for speeding and they had the headlines, in big black print it said: "They often call him Speedo, but his real name is Elvis Peedo." (Laughs.) And it went on to read about…this guy who wrote the article in a canned "cat" language. He don't know "chain gang," or, you know.

[R.C.B.] You don't talk much like that, do you? Do ya at all? Got any expressions that you use a lot?

No I don't.

[R.C.B.] Just talk English.

Not with the people I'm seeing. Well, if you start puttin' on cat talk, everybody'll start thinkin' there's a square side of you.

[R.C.B.] I never hear any musicians talk that way. I hear you used to go to a lot of movies when you were a kid.

I still do.

[R.C.B.] Yeah, how many?

Well, every time we play where I've got any time, I maybe go to a movie.

[R.C.B.] What ones have you liked the best recently?

Recently, I liked Helen of Troy. *I liked that. I liked* The Man with the Golden Arm. Picnic, *I liked.* Picnic.

[R.C.B.] Gee, I have no more questions. You got anything you want to say?

No, I guess that's about it.

[R.C.B.] How do you feel? It's time to go to work out there.

I am. We're on the blocks.

[R.C.B.] I shouldn't do this to you.

Nah, it might have helped me (laughs). But I gotta do somethin' before I go on.

LOCATION: *Municipal Auditorium, Wichita Falls, Texas.*
INTERVIEWER: *Jay Thompson.*
SOURCE: The Sun Years *(LP).*

[Jay Thompson] Well now, country-and-western fans of our Hillbilly Hit Parade, this is an interview we're gonna give you with Elvis Presley, taken from the Municipal Auditorium up in Wichita Falls, Texas, where we were last night. Elvis played a big show, I think many of you are familiar with that. In fact, a lot of you were up there. We're gonna ask Elvis some questions, let him tell you straight because I think you'll get more out of it that way. And I know that each and every one of ya are just waitin' to hear him talk. Elvis, boy, we want to first ask you how old you are?

Uh, I'm twenty-one, sir.

[J.T.] You're twenty-one years old. Sureheart, you got a few months on me, I'll tell you for sure. Tell us, before you got in this music business, what were you doin' for yourself?

I was drivin' a truck.

[J.T.] Drivin a truck.

Yeah, I was.

[J.T.] Was that back in Tennessee?

Yeah, it was back in Memphis, where I live now. I was tryin' to say I was learnin' to be an electrician.

[J.T.] You decided to stick to truck drivin', uh?

Well, I was drivin' a truck and I was studyin' to be an electrician too, see.

[J.T.] I see and you got all mixed up in this crazy music bidness, and that tore the electrician deal all to heck.
Tore the electrician and the trucks all up.

[J.T.] Tell us, how'd you get your first break, to make your first record with Sun Records?
Well I went into Sun Records and there was a guy in there that took down my name; told me he might call me sometime. So he called me about a year and a half later. I went in and I made my first record, "That's All Right Mama."

[J.T.] Yeah, and then from there on, why we know a little bit about what happened, 'cause, boy, those things been on the turntables like nobody's bidness. How'd you get your start on the Louisiana Hayride? What brought that all about?
I went down there just to try out, more or less. I went down there once, and I went back again couple weeks later and the people, they seemed to kinda go for my songs a little bit, so they gave me a job down there.

[J.T.] So from then on, you was a regular? You're not with the Hayride anymore, are you?
No. Last Saturday night [April 7, 1956] was my last night down there.

[J.T.] Last night with the Hayride. How'd you pick up these boys, Scotty and Bill? You known them a long time? They live there around ye?
They live in Memphis, but I never knew 'em until we made our first record.

[J.T.] That right?
Yeah.

[J.T.] Well, tell us…what'dya doin' now, just makin' personal appearances 'round the country, is that all you're doin'?
Yeah. We just tourin' the country, different place every night (laughs).

[J.T.] (Laughs.) I got a kick out of that on the Hayride last Saturday night, I'll tell you for sure. El, anything else in particular you wanna tell us before we break this little interview up?
Well, I'd like to tell you that I sure appreciate all the spins you been givin' me. You really helped me a lot and I'd like to tell you how much I appreciate it and all the wonderful people that have been writin' in and buyin' my records and comin' out to see our shows, because that's really what makes anybody…is the people. You can make 'em or break 'em.

[J.T.] Well, I'll tell ya for sure, they sure go for your style, I'll tell ya for sure. Because, we get the cards and letters ever'day, we play the records, and incidentally, your new album's just takin' over our Hillbilly Hit Parade.
Yeah?

[J.T.] That thing's goin' like a storm.
That's good, and, I'd like to tell you that it's been a pleasure talkin' to you and I'll be seeing you again real soon.

[J.T.] We'll be lookin' forward to it. Thank ya.

APRIL 15, 1956

LOCATION: *Municipal Auditorium, San Antonio, Texas.*
INTERVIEWER: *Charlie Walker (KMAC Radio, San Antonio, Texas).*
SOURCE: The Sun Years *(LP).*

[Charlie Walker] We're still backstage at the Municipal Auditorium here in San Antonio and we, it's really a pleasure to get to interview the next artist on our big Elvis Presley Show because this is the boy that, in the last year or so, has become the outstanding show business personality in the entire world. Not only the United States but all over the world. This boy, I think, is probably the hottest show business personality in the last twenty-five years, and we'd like to get him over here to say hi to you— that RCA Victor recording star, Mr. Elvis "The Cat" Presley. Elvis, it's wonderful to have you on our show, buddy.

With deejay/country singer Charlie Walker, Memphis, 1955.

Thank you, Charlie, for that wonderful build-up and everything. I just hope I can live up to what you just said, I'll be alright.

[C.W.] Well, I'll guarantee ya that the two shows that you did here this afternoon and tonight in San Antonio is proof to us that you'll be here for many, many years to come.
Thank you very much, Charlie. I hope so.

[C.W.] It hadn't been but about three months since you was here.
That's right. It's about three months I was here. Who was on the show with me then?

[C.W.] Gosh, I can't remember right off, but I know that in that time since you been here, you been on so many big shows, and so many wonderful things happened to you. I know that you'd like to tell the folks about it. Of course we've seen a lot of publicity on it and I know that I guess one of the outstanding things that has happened is the new movie contract that you have. Would you like to tell us about that?
Yes, actually I guess that's about the biggest

thing. Of course it's a dream come true, and everything. It's somethin' I never thought would happen to me…of all people. But it just shows that you never can tell what's gonna happen to you in life.*

[C.W.] Is that with Paramount?
Yes, Paramount Pictures, and a seven-year contract.

[C.W.] Seven-year contract, well that's really wonderful.
I've had people ask me was I gonna sing in the movies…I'm not, I mean as far as I know, 'cause I took strictly an acting test and I wouldn't care too much about singin' in the movies.

[C.W.] Um-umm. Well we saw you…
I get enough singin' around the country without…

[C.W.] We saw you on the Milton Berle television show here recently and I'll guarantee ya the job you did with your dialogue and acting on that show was really wonderful and I know that you'll do real great in motion pictures as an actor.
Thank you very much, sir, and I'd like to tell you that it's really been a pleasure seein' you again, Charlie, and all these wonderful people here in San Antonio. They really accepted us well here and we're just thrilled today and we hope we can keep on pleasin' 'em and givin' 'em things they wanna hear.

[C.W.] Elvis, I understand that you received a Gold Record this week for your "Heartbreak Hotel." It sold over a million.
Yes, that's right, yesterday. I had a session in Nashville, Tennessee, and they awarded me with a Gold Record.

[C.W.] We talked with ol' Jesse Snyder, the RCA Victor man here in San Antonio, and it looks like this album [*Elvis Presley*] I believe is gonna be the biggest album seller that RCA Victor's ever

had, in the history of RCA Victor Records. That's really gonna be somethin', isn't it?

It really is. It's really great. Actually, I didn't think it would do as well as it has in the ratings when they put it out. But it's doin' okay.

[C.W.] Elvis, I don't know if you can hear that or not. I think you can, but I doubt if it's pickin' up on the mike, but outside the window here, while we're talking, about five thousand kids are hollerin' "We want Elvis." I wish we could get this…let me see if we can get this on the microphone here.

[Crowd.] We want Elvis! We want Elvis!

[C.W.] Well, there it is, Elvis. There's the proof, about five thousand are standing outside the window here, and just was lucky enough to get our microphone in…did that pick up okay there, Wayne? Gee whiz, boy, they're hollerin'…like it was this afternoon…was a regular riot and I know that a lot of the newspapers here in San Antonio are gonna have stories on it tomorrow, about the regular riot that was caused here this afternoon. In fact it was so bad I don't think you had a chance to do much autographin', did you?

No I didn't, actually. You know I hate not to but if a lot of people start gettin' hurt, and there's a lot of little bitty kids in the crowd and they get trampled on and everything. And the police make us quit, you know.

[C.W.] Well I know that you couldn't possibly have gotten out there and autographed this afternoon, because with that many people and they were pushin' and shovin' and everything, why you'd a probably gotten killed and a lot of the people that was out there would have too. And I know that you would've like to autographed…

I sure would.

[C.W.]…if you could've possibly gone out. Well Elvis, I know that you have a long sched-

ule ahead of you, you got I think you go to Corpus Christi tomorrow…

That's right.

[C.W.]…or it's today…when this tape is being played…

Yeah.

[C.W.]… Monday… you're in Corpus.

That's right.

[C.W.] So we won't take up too much more of your time. We'd just like to say a million thanks to ya, and lots o' luck to an ol' Mississippi boy that's doin' real great.

Thank you, Charlie.

[C.W.] And keep makin' those wonderful records, and we'll be lookin' fer that movie when it comes out, and I wanna get right on the front row.

Thank you very much, Charlie. And I'd like to say that the noise people been hearin' is me chewin' on some ice (laughs). There's nothin' wrong with the tape recorder. And I'd like to say thanks for all the spins, Charlie, you been givin' me. And you really been a friend to me, and I want you to know I really appreciate it, and I'll be lookin' forward to comin' back and visitin' with you again real soon.

[C.W.] Elvis, do that. And you keep makin' those great records, and we'll be seein' you I hope again real soon.

Thank you very much.

[C.W.] Bye now.

Bye-bye.

MAY 6, 1956

LOCATION: *New Frontier Hotel, Las Vegas, Nevada.*

SOURCE: Elvis Aron Presley *(LP).*

Closing Night

Thank you very much, ladies…and gentlemen. I'd like to tell you that it's really been a

With D.J. Fontana, Bill Black and the Freddy Martin orchestra, Las Vegas, 1956.

pleasure bein' in Las Vegas. This makes our second week here and tonight's our last night. We've had a pretty hard time stayin'…ah…had a pretty good time while we were here. We got a few little songs we'd like to do for you that we have on record, in our style of singin'…if you wanna call it singin.'

About the First Gold Record

Thank you very much, friends. Here's one more little song we'd like to do for you. To do this song, we'd like to call on Mr. Freddy Martin and his very wonderful orchestra to back us up…back us completely up. The night before last on the stage of this auditorium… of this place here, RCA Victor awarded me a Gold Record for the millionth sale of "Heartburn Motel," that we did earlier out here. And we're real proud of it 'cause it's made so much mon…it's done so well for itself. And here's another one that's comin' right up behind it, we hope it will hit the million mark. This song here is called "Get Out of the Stables Grandma, You're Too Old to Be Horsin' Around."…You know that

song, Mr. Martin, "Get Out of the Stables." You know that? You do? (Laughs.) Well, do you know that one about "Take Back Your Golden Garter, My Leg Is Turnin' Green"? Did you ever hear that one?

Introduction of Guests

Oh yeah, friends, I'd like to do my whole part of the show and I hope that you like somethin' we do up here even if it's wrong. Two celebrities that we have in the house. We may have more but these two fellows I know are here. I'd like to do this little song here for them. Mr. Ray Bolger is in the audience, Mr. Ray Bolger. And also for Mr. Phil Silvers, he's in the audience. And Roy Acuff, he's out here somewhere.

A Violent Song?

I'd like to do a little song right here that I hope you people like. This one's called "Darling, You Broke My Heart When You Went Away, but I'll Break Your Jaw When You Come Back." Did you ever hear that one?

About Tomorrow Night

Thank you very much, ladies and gentlemen.

I'd like to stand out here and shake, rattle and roll for ya all night, but we're booked in Alcatraz tomorrow night, we got a long drive ahead of us.

MAY 14, 1956

LOCATION: *Sawyer Auditorium, Lacrosse, Wisconsin.*
INTERVIEWER: *Unknown.*
SOURCE: Elvis Answers Back, Vol. 2 *(LP).*

[Media] Well, ladies and gentlemen, we're in the stars' dressing room of the Mary E. Sawyer Auditorium, and what a fabulous night this has been. We're very happy to have with us here Mr. Elvis Presley. How are you, Elvis?
Fine sir, how're you?

[Media] Terrific. You know I've lived in Lacrosse all my life and this is the first time I've seen anything like this [Elvis' matinee show] happen.
(Laughs.) Well that…it's good. It's the first time I've been up in this part of the country.

[Media] Where do you hail from, Elvis?
I was born in Mississippi but I live in Memphis, Tennessee, now.

[Media] I see. And this is a very controversial question, how old are you? They say eighteen, nineteen, twenty, twenty-one. Give us the official dope now.
I'm twenty-one.

[Media] Twenty-one. Uh-huh. Another thing I'm gonna ask you, I've been reading up on your career. You've been in the business for about two years now and what was the first song that you ever sang to an audience? Could that have been the Red Foley thing of "Old Shep"?
"Old Shep," that's right. Well, that was when I was about seven or eight year old when I sang that song.

[Media] I see. And the gentlemen that accom-

panied you tonight, that was Scotty [Moore] and Bill [Black] out there?
Scotty and Bill, and D. J. Fontana.

[Media] On the drums, uh?
Yes.

[Media] And they've been with you ever since you started your fabulous career?
Scotty and Bill have. The drummer has been with me for about two or three months.

[Media] I see. The first record you ever cut for the Sun label, was it "Blue Moon of Kentucky"?
Yes, that's right.

[Media] And I understand it had real great response down there when it was first played by the deejays.
Well, it did okay, but it kinda surprised me. I thought they would laugh me out of town (laughs).

[Media] (Laughs.) I noticed there was a very heavy echo effect in that. More than some of the others.
Yes, there was a lot of echo in it.

[Media] The people around town here thought that the first recording you ever made was "I Forgot to Remember to Forget," because that was the first one we…
That was the fifth one. "I Forgot to Remember to Forget."

[Media] I see, but the first one released on the Victor label, right?
Yes.

[Media] Um-mm.
That's right.

[Media] Well, you certainly are without a doubt the number-one-selling artist in the nation now. You have the number-one record ["Heartbreak Hotel"] and the top-selling album [*Elvis Presley*]. Now what do you do in

your spare time? (Laughs.)…if you have any.
I haven't got any, really. But when I do get some time off I usually…I always go home and see my folks and oh I ride a motorcycle and do different things.

[Media] You have a favorite sport, haven't you, waterskiing?
Yeah, I do a little waterskiing, and I like football, I like boxing.

[Media] Teenagers have inquired about your forthcoming movie career too. Now maybe that's a little too early to talk about but I see you're signed by Hal Wallis and Company out of Paramount.
Yes.

[Media] Can you tell us anything about the first movie that will be made?
I couldn't tell you the name of it because I don't know. They're writing me a play. I was offered a part in The Rainmaker.

[Media] I see.
With Burt Lancaster.

[Media] Quite a dramatic bit, isn't it?
Well it was, but it wasn't the character in it, I didn't think. I mean, I didn't feel I could do it the way that it should be done.

[Media] I see. Well you're certainly in the position to pick the role that you want right now, I'll say that. Where do you go from here, Elvis?
I play Memphis tomorrow night, which is Tuesday night.

[Media] Boy, that's a lot of traveling there, about seven hundred miles or so.
Seven ninety-five. I'm gonna fly down.

[Media] Fly, uh-huh. Well let's see, the fans have asked me so many questions here. Do you have any particular experience that sticks in your mind? Something that has happened during your two-year career? Anything that you'd like to tell us about?

There's so many things that have happened, but I can't think of any…any particular…

[Media] How about the Las Vegas incident? You were down there just about two weeks ago.
Yes.

[Media] A completely different type of audience, I understand.
Well it was. It was strictly an adult audience, and mostly elderly people.

[Media] Did it take a little while to warm them up to your style of singing?
It took…well, the first night, especially, I was… I was absolutely scared stiff.

[Media] Uh-huh.
And ah…(laughs).

[Media] But from reading some of the reviews, I understand they responded quite well though, after awhile.
Afterwards I got a little more relaxed and I didn't…I worked a little harder and I finally got 'em…finally got 'em on my side a little bit.

[Media] You sang this "Only You" tonight. Do you have any plans of recording that for RCA Victor?
No, I've been doin' it ever since it's been out.
    [Though Elvis indicates he'd been doing "Only You" since it came out—in May 1955—a recording of it is, as of this writing, not known to exist. Interestingly, two days later, in his May 16th Little Rock concert, which has been issued, he does not sing "Only You."]

[Media] Your new release ["I Want You, I Need You, I Love You"], I understand, has sold over three hundred thousand copies for RCA, and they had that many orders before it was released.
Well.

[Media] So this could be another second million for you.

The last count I had, it had reached a half a million.

[Media] It's really fabulous.
I don't know how many it will sell.

[Media] Another thing that the teenagers are interested in is future television appearances. I understand you're gonna be on the *Milton Berle Show*.
Yes, the Milton Berle Show *the fifth of June. After that, I don't know where I'm going.*

[Media] Well we certainly don't want to keep you, Elvis, 'cause I know you have a lot of things to do and the next [evening] show will be coming up very, very shortly. I want to thank you very much for talking with us this evening.
Thank you very much. And thanks a lot for playin' my records.

[Media] You bet'cha.
And I'll keep trying to give you something to play.

[Media] (Laughs.) The ones that you've had out so far have been terrific. They've all been great sellers.
Well thank you very much.

[Media] You know this [*Elvis Presley* extended play] album of "Blue Suede Shoes"? We sold that like a single. We sold more of that than we averagely sell a single. That's what amazed us down there. You're about the first guy to have ever done that for RCA, I'm sure of that.
Well, I don't know. I hate to say yeah…it'll sound like I'm bragging.

[Media] (Laughs.) Well thank you very much, Elvis Presley. It's been great.
Thank you sir. Thank you.

MAY 16, 1956

LOCATION: *Robinson Auditorium, Little Rock, Arkansas.*

INTERVIEWER: *Ray Green.*
SOURCE: Elvis Exclusive Interview *(LP).*

[Ray Green] Elvis, welcome to Little Rock.
Thank you very much. It's a pleasure to be here, sir.

[R.G.] Well, would you tell the folks your favorite movie star…in the female sex?
Oh, well I like a lot of 'em, but I guess I like Kim Novak.

[R.G.] Kim Novak… what about the male sex?
Well, I like Brando's acting…and James Dean…and Richard Widmark. Quite a few of 'em I like.

[R.G.] I noticed in your write-up in *Time* magazine that you liked football a little bit. Would you tell the folks something about your football experience, or just what position that you like to play best?
Well I played end for two years. I never made real good at it, but, I mean, I enjoyed playing.

[R.G.] Well okay…now what about your favorite recording, Elvis? Since you've been in the business…your favorite recording.
Well I guess I would say "I Was the One" I like… I like the song, especially. But "Heartbreak Hotel" I would like because it's outsold any of the rest of 'em.

[R.G.] That's right, I noticed from the hit parade magazines, and from the record sales throughout the country that "Heartbreak Hotel" has been right on top for about the past six or seven weeks. Well, would you care to make some comment about Little Rock, or about something like that?
Well this makes my third visit here.

[R.G.] Your third visit…well, what do you think about the people?
Well, it's really wonderful, and especially tonight. I think the crowd is much larger than it's ever been, and the people were more respon-

Backstage interview with a reporter, 1956.

sive. But every time I've ever come over here I've had a real nice time and met a lot of real wonderful people.

[R.G.] Well very good, Elvis. Thank you very much. I'm sure that the guys and gals and the people of Little Rock will be thrilled to hear that. Well what are you gonna do on your late show tonight? You gonna do any deviation from your first show?

No I'm not. I usually do about the same. I do the songs that I get more requests for, which is the ones I did on the first show.

[R.G.] Okay Elvis, this is sort of off the cuff, but tell me, how does it feel to be right up there on top? I mean right with the…well, with the best of 'em, since you are one of that class. How does it feel?

Well, as I was telling you earlier, it feels pretty good (laughs). It all happened so fast till I don't know I'm afraid to wake up, afraid it's liable to be a dream, you know.

[R.G.] Okay folks, that's been Elvis Presley, the star that's been right up on top now for about these past…well, he's been right up there on top for quite a while. Say Elvis, before we get away, we'd like to ask you about your

favorite music. **What what type of music really appeals to you?**

I like different types. I like rock and roll, and hillbilly, pop, some classical. I like different kinds of music. I like anything, any kind if it's good.

[R.G.] Well, speaking of rock and roll, what's your opinion on this rock and roll phase that's going through the country right now?

Rock and roll has been in for about five years. I'm not gonna sit here and say that it's gonna last because I don't know. But all I can say is that it's good, the people like it, it's sellin'… I don't mean mine, I mean rock and roll.

[R.G.] Uh-huh.

It might change. Like years ago when the Charleston was real popular, or the vaudeville acts, stuff like that. You could'a told those people maybe it was gonna die out and they wouldn't of believed you. But it's dead now, see. And maybe four or five years from now, well, rock and roll will be dead.

[R.G.] But as far as rock and roll goes, you really like it, huh?

As far as rock and roll goes, I really like it. I enjoy doin' it, and the people have really accepted it great and it just makes me wanna knock myself out to keep givin' 'em somethin' that they enjoy.

[R.G.] Well that's fine, Elvis, and I notice you really do knock yourself out. Say something about your unique style. Where did you get the idea for this?

I just landed upon it accidentally. More or less I [am] a pretty close follower of religious quartets, and they do a lot of rockin' spirtuals.

[R.G.] Uh-huh.

And so that's where I got the idea from, is religious quartets.

[R.G.] Well, it's really proving to be a good one

for you. I notice the fans really go wild when you start, as the expression goes, cutting loose. Well, what type of girls do you like?

Female only.

[R.G.] (Laughs.) He likes female girls. Oh I notice the music is just going on. It's almost time for you to go back, Elvis, but before you get away, would you tell us just a little bit about your latest release? I understand you had a little bit of plane trouble and everything. Would you tell us just a little bit about that?

When I left Amarillo, Texas, going to Nashville to record my latest record, "I Love You, I Need You, I Want You"…"I Want Ya, I Love," whatever it is, anyway…the plane we were ridin' ran out of gas about six thousand feet up in the air.

[R.G.] Then what happened?

The engine just died. Of course he just happened to get it switched to another…to a spare tank he had.

[R.G.] I understand you had a little difficulty getting started. How many cuts was that you made on your recording? How many different cuts before they found a perfect one?

Which recording are you speaking of?

[R.G.] Your latest recording, "I Need You, I Want You, I Love You"?

I recorded it about eight times…ten.

[At no time during this interview did either Elvis or the interviewer get this song title right. It is, of course, "I Want You, I Need You, I Love You."]

[R.G.] About eight? I understood it was something about twenty-seven.

Nah.

[R.G.] Just eight or nine times before you found a perfect cut. Okay Elvis, would you make one closing comment then, please?

Yes I sure would. I'd like to tell you that it's a pleasure talkin' to you and thank you very much for the spins you've given me on my records…

and thank all the wonderful people that have really, really backed me up. And I hope…

[R.G.] Okay Elvis, thank you very…

…I hope I can keep givin' 'em stuff that they like.

[R.G.] Okay Elvis, thank you a lot. It's been fine talkin' to ya. And folks, that's been Elvis Presley, the man that's been right up on top for the past, well, as I said a moment ago, quite a long while. And it's been a pleasure for me to talk to him, and thank you very, very much.

JUNE 5, 1956

LOCATION: *NBC Studios, Burbank, California.*
EVENT: *Second of two appearances on* The Milton Berle Show.
SOURCE: *Videotape.*

> *[Appearing on* The Milton Berle Show *was Elvis' first time on television in color, actually billed as "in color and compatible black and white."]*

[Milton Berle] Elvis, if I did that thing the same way you did it, do you think I could get all the girls the way that you do?

Well, it might not help you get girls, but it'd sure aid you to keep your blood circulating.

[M.B.] At my age…you make me feel like a used car. My tail light may be dragging, but my battery is still charging. I wanna…what do you do with your hair? Toni [home permanent], do you use here?

Prom!

[M.B.] Prom? No [product] plugs, you understand. I wanna tell ya, how can I get these girls to scream over me? I really mean that. How can I do that?

Mr. Berle, I don't think you'd like it.

[M.B.] I wouldn't like what? What do you mean?

I don't like it. All these girls screaming, always

TV show rehearsal with Milton Berle, New York, 1956.

tearing your clothes off, always trying to rip you apart, always kiss ya. I don't like it.

[M.B.] You don't? Somebody must have stomped on his head with those blue suede shoes. You must be kidding. Are you kidding, you don't like it?
I'll tell ya, I'd rather have a quiet type of a girl. Someone more sedate, someone that'll calm me down and relax me, you know?

[M.B.] You don't want a girl, you want a Miltown [tranquilizer].
Really, Mr. Berle.

[M.B.] Yeah.
I'll tell you the type I dig, is someone like that Debra Paget.

[M.B.] I can't hear ya. I'm next to you but I can't hear ya.
I said…

[M.B.] Somebody like Debra Paget.
Somebody like Debra Paget.

[M.B.] Oh, you like that type. No, look…
Man, she's real gone.

[M.B.] I know she's real gone, but look. Debra Paget, Elvis, she's not in your league, you know what I mean? Stick to Heartbreak Hotel and stay away from the Waldorf, you know what I mean? Elvis, she'd never go out with a guy like you, I mean she's much too sophisticated. She's a beautiful woman, she really is. I'll prove it to you, she's too sophisticated for you. Debra, Debra, would you come out here, please. Debra Paget, I want you to meet Elvis Presley.

[Debra Paget] [Screaming and grabbing Elvis.] Elvis!

[M.B.] Well, how do you feel now, man?
Cool man!

[M.B.] How do ya like that? She kissed him and he feels cool. You better get ready for your next number—your hit record ["I Want You, I Need You, I Love You"], and we'll be right back to you. See you later. Yeah, dig you later. I don't know what they see in him. I can sing as well as he can. If I were only bowlegged. Debra, I can't understand why all the girls—of course he's number one across the country—I can't understand why they go for this guy. Why, why, why? What's he got?

[D.P.] Milton, he's young and handsome. He's sexy, and virile, and…ooh, he's the handsomest.

[M.B.] What about me?

[D.P.] You're the hippyest.

[M.B.] Incidentally, ladies and gentlemen, I don't think that I'm revealing any secrets when I say that Elvis Presley is the fastest-rising young singer in the entertainment industry today, and as proof of this, I would like to present this to you. It's a special…well, it's a great award from one of the great theatrical periodicals of all time. It's the *Billboard*, back east and all over the country. They present you this, I'd like to read it for you. "The Triple Crown Award, presented to Elvis Presley for his RCA

Victor recording, of Heartbreak Hotel." There it is, ladies and gentlemen, let's hear it. *Thank you.*

JUNE 8, 1956

LOCATION: *Shrine Auditorium, Los Angeles, California.*
INTERVIEWER: *Lou Irwin.*
SOURCE: Earth News *(LP).*

[Lou Irwin] Elvis, how does someone like you come out from Tennessee out here to Hollywood and break into this business the way you have?
That's a pretty tough question. I don't know. Like I said, I've just had some good breaks.

[L.I.] How'd the breaks come?
I mean television and stuff like that. And records, I got an RCA Victor contract. Then I got on some of the big television shows and I got better known by the people and started sellin' my records more, and then I got a movie contract. And everything just…

[L.I.] Seemed to snap…seemed to click?
…Seemed to snap. Yes, that's exactly right.

[L.I.] What happens with rhythm and blues? Is this just a fad? Are you just a fad? What happens next?
You tell me (laughs). I wish I knew.

[L.I.] What is rhythm and blues?
Rhythm and blues is just rock and roll. It's a music. Rhythm and blues, it's a craze, but it's a very good craze in that there is some very beautiful songs recorded in rhythm and blues, if the people will just take time…some of the people that don't like it…would just take time out to listen to it. There's some very beautiful songs, for instance "Ivory Tower."

[L.I.] How do you explain the controversy over your music?
Well it makes the crowd go wild. I mean, if the people like it, they feel it. In other words, they can't sit still when they hear it.

[L.I.] You've probably heard that rock and roll was outlawed just last week in a northern California city. People have been saying that it's contributing to juvenile delinquency. I'm sure you don't agree with that.
I don't! I do not agree. Not only because I do it, but because it's untrue. Rock and roll is a music. Why should a music contribute to rock and roll…I mean contribute to juvenile delinquency. If people are gonna be juvenile delinquents they're gonna be delinquents if they hear Mother Goose rhymes. Rock and roll does not contribute to juvenile delinquency at all. The only thing about it is, in some of the auditoriums the kids get up and start dancin' in the aisles, and they start squealin' and everything and kickin' the seats. Now that's the only thing that I know of. And that doesn't happen all the time. It just happens in some cases.

TV show rehearsal with Debra Paget, New York, 1956.

[L.I.] Overall, how has the reaction been?

The reaction has been very well. I don't want to sound like I'm braggin' or anything, but reaction has been very good, and the people have accepted me very well.

[L.I.] Why do you think you didn't go over so well in Las Vegas?

There was no teenagers. I mean the reaction was as well as anybody could expect, but it was only my imagination because I was used to a bunch of howling, screaming teenagers, and in Las Vegas there's no teenagers. They're all elderly folks…they are all older.

[L.I.] So rock and roll is a music for teenagers, you would say?

No, I didn't mean it that way. It's just that I was used to the screamin' teenagers and there was none out there.

[L.I.] It will be accepted, you think, more by older people soon?

I don't know about that either. But I just know that right now it's the biggest record-selling business there is…is rock and roll.

[L.I.] How many records have you sold?

You mean all totaled or on one…each individual record?

[L.I.] All totaled?

Oh, I guess I've sold two and one-half million.

[L.I.] Two and one-half million. How do you explain your success?

I've had some very lucky and wonderful breaks, and the people have really been accepting me very well everywhere we've been. And a lot of different things.

JUNE 16, 1956

LOCATION: *Memphis, Tennessee.*
EVENT: *Wink Martindale's* Dance Party *show on WHBQ-TV. Includes visit by deejay Dewey Phillips.*

SOURCE: That Was Elvis to Me *by Wink Martindale (CD).*

[Dewey Phillips] Hello Mother!

[Wink Martindale] Now you see him. There he is.

[D.P.] There's your boy, right there, Wink.

[W.M.] Is this the fella you were going to bring to see us today?

[D.P.] That's lover boy!

[W.M.] Lover boy.
Ahhhh! Ahhhh!

[W.M.] Dewey Phillips and Elvis Presley! Dewey, thanks a lot for getting him here today. You were really one of the guys who helped to get this fella started, weren't you?

[D.P.] I helped a little.

[W.M.] Weren't you one of the first to play his records?

[D.P.] You ask Elvis, I don't know. What about it, Elvis?
Nahh! (Laughs.) I guess he was the first one in Memphis to play my record.

[D.P.] I'll tell you what happened, Wink…
It didn't cost me much.

[W.M.] Didn't cost you much, huh?

[D.P.] He went out there. He recorded a record for Sam Phillips and one night Sam brought the record up to the radio station, and I listened to the record…and I said, "Man, one of 'em has got to go!" That "Blue Moon [of Kentucky]" and "That's All Right." And I got Elvis' home phone number. And I called, and his mother answered the phone. I said, "Mrs. Presley, is Elvis at home?" She said, "No, he's down there watching a Western at the Suzore." And I called down to the theater and asked Presley to come up there [to the radio station]. And he came up to the station and we cut loose

with that record, "That's All Right." You know what made that record?

[W.M.] What?

[D.P.] [Singing] Dee Dee Dee Dee! How's it go, Elvis?
I forgot.

[W.M.] That's been a long time ago.

[D.P.] How about me singing a song here?
[Singing.] Yes it's me and I'm in love again.

[D.P.] [Singing.] Yes it's me and I'm in love again.

[W.M.] That's the only one you know, isn't it?

[D.P.] Naw. I know… well, I better not give that one.

[W.M.] Alright, do one chorus. C'mon, one little chorus right quick here.

[D.P.] You with me, Elvis?
I'm with you.

[D.P.] You got your knife with you? You got your pick? [Looking up.] Man, there's a flock of 'em flew over then.
[Though the "flock" reference may not make sense now, those in Memphis at the time knew it to be a comic reference used frequently by Phillips on his radio show.]
How about "Gee Dad, It's a Wurlitzer"?

[D.P.] Gee dad it's a Wurlitzer. Let's go. Let's go, cat. You ready?
You go ahead. I'll wind it up.

[D.P.] You gonna wind me up? [Singing.] Well, the landlord rang my front…where's the mike at? I don't see no mike. That the mike?

[W.M.] That's it. Go ahead.

[D.P.] You ready? I'll tell you what you do, Elvis. You hold the chord. I don't know how to hold it.
You're left-handed. I can't. I can't.

With Dewey Phillips, Downtown Memphis, 1956.

[D.P.] Don't break it! That's it right there, isn't it?
Well, you got me. I can't play right.

[D.P.] Here it is. Let's go. That's not the song. What are we gonna sing?
You were singing "Money Honey."

[D.P.] [Singing.] Well the landlord rang my front door bell, I let it ring for a long, long spell. I went to the winder and I jumped straight out. I said what is it baby that's on your mind. She said, money honey, money honey. Ooh baby.

[W.M.] Thanks a lot, Dewey.

[D.P.] Martindale, [I] want you to meet one of the nicest guys in show business—Elvis Presley. He's a clean boy [applause]. He's one of the hottest guys that's ever hit show business.

[W.M.] I realize that, and I…
You ain't kidding.

[D.P.] See ya, old buddy.

[W.M.] Thanks a lot, Dewey.

Visiting Dewey Phillips at WHBQ radio, Memphis, 1956.

[D.P.] Anytime you want me, if you got the money I'll be back, old buddy.

[W.M.] Okay. You cost too much!

[D.P.] Bye mother!

[W.M.] Elvis, it goes without saying that all of us here at *Dance Party* appreciate very much you taking time out today to come by and say hello to all of our friends that watch *Dance Party.* And also the people who are here on the floor today. And it's nice that you were able to spend these past few days at home. How is it you've been home so many days in a row here?
Well, it's the first time I've been off in months. I've been on the road. I've been out on the West Coast and everything. And I decided I needed a little rest.

[W.M.] A few days off, huh?
Yeah.

[W.M.] You don't want to go too fast now.
And I'd like to tell you that I really enjoy…I mean out here, all these people…

[W.M.] Well we're certainly glad to have you here. Elvis, we want to ask you a few questions, and, uh…
Shoot.

[W.M.] Here we go. Let's go back to the beginning first of all, to your quick rise to fame. First of all, how old were you when you first remember being attracted to music and singing? And, well how old were you? How'd you get started? And when did you get that first guitar, and where did you get it?
Whew!

[W.M.] That's a lot of questions.
Let's start with the first question again.

[W.M.] Okay. How old were you when you first…
… When I first started singing? Well, I never sung in my life until I made my first record, you know.

[W.M.] Uh-huh.
I, ah…

[W.M.] Where did you get that guitar?

I got it in [Tupelo] Mississippi. It cost twelve dollars I think.

[W.M.] Twelve-dollar guitar, huh?
It was a Gene Autry guitar. I got a Roy Rogers now.

[W.M.] What did you do with that first guitar? What happened to it?
Well I had some uncles that picked a guitar a little bit; and I sat down and watched 'em all the time. And I just picked it up watching 'em. But I mean, I never thought I'd make anything doing it, ya know.

[W.M.] Uh-huh.
You know.

[W.M.] Well now, when you were graduated from Humes High School, did you expect to pursue singing and…
I didn't even expect to get out of Humes High School (laughs).

[W.M.] That takes care of that question. Very well answered.
No, I'll tell you. I never even thought of singing as a career. In fact I was ashamed to sing in front of anybody except my mother and daddy.

[W.M.] Then all of a sudden you started singing in front of people and that was it.
And all of a sudden one day I got a sudden urge to go into this recording studio, which is Mr. Sam Phillips's Memphis Recording Service. And he told me he might call me sometime, ya know.

[W.M.] And he called you.
So he called me. It was a year and a half later, and I was…I was an old man.

[W.M.] Elvis, regarding your hobbies and so forth. Would you consider cars or sports cars an interest?
I don't have any cars.

[W.M.] You don't have any cars?
Naw, uh.

[W.M.] I heard the opposite of that.
My daddy's got Presley's Used Car Lot out on Audubon Drive (laughs).

[W.M.] How many cars do you have, by the way?
I've got four and a Messerschmitt, and a motor-cycle.

[W.M.] What kind of cars are included in the four cars?
All Lincolns!

[W.M.] He said that for the benefit of Dewey Phillips. But actually, they're what?
[Reference here is that Dewey was then the proud owner of a huge new Lincoln. Elvis actually owned Cadillacs at the time, but would buy a new Lincoln the following month, July.]
They're…I don't want to tell.

[W.M.] Okay, okay. Now…
I'll tell you…the reason I bought those cars. Maybe someday I'll go broke and I can sell one of 'em.

[W.M.] And have a little extra money on hand.
Right.

[W.M.] You have experienced a phenomenal rise in popularity, Elvis, in the course of a few months' time. How did you first feel when your records first started to be accepted by the people and bought by the public? Did you have a sort of sensation and…and…
Well I'll tell you, Wink. It all happened so fast and so I didn't even have time to think about it. It, ah…everything just…just (whistles) just like that.

[W.M.] Just like that.
And it just kept goin' and it's still doin' that way and I can't even think about it. In fact I don't even like to wake up mornings. I'm afraid I might wake up…

[W.M.] Afraid it might be all over.

...Afraid I might be back driving a truck again (laughs).

[W.M.] Some people have said they don't like the way you jump around… move… when you sing. Elvis, now does this help you or is it an unconscious motion which sorta goes with the mood of the song? Is that a hard question to answer?

Well I'll tell ya. I'm not doing it on purpose. I mean, I'm aware of everything I do at all times. But it's just the way I feel. I mean…If I…I can just picture somebody singing a rock and roll song standing real still. Actually I'd go nuts standing there, ya know.

[W.M.] Uh-huh.

I just…yeah.

[W.M.] People everywhere say, well, I know—and you've heard it too, more than likely—all this type of thing is just a craze and a fad like other fads and personalities in the past. Presley and rock and roll music will depart in due time. What is your feeling about this, along this line?

Well I…I'm inclined to agree with them. I mean, people change. I mean, some time they like you and then again…later on they don't.

[W.M.] Uh-huh.

And the rock and roll is…is real hot right now.

[W.M.] Uh-huh.

And I like it. It's very good. It has a feeling and people enjoy it. People enjoy dancing to it. And there's some very beautiful records made in rock and roll style. Stuff like "[You've Got] The Magic Touch" [Platters], "The Great Pretender" [Platters], and stuff like that. I mean, they just don't make any prettier songs than that.

[W.M.] Well now, speaking of records, "Heartbreak Hotel" sold over a million copies and undoubtedly that was a pretty thrilling experience to be presented by the RCA Victor record people with a gold copy for you to keep

for the rest of your life. Now, actually, didn't you like the other side better than "Heartbreak Hotel"?

I liked "I Was the One," but I liked the royalty checks better on "Heartbreak Hotel."

[W.M.] Well, which record, in your opinion, of all the ones you've recorded, do you like the best?

"I Was the One."

[W.M.] "I Was the One," huh?

Yeah.

[W.M.] And that was on the other side of "Heartbreak Hotel." We could say that both of them helped to sell a million copies. Well, how are things looking regarding your latest releases?

My latest record, "I Want You, I Need You, I Love You," has sold almost a million. It's only been out fifteen days.

[W.M.] Uh-huh.

Sold right close to eight hundred thousand.

[W.M.] Pretty fast work, isn't it people, huh? [Applause.] Elvis, you've made many personal appearances. You've played many one-nighters and you've appeared on several big-time television shows. And you've sang. Now which do you get the biggest kick out of? Which do you enjoy the most? Do you like the live personal appearances or television better?

I like live personal appearances better.

[W.M.] Any particular reason?

Well, I enjoy it. I mean, on television you're limited, ya know. You can only do so much. And [there are] so many rehearsals.

[W.M.] You rehearse and you rehearse and you rehearse some more, don't you?

By doing only so much, I mean, that you know, you can only do a couple of songs and by the time you get warmed up, well, they're dragging you off.

[W.M.] That's it. Well, in the cities and towns

you've visited the past several months you've met lots of people. You've signed lots of autographs and I understand you've lost several shirts in the process.

Well, there's been some pretty wild stories, like the one in Kansas City where my drummer [D. J. Fontana] was thrown in the orchestra pit [May 24, 1956]. Ah, there wasn't even an orchestra pit there. What it was, was a barn. Well, actually it was. It was more or less a great big barn we were playing in, and they overran the police, I think there were six policemen around the stage. And the people overran the police. And I was singing "you ain't nothin' but a hound dog," and I was right in the middle of the song, and I said "you ain't nothin' but a hound," and out I went, man, right in the middle of the song. And there was a door backstage that I ran through. I mean, I knocked the lock off of it. I hit it. It was dark and I couldn't see where I was going. I just knew where the door was.

[W.M.] You made a new door, in other words.
I mean…there's a lot of stories start, but…

[W.M.] Well now, that brings us around to something else, and we're getting around to the end pretty soon here. Some people, and we discussed this the other day…
Aw, we got plenty of time. And about this Judy Spreckles, I've been gettin' a lot of publicity with Judy Spreckles.

[W.M.] Uh-huh.
All that got started when Judy gave me a ring, out in Las Vegas. She gave me this ring here, and that ring there.

[W.M.] It is a pretty big ring, isn't it? Would you show it to us up close there.
Sure.

[W.M.] Pretty big. Beautiful ring too.
She gave me this ring because, oh, I saw it in the window and I just admired it. But Judy is a very good friend. Judy is older than I am and

she's engaged. She's gonna get married next month. And she's a real good friend, nothing else. Somebody had started that she was wearing my ring and I was wearing her ring, and we were wearing each other's rings.

[W.M.] That's the way it goes. How about the big show at Russwood Park, scheduled for July Fourth? Bob Johnson, surely I know, wants us to mention that and we want to mention it. I believe the proceeds from this show go to the Cynthia Milk Fund. Is that right, Elvis?
[Through donations, the Cynthia Milk Fund, established in 1914 by Cynthia Gray of the Memphis Press, assists indigent families with life's necessities.]
Yes sir, that's right, and…let's see, what would I like to say (laughs)? I'd like to say that we have a diamond ring that we're gonna have as a door prize.

[W.M.] Uh-huh.
It's my initial ring. I've had it for some time and it has fourteen diamonds in it, and we're gonna give it away at the door as a door prize.

[W.M.] I see.
And everything.

[W.M.] And all the proceeds from this particular show…this is July Fourth at Russwood Park, Elvis is gonna be there. He's gonna sing and play, his band will be there. Many other stars will be there too. We will certainly want you to watch Bob Johnson's column in the *Memphis Press-Scimitar*. Watch all the publicity on it and get your tickets in advance. Elvis Presley, I want to thank you again.
Thank you.

[W.M.] Because we know you're a busy man and thanks a lot for coming by and seeing us at the *Dance Party* and saying hello to all your friends here in Memphis and the Mid-South. And anytime you're in town and wanna come by we certainly will welcome you.

A quiet moment at home, Memphis, 1956.

Well, thank you very much, Wink. And I'll see you again.

[W.M.] Okay. Thanks a lot. Elvis Presley [applause].

JULY 1, 1956

LOCATION: *Hudson Theater, New York, New York.*

EVENT: *Guest appearances on* Steve Allen Show.

SOURCE: *Videotape.*

[Steve Allen] Elvis, I must say you look absolutely wonderful. You really do, and I think your millions of fans are really going to get kind of a kick seeing a different side of your personality.
Well, thank you, Mr. Allen.

[S.A.] You want a guitar here?
It's not too often that I get to wear the suit and tails, but ah…

[S.A.] Uh-huh.

But I think I have on something tonight that's not quite correct for evening wear.

[S.A.] Not quite formal, what's that, Elvis?
Blue suede shows.

[S.A.] Oh yeah! Well, Elvis, you're certainly being a real good sport about the whole thing. And now I have a little surprise for you. Gene, could I have the surprise?

[Gene Rayburn] There you are.

[S.A.] Thank you, Gene Rayburn. This, Elvis, believe it or not, is a giant petition—it was signed by three giants out in the alley. No, seriously, this was signed by over eighteen thousand of Elvis' loyal fans saying they wanted to see him again soon on television, it was sent in to us just the other day by our good friend, deejay Don Wallace, in Tulsa, Oklahoma. Eighteen thousand signatures on this! Elvis, it's a fine thing.
It's wonderful, Mr. Allen. I'd like to thank…I'd like to thank all those wonderful folks, and I'd like to thank you too.

[S.A.] Well, that's okay, Elvis. Now what you gonna sing for us first tonight?
"I Want You, I Need You, I Love You."

[S.A.] Here's the big RCA hit!
[Sings "I Want You, I Need You, I Love You."]

[S.A.] Thank you, Elvis. That was his great vocal group, the Jordanaires, in the background. Elvis, your new record hit—I predict it's gonna be one because I've heard you rehearse it and you're gonna record it tomorrow—called "Hound Dog." I got you a very cute little hound dog right here. And away you go.

JULY 1, 1956

LOCATION: *Warwick Hotel, New York.*
EVENT: *Hy Gardner telephone interview (broadcast on WRCA-TV).*
SOURCE: *"From Introduction to Demob" (Videotape);* This Is Elvis *and* TV Guide Presents Elvis *(LPs).*

[Marilyn] Hello, I'm Marilyn, Hy Gardner's secretary. Tonight, as usual, the *Herald-Tribune* syndicated columnist will be checking stories, live and unrehearsed, with names that make news. We'll talk with veteran bandleader Ted Lewis; Egyptian dancer Nedula Ace; the unidentified author of the shocking book titled *I Was a Dope Addict*; and to get right into action immediately with the most controversial entertainer of the year…well, you'll hear who.

[Marilyn] Hy.

[Hy Gardner] Umm.

[Marilyn] I have Elvis Presley on the phone. Hello.
Hello.

Hello Elvis, just one moment.

[H.G.] Hello Elvis.
Hello.

[H.G.] Did you have fun tonight on the *Steve Allen Show*?
Yes sir, I really did. I really enjoyed it.

[H.G.] First time you ever worked in a tux or tails?
It's the first time I ever had one on, period.

[H.G.] You mean you've got, as they say, four Cadillacs but no tuxedos?
No tuxedos. I usually drive the Cadillacs in blue jeans.

[H.G.] (Laughs.) That's very interesting, especially when a cop stops you and wants to know if you own the car.
That's right. You have to show 'em all your ownership papers and everything.

[H.G.] You know, less than two years ago you were earning fourteen dollars a week as a movie usher, and then thirty-five dollars a week for driving a truck in Memphis. Today you're the most controversial name in show business. Has this sudden notoriety affected your sleep, your appetite, or the size of your head?
Not the size of my head. It's affected my sleep.

[H.G.] How much sleep do you get?
Oh, I average about four or five hours a night, I guess.

[H.G.] Is that enough?
Well it's really not but I'm used to it. And I can't sleep any longer.

[H.G.] What do you keep in mind mostly? I mean, some of the songs you're going to do or some of your plans or what? What goes through your mind?
Well, everything has happened to me so fast in the last year and a half, till I'm all mixed up. I mean, I can't keep up with everything that's happening.

[H.G.] Well I think that you've got very good company in Colonel Tom Parker. His feet are on the ground and I think he's doing a wonderful job of keeping things rolling nicely. I want to give you an opportunity here to go over a lot of the rumors that have been printed about you, including a few that I've printed myself. Because some of these things can be checked and some can't and I think that we ought to sort of fix up the record. Now, your style of gyrating, while you sing, has been heavily criticized, even by usually mild and gentle TV critics, like Ben Gross. Now, do you bear any animosity towards these critics?

Well…not really. Those people have a job to do and they do it.

[H.G.] And do you think you've learned anything from the criticism leveled at you?
No I haven't.

[H.G.] You haven't, huh?
Because I don't feel that I'm doing anything wrong.

[H.G.] Do you read this stuff?
Do I read the…

[H.G.]…the reviews?
Not if I can help it.

[H.G.] (Laughs.) Do you keep a scrapbook at all?
Only of the good stuff.

[H.G.] Only of the good stuff, that's fine. Tell me, what kind of a teenager were you? Were you a…would you consider yourself well behaved?
Yes, well I was raised in a pretty decent home and everything. My folks always made me behave whether I wanted to or not.

[H.G.] Well, how do they feel about your success, and the things that some of the critics have said about you, both good and bad?
Well, I guess they're just like myself. They're very thankful for it. I mean we always led a kind of a common life. We never had any luxuries but we were never real hungry.

[H.G.] Uh-huh.
I guess they're just real proud, just like I am.

[H.G.] Well now, there are two or three columns this week that carried items that you had bought four Cadillacs. Now what is that, Elvis?
It's the truth. I do have four Cadillacs.

[H.G.] What do you do with four Caddys?
(Laughs.) Well I…(laughs) I don't know. I haven't got any use for four, I just, ah. Maybe someday I'll go broke and I can sell a couple of 'em.

[H.G.] Well, some people collect stamps and government bonds. I guess Cadillacs are probably in the same category. I understand you gave one of them to your folks. Is that right?
Anything that's mine is theirs. I mean, all four of 'em is theirs. I'm planning for seven. I want seven.

[H.G.] You want seven, uh?
Yes (laughs).

[H.G.] You know what's going to happen, you'll wind up. It'll be the Presley Car Renting Corporation.
Yeah, I was thinking about the Presley Used Car Lot.

[H.G.] Uh-huh. I understand that you bought a home for your folks, and even though your father was only thirty-nine, you insisted that he retire. Is that true?
Yes. Well he's more help at home than he is anywhere else, because he can take care of all my business and he can look after things when I'm gone.

[H.G.] Well I think that's great. When you shake and you quake when you sing, is that sort of an involuntary response to the hysteria of your audience?
Involuntary?

[H.G.] Yeah.

Well I'm aware of everything I do, at all times. But, it's just the way I feel.

[H.G.] I mean, for example, if someone is playing…they try a little bit harder when the fans root. And I was wondering whether this had anything to do with it.
Oh sure, I guess any artist, if the audience acts like they're enjoying it, if they act like they're with you, it makes you put more into it.

[H.G.] Do you think that your rocking and rolling has had an evil influence on teenagers?
I don't see that any type of a music would have any bad influence on people, when it's only a music, I mean.

[H.G.] Uh-huh.
I can't figure it out. I mean, in a lot of the papers they say rock and roll is a big influence on juvenile delinquency. I don't think that it is. Juvenile delinquency is something that's…I don't know how to explain it but I don't think that music would have anything to do with it at all.

[H.G.] I've got a couple of questions here I'd like to sort of clear up. One of 'em, and it's sort of a silly one to me after having talked with you at some length earlier, is what about the rumor that you once shot your mother?
(Laughs.) Well I think that one takes the cake, I mean (laughs). That's about the funniest one I've ever heard.

[H.G.] Where'd that one come from? Have you any idea?
I have no idea. I can't imagine. When you mentioned it to me, it's the first time I ever heard it.

[H.G.] Is that right?
It's the first time I ever heard it.

[H.G.] Well there's another one too, you may not have heard before. Several newspaper stories hinted that you smoked marijuana, or hit the bottle, in order to work yourself into a

frenzy while singing. What about that?
(Laughs.) Well, I don't know.

[H.G.] You won't even bother answering that? Well, here's one that's very interesting. I don't know if you noticed the column the other day…they predict that Elvis Presley will be another James Dean. Now, have you heard that?
I've heard something about it. But I would never compare myself in any way to James Dean, because James Dean was a genius in acting.

[H.G.] Uh-huh.
Although I'll say that I sure would like to. I mean, I guess there's a lot of actors in Hollywood that would like to have the ability that James Dean had.

[H.G.] Uh-huh.
But I would never compare myself to James Dean in any way.

[H.G.] Now, if you had your choice, would you prefer to be an actor to being a singing entertainer?
If I were a good actor—of course I'm not a good singer but if I were a good actor—I think that I would like that a little better. Although if I ever break into the acting completely, I'll still continue my singing. I'll still continue making records.

[H.G.] Well that's always a very, very good sideline. It was just fine talking with you and I hope that you'll enjoy a long career, whether it's acting or anything else, and I think that all the things said about you, while they've been extremely critical, I think they have helped to make you the kind of a big name that has made it possible for you to do the things for your folks you always wanted to. So I sort of figured I'd look at it that way, Elvis.
Well sir, I'll tell ya. You gotta accept the bad along with the good. I've been gettin' some very good publicity, the press has been real wonderful

to me. I have been given some bad publicity, but you gotta expect that, and I know that I'm doin' the best I can. I have never turned a reporter down, I've never turned a disc jockey down, because they're the people that help make you in this business.

[H.G.] Uh-huh.
And as long as I know that I'm doin' the best I can.

[H.G.] Well, you can't be expected to do any-more. And I wanna tell you it's just been swell talking with you, and you make a lot of sense.
Thank you very much.

[H.G.] Give my thanks to the Colonel now.
Sure will.

JULY 9, 1956

LOCATION: *WNOE Radio, New Orleans, Louisiana.*
INTERVIEWER: *Unknown.*
SOURCE: Loving You Session, Vol. 1 *(LP).*

Summertime on the Gulf Coast with June Juanico, Biloxi, 1956.

[Media] Ladies and gentlemen, you have no doubt heard that we have had comments from June Juanico, down in Biloxi [Mississippi], concerning her purported engagement to Elvis Presley. And we understand that, as of this morning, they are not engaged nor is Elvis Presley engaged to anybody. And we were shocked a few minutes ago by the man himself, the man of the hour, walking into the studio. Here he is: Elvis Presley.
Hello.

[Media] Elvis, how are you?
Fine. How are you, sir?

[Media] Wonderful. When did you come into town?
Well I just came in a few minutes ago.

[Media] You drove up from…
A few minutes ago (laughs). Yeah, I was in Biloxi and I heard on the radio where I was supposed to be engaged to somebody, so I came down here to see who I was supposed to be engaged to (laughs).

[Media] Well just what is the story? Are you engaged to anybody?
No I'm not. The girl they were talkin' about, June Juanico, I've dated a couple times.

[Media] Are you…
We're not engaged.

[Media] Are you serious about anybody?
No I'm not.

[Media] Just serious about the music business.
I'm serious about my career right now, that's right.

[Media] Well your career has been meteoric. It has been fantastic! And I know down here, as you probably know yourself, there are hundreds of thousands of your fans and they're all proba-bly wondering about your new releases and what your plans are for the immediate future.
I don't know when a new release'll be out. My

last one, "I Want You, I Need You, I Love You," is doin' okay.

[Media] That's the biggest understatement of the year, Elvis. This is one of the biggest smash hits in America today.
(Laughs.) Well it's doin' okay...I'll say it's doin' okay. And my next one will probably be "Hound Dog," the one I've been doin' on television a lot.

[Media] There's been a lot of people ask about it.
We've had a lot of requests...RCA Victor has had a lot of orders...

[Media] Uh-huh.
...wantin' the record, and I haven't even made it yet.

[Media] Elvis, where is your hometown?
Memphis, Tennessee.

[Media] When was the last time you were back in Memphis?
I liked to swallowed my chewing gum. I was in Memphis yesterday.

[Media] Can you, in your own words, Elvis, tell us why you think you are the big success that you are? Is there any one or two things you can point out?
No, I don't. I can't think of anything...

[Media] Uh-huh.
...specific. Just the great backing that I've had. And the people and my managers and my assistants and all that sort of stuff, have really done a wonderful job. Milton Berle, Steve Allen, the Dorsey Brothers, and all of 'em have really helped, RCA Victor. Everybody's just been really really helpin' me.

[Media] Well wonderful. How old are you, Elvis?
Twenty-one.

[Media] What age do you think might be the best for you to get married?
I never thought much about it. In fact, I have

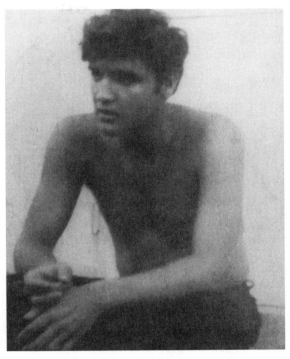

Cooling off on the porch, Memphis, 1956.

never thought of marriage. I've never even thought of it. I'll say this much, I'm not thinkin' of it right now, but if I were to decide to get married at all it wouldn't be a secret. I mean, I'd let everybody know about it. But I have no plans for marriage. I have no specific loves. And I'm not engaged, and I'm not goin' steady with nobody or nothin' like that.

[Media] Well you know how this whole thing started last night. We got...
Well, I don't (laughs). Excuse me for buttin' in, but I don't know how it got started, but everywhere I go, I mean I'm either engaged or married, or I've got four or five kids or somethin' like that.

[Media] But you're not.
Everywhere I go. Nah.

[Media] You're as free as the breeze.
That's right. I don't know how they get started. I guess they get started about everybody.

[Media] Well Elvis, thank you so very much for taking your important time to come down here today to WNOE.
Well, my time's not important right now, I'm on vacation (laughs).

[Media] Oh, wonderful! How long are you on vacation?
About a month. I'm off for about three more weeks.

[Media] Where do you expect to go?
I plan to go to Florida, probably Miami.

[Media] Uh-huh.
And then, when I go back on the road…on tour…I'll open up in Florida, I think Tampa.

[Media] Well you probably won't have too much of a vacation, because of the tremendous amount of kids who'll be down there, and fans who'll be spotting you.
Well I don't mind. Without 'em I'd be lost (laughs).

[Media] Well Elvis, thank you so very much again and we wish you lots and lots of good luck in your continued meteoric rise to stardom, which has been so phenomonal during the past couple months. And again, our many, many thanks from all of us here at WNOE.
Thank you very much. I've enjoyed talkin' to you, and I hope that we got the little rumor cleared up, because it's just a rumor and nothin' more. If it wasn't, then I wouldn't care for tellin' anybody. I wouldn't be ashamed of it.

[Media] Why don't you say it just one more time, so people still don't get the wrong idea?
(Laughs.) Well, I'm not engaged, if that's what it's supposed to be.

[Media] Okay Elvis, thanks a million.
Thank you.

JULY 10, 1956

LOCATION: *Radio Station Studio, New Orleans, Louisiana.*
INTERVIEWER: *Jim Stewart.*
SOURCE: Loving You Session, Vol. 1 *(LP).*

I've been gettin' some pretty bad publicity lately, especially after The Milton Berle Show. *I got quite a bit of bad publicity about my actions on the stage out there.*

[Jim Stewart] I'll tell you one thing, Elvis Presley, we have fifty thousand watts and they're very strong here in the New Orleans area, and you'll never hear anything other than "Elvis Presley is a very fine person" here. I can speak in behalf of Larry Monroe, and Hal Murray, and Jim Edwards on the Night Train, Mickey Scott, and all the personnel here who have talked with you. We've been playing your records for a long time.
Thank you very much. I've been listenin' to your station for the past couple of days, ever since I been down here. And I can say that I certainly appreciate it a lot because if there wasn't somebody on my side, I'd be lost.

[J.S.] I have a little little note here. Ellery Wagner is the new president for the New Orleans fan club, for Elvis Presley, I take it. Have you met…is it a young man, is it? Ellery? Oh, it's a girl. I see. Have you met Miss Wagner?
I don't believe I have. If I did it was a long time ago and I forgot it, back when I was first in New Orleans, when I first started out in the business.

[J.S.] Oh you were in New Orleans?
Yes, I was at Ponchartrain Beach, and that's back when I first started out. And I've been around quite a bit since then. I've met so many people till it's hard to remember.

[J.S.] Well I heard the Democratic Party is trying to buy the Elvis Presley block of votes (laughs). That's what I hear.
Well I'm afraid that the biggest part of 'em would be kinda too young to vote (laughs).

[J.S.] I want to ask you one other thing. I was reading in one of the trade magazines you made the statement—whether or not you made it or not, we'll find out—that "I want to make it while I'm hot." In reference to a—I mentioned

earlier—disc jockey who said he would pay you a dollar a minute for every minute you…he interviewed you on the air. And Elvis, please don't hold me to that because I'd have to sell the station.

Well that's one of the most untrue rumors that I've heard yet. I've never even…in fact, it's the first time I've even thought of anything like that, when you mentioned it. But I think it's a good idea, so (laughs).

[J.S.] (Laughs.) There are a lot of people that possibly don't like ya, you know. And there are a number of people that don't like me, and probably…Bob Hope, and right down the line, but what you do, you do well, so I don't know why people just…there's a certain amount of integrity that should go with this. Like these quotes here and there that you read about you, now that you say there's no truth to them.

Mr. Stewart, I'll tell you like this. I was tellin' a reporter a little earlier today, regardless of who you are or what you do, there's gonna be people that don't like ya. There were people that didn't like Jesus Christ. They killed him and Jesus Christ was a perfect man. And there's gonna be people that don't like ya regardless of who you are or what you do because if everybody thought the same way they'd be drivin' the same car, everybody'd be marryin' the same woman, and that wouldn't work out, you know.

[J.S.] That's right. A lot of philosophy there, very, very much so. Well how about your new release? I've got a million calls…I know that Mickey, and Larry Monroe, and Hal Murray and Jim Edwards have all received the same call: "Why don't you play 'Hound Dog'?" And we can't find it!

(Laughs.) Well it's probably because I hadn't made it yet (laughs). "Hound Dog" should be out in the next three or four weeks. I'm not sure. I've got it to record yet, but after you record, it don't take 'em but just a week or two to get it out.

[Interestingly, Elvis had already recorded "Hound Dog," as well as "Don't Be Cruel," on July 2, in New York. The record came out on July 13.]

[J.S.] Elvis, do you think there's any chance that you might send us an exclusive on it?

I'll see if I'll get my manager to send you one of the first copies that comes out.

[J.S.] Oh, we'd appreciate that and we'll play it till the old dog's [Nipper] tongue's hanging out (laughs).

(Laughs.)

[J.S.] Do you write most of the lyrics for your tunes?

No. I've never written a song.

[J.S.] Never written a song?

I never written a song in my life. I wish I could. I wish I was like some of my rivals— Carl Perkins and Gene Vincent. Those guys, they're pretty good songwriters. But me, I did good to get out of high school (laughs). I've never written a song.

[J.S.] Well Elvis, you don't need…you just keep singing. But tell me one thing else. How long do you plan to be in Biloxi? Are you going back to Biloxi now?

No I'm not. I'm going to Miami, Florida.

[J.S.] Miami, Florida.

Yes I am.

[J.S.] Are you booked down there?

No, I'm on vacation. I'm off for about three weeks. It's the first vacation I've had since I've been in the business.

[J.S.] I see.

And I been in the business about forty-three years now (laughs).

[J.S.] (Laughs.) Let's see…energy he uses eating sugar, take box candy, take half box candy.

What does that mean?

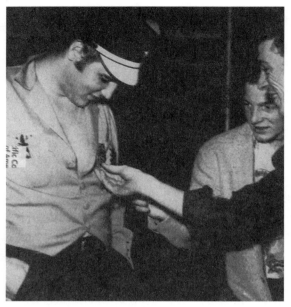

With Gene Vincent (far right) and friend, 1956.

[J.S.] Oh, sugar, ate half box…oh! Elvis, did you eat up that box of candy I gave June? *(Laughs.)*

[J.S.] I got one piece.
Well, it was very good candy.

[J.S.] (Laughs.)
I saw the price tag on the bottom of it, you know, ninety-eight cents (laughs).

[J.S.] Don't worry, I stole it.
No, it was very good candy. I didn't know who it belonged to. It was just sittin' in front of me and I was eating it.

[J.S.] I see (laughs), just sittin' in front of him. Well I'd like to play an Elvis Presley tune here.
Who? (Laughs.) Gene Vincent himself!

[J.S.] This boy's come on, but…
I met Gene in New York. I met him last week. He was in the train station up there. I was goin' from New York to Memphis, and Gene Vincent was in a train station, and I didn't know who he was. One of the boys in my band knew him and I walked over and introduced myself to him. And it's the first time I had ever seen him. He had seen me on shows but I had never met him. I told him, "Gene," I said, "Congratulations on your record" ["Be-Bop-A-

Lula"]. I said, "You really got a hit." And right immediately, the first thing he said was "Well I wasn't tryin' to copy you," he said (laughs).

[J.S.] (Laughs.)
He said, "I wasn't tryin' to sound like you." I mean, just right off of the bat he said that, see, without it even bein' asked.

[J.S.] Yeah.
I told him, "Oh, I know that." I said, "That's just your natural style" (laughs). But the boy has got out a very good record. I mean, I have people ask me all the time what I think about these people that sound a lot like me, I mean well, I was the first one to come out with it, I reckon, as far as I can remember. But those people that are using the style, I don't blame 'em. I'd probably jump on the bandwagon too (laughs).

[J.S.] Well, one last question: How long do you think that rock and roll will last now?
I wish I knew. That's a question that if I could answer, I'd be makin' plans for the future, but I don't know. I'll say this, it is very hot now and I like it. I enjoy rock and roll. A lot of people like it, a lot of people don't. But as long as it lasts, as long as it sells, I'll continue doing it, as long as that's what the people want. And if they change, if it dies out, I'll try to do somethin' else, and if that doesn't work, I'll just say, well I had my day.

AUGUST 5, 1956

LOCATION: *Tampa, Florida.*
INTERVIEWER: *Ray Pillow.*
SOURCE: Elvis: A Legendary Performer, Vol. 4 *(LP).*

[Ray Pillow] [Talking about *Elvis Presley* LP]
It's got songs I never recorded before and everything.

[R.P.] Uh-huh.
It's got stuff like "Tutti Frutti," "I Got a Woman Way Over Town."

[R.P.] Yeah, Pat Boone put that ["Tutti Frutti"] out didn't he?
Yeah, Pat Boone recorded it.

[R.P.] Yeah, I had a lot of arguments about that song, who does it the best. Well there's no doubt in my mind how it sounds the best, as far as rhythm. Well I appreciate a whole lot talkin' to you, Elvis, and I'll be lookin' for ya to come back around again.
Ray, it's a pleasure and thanks a lot.

[R.P.] Have you ever played Detroit?
Never have.

[R.P.] Well thanks a lot. And I'll play you [your songs] for long time to come.
Thank you, Ray.

AUGUST 5, 1956

LOCATION: *Tampa, Florida.*
INTERVIEWER: *Norma Pillow.*
SOURCE: Elvis: A Legendary Performer, Vol. 4 *(LP).*

[Norma Pillow] Elvis!

[Unidentified person] What station are you with?

[N.P.] WJBK

[Unidentified person] In Detroit?

[N.P.] Detroit. I'm from Detroit, Michigan. I'm with WJBK.

[N.P.] Elvis, when will you be on TV next?
September the ninth.

[N.P.] Any plans for marriage?
Just keep cool.

[N.P.] Just keep cool, uh? Well what do you think of the future with rock and roll music?
I wish I knew.

[N.P.] You wish you knew?
Yeah.

[N.P.] Well, I wish you the best of luck.
Thank you very much. Don't be so nervous, I'm not gonna bite ya.

[N.P.] (Laughs.) And was "Good Rockin' Tonight" your first recording?
No "Blue Moon of Kentucky" and "That's All Right Mama" was my first recording.

[N.P.] Well, you know I traveled all over the city of Detroit lookin' for "Good Rockin' Tonight."
Is that right?

[N.P.] I sure did.
Well why didn't you come down to my house and I'll give it to ya.

[N.P.] Well, I woulda loved to. Where're you from?
Memphis, Tennessee.

[N.P.] Memphis, Tennessee. And how old are you?
Twenty-one.

[N.P.] Twenty-one.
Yeah.

[N.P.] Ya still out lookin' for a girl?
I think I found her.

[N.P.] You found her, uh?
You!

[N.P.] Oh well, thank you. You like blondes or brunettes?
Oh I like all kinds.

[N.P.] All kinds.
Yeah. Female kinds.

[N.P.] Elvis, it's been real sweet talkin' to you.
Thank you very much, honey, and don't be so nervous. Because there's nothin' to it.

[N.P.] (Laughs.) Nothing to it. I think I could'a gotten an interview with the president quicker than I could with you.
(Laughs.) Well I've enjoyed talkin' to ya, honey, and I'll see you around.

[N.P.] Yeah, I'm gonna stick around and listen to the show. Thank you.

LOCATION: *Polk Theater, Lakeland, Florida.*
EVENT: TV Guide *interview (backstage before Elvis' show).*
INTERVIEWER: *Paul Wilder.*
SOURCE: Uncensored *(CD) and* Elvis Presley Interview Record—An Audio Self-Portrait *(LP).*

[Paul Wilder] What is Presley's answer to his critics?
Well, those people got a job to do and they do it.

[P.W.] That's a good answer. Let me read to you an article from the *Miami [Herald].*
I've already read the article.

[P.W.] You read that one? How did you feel about it, generally?
Well he called me "idiot's delight." He said that all the kids was a bunch o' idiots, they should all be slapped in the mouth. What I'd like is to...

[P.W.] Let me read it to you. I think it's a little bit different. It says: "When this day is over, an unhealthy hunk of Miami's teenage girls will have unashamedly screamed their lungs out to frank adoration of the biggest freak in modern show business history. In seven stage shows at the Olympia yesterday [August 3] and today [August 4], Elvis is a no-talent performer riding the crest of a wave of mass hysteria."

[P.W.] How's your feeling on that item: "[Elvis is a] no-talent performer"?
I don't know. I don't even want to think about it. He ain't nothin' but an idiot or he wouldn't sit up there and write all that stuff. He just hates to admit that he's too old to have any more fun.

[P.W.] (Laughs.) "He's drawing an average of two thousand kids a show and nearly all of

them are girls. Elvis can't sing, can't play the guitar."

[P.W.] Ah, can you play the guitar?
No, and I can't sing either but somebody likes it.

[P.W.] (Laughs.) "And he can't dance."
No, can't dance.

[P.W.] (Laughs.)
I can't do nothing but read Herb Rowe's article in the newspaper. That's all I can do.

[P.W.] "He had two thousand idiots per show yelp every time he opens his mouth, plucks a guitar string or shakes his pelvis like any strip tease babe in town."

[P.W.] Do you shake your pelvis "like any strip-tease babe in town."
Well he should know. I guess that's where he hangs around.

[P.W.] (Laughs.) "In over a decade of active professional participation on the fringes of show business, we've never seen anything like it, nor can we understand it. A division of Infantrymen, fresh from the front lines, never screamed at Bob Hope like Miami's teenagers are screechin' for Elvis Presley. Judy Garland killed them at the Palace, but they never heard anything like this Olympia wingding. Nor did Al Jolson at the height of his glory, or Frank Sinatra, or Will Rogers, or Jerry Lewis, or Bing Crosby. If what Elvis Presley dishes out is entertainment, then we give up. We're beyond our teens yet not so ancient we can't appreciate what might appeal to a youngster. Except in regard to Presley. There is a 'warm-up' scream program prior to the proceedings on stage. Running among the movie shorts is a rock and roll thing featuring Bill Haley and His Comets. They yell and scream through this too, and if it weren't for the cops and firemen on hand they'd dance in the aisles also. The scream warm-up routine is reminiscent, in staging, of another kind of film prior to another kind of performance in another kind of house."

Sir, those kids that come here and pay their money to see this show, come to have a good time. What's-his-name here, probably, might have had a little fun when he was young. But I doubt it.

[P.W.] Rowe. Herb Rowe.

Herb Rowe, whatever his name is. I mean I'm not runnin' Mr. Rowe down, but I just don't see that he should call those people idiots. Because they're somebody's kids. They're somebody's decent kids, probably that was raised in a decent home. And he hadn't got any right to call those kids idiots. If they wanna pay their money to come out and jump around, and scream and yell, it's their business. They'll grow up someday and grow out of that. But while they're young let 'em have their fun. Don't let some old man that's so old he can't get around, sit around and call 'em a bunch o' idiots, because they're just human beings like he is.

[P.W.] Okay. We'll go back to a quotation. "They can't like Presley for his voice or his guitar playing (laughs) no matter how lousy both may be. They can't adore him for these things because they screamed so loud they can't even hear him sing or strum his guitar." Do you strum your guitar?

Well I beat on it. I have for quite a number of years. So, I'm not an expert on it. I'll say this and I'd like to add it to what I just got through saying about him. As a rule, most of the adults are real nice. They're understanding. I've had 'em come 'round to me by the hundreds and say I don't personally like your kind of music, but my children like it and so on. And if they like it, well I hadn't got any kick about it because when I was young, I liked the Charleston, or I liked the fox trot. I liked this and that. They are adults with a little intelligence. I mean, they don't run the people in the ground for havin' a nice time.

[P.W.] Okay, back to the clipping. "What remains, unfortunately, are his pelvic gyrations. And that's the core of the whole appeal—sex stimulation."

[P.W.] Any answer to that one?

Well I don't roll my—what'd he call it—pelvic gyrations…

[P.W.] Uh-huh.

…my pelvis had nothin' to do with what I do. I just get kinda in rhythm with the music, I jump around to it because I enjoy what I'm doin', I'm not tryin' to be vulgar, I'm not tryin' to sell any sex, I'm not tryin' to look vulgar and nasty. I just enjoy what I'm doin' and tryin' to make the best of it.

[P.W.] Where did you get the name "Elvis the Pelvis"?

From somebody just like the character that's writing this article here.

[P.W.] Do you have any idea who?

No sir. I wish I knew, I don't know. Course I don't like to be called Elvis the Pelvis, it's one of the most childish expressions I've ever heard, coming from an adult. Elvis the Pelvis. But if they wanna call me that there's nothing I can do about it, so I just have to accept it. Just like you gotta accept the good with the bad…the bad with the good.

[P.W.] Okay. Back to the quotation. "We're no prude but we might suggest a gift to our fourteen thousand Miami girls who—as if it were a fetish, of vocally and mentally genuflecting to Elvis Presley—a solid slap across the mouth." He means…Rowe means a slap across the mouth to these girls. Have you any comment to that?

Yeah, but I don't think I should say it.

[P.W.] Okay. Okay. This isn't over the air. This is for *TV Guide*.

TV Guide. I don't think I should say it.

In the showroom, signing autographs, 1956.

[P.W.] Okay.
'Cause I'm a singer, not a fighter.

[P.W.] They also ask...I'll ask...where did you pick up your style?
Well sir, I don't know. I really don't know. I just started out doing what I'm doing now (laughs).

[P.W.] Ah, have you ever seen anybody else do it?
No sir. Never have.

[P.W.] Have you got any techniques that you've added since you started show business, or are these all?
No sir, I been doin' the same thing. I've only been in the business about a year and a half.

[P.W.] Uh-huh.
And I'm doin' the same thing that I started out doing. I haven't added or taken anything away.

[P.W.] Did your first appearances...I mean did your first success occur in records or in personal appearances?
My records started sellin' pretty well and then I...

[P.W.] Your records sold before you made any success as an important performer?
Yes sir.

[P.W.] So do you think that your gyrations merely add to the performance you give? Do you think that the movements you make have made you famous, or your style of singing?
I don't know, sir. I can't answer that.

[P.W.] You haven't any idea?
I can't answer that.

[P.W.] Okay. I read a clipping somewhere where you were attributed as saying that the Holy Roller...you had...
I have never used that expression. That's another deal. See, I belong to Assembly of God church...

[P.W.] Uh-huh.
...which is a Holiness church. I was raised up in a little Assembly of God church, and some character called 'em Holy Rollers.

[P.W.] Oh, I see.
And that's where that got started. I always attended church where people sang, stood up, and sang in the choir and worshiped God.

[P.W.] Uh-huh.

I have never used the expression "Holy Roller."

[P.W.] Do you still attend church?

Every opportunity I get. I don't have as much opportunity as I used to, because I'm on the road most of the time.

[P.W.] In the Holiness church, do they have peppy music?

Peppy music?

[P.W.] Uh-huh.

They sing hymns and spirtuals…they sing spirtual songs every once in awhile.

[P.W.] Do they sing 'em at a fast tempo?

Yes sir, they do sometimes.

[P.W.] How long you been goin' to that church?

Ever since I was old enough to walk.

[P.W.] About five or six, uh?

Yes sir.

[P.W.] And do you think you transfer some of that rhythm into your singing?

That's not it! That's not it at all. They was some article came out that where I got the jumping around from my religion. My religion has nothin' to do with what I do now, because, the type stuff I do now is not religious music. My religious background has nothing to do with the way I sing.

[P.W.] Do you recall the first time you sang in public? Do you remember when the first time you sang in public was?

Yes sir, it was back when I was about a ten- or eleven-year-old. I was in an amateur program at a fair.

[P.W.] And did you use a lot of gyrations then?

Well, I wasn't doin' the type songs I doin' now. Nobody knew what rock and roll was back in those days.

[P.W.] So when you hear rock and roll, it gets you on fire?

Not when I just hear it on the radio. When I'm doin' it on stage…you have to put on a show for the people.

[P.W.] Yeah.

In other words, people can buy your records and hear you sing. They don't have to come out to hear you sing. You have to put on a show in order to draw a crowd.

[P.W.] Yeah.

If I just stood out there and sang and never moved a muscle, the people would say well my goodness, I can stay home and listen to his records.

[P.W.] That's right.

But you have to give 'em a show, somethin' to talk about.

[P.W.] Now in this show—we've established that it is a show that you put on—how did you get the idea for the rapid amount of action? Have you ever seen anybody move around as much?

No sir, I never have. I just…

[P.W.] Never had any old showman advise you you oughta do it?

Nobody has ever told me.

[P.W.] Where is the first time that you used the rapid action?

The very first appearance after I started recording. I was on a show in Memphis where I started doin' that. I was on a show as an extra added single, a big jamboree at an outdoor theater…outdoor auditorium. And, uh, and I came out on stage and I was…I was scared stiff. And it was my first big appearance in front of an audience.

[P.W.] Uh-huh.

And I came out and I was doin' a fast-type tune, one of my first records, and everybody was hollerin' and I didn't know what they were hollerin' at. Everybody was screamin' and every-

thing. And then I came offstage and my manager told me they was hollerin' because I was wigglin' my legs.

[P.W.] Uh-huh.
And I was unaware of what I was doing.

[P.W.] And who was your manager at that time?
Bob Neal.

[P.W.] Bob Neal, okay.
That was my manager. And so I went back out for an encore and I did a little more. And the more I did, the wilder they went.

[P.W.] Okay, now we're down to the question…in other words, you picked up your style when they…from when they appreciated just a little wiggle, you figured they'd appreciate more of a little…more wiggle, and they did. So now you really give 'em the works. Right?
That's right.

[P.W.] Okay.
I'll say this, sir, before we go any further. It's back on the subject we were talkin' about at first—ah, talkin' about reporters. There's a rumor has gotten out that I don't have time… no time for reporters; that I just answer with a "yes" or "no" and it's very untrue. I have my first one yet to turn down. I've never turned down a reporter. I've never turned down a disc jockey. I know that I can't visit radio stations like I'd like to, but I don't have time. And I have never turned down a reporter. I have never been sassy to one. In fact, I never been sassy to anyone. And I've always stayed and talked to 'em as long as they wanted to talk. And I admire 'em.

[P.W.] Why?
Well, because they keep us in business. I mean, the newspaper columns, the reporters, the disc jockeys…we all work hand-in-hand.

[P.W.] Do you recognize, or do you have any idea one way or the other whether crit-
icism has helped or hurt your career?
I don't know, sir. I wish I knew.

[P.W.] Would you agree with myself in the opinion that the criticism has helped skyrocket you, with a defense comin' to your rescue every time somebody knocks you. Every knock was a boost, in other words.
That makes a lot of sense.

[P.W.] Here's a new question now. What was your reaction to the NBC comment, after they learned [Ed] Sullivan [CBS] hired ya, that you are just a flash in the pan?
Maybe they're right. I don't know. Nobody knows, in fact. If I knew, I would be a mastermind.

[P.W.] Uh-huh.
I'm not.

[P.W.] Okay. That's a good answer. Next question is…what about your acting career? Do you have any plans for an acting career?
Yes I do.

[P.W.] You have a contract now with…
I have one with Paramount.

[P.W.] And how long is it?
Seven years.

[P.W.] Seven years. And how many pictures?
A picture a year.

[P.W.] Picture a year. Can you give me an approximation of the amount of that contract over the seven years. Or the amount of fee that you'll receive?
No sir, that's never been released.

[P.W.] Have you ever had any experience in acting before?
I've never read a line in my life.

[P.W.] How do you figure to go about learning to become an actor?
Sir, I don't think you learn to become an actor. I think you just, maybe you've got a little bit of

acting talent, you develop it. I don't think you learn to become an actor. If you learn to be an actor…in other words, if you're not a real actor…you're false.

[P.W.] Well, are you learning, in your acting, are you taking advice from anyone? Tom Parker or…
I'm not takin' advice from anybody.

[P.W.] Well I mean, is anyone responsible for assisting you in that?
The Colonel is responsible for assisting me in everything.

[P.W.] Uh-huh.
But I've talked to veteran actors. I've talked to a lot of the producers and directors in Hollywood, and they all give you advice.

[P.W.] They think you're a natural?
Well I wouldn't say that. But they told me that I had good possibilities because when I took my screen test—like I said, I have never read a line, I never studied acting, never been in any plays or anything—I just got out there. I knew my script, they sent it to me before I came to Hollywood.

[P.W.] How big a script was it? How many pages or lines, do you remember?
Oh, it was about fifteen pages, I guess.

[P.W.] Go ahead.
And I knew my script when I got out there and I just tried to put myself into the place of the character I was playing. Just tryin' to act natural as I could.

[P.W.] And did you have any wheels that approved the test, that you know?
You mean, uh?

[P.W.] Any of the movie wheels [executives]?
Well, all of 'em saw it.

[P.W.] Do you look forward to your acting career?

Yes I do. I think I'm gonna enjoy it. I really do.

[P.W.] Do you think that will eventually become your main choice of income?
I don't know (laughs).

[P.W.] Wait and see. Are you looking for a TV show of your own?
No I'm not. I never thought about it.

[P.W.] If not, why not?
I'm just not ready for that yet.

[P.W.] You mean in experience…in your own experience, you're not ready yet?
That's right.

[P.W.] Next question: Who are your most avid fans? What age group would you say?
Well, I don't know. Mostly the teenagers, I guess…probably.

[P.W.] Have you had many older people go real excited when you're around… that you recall?
Well, not when I'm around. I've had 'em…

[P.W.] Or tried to get to ya?
Yes, I've seen quite a few adults…

[P.W.] Men or women?
…mostly women, jump up and down and scream and everything.

[P.W.] Do you recall seeing any gray-haired women jump up and down?
Well, there was one in Tampa, Florida… yesterday.

[P.W.] That was on August the fifth.
August the fifth, yeah, there was one maybe. About sixty-five years old, she was completely gray-haired.

[P.W.] What'd she do?
She was clapping her hands and everything, right along with the other people.

[P.W.] But most of 'em are teenage girls. How about the boys?
Well, the boys they seem to like the music.

[P.W.] Who's this boy that just came up to see me? What's your name?

[Jerry Gambrell] Jerry Gambrell.

[P.W.] How do you spell it?

[J.G.] G-a-m-b-r-e-l-l.

[P.W.] Now let me get that name again. Jerry, J-e-r-r-y G-a-m-b-r-e-l-l. And give me your comment that you told me in the car when we were coming up to the show tonight…once again.

[J.G.] I said I liked Elvis Presley 'bout as good as some girls.

[P.W.] And why?

[J.G.] I just like his style.

[P.W.] And the rhythm he presents?

[J.G.] Yes sir.

[P.W.] Okay, that's an intervention there of… and how old are you, son?

[J.G.] Fifteen.

[P.W.]…Of a fifteen-year-old boy who came to see his show tonight and said he liked his show as well as the girls did almost, because of the rhythm and the action. The next question: How 'bout tiny children? Do you have any tiny children, before I go to the next question?
Quite a few of 'em. In fact, I guess I get more real tiny ones than I have adults.

[P.W.] How do you handle autographs?
What do you mean, how do I handle it?

[P.W.] How do you keep from…do you autograph every one that reaches you?
Every one that gets to me, I always do. I never turn anybody down.

[P.W.] Sometimes you seem to disregard the protection given you by people in the theaters, and the ushers and so forth, and maybe shake hands with someone, reach over the rail or

somethin' like that. Or you open a window when you're ridin' in a car, when you know it's…you shouldn't.
Yeah.

[P.W.] Why do you do that?
If it wasn't for gettin' mobbed, maybe clothes torn off, stuff like that, I would go right out in the middle of those people, but I hate to turn anybody down that wants autographs…buys pictures and wants to get 'em signed tonight…

[P.W.] How many autographs do you sign a day, do you know?
I don't know. But, I hate to turn anybody down. But in a situation like, well, most of the time the people…the crowd is so large you couldn't autograph everybody.

[P.W.] Have you noticed the girls who scream and shout the most—are many of them blondes? Have you noticed?
No, that doesn't mean anything (laughs).

[P.W.] No…it seemed like so many of the girls I've seen are bleached blonde. You don't notice?
I haven't seen that many. I saw more in Tampa, Florida, on the same date, than anywhere else.

[P.W.] Oh. That just seems to be a local situation.
Yeah, I guess. Probably happened. Maybe it's a fad goin' around town…nothin' to do with me. That doesn't make…I mean there's girls, brunettes, redheads, streaked heads, everything (laughs).

[P.W.] Most of the boys…do most of the boys wear long sideburns, or do you notice?
No. There's a lot of 'em wear 'em, but I guess there's more crew-cuts than anything else.

[P.W.] How did you happen to adopt long sideburns?
I just always wanted to. When I was growin' up I always wanted to grow 'em because…

[P.W.] Make you feel like a bigger man, or older.

It makes you look a little older, and I always liked 'em.

[P.W.] Did you ride motorcycles when you were a kid?
No sir. I ride one now but not when I was growin' up.

[P.W.] Generally you think of a motorcycle rider as being [with] long sideburns. That's why I asked.
That's right.

[P.W.] How's showtime? Are we doin' all right?
Yeah, we got a few more minutes.

[P.W.] Next question: Do you have any opinions why you are such a big hit? Now this is a question a lot of people want to know, so stop and think about it if you have to.
Well…pretty stiff question. I don't know how to answer you. It's all happened so fast to me. I don't know…I don't know what it is.

[P.W.] Well now, when you're performing and the screams, you realize that every movement will bring a surge of screams from the crowd, do you enjoy making a movement that will make the crowd scream?
Mmmm. Yes sir.

[P.W.] And do you sort of play the audience? I mean, see which side of the auditorium you can make scream. Or do you try to work the audience in any way?
I just try to work the audience. Half the time, I can't even see the audience.

[P.W.] Half the time?
In most theaters and auditoriums, the lights keep you from seein' anything…anyone.

[P.W.] Sometimes on occasion I notice you throw your head back and laugh. Is it because you enjoy making a surge of noise come out?
No I get tickled. I get tickled sometimes, maybe some little girl, or individual girl in the front row will do something real funny, like grab her hair or somethin' like that.

[P.W.] What's the funniest thing that you recall seein' happen in the front row…
Mmmmm.

[P.W.]…that made you laugh? Have you ever gotten broken up on your show by somethin' that happened in front of you?
Yes. The whole band has several times.

[P.W.] Where was the last time?
I don't remember exactly where, but a couple times I had to walk off stage, I got so tickled at somethin'.

[P.W.] Because of the roughhouse or because you got tickled?
Because I got tickled.

[P.W.] Can you remember that incident, when you had to walk off stage?
I remember what was happening. This one girl in Atlanta, Georgia, had come to three different shows and sat in the front row and screamed all through all of 'em. Then the night we closed, well she decided to come up on the stage. So she made a dive for the stage and got almost up there. About five policemen grabbed her and she was fightin' 'em just like some man would and everything. And the audience…it just broke the audience up. She was screamin' "let me at him," stuff like that.

[P.W.] Yeah.
And I got so tickled I had to walk off stage.

[P.W.] Well, did you leave for her protection, or just because you was tickled?
Because I got tickled.

[P.W.] Then did you come back out?
Yes.

[P.W.] And by that time, what'd happened to the girl?
They had carried her… I don't know.

[P.W.] You don't know.

Elvis with Eddy Arnold, RCA's Frank Folsam, and Col. Parker.

I didn't see her anymore. They must have taken her outside.

[P.W.] I'll ask another question that I've already asked you before but I'll ask it again. How do you feel about having to calm down for *The Steve Allen Show?* You say you didn't have to calm down.
No, I didn't have to.

[P.W.] Nobody asked you…your manager?
Yes. People asked me, but I still didn't have to unless I wanted to, but I didn't want to make anybody mad, so I did.

[P.W.] Let me ask you a question or two about Tom Parker. That's the Colonel Tom Parker of Madison, Tennessee, who managed Hank Snow, Eddy Arnold, and some of the others. How did you first meet Tom Parker?
When I was with Bob Neal—Bob Neal was my manager—but the Colonel used to take shows out on the road, he'd hire me for an extra added single.

[P.W.] Uh-huh.
And he undoubtedly liked the performance that we did, so we decided to start workin' together, him as my manager.

[P.W.] Was it Bob Neal turned you over to Tom?
Yes. Well his contract was up.

[P.W.] His contract was up?
Yes sir. I had been with him a year.

[P.W.] And when did you pick Parker, or did Parker come for you?
No, we more or less picked each other. It was like this, the Colonel [said]…"If you want me as your manager, I will do the best I can." And I told him, "If you'd like to manage me I'll work for you…" It was a deal like that.

[P.W.] What date did Tom Parker take over?
It was March the fifteenth.

[P.W.] That was what year? This year?
Yes sir.

[P.W.] Nineteen fifty…
Fifty-five.

[P.W.] Fifty-six.
Uh, fifty-six.

[P.W.] This is August.
Oh, that's right.

[P.W.] You just been with him for three months.
Now wait now. March, April, May, June, July, August. He's been with me 'bout six months.

[P.W.] Has that been the period of your biggest rise in popularity?
Yes, it has definitely been.

[P.W.] Do you ascribe any of that popularity to his operation?
Most of it, yes sir.

[P.W.] A while ago, I asked you a question: Do you have any idea why you're such a big hit? Do you think that the promotion which Parker handles, has anything to do with that…you becoming a solid hit? Or do you think you would have been a hit anyway?
Oh…

[P.W.] That's kind of a tricky question, but… how were you doin' before?
Well I was makin' quite a bit of money, but I mean I wasn't as nationally known as I am now. 'Cause the Colonel has a lot of friends in the entertainment business. He has a lot of connections.

[P.W.] Oh yeah.
[He] knows lots of people that are important wheels in the business.

[P.W.] So you weren't well-known before Tom Parker took over.
I wasn't known at all until Colonel Parker started managing me, see, then I got on RCA Victor and on television and then I started being known. I was known in certain sections, you know, but I wasn't known all over.

[P.W.] Do you recall any publicity gimmick or promotion gimmick that amused you particularly, that worked out?
He's a very amusing guy. He plans stuff that nobody else would even think of. Oh, I could tell you lots of things but I don't have the time right now.

[P.W.] Okay. Ah, gettin' close [to showtime]. Okay, well I'll thank you. Good evening.

AUGUST 7, 1956

LOCATION: *St. Petersburg, Florida.*
INTERVIEWER: *Bob Hoffer.*
SOURCE: In the Beginning *(CD).*

[Bob Hoffer] Well kids, like I promised you about, ooh, twenty-four hours ago from this very minute, I would do my best to get the boy himself to say something to you. And lots of you have written and asked if we couldn't get him on the show. Well the problem there is that the guy just has to have a little time of his own, and he has little enough of it. So he is gracious enough to ask us to come up here and talk with him in the dressing room. And there are, let's see, three of his buddies here and Joanne is over in the corner. So you're in good company with Elvis Presley. Elvis, I'm awfully glad to take this opportunity to talk with you a little bit.
Well thank you very much, Bob, it's a pleasure too. And is that your wife over in the corner?

[B.H.] That is my wife Joanne, yes.
Whooooh!

[B.H.] Now Joanne will be the envy of everybody at the Platter Party tonight. She has been whooooed at by Elvis Presley. And I thank you, Elvis. I agree with you, incidentally. Sure I do. You know what I was impressed first of all when I saw you, you're a taller boy than I had figured. How tall are you, incidentally?
An even six foot.

[B.H.] Are ya? I had not pictured you as quite so tall. You…what sports have you indulged in…any? When you were in school?
Well I tried to play football, only I never could make it. I never was very good at it. So I…

[B.H.] Gave it up for the git-fiddle slinging, uh?
Yeah.

[B.H.] I don't blame you a miserable bit, not as well as you've done. What I would like to find out from ya…I know that probably your top problem on these tours is getting enough rest to do the job you do on the stage. How do you manage the confounded rest on these tours?
Well, I don't. In fact, don't any of us get much rest. We just, and it's a lot worse when you do two or three shows a day…three and four. We do four sometimes.

[B.H.] So you just have to catch it when you can. Is that right?
That's right. And then usually when it's all over with there's a lot of people around and you just don't get much rest at all.

[B.H.] So just between tours you've got to climb in the sack somewhere and rest a little while. Is that the idea?
Yes, that's right. We average maybe four or five hours a night.

[B.H.] Where do you call home now?
Memphis, Tennessee.

[B.H.] Your parents up there now, in that nice big house you bought 'em?
Yes sir.

[B.H.] Good. I've heard a lot about that and it's a fine thing. Something else I've heard about too, on a piece of your property, I heard the bad luck you had with the Lincoln over in Tampa. Is that true? About in the garage?
Oh that wasn't too bad. Some of the kids got my gas cap and some o' my cigarette lighters, but that was the fault of the garage.

[B.H.] Somebody said they'd gotten the hub caps too. Is that not true?
No, that's not.

[B.H.] Oh, am I so glad. I could just see you buyin' four hub caps for a Lincoln. That would cost more than the car I drive, believe me.

I think the Continental hub caps are fifty dollars each. That's two hundred dollars for a set, you know.

[B.H.] Wow! What's this three-hundred-and-fifty-dollar hood ornament you were telling Ann Rowe of the *St. Petersburg Times* about?
Yes, the ornament on the Lincoln Continental is three hundred and fifty dollars 'cause it's white gold plated.

[B.H.] Listen, one thing I did want to check with you on, I know you don't get the chance to keep up with things too much when you're on the tour. Did you know that Ed Sullivan was injured in an automobile accident the other night [August 6]?
Yes sir, I read that in the paper.

[B.H.] He is not going to be able to make his show until the nineteenth of August.
Is that right?

[B.H.] That's the first one he'll be able to make. I thought you might be interested in that. And when are you due on the Sullivan show again?
My first one is September ninth.

[B.H.] Ninth, uh?
Yeah.

[B.H.] Maybe have a new platter out for Victor by that time?
I doubt it.

[B.H.] You doubt it, really?
I shouldn't have because I just had a release, see.

[B.H.] Oh yes, and you've done pretty well with it too. Over a million copies in something like two weeks for "Hound Dog" and "Don't Be Cruel." Is that right?
Yeah.

[B.H.] Three gold platters you've got yourself now for Victor, and I think it's a fine thing.
Four!

[B.H.] Four? Excuse me, four.
I got one for "Heartbreak Hotel."

[B.H.] Yeah.
One for "Hound Dog," one for "I Want You, I Need You, I Love You," and one for my album [Elvis Presley].

[B.H.] The album too has gone over a million?
Yes sir.

[B.H.] No kidding. That's almost fantastic in the record business, isn't it? Well, Elvis, there are a couple other things. I saw in the paper the night before last that Hal Wallis is thinking of starring you in a picture with Jerry Lewis. Had you heard that one?
Jerry Lewis?

[B.H.] With Jerry Lewis. Have you heard it? Really.
No I hadn't.

[B.H.] Well there's somethin' for you to think about.
You know Dean and Jerry broke up.

[B.H.] Yes, that's true, soooo.
I heard somethin' about that but, I don't think I'd (laughs)…

[B.H.] What's the…what do you mean?
I don't know.

[B.H.] You don't think you and Jerry would get along (laughs)?
That's Dean Martin. Well, it's not that, but that's Dean Martin and it'll always be Dean and Jerry, nothin' else.

[B.H.] Well I sort of agree with you on it. Speakin' about partners and enemies and so forth, what's the Pat Boone situation with you? Do you know Pat?
Well, I know Pat very well. I didn't know anything about anything like that except when I read this Radio-TV Mirror, *or whatever it is, where they said "Presley and Boone battle it out." Why that's nothing. I mean Pat Boone and I are very good friends.*

[B.H.] And you're not fighting with Pat Boone at all?
Never. Pat's one of the nicest guys I ever met. I don't think he'd say anything bad about me.

[B.H.] I think the only time you've crossed swords on songs is "Tutti-Frutti," isn't it? It's the only tune that both of you have cut.

Well, both of us had a flop on it so we didn't have anything to fight about, really.

[B.H.] (Laughs.) Good. Okay. Well we've had quite a time here with Elvis and he's getting ready to take off, I know, and to finish that lunch I guess that he had here.
Well I didn't have enough. They didn't bring me but one sandwich and that's just an appetizer.

[B.H.] There was one other thing I wanted to check with you. What has been your own personal reaction to the reaction of your fans as a result of the Steve Allen appearance?
Well, the kids didn't like it. In other words, they were writing letters in and telling 'em to leave me alone, leave me the way I was, and all that. But I believe that I won a lot of new friends by doing that.

[B.H.] Sure.
By showin' 'em that I could act like a gentleman if I wanted to (laughs).

[B.H.] Well you...he doesn't mean it. Go ahead (laughs).
Which is not the way that I started out.

[B.H.] Sure. Well, Elvis, I don't want to take up any more of your time. Gosh, I know you've got a thousand things to do and I thank you for this five or six minutes. It's been wonderful and Joanne and I can go home and Joanne can sit there starry-eyed after having been whooooooed at, and I thank you so much for this time and I personally want you to know that on the Bob Hoffer show there are no anti-Elvis Presley fan clubs at all. It's all "for" Elvis Presley, and that we spin at least three to four of your records each evening in a forty-five-minute period, as a result of the demand of the kids. So I, and I also want you to know that as a result of our poll at our Platter Party Saturday night, "Hound Dog" and "Don't Be Cruel" were number one and two in St. Petersburg, in that order, with the kids. And I think that ought to be good news to you.

Yes it is.

[B.H.] Okay, thanks very much, Elvis.
Thank you, sir.

[B.H.] And lots of luck in the future.
Thank you very much.

[B.H.] Right. Bye.

AUGUST 8, 1956

LOCATION: *Orlando, Florida.*
INTERVIEWER: *"Happy" (of NBC's* Monitor*).*
SOURCE: When All Was Kool *(CD).*

[Happy] Many a teenager would like to be in my shoes right now, for we have beside us the one and only Elvis Presley. It's good to have you on NBC's [Radio] *Monitor*, **Elvis.**
Thank you, Happy. It's a pleasure bein' here, sir.

[Happy] Might tell you right now that eight thousand fans are anxiously awaiting for your performance here, but let's ask you a few questions for our NBC listening audience. How do you like this traveling?
Well sir, I liked it a lot. In fact I don't like to stay in one place very long.

[Happy] What about your future plans, Elvis?
You mean as far as the music business? Well, everything's happened so fast I hadn't had time to make many plans, but I just hope to continue makin' records and everything, and hope I can get some good material so...might like it.

[Happy] Do you think maybe the movies will occupy most of your time if you make a picture?
No sir, they won't occupy most of my time, just...I don't know...

[Happy] Do you like traveling around the country?
...In other words, we'll cross that bridge when we come to it.

[Happy] Do you like playing nightclubs, Elvis?
No sir.

[Happy] You don't?
I do not, not particularly.

[Happy] How did you ever start those long sideburns? You're starting a fad now.
Well, I've had 'em for twenty-eight years.
[At a time when Elvis was twenty-one years of age, it is quite mysterious that he states the impossible—having sideburns for twenty-eight years—unless he was joking. Strangely, there is no indication of joking or kidding, nor is there any laughter here.]

[Happy] Twenty-eight years.
Twenty-eight long years.

[Happy] And you don't mind wearing 'em, uh?
No, I don't. I've had 'em ever since I was old enough to grow 'em.

[Happy] What's your favorite song, Elvis?
Out of mine, or out of…

[Happy] Out of any song?
"Don't Be Cruel" is my favorite of mine now. Of other records I like [The Platters'] "My Prayer" probably.

[Happy] And what is the biggest thrill that you've had so far?
Well I've had quite a few of 'em. I've had quite a few.

[Happy] "Heartbreak Hotel" the first one?
That's my biggest hit…it wasn't my biggest thrill, I don't guess. Course I hadn't seen the royalty check from it yet (laughs).

[Happy] Well it's nice to have you on *Monitor*, Elvis Presley, and thanks for being with us.
Thank you, Happy, very much.

[Happy] Now back to Radio Central in New York.

AUGUST 9, 1956

LOCATION: *Peabody Auditorium, Daytona Beach, Florida.*

INTERVIEWER: *Ed Ripley and "Peggy."*
SOURCE: Rockin' Rebel *(LP).*

[Ed Ripley] Ladies and gentlemen, this is your ol' buddy, Ed Ripley, and we're here at Peabody Auditorium in Daytona Beach. And I'm in Elvis Presley's dressing room, where one of our girls from Deland High School is interviewing Elvis. Let's listen in on it:
[Interview in progress, so comment or question preceding response below is not known.]
Don't you know that's what I'm talkin' about on the stage version.

[Peggy] Okay. How many cars do you really have?
Four.

[Peggy] Do you like the girls going wild over you?
That's what keeps me in business (laughs).

[Peggy] Are you going to shave your sideburns off?
Never.

[Peggy] Is it true that you don't collect stuffed animals?
I don't collect 'em, no. A lot of people have gotten the idea that I do and have sent 'em to me. But, I mean, I'll keep 'em if people send 'em to me. But I never thought about makin' a collection of 'em.

[Peggy] Are you bothered by anybody who says that they're real good friends of yours now, when they didn't even speak to you before?
Nah.

[Peggy] Well, I have another one, but I don't know if I should ask it or not.
You can ask it.

[Peggy] Are you a dope fiend?
Yeah! (Laughs.) What stage.

[Peggy] (Laughing.) What's your favorite color?
What's my favorite what?

[Peggy] Color?

As far as clothes, I like black. As far as cars, I like white.

[Peggy] Okay, thank you.

[E.R.] Well, Elvis, what's this I hear about pink Cadillacs? I thought you took a fancy to that.

Well, my first one was a pink one.

[E.R.] Yeah.

And I got a kind of a, you know, a sentimental feeling about it.

[E.R.] Elvis, just how'd you get your start in the entertainment world? I understand you were in Memphis, and signed up with Sun Records Company. Just how'd you get your big break?

Well, let me see now. I told the story so much I've gotten it confused. Hang on just a minute.

[E.R.] We'll hang on. Elvis is signing one of his pictures here right now. It's pretty busy here in the dressing room this evening, and we got movie cameras, autographs, and everything else going around here. We even got some people out here knockin' on the windows.

I'm ready now. Now ask me that question you asked me.

[E.R.] How'd you first get your start as a recording artist and everything?

Well I started out in Memphis. Just started out makin' records. I made one record and it kinda caught on.

[E.R.] What was that first record you made?

"That's All Right Mama" and "Blue Moon of Kentucky."

[E.R.] And how'd you go about gettin' your contract with RCA Victor?

RCA Victor just bought my contract from Sun Records. I didn't have much say-so, although I am glad they did, you know.

[E.R.] Yeah, I guess it did kinda help, a big label and everything. Oh, one more question, Elvis, before we sign things off. Of all the records you've made, both on Sun and now on RCA Victor, what one do you think you like best personally?

I like "Don't Be Cruel" probably better than any of 'em I've made.

[Peggy] Oh, good!

[E.R.] (Laughs.) Well I think I'm inclined to agree with you. Peggy over here, she kinda likes "Don't Be Cruel" too.

And I like Peggy!

[E.R.] (Laughs.) Well, how 'bout that? That's quite a ring. Folks, Elvis has got…looks like a horseshoe there with diamonds in it.

Yes sir.

[E.R.] And that's on his right hand. On his little finger of his left hand…what is that there?

A black sapphire.

[Peggy] Oh, that's neat!

[E.R.] A black sapphire. By the way, do you know what your next record's going to be for RCA?

No sir, I don't know what.

[E.R.] Don't you give out that kind of information?

Well, if I knew I'd tell you, but, I haven't made anything. "Hound Dog" and "Don't Be Cruel" just came out and I haven't made one since then.

[E.R.] I hear you're gonna get a golden record for those two sides. Is that right?

I get a gold one for "Hound Dog," and I get one for "I Want You, I Need You, I Love You," and one for my album [Elvis Presley].

[E.R.] The album sold a million too?

Yes.

[E.R.] Well, by golly. So when do you think your next release will be out? After your tour is

WESTERN UNION
TELEGRAM
W. P. MARSHALL, PRESIDENT

The filing time shown in the date line on domestic telegrams is STANDARD TIME at point of origin. Time of receipt is STANDARD TIME at point of destination

NSA052 LA109   10 L

L HDA084 PD=VGP HOLLYWOOD CALIF 21 856A MP=

MISS JUNE JUANICO=

505 FAYARD ST BILOXI MISS=

HI WIOOLE BITTY. I MISS YOU BABY. HAVENT HAD YOU OUT OF
MY MIND FOR A SECOND. ILL ALWAYS BE YOURS AND YOURS
ALONE TO LOVE. DREAMED ABOUT YOU LAST NIGHT. LOVE YA
YEA UH-HUH=

EP=

over, around the country here? [Sound of breaking glass.] Oooh! Somebody just broke a window here in Elvis' dressing room. Ah, gettin' back to you, Elvis, just this one more thing now—when do you think your next release is comin' out?

It'll probably be (laughs)—they let him out the window—probably be a couple months yet.

[E.R.] Well, Elvis, it's been mighty nice talkin' to you. And I know all the fans over on Dayta [Daytona] music over here on WJBS will really appreciate your givin' 'em all a little word there. Thanks a lot.

Well, thank you very much.

AUGUST 21, 1956

ITEM: *Telegram from Elvis Presley (Hollywood, California) to June Juanico (Biloxi, Mississippi).*

SOURCE: *Document photocopy.*

Miss June Juanico,
Hi wioole [widdle] bitty. I miss you baby. Haven't had you out of my mind for a second. I'll always be yours and yours alone to love. Dreamed about you last night. Love ya. Yea uh-huh.

EP

AUGUST 28, 1956

LOCATION: *20th Century-Fox Lot, Hollywood, California.*

SOURCE: Elvis Answers Back *magazine.*

Hi! This is Elvis Presley! Well at last I'm getting the chance to sit down and talk to you, to speak right out and tell you all the things that are on my mind. I've wanted to tell you about myself for a long time, a real long time. And now that I've got the chance to speak right out to you, I hope you won't mind if I get a lot of things off my chest.

Telegram to
June Juanico,
1956.

Things I think you'll understand, though I know that a lot of people don't. I want to tell you in my own way and in my own words why I do the things I do and why I feel the way I feel. And I know that if I can just sit down with you alone somewhere, if I can just talk with you personal like, you'll understand.

That's why I made the gold record on the cover of this magazine. In the record business, giving a gold record has a special meaning. It's kind of like an engagement ring or a new car or a thousand dollars. You just don't pass 'em around to just anybody. When you give someone a gold record, you're saying, "This is something pretty important to me, something pretty special…from me to you." That's just how I feel about this record of mine in the magazine. That's why it's gold. And that's why I wanted to make it up. Because I wanted, more than anything, the chance to get together with you!

One of the biggest kicks I ever had in my life was making this special gold record for you. I wanted it to say just exactly the way I feel, and I've played it over and over, trying to be sure it's just exactly right. You know, one of the things they write about me is that I try to do everything perfect. Maybe I try too hard sometimes. But they're right. I feel I've got to do my best, whatever I try. I'll bet you feel that way, too.

About the "Criticism"

When I first started doing my performances, everyone was happy. All the kids came out and had a good time and released a lot of energy and no one was getting hurt. It lasted that way about two years. I kept singing the songs everyone liked, and kept doing what I'd always been doing on the stage.

But during the past six or seven months, I've gotten criticism from a lot of people for "losing myself" in my performances, for

singing the way I do on stage. I can't really understand it. This is the only thing I can say, this is the only explanation I've got for it.

I've been doing the same thing ever since I started in singing on stage, for at least two and a half years now. It's only been the past few months that I've felt criticism. So I guess it's because my records have become bigger and everything. I guess the more popular you are, the more criticism you get. If I was still back at a Music Jamboree in Memphis, nobody would care what I did when I sang. But now, as I'm meeting more and more people every day and singing more and more places all the time, it's a different story.

I can tell you this, though. I don't scheme up any actions for the songs I sing, like I've heard some people tell. I sing the way I do, and act the way I do, because it comes natural to me while I'm singing. I wouldn't do it if I thought it wasn't the right thing to do, or if I thought someone was being hurt by it. If I thought that, I'd pack up and go back home and never sing another note.

About the "Show"

There's one other thing, too, that I think people should try and realize. There's a big difference in singing on a record and singing for an audience. People can stay home and listen to your records on the radio or phonograph and it doesn't cost 'em anything. But when they pay their money to come out and see you at a personal appearance, these people want to see a show. They pay their money to see something with life in it, not just to hear something on a phonograph. If I stood up in front of an audience and did nothing but sing, I'd be holding myself back deliberate. I wouldn't enjoy myself, I couldn't enjoy myself if I did that. And the audience would know it. They'd know I didn't enjoy what I was doing, and they wouldn't come out to see me again the next time.

So I'm Never Nervous, Huh?

One of the things they've said about me is that I'm never nervous. They say I don't worry about a thing and they say I get eight or ten good hours sleep a night. I wish they were right.

But they aren't. I've been kind of nervous all my life. And now, going out on personal appearances all the time, I get so keyed up that I just can't relax. After a show I'll go back to my hotel room and go to bed and try to get some sleep. But you know how hard it is, getting to sleep in a strange room and in a strange bed away from home, particularly when you're kind of nervous and jumpy. I'll go to bed at night and close my eyes and just lay there. And then I'll start turning. And twisting. And a couple of hours will pass, and I won't have had a lick of sleep. They say you learn how to relax when you get older. I hope they're right.

I can't help it. I just feel restless sometimes. I don't know what it is. Maybe it's that I've never been away from home and all my folks and friends for so long. I don't know. But it's a funny feeling. A lonesome feeling. I guess everyone's felt it, sometime or another.

I like the sun and the outdoors and swimming. I have to be careful of chlorine, though, because I react to it. That's why we don't use it in the pool we just had built back home. The neighbor kids love the pool. They come on over all the time. And momma, my best girl, is learning how to swim, too.

My Special Girl

I know what you've read about that "special girl" I have back home in Memphis. You've read that we went steady through high school, and that we've been dating each other steady for the past three years. I know. I've read about her, too. But that's the only way I know about her, because to tell you the plain facts, I don't have a special girl. Now or ever. I've never gone with any one girl three weeks, or three months in a row, let alone three years. And right now, with all the traveling and work I'm doing, I don't have time to date very much. I'd like to, of course, but I just don't have the time.

When I get back home to Memphis every so often, it's easier to get me a date because I still know a lot of girls I went to school with. But I've never gone steady with any of them. We all have a good time together, and that's about all there is to it as far as any "special girl" is concerned.

Maybe it won't always be like that. I hope not.

Yes, I phone home to my folks in Memphis a lot. Almost every day. But I like to know how they are and how things are going. And I don't get time to write much or like that, so I call instead. It sure sounds good, hearing their voices. Makes me a little homesick sometimes.

I'm not a loner, I don't think. But I've got to admit. Sometimes I like just getting off by myself. You know. Just off somewhere alone. No crowds or anything. Where it's just peaceful. And quiet. And you can think.

What, No Singing Lessons?

Nope. I've never had a singing lesson in my life. No music lesson of any kind, in fact. I just started singing when I was a little kid, like I told you, and I've been doing it ever since. I was 11 years old when I went in front of a real audience for the first time. It was at a fairground in the town I was born, Tupelo, Mississippi. I was shaking like a leaf, but I'd set my heart on singing, and nothing in this world could have stopped me from going ahead and entering the talent contest

Backstage interview with a reporter, 1956.

at the fair. I did it all on my own, and I didn't have any idea what I was going to do once I got out there in front of all those people. All I had in my head was the idea that I was going to sing.

I didn't have any music or anything, and I couldn't get anybody to play for me and I couldn't play for myself because I didn't know how. So I just went out there and started singing. I sang a song called "Old Shep," the story of a dog, and I know they must of felt sorry for me because they gave me fifth prize and everyone applauded real nice. Man I'll tell you I was really scared and shaking and all turning over inside. But I felt good, too. I'd been on a stage for the first time in my life.

Later on, when I was 13 or so, me and a bunch of the kids would fool around singing. I never tried to go into any of the High School shows or anything like that, but I sure enjoyed beating up a storm with the other kids. And you know how it is. You get to trying different ways of using your voice and

singing the words and such, and pretty soon you're singing in a style all your own. Everyone does it, no matter whether you want to be a singer or not. So that's how I got my practice in singing, just experimenting around and singing with the other kids and having a good time. And most important, singing the way I felt. And to tell you the truth, I think it's the best kind of practice I could have had.

The Green Scrapbook

Yes, it's true that I keep me a scrapbook of a lot of the stuff that's printed about me. But you know something? I don't save the articles or stories that tell nice things about me. My scrapbook only has stuff in it that isn't very friendly. I'll tell you why this is.

When I first started out, my momma wanted to save all the programs and pictures and things that everyone put in the papers and magazines. I wasn't much interested in doing this, because I was so busy singing and working and learning that I just didn't want to take the time to sit down every so often in the middle of something and start cutting out pictures and things. Momma bought her a big green scrapbook, though, and asked me to send her stuff whenever I got the chance. For the first year or so, I didn't send nary a thing, and the scrapbook was empty, except for a couple of clippings she got out of the Memphis papers.

Then one day I saw this article about me not being a very good singer. I cut that out and sent it to momma and she wrote back and told me I didn't want to fill my scrapbook with things like that. But I wrote back and told her, "Momma, anyone can fill a scrapbook with good things. But what good does it do? I'd like to know the things people don't particularly like and study them and try to make myself better if I can." So that's *how The Green Scrapbook got started. I've got a lot of the pages filled, and a lot of them are still empty, but I'll tell you this. Every time I go home to Memphis, I take down that scrapbook and study it. I know most of the things in it by heart, and I'm always going to do my best to improve whenever and wherever I can.*

My Greatest Ambition

I know I've been lucky in an awful lot of ways. But I think the luckiest thing that ever happened to me is that I'm already beginning to realize my greatest ambition.

All of my life, I've wanted to be an actor, though I never was in any school plays or recited a line other than the Gettysburg Address for my sixth-grade homeroom class. But always sticking in the back of my head was the idea that somehow, someday, I'd like to get the chance to act.

I came out to Hollywood almost three months ago, and Mr. Hal Wallis of Paramount Pictures asked me to take a screen test. I jumped at the chance. I went in to take the test and Mr. Wallis told me not to worry about trying to act like John Barrymore or anybody. He told me to just act like myself. I studied up on what they wanted me to do, and then before I knew it I was in front of the camera. I wonder if you can ever know what it's like to be standing on a movie sound stage and hear a bell ring and people shout "Quiet," and then all of a sudden realize that everyone's watching you, and you're supposed to be acting out a part. I'll tell you, it's enough to make your legs slide out from under you.

Whenever I get excited, I stutter a little bit. I have a hard time saying "when" or "where" or any words that start with "w" or "i." Well I can tell you I really had a hard time with the w's and i's that day.

When the test was over, I thought I'd been awful. But Mr. Wallis came up to me and he told me that things like my missing letters of some words is actually good in acting… it makes the performance more natural. I kind of smiled and thanked him, but you can bet I didn't say a thing about not missing those letters on purpose! If that was natural, what I'd done, and they were satisfied with it, then it was great by me. And it was a real relief, too. My screen test was over. I'd gone through the first step of realizing my life's ambition.

My Sideburns

I've heard so many stories about why I grew my sideburns that I just can't help from laughing sometimes. One magazine said "… he started wearing sideburns at 15 because they made him feel mature and important. He still wears them for the same reason…"

Man, that magazine made me laugh because there wasn't a lick of truth to the things they said. Heck, I couldn't have grown sideburns when I was 15 if I'd wanted to! I wasn't hardly even shaving by then! I was 17 when I first started growing 'em. And I sure didn't feel "mature and important" when the sideburns started coming in. I grew them for one reason only…because I'd always admired them. I never thought they make you look older, and I certainly never thought they made me look important. Nope. I just like them, that's all. That's why I wear 'em. A lot of people ask me why I don't cut them off now. You know what I tell them? I tell them that I got started off wearing sideburns and I'm like those folks who don't like to change horses in the middle of the stream. All my friends have liked me with the sideburns on, so I don't really see any reason for cutting them off. And, oh yes, there's one other thing, too. I still admire them very much, just like I did when I was a little kid.

They ask me why I wear the clothes I do. What can I say? I just like nice clothes, that's all. I like color and such. Is there something wrong with that?

My True Religion

The other day, I read this: "…Presley got his start by singing in a church choir, but fame has made him forget all about religion…"

I sat right down and cut that out of the paper and put it in an envelope and sent it home for my momma to put in my scrapbook. I expected they'd start saying things like that. About me not being religious. I mean. But this was the first time I'd seen it anywhere.

Well, I'm not exactly sure what they mean by "religious" in that article, but I can tell you this much. I don't think they're right in saying things like that. No, I don't go to church regular anymore, if that's what they mean by religious. Being on the road all the time, and traveling every minute I'm not working, I can't ever be sure when I'll have a Sunday free to myself. I wish I could, just like I wish I could be with my folks more often, but I can't. So if they mean just going to church regularly makes you religious, then I guess I don't fit up to what they want.

But I want you to know this. I believe in God, I believe in Him with all my heart. I believe all good things come from God. That includes all the good things that have come to me and to my folks. And the way I feel about it, being religious means that you love God and are real grateful for all He's given, and want to work for Him. I feel deep in my heart that I'm doing all this. And I pray that if I'm wrong in feeling the way I do, God will tell me. Because I owe everything that's happened to me to Him.

Have I Changed?

I guess everyone wonders what he'd do if he got lucky and got in front of the public and got real well-known. I remember I used to think about that, when I was driving a pickup truck in Memphis I used to dream about being a success and wondered how my life would change if it should ever happen. Well, I can tell you how I feel about it now. I don't feel a bit different now than I did before all this happened. I'm just like I always was.

Of course, I guess everybody says this. And even though they say it, a lot of people change anyway, without knowing it. But actually, I'm sure I haven't. I've never felt a change. I feel the same now as I did five, ten years ago. The only difference I've felt since then is happiness, and that things have gotten better for me… that God has blessed me and that he's given me a lot of the wonderful and good things in life. I hope I won't change. I hope I'll never be like some of the people I've seen, who forget that they never could have been successful or happy at all without God's help. And I wish, I just wish, that everybody could know the same kind of happiness I've known from all this. I wish that, more than anything, with all my heart.

Who Am I Going to Act Like?

There've been a lot of articles come out lately that I was going to imitate or copy the late James Dean. Well, I want to set you straight on that.

Like I told you with my singing, I don't want to copy anyone. The same thing goes for my acting. I was a powerful admirer of James Dean. I think he was one of the greatest actors I've ever seen. He and Marlon Brando, and a whole bunch more I could call. But I'm not going to try and copy anybody. I'm trying to be myself in my acting, with my own name and my own kind of style. Sure, I hope I can be even half as good as James Dean some day. He was the greatest.

But I won't try and copy him. I know I couldn't, even if I tried.

And another thing. Some magazine a month or so ago already had me playing in the life story of James Dean on the screen. Well, I'm not. It would be a great privilege to be good enough to play the part of James Dean in his life story, but it certainly isn't being planned for now. All I hope is that I'll do an acting job that will make you proud of me. And I want you to know, I'm going to keep on trying always to do my very best.

I'll tell you something about Hollywood. It's really a great place. At least, I've had the kicks there. I just finished my first movie for 20th Century-Fox, called Love Me Tender, *and you know, it was the biggest thrill of my life. Making pictures is, well, I don't know exactly what to call it, except that it's different. It's something I've always wanted to do. And I just hope you'll like me on the screen because I'd sure like to keep on making pictures for you.*

Do I Really Play the Guitar?

There's been another rumor of sorts that's kind of amusing. I read in one magazine that I can't play a note on the guitar, and in another, the same week, that I'm the best guitar player in the world. Well, both of those stories are wrong.

I've never had any music lessons, like I told you. But I've always enjoyed music of any kind, and musical instruments. My daddy bought me a department store guitar when I was pretty young. I learned to pick out a couple of chords on it, but I didn't try to get fancy or anything like that. I can plunk on it pretty good, and follow a tune if I'm really pressed to do it. But I've never won any prizes and I never will.

Then when I went out on stage in my first personal appearance, I just naturally took my guitar along with me, to sort of keep me company. I used it as a prop or whatever you want to call it. To me, in that first appearance, it was the best friend I ever had because it kept me company and I knew I wasn't alone out there making a fool of myself. I've just kept on taking it out there with me, and I've got a new one now, a gift to me, that even has my name carved on it. There's always another fellow in the band who does most of the playing, and if you'll watch me real close in a performance sometime, you'll see how it works. He follows my motions and hits the chords at just the right time.

Along down the years, I've just naturally taken to some other instruments, though. I like the drums, and I really would like to take lessons on them some day. I try 'em now just for fun, and sometimes it almost sounds like I know what I'm doing. I also like the piano, though I guess I don't play it exactly the way you're supposed to. I just hit whatever keys look good to me. It's a lot of fun, and sometimes I'll play along while I'm singing. Never in a performance or on a record though. I'm not that good. I bought my mama an electric organ, which we now have in our home in Memphis. The whole family takes a whack at it, and I guess it's about the easiest thing of all to play. Sounds great, too, when you've got the volume on just right and when you're in the mood to experiment around.

Maybe someday I'll learn to play some of these things better. But in the meantime, I keep trying out all kinds of instruments. As I say, I do it because, of everything I know, I like music the very best.

Do I Say All Those Things?

It's not just the rumors. It's the things they claim I say that kinda gets me down ever so often. I don't know why people claim I say things that I don't, but that's what happens sometimes. And they go off on a whole big business about teenagers being so different today and that kind of stuff. I'll tell you honestly. I can't understand it.

And you know something? I'm sorry that these people who try to put words in my mouth and read something into my actions on the stage don't try, instead, to understand about kids our age. I'm sorry that they don't try to understand that we've got a lot of energy that we've got to do something with, and that the main reason we stick together is that we understand each other, and that we can help each other work off some of this energy by sharing our feelings together. Is this wrong for us to do? I can't believe that it is. And I'll bet that if the people who criticize us would only try to understand instead, they wouldn't feel we were so bad either.

I'll tell you, though. I guess no matter how hard you try to be fair and good with people, there're always those few who are gonna make up stories no matter what you do.

One fellow wrote in a magazine that he knew a "secret" about me. His piece went, "… Presley's secret? Simple. He's popular because he throws himself around the stage. Without his contortions, he wouldn't stand a chance in the big time music business." I wonder what this fellow would say if I told him that most of my records have been bought by people who have never seen me in person!

On Amusement Parks

Sure, I like amusement parks. I like 'em a lot. And I like winning pandas and that kind of stuff. That's about the only relaxation I get when I'm on the road. That, and going to movies. And as for food, give me home cooking. My mouth waters every time I think of momma's bacon and egg breakfasts. I sure fill up on 'em when I'm home!

Why Do I Sing Like I Do?

Everybody asks me: Why do I sing like I do? I know as well as you do what some people are saying. I'm not deaf. I can hear it same as you. They don't like dancing. They don't like western music. They don't like rock and roll. And they don't like me.

Well my momma taught me one thing right from the very beginning, and that's that everyone's got a right to his own opinion. I believe that. And I also believe that you can't make everyone like you, no matter who you are.

I can't explain it. I can't explain what happens when the music starts. But I think you know. I think you know what it is to get all tied up in something, to get lost in it. That's what singing and music does to me. It ties me up. It makes me forget everything else except the beat and the sound. It tells me more than anything else I've ever known, how good, how great it is just to be alive.

I've been singing the way I do now as far back as I can remember. I don't know what style you'd call it or anything like that. All I know is I sing the way I do because it comes to me natural.

A lot of people ask me, "Are you trying to copy somebody, the way you sing?" All I can tell 'em is what I honestly know in my heart. I've never tried to copy anybody.

One girl said I reminded her of Johnny Ray, but I laughed and told her that I don't pull my hair or roll on the floor or anything like that. And I never intend to. No, I've never copied anybody, and I've also never heard any style like mine. I just originated it accidentally, more or less.

When I was called to make my first record, I went to the studio and they told me what they wanted me to sing and how they wanted me to sing it. Well, I tried it their way, but it didn't work out so good. So while most of 'em were sitting around resting, a couple of us just started playing around with "That's All Right," a great beat number. We were supposed to be resting for ten minutes or so, so we just did it natural. It came off pretty good, and Mr. [Sam] Phillips, the man who owned the recording company, said I should go ahead and sing all the songs my own way, the way I knew best. We tried it, and everything went along a lot better. They decided to put "That's All Right" on record, and backed it up with "Blue Moon of Kentucky."

That was my first record. I'll never forget it. Lately, as you probably know, there's been a lot of talk about all the "bouncing around" that goes on during one of my shows. I'd like to tell you how the bouncing around all got started.

When Mr. Phillips called me in to make that first record, I went into the studio and started singing. I started jumping up and down, they tell me, and I wasn't even aware of it. My legs were shaking all over, mostly because I was so nervous and excited, but also because I can feel the music more when I just let myself react. After the third rehearsal Scotty Moore, the guitar player for the band, came over to me and said, "You still scared, Elvis? You shake all over when you start singing." I told him I wasn't scared once the music started, and that I didn't even realize I was moving around at all while I was singing. I told him I'd try to just sit still during the next rehearsal.

But at the next rehearsal the same thing happened. The minute the music started, I wasn't me anymore. I couldn't have stopped moving around if I'd wanted to. Because all that motion was just as much a part of the music to me as the words I was singing. I

told Scotty, and he said, "Okay, then, do whatever comes natural." So that's what I did.

After that first record was a success, I appeared on this big Music Jamboree in Memphis, my hometown, in an open-air theater. I'll never forget how it was, standing backstage and listening to all these great performers and knowing that I'd have to get out there in just a couple of minutes and try to be as good as all the others. When my time came, I was scared completely stiff. Me and my band went out there and set up and we were ready to begin. But man we couldn't move! We were all like a bunch of dead people, we were scared so bad. I guess there were four or five thousand people in the audience, and they stared at me and I stared at them. Then someone in the bass section got up nerve and started playing, and the others followed, and before I knew it I was singing. And then the audience got to squealing a little, and then someone started hollering, and then they all got with it and we really had a ball. I left the stage and they applauded and called me back and kept calling me back. I couldn't figure it out. I didn't have any idea what I was doing that they liked. My manager gave me a push toward the stage and told me to get back out there and do what I'd been doing, and I said, "What have I been doing?" and he said, "You've been shaking all over." He said, "Your legs have been shaking with the music and your eyes twitching and your shoulders twitching and everything! Get out there and keep doing it!"

So I went back on, and we picked another rock and roll song real quick. And I said to myself, "Now listen, try and do it again." And then the music started, and I never did remember to do what I'd said to myself, but I must have done it again anyway because the *audience was whooping and hollering like crazy when the song was through. That's when it really started, that night, and it's happened ever since.*

I wish—how can I explain it—that I could do everything with music. I wish I could play every instrument. I wish I could know every song. And I wish I could thank all of you who feel the same way about music and who tell me so. I've been so lucky. From that first wonderful start on the Stage Show *TV program until now, and Mr. Sullivan. I've been so lucky. I just can't believe it sometimes.*

And Now, What Can I Say?

I just don't know what to say about how I feel now, about all this. Since that first night, things have happened so fast that I really don't know. I like it, of course. It's been the most wonderful thing in the world. The way you've bought all my RCA Victor records, and come out to my performances and watched me on Mr. Sullivan's TV show, and all the others. I just don't know exactly what to say.

And now that I've made my first movie out at 20th Century-Fox, I'm hoping to learn how to become as good an actor as I can. Making Love Me Tender *was something I'll never forget. You'll never know how nice Debra Paget was to me, helping me learn my lines and study and such. And the same goes for everyone out there. What can I say, except that I'm thankful to all of them.*

And what can I say to you? All I can say is the same thing. Thanks. I know it's not enough, but I want to tell you something. With that one word goes out a big part of me. A part of me that never could have existed at all save for your help and encouragement.

And I want you to know that my thanks to you comes from right down here, right from the deep bottom of the happiest heart in this whole great big old world.

Yes, I've been lucky. And you know something? I just feel sometimes like it's all a dream, like I'll rub my eyes and wake up and it'll all be over. I hope not. I hope it never happens. I hope it never ends.

Address Change

I'm ever grateful to my fans everywhere. They really are responsible for my acceptance and success. So that the ever increasing mail from these wonderful people can be properly and quickly approved, we are moving the Elvis Presley Fan Club Headquarters to Hollywood. Now that I have finished Love Me Tender *for 20th Century-Fox, and am making another picture for Paramount, it looks like I'll be spending a lot of time in Hollywood. So please address your mail to me to Box 94, Hollywood, California. A million thanks!*

AUGUST 29, 1956

LOCATION: *20th Century-Fox Lot, Hollywood, California.*

INTERVIEWER: *Unknown. The voice heard on the CD asking questions is not that of the original interviewer.*

SOURCE: Elvis Answers Back / The Truth About Me *(CD).*

[Since the volume level of the original interviewer's voice was too low for satisfactory reproduction, a studio person recorded the questions and edited them to precede Elvis' responses. This explains the unnatural-sounding interaction between Elvis and the interviewer.]

Hi! This is Elvis Presley. I just got into Hollywood, by Delta Airlines, and there was really a nice crowd out here at the airport, and a lot of newspaper reporters and photographers and everything. It really makes me feel good because this is the place of places out here.

[Media] What have I been reading in the fan magazines about your acting abilities?

There have been a lot of articles come out that I was gonna imitate or copy the late James Dean, er, something like that, but I've never thought about it, although James Dean was one of the greatest actors I've ever seen. He and Marlon Brando, and a whole bunch more I could recall. But I'm not going to try to copy anybody. In fact, I don't even know if I can act or not. I'm just gonna give it a try.

[Media] Did they tell you at the studio that they thought you were a good actor?
Well (laughs) no. They didn't say I was good. They just told me that my test turned out real well.

[Media] I thought you were gonna make a picture at Paramount first. What are you doing at Fox?
I was supposed to have made for Paramount first, but something happened and Mr. Wallis said he didn't want to make anything until December.

[Media] Until December?
That's right.

[Media] Do you think you'll make a film for Paramount then?
I'm pretty sure I will. I don't know what it'll be yet.

[Media] Where did you go to high school?
Humes High School in Memphis.

[Media] Have you ever gone to any college of any kind?
No.

[Media] Where'd you go to school in the early years?
I went to grammar school in Mississippi. Tupelo, Mississippi.

[Media] Do you really have four cars?
Yeah. One of them's pink, one's blue, and two of 'em's white.

[Media] Are they all Cadillacs?
No. One of them's a Lincoln Continental.

[Media] What's the other car you have?
I have a Messerschmitt.

[Media] A Messerschmitt! What is that? Is that a car?
It's a three-wheel car, German made.

Getting adjusted in his tiny Messerschmitt, 1956.

[Media] Which one do you like the best of all of 'em?
Motorcycle.

[Media] Is that right? How tall are you?
Six feet even.

[Media] How much do you weigh?
A hundred and eighty.

[Media] Blue eyes, right?
Greenish blue, yeah.

[Media] Tell us about this sideburn business. Why did you decide to start growing sideburns?
I just always wanted to grow 'em, when I was growing up. I always admired sideburns.

[Media] How old were you when you first let 'em start growing?
When I was old enough to grow 'em, I guess I was about 17.

[Media] Do you have any brothers or sisters?
No I don't.

[Media] Elvis, where do you live at home in Memphis?
Where do I live at home…I live at home (laughs).

[Media] No, I mean do you have your own house or apartment?
Yes, we have a house in Memphis.

[Media] You and your parents?
Yes.

[Media] And you actually do ride these motorcycles?
Yeah.

[Media] Do you own one?
Yes, a Harley-Davidson. That's my favorite sport…motorcycle riding.

[Media] Do you horseback ride at all?
Not very much. I'm gonna have to learn though (laughs).

[Media] Now, we've heard you like amusement parks. Tell us about that.
They just amuse me, because it's so much to do. They take your mind off everything.

[Media] What do you like to do there the most?
Oh I try to win prizes…playing their crooked games (laughs). Don't print that, please, I was just kiddin'.

[Media] Now, you don't actually have a girl right now, is that true?
Not a special girl. I date a few different ones, but nobody in particular.

[Media] I read somewhere that you have a girlfriend that you've been dating three years. Is that true?
It's very untrue. I've never dated a girl three years. I've never dated one three months (laughs).

[Media] Were you ever in love at all?
Ah, I thought I was when I was growing up, but I wasn't. You know when you're growing up, you sometime think you're in love. You sometime think that this is it, you'll never find another one, you know. But then you grow up and you laugh at yourself.

[Media] Right. Do you think you're any different now than you were two years ago, or a year ago?

You mean as far as character's concerned?

[Media] As far as the way you feel now in comparison to when you were a nobody.

Oh I don't feel a bit different. I'm just like I was. In other words, course I guess everybody says this. A lot of people change but actually I haven't. I've never even felt a change. The only thing I've felt is that…is happiness, that things have gotten better for me. That God has blessed me and that he's given me a lot of things that a lot of other people would like to have. That I would like to see other people have. In other words, I wish that everybody could have, you know, luxuries in life, but I guess that's impossible.

[Media] Do you consider yourself to be religious?

Well I don't attend church regularly or nothing like that, but I'm a true believer of God if that's what you mean. I believe that all good things come from God.

[Media] When did you first start singing…do you call it singing…the stuff you do?

Do I call it singing?

[Media] Yeah, that is what you call it, right?

Well I've sold five million records! Somebody calls it singing (laughs).

[Media] I mean this is what the critics say. I guess you read this all the time.

Well I'll tell you. This is the only thing…the only explanation I've got for it is the people always… I get a lot of criticism for the actions I use on stage. I have been doin' it for two years. I've been doing the same thing for two years and it just got, in the last four or five months, that I've felt criticism. I guess it's because my records have become bigger and everything. In other words, the more popular you are the more criticism you get. But, in other words, people can stay home

and hear you sing, but when they pay their money to come out and see you on a personal appearance, those people want to see a show. They come out to see some action. And if I stood up in front of an audience and did nothing but sing, if I didn't put on a show and if I didn't act like I enjoyed what I was doing, they wouldn't come out to see me the next time I went back.

[Media] Do you really enjoy being up there on the stage as much as you seem to?

I get such a thrill out of it till I wear myself completely out. And sometime we have three or four shows a day and it's the same thing as a fighter goin' into the ring three times in one night. And not many fighters will do it (laughs).

[Media] Were you self-conscious when you first started? I mean, did you have stage fright at all?

Ah, well I still do.

[Media] You still do?

Still do. And I've been in front of a lot of audiences, but I always get nervous.

[Media] Are you nervous throughout the show?

After the first couple of songs I feel okay. But I always go out with the thought in my mind, "Are they gonna like me, or are they gonna throw rocks at me?" or somethin' like that.

[Media] Tell me about the craziest audience you ever had.

The craziest audience?

[Media] One of the craziest.

Well I've run across quite a few crazy audiences…not "crazy" audiences…I don't mean that.

[Media] Unusual.

Kind of wild and exciting. I couldn't tell you one particular place 'cause it's happened quite a few times. In fact, it happens more that way than it does conservative-type audience.

Anywhere you get a bunch of young people together there's gonna be excitement.

[Media] Do you remember the first time you performed in front of an audience?

First time I performed…ah, let's see. In my life you mean?

[Media] Yeah, is there any time that stands out as being the first time you had to get up there?

Yes, I was in front of an audience at a fairground when I was an eleven-year-old. There was a fair, an annual fair, and they had a talent contest and I sang a song called "Old Shep," story of a dog, and I sang it, and I won fifth prize. I won five dollars. That's the first time.

[Media] Where was this?

It was in Tupelo, Mississippi, and the first time I ever sang in front of an audience.

[Media] Were you nervous?

I was shakin' like a leaf.

[Media] How did the song go over?

I didn't have any music or anything. I couldn't get anybody to play for me and I couldn't play anything myself, so I just went out and sang it. And I believe that they felt sorry for me back then, is why they let me win fifth prize (laughs)…'cause I was scared so bad.

[Media] Do you think your style of singing is different than anybody else's, or do you follow a pattern? Do you, say, sing like Johnnie Ray, for instance?

No, no. I don't pull my hair and roll on the floor.

[Media] Do you feel that this is your style alone, the way you sing?

Well, I mean, I don't know. I have never heard a style like it, I mean. I'm not saying that it's good or nothing like that, I mean I have never heard anything…I never copied anybody. I just originated it accidentally, more or less. When I was called to make my first record, I went into

the studio and I started singing, I started jumping up and down. And, uh, I mean, I wasn't even aware that my legs were shaking, and all over. And then, after my first record became a hit, well, I was on this big jamboree in Memphis, at an open-air theater. And I came out on stage and I was scared completely stiff, and my band…we all looked like a bunch of dead people, we were scared so bad. I guess there were four or five thousand people in the audience.*

[Media] They're telling me here that we're running out of time.

Well let me go ahead and finish this. Anyway I came out on stage and I was singing a couple of these rock and roll songs, and the audience got to hollerin' and squealin' with me, and they had been very quiet through the whole show. I was the last one on the show and they had been very quiet and the audience started squealin' and I left the stage and they kept callin' me back, and I didn't know what I was doin' that they liked, because I never even thought about it. And my manager told me, he said, "Go back out there and do just what you been doing." So I asked him "what have I been doing?" And he said, "You been shakin' all over." He said, "Your legs have been shakin' with the music, and your eyes twitchin' and your shoulders twitchin' and everything." And so I stuck with it and I been doing it ever since.

[Media] "The Truth About Me" as issued on the 78 rpm flexi-disc attached to the front cover of the *Elvis Answers Back* magazine:

Hi, this is Elvis Presley.

I guess the first thing people want to know is why I can't stand still when I'm singing.

Some people tap their feet. Some people snap their fingers. And some people just sway back and forth. I just sort of do 'em all together I guess.

Singin' rhythm and blues really knocks it out. I watch my audience and listen to 'em and I know that we're all getting something out of our system. None of us knows what it is. The important thing is that we're gettin' rid of it and nobody's gettin' hurt.

I suppose you know I've got a lot of cars. People have written about in the papers and a lot of them have write and ask me why.

Well when I was drivin' a truck, every time a big shiny car drove by it started me sort of daydreaming. I always felt that someday, somehow, something would happen to change everything for me, and I'd daydream about how it would be.

The first car I ever bought was the most beautiful car I've ever seen. It was second hand but I parked it outside of my hotel the day I got it, and sat up all night just lookin' at it. And the next day, the thing caught fire and burned up on the road [June 5, 1955].

In a lot of the mail I get, people ask questions about the kind of things I do and all that sort of stuff. Well I don't smoke and I don't drink, and I love to go to movies.

Maybe someday I'm gonna have a home and family of my own and I'm not gonna budge from it.

I was an only child but maybe my kids won't be.

I suppose this kind of talk raises another question: am I in love? No (laughs). I thought I been in love but I guess I wasn't. It just passed over. I guess I haven't met the girl yet, but I will. And I hope I won't be too long 'cause I get lonesome sometimes. I get lonesome right in the middle of a crowd. But I've got a feelin' that with her—whoever she may be—I won't be lonesome, no matter where I am.

Well thanks for letting me talk to you and sorta get things off of my chest.

I sure appreciate you listening to my RCA Victor records, and I'd like to thank all the disc jockeys for playing 'em. Bye-bye.

"THE TRUTH ABOUT ME" OUTTAKES

Take 1

Ah, oh, the script, okay.

Hi, this is Elvis Presley. I'm glad you bought this magazine, so I can have a chance to speak to you and tell you a few things about the way I feel, why I do the things I do and see if maybe you don't feel the same way.

That's not my voice.

Take 2

Hi, this is Elvis Presley. You know, I'm glad you bought this magazine, so I can have a chance to speak to you and tell you a few things about the way I feel, why I do the things I do and see if maybe you don't feel the same way.

I guess the first thing people want to know is why I can't stand still when I'm singing.

Well I don't think I have to explain that to someone like you, or anyone who feels…

Let me start over again.

Take 3

Does it make you feel good, like you got some-

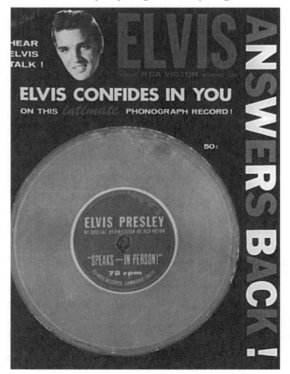

Elvis Answers Back magazine, with bonus recording, **"The Truth About Me,"** 1956.

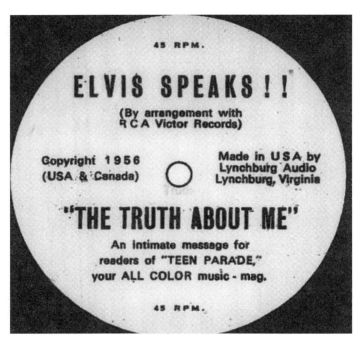

45 RPM.

ELVIS SPEAKS!!

(By arrangement with R C A Victor Records)

Copyright 1956 (USA & Canada)

Made in USA by Lynchburg Audio Lynchburg, Virginia

"THE TRUTH ABOUT ME"

An intimate message for readers of "TEEN PARADE," your ALL COLOR music - mag.

45 RPM.

"The Truth About Me" monologue as first issued on vinyl 45 soundsheet, 1956.

thing out of your system? I get all tense and tight inside sometimes, not for any particular reason that I know of. It just, it just happens like that 'cause I've got too much energy and I wanna do somethin' with it.

Listening to music helps, helps. Listening to music helps but singin' rhythm and blues really knocks it.

I watch my audience and listen to them and I know what their all...I know that their all gettin'...shhh.

Take 4

I watch my audiences and listen to them and I know that we're all getting something out of our system and none of us knows what it is. The important thing is that we're getting rid of it and nobody's gettin' hurt.

I've always liked music. My mother and dad both loved to sing. They tell me that when I was about three or four years old I got away from them in church and walked up in front of the choir and started beatin' time.

So I'm acting like it's the dream now.

I guess the most wonderful part is that I got a nice home for my folks, and a car for 'em, and the whole family's doin' fine. And I

can still buy things just 'cause I feel like buyin' 'em.

I've got more of 'em now [cars] but no one will ever take the place of that first one. I had plans for it. I wasn't goin' to sell it after I got through using it. I was sorta gonna put it out in a pasture and look at it.

I think I learned a lot from studying the movies I've been to, and watching to try to find out how it's done. But you'll be able to tell when my picture [Love Me Tender] comes out. It'll be fun to stay in one place long enough to make a picture. It's pretty hard work traveling the way I been doing. I've been to a lot of places, but I haven't seen any of 'em, really. Lots of times all I get to see of a city is a hotel room, my dressing room, and the stage. Course, I don't mind the hard work. I don't guess anyone would mind it after all the good things that's happening to me.

The only part I don't like is staying away from home so much.

The happiest times I've ever had have been with my family. In fact, I can't wait to get home every once in awhile to be with my mother and daddy. And we all have fun together. We sit around and watch television, go to movies, go for drives on Sunday afternoons. Different things.

I buy a lot of little gadgets for the home when I'm out traveling around, and send 'em home. Mother always puts them up. It makes me feel a little more like I'm there with them.

I love going out on dates, especially with a girl that likes to have fun. The kind of fun I mean is just goin' out and lookin' around places and things, wondering about people, and tryin' to win prizes at the amusement parks. And just generally havin' a good time.

Well, thanks for letting me talk to you and sorta get things off of my chest.

I sure appreciate you listening to my RCA

With actor Richard Egan on *Love Me Tender* set, 1956.

Victor records, and I'd like to thank all the disc jockeys for playing 'em.

That's all the time we've got now, so I'll say bye-bye.

Take 5

Well thanks for letting me talk to you and sorta get things off of my chest.

Oh, by the way, you know my fan club headquarters is in Madison, Tennessee, Box 417, and we have nine secretaries in Nashville that does nothing but answer mail. And they're about 25,000 letters behind right now, and so if you don't get your card or letter answered, well don't think that we're just ignoring you because you will hear from us. It may take a little time but, uh, just as quick as they can get caught up, we'll...I'll make darn sure that you get an answer because, because we certainly appreciate all the thousands of letters that are comin' in every day. And at least we've given the postmen in Nashville something to do (laughs).

Ah, well, I guess that's about all we've got to say, so you keep writing in and don't feel bad if you don't get an answer right away, because we'll answer you as quick as we can.

Take 6

I always felt that someday, somehow, something would happen to change everything for me, and I'd daydream about how it would be.

Oh, and by the way, about all the fan mail that's been comin' in, I want you to know that I certainly appreciate all the letters that you've been sending me, and that if you haven't gotten your answer back yet, well don't feel bad, because we'll answer just as quick as we can get to it.

Well thanks for letting me talk to you and sorta get things off of my chest.

I sure appreciate you listening to my RCA Victor records, and I'd like to thank all the disc jockeys for playing 'em. Bye-bye.

Take 7

Hi, this is Elvis Presley.

You know I'm just sittin' here in my real fancy dressing room at 20th Century-Fox, just before we start shooting The Reno Brothers, and I'd just like to tell everybody

With reporter Jules Archer on the *Love Me Tender* set, 1956.

how good it makes me feel to see my name on the door of my own private dressing room and everything.

AUGUST 1956

LOCATION: *Madison, Tennessee.*

ITEM: *Letter sent to Elvis Presley Fan Club members from their national headquarters. Printed on pink stock with a picture of Elvis at upper left.*

[Exact date not known. Though letterhead reads "A Personal Note to You from E.P.," this particular flyer is anything but personal, and was more than likely drafted by someone on Colonel Parker's staff.]

Dear Fan Club Member: Say, thanks a lot for writing in. I enjoyed reading your correspondence and hope I'll be hearing from you again.

I guess you'd like to know something about me. I was born in Tupelo, Mississippi, and am now a happy 21 years old. I carry 160 pounds on my 6-foot frame and have dark brown hair and blue eyes.

Never have thought much about getting married—in fact, just being near girls makes me kinda nervous and tingley all over, like getting shocked, but I like it!!

You ought to see my cars, and my motorcycle! My two favorites are a pink and black Cadillac Fleetwood sedan, and my home car, a canary-yellow Caddie convertible. Boy, they'll really scorch the wind!!

'Cat' clothes are absolutely the most as far as I'm concerned. My favorite hobby is collecting these real cool outfits, and I'd almost rather wear them than eat! Man, I do like to eat though!

If you get the chance, drop your local disc jockey a card and, say, by the way, ask him to spin one of my songs for you. He'll be glad to do it, and you remember that I'll be singing it just for you!

I'll be on a lot of personal appearances, probably near your home, so I'll be hoping to see you. Well, I'll say bye for now.

Your pal, Elvis.

P.S.: Hope you are getting as much of a thrill out of listening to "Hound Dog" and "Cruel" as I got out of singing them for you!

EVENT: *Random comments made during the first* Ed Sullivan Show *appearance.*
LOCATION: *Los Angeles, California.*
SOURCE: *Videotape.*

[In place of Ed Sullivan, who is recovering from injuries received in an automobile accident, Charles Laughton is hosting the show.]

Growl. Thank you Mr. [Charles] Laughton, ladies and gentlemen. Wow! This is probably the greatest honor that I've ever had in my life. There's not much I can say except that it really makes you feel good. We wanna thank you from the bottom of our hearts. And now…"Don't Be Cruel."

Thank you very much. Thank you, ladies. And now friends, we'd like to introduce you to a brand-new song. It's completely different from anything we've ever done. And this is the title of our brand-new Twentieth Century-Fox movie, and it's also my newest RCA Victor escape, er, release. And I would like to say right now that the people over at Twentieth Century-Fox have really been wonderful, all the great stars in the cast, the director, the producer. This is our first picture and they really helped us along. With the help of the very wonderful Jordanaires, a song called "Love Me Tender."

Thank you very much. Whew! Mr. [Ed] Sullivan, we know that somewhere out there that you're lookin' in. And all the boys and myself and everybody out here are looking forward to seeing you back on television. And we'll be seeing you October 28, when we're back on your show again. Friends, as a great philosopher once said…[sings "Hound Dog."]

SEPTEMBER 26, 1956

LOCATION: *Tupelo, Mississippi.*
INTERVIEWER: *Jack Christal.*

SOURCE: Elvis Presley Interview Record— An Audio Self-Portrait *(LP).*

[Jack Christal] Elvis, welcome to Tupelo.
Thank you, sir.

[J.C.] It's certainly nice to meet you, Elvis. I'd like to ask you just a few questions, I know you're in a terrible hurry. First of all, how does it feel…all this tremendous reception…to be back home after these years, and have everybody come out to see ya and meet you like this?
It really feels great. I've been lookin' forward to it for a long time.

[J.C.] Have you met a lot of your old friends tonight?
I sure have. I met a lot of people I went to school with and a lot of my kinfolks I haven't seen for a long time…and it's really been a great day.

[J.C.] I know it has, and it's been a great day for the people of Tupelo too. They had a terrific parade in your honor this afternoon. I wish you could've seen it.
I wish I could've been here, but I couldn't make it.

Stopping to greet fans and sign autographs, 1956.

[J.C.] It was great. We met your parents tonight and they're awfully proud of you, and I know you're proud of them. And Tupelo is certainly proud of you. Like to ask you a couple of questions…other now…before we quit. One is, how do you feel now about the reactions of the teenagers, like the young lady [Judy Hopper] that jumped on the stage this afternoon, and the way they act down in the audience? How do you feel about it?

I really enjoy it. I think it's real great that they care that much about you, you know. I had people ask me, did I think it was silly. I do not. I think it's wonderful. I'm glad that they think enough of me.

[J.C.] Well they certainly do think enough of you, and I think that's evident by the fact that they're out there just chompin' at the bits right now for you to come on out. And I wonder if you have anything you'd like to say to all the people of Tupelo, and your friends and relatives here.

I'd like to say to all the people that brought me down here…Mr. James Savery [Fair Administrator], the [Tupelo] mayor [James L. Ballard] and the [Mississippi] governor [J. P. Coleman] and all, thanks for givin' me the most wonderful time of my life, and all the wonderful people that came out to see us.

[J.C.] Elvis, thank you so much. It's been terrific to interview you. Would you like to say one thing about your movie before we sign off?

It'll be out in November. It should be released the first of November. That's all I can say about it.

[J.C.] Have they planned any kind of premiere for it?

No, not yet. I wish I knew.

[J.C.] Well good luck to you, Elvis, and thanks a million for the interview. We'll see ya.

ITEM: *Signed letter, titled "Rock 'N' Roll 'N' Drag," from Elvis Presley to* Rod Builder and Customizer *magazine.*
SOURCE: *Document photocopy*

I've been wild about cars almost since I can remember. When I was six years old, singing songs for folk gatherings in Tupelo, Miss., I recall feeling sad because we had to walk while all those sleek cars passed us on the road.

Yes, way back in those rough old days, when dad couldn't spare the cash to buy me a guitar, I used to dream about ridiculous things like Cadillacs and such.

As I got older, my car tastes began to change a little. I remember craving a Lincoln Continental, a classic Packard, then a Model T, and finally a '32 Roadster. I wanted a '32 so bad I think I'll never crave anything as much again. I dreamed of souping it up, customizing it and maybe dragging it out a little.

As I grew older—I'm twenty-one now—I looked more and more longingly at the antique cars I used to see in the magazines. Once, I even saw a beautiful Bugatti parked in front of a big house in Biloxi [Mississippi]. I knew it would take money to own one of those classics. And I was sure I'd never have enough.

Cars—any kind—were out of the question for me. I was picking out tunes on a two dollar and ninety-eight cent guitar, so how could I afford anything that cost two thousand dollars? Nearest I ever got in those days was a part-time job cleaning up a garage in town.

Then, I finished high school and began to try real hard for the big time. Cut some records and almost before I knew it, I had cash. Enough of it to fix the family up comfortable and buy myself a dozen guitars. And a dozen cars, if I wanted them.

Well, I'm a little ashamed to admit it—but I

bought me three little old Cadillacs, the kind I first craved 15 years ago. There is a yellow sedan, a pink convertible, and a big black limousine which I can take the folks around in. Then, after I got those off my chest, I bought a three-wheeler—a Messerschmitt. This is a cool little buggy, if ever there was one, perfect for zooming around town when I'm home. And she gives me almost 50 miles to the gallon. I have a motorcycle, too, but I don't get much of a chance to ride it these days.

The most important thing, though, I still haven't forgotten. It's that '32. And one of these days—very soon as a matter of fact—I'm going to have enough time to shop for it. And as soon as things quiet down, you'll find me in the garage chopping and channeling away like crazy. If there's any time left over, I'll be out at the strip, maybe even competing. Rodding is for me.

Before I finish, I want to say a couple of things that need to be said. Some people make nasty remarks about hot rodders—just the way they sometimes do about rock 'n' roll music and the kids who love it. Neither are fair.

Sure, there are some irresponsible kids who break the rules. But, they are the exceptions—and that holds true about rodding as well as rock 'n' rolling.

Outlaws never set the pace.

All you can ever do is your honest best and as long as it's constructive and peaceful, you can feel proud. There is little we can do about the few people who would like to destroy everything because a little part of something is bad.

Elvis Presley

OCTOBER 14, 1956

[Al Hickock] Good afternoon. This is Al Hickock at the County Coliseum in San Antonio, Texas, where at this very moment the Elvis Presley show is going on, and being acclaimed by the shouts and stamping of many thousands of young Texans right here in San Antonio. Right now we'd like to bring you the one and only, the remarkable Mr. Elvis Presley.
Hello sir, how are you? Thanks for the big buildup. I remembered your face when I first walked in the door. I really did, but I'd forgotten where, you know.

[A.H.] How did you like the movies, Mr. Presley?
I loved it! I really enjoyed making it. It will be released Thanksgiving…Thanksgiving Day.

[A.H.] Do you have any plans for any more pictures?
Well, I have a contract. I have to do about ten more.

[A.H.] Ten more?
I don't know what they are or when they'll be. They maybe ten years from now, I don't know. But I have a contract for ten pictures.

[A.H.] How do you like picture work?
I love it!

[A.H.] Oh good. I think you'll make a real good actor.
Well I'm trying to learn. I'm not very good at it but I'm trying to learn.

[A.H.] Tell us what type picture this is? Is it a Western or a musical, or what?
It's not a Western, honey. It's not a musical. It's a dramatic picture. It's a love story, but it's not Western.

[A.H.] Who are the stars? Who plays opposite you, Elvis?
Debra Paget and Richard Egan. It's a very good cast. And they have a lot of big stars in the supporting cast.

[A.H.] When is your spectacular coming up, Elvis?

My spectacular?

[A.H.] Aren't you signed for a spectacular soon?

Spectacular? Not that I know of...I haven't heard anything about it yet.

[Fan] On behalf of the Elvis Presley Fan Club, the officers, and Sharon and myself, which we're both co-presidents, I'd like to give you this plaque to show how much we really like you. How much we really adore you, and how much we like your entertainment.

Thank you, darling.

[Fan] And I wanna say, just keep up the good work, because we're so happy to give you this plaque. We've worked for it.

Bless your heart. I'll do my best, honey. I'll do everything I can.

[Unknown Person] Is there one factor that you owe your success to, do you think?

I owe it mainly to the people.

[Unknown] Mr. Presley, what are you doing with your money, if it's polite to ask?

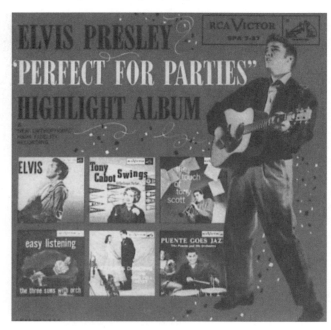

On this 1956 promotional EP, Elvis introduces six new RCA albums.

Oh...saving it.

[Unknown] Mr. Presley, I'd like to ask a question.

Okay.

[Unknown] Just what are you trying to do? Are you trying to raise money, or are you trying to establish this type of music as a standard?

Am I trying to raise money?

[Unknown] Well... I mean, ah...just, ah (laughter)...well naturally you're getting a lot of money out of it, but do you want to establish this type of music as a standard in the United States!

Honey, I'm just doing the best I can. I don't know what I'm trying to do or what I've done. I'm just takin' every day as it comes along. I don't know what's gonna happen tomorrow.

[Unknown] Mr. Presley, do you like just appealing to the teenagers or would you rather appeal to the whole crowd?

Honey, I'd appeal to the apes in Africa if I could (laughs).

[A.H.??] Is "Love Me Tender" [recording] an indication of things to come?

Well, if I can get another one that sells like "Love Me Tender"...yeah.

[A.H.??] Do you like slow music, as a whole?

Yeah.

[A.H.??] How do you feel about your rapid success, Elvis?

Well it kind of scares you a little bit. Everything has happened so fast, as you know. I haven't had time to even think about it, really.

[A.H.] I've talked with some of your associates—people that work with you—and they say that you're still the same Elvis Presley that you were when you started out.
That's right.

[A.H.] I think that's a fabulous thing, Elvis. And thanks a lot for saying hello to us. I know you're pressed for time and your show's just about to start. Thanks a lot.
Thank you.

OCTOBER 25, 1956

EVENT: *Recording of personal introductions for latest RCA Victor albums.*
SOURCE: Perfect for Parties *(EP)*

Hello everybody! This is Elvis inviting you to sample some of the tunes from RCA Victor's wonderful Perfect for Parties *albums.*

Our first song is from my new RCA Victor album called Elvis. *We had a lot of fun recording these tunes, and I sure hope you like 'em.*
[Introduction for "Love Me."]

Our next selection is from the new Perfect for Parties *album, "Tony Cabot Swings on Campus." This is the biggest and the best selection of college songs ever. Here's Tony Cabot and a really swingin' version of "Anchor's Aweigh."*
Now here's a sample from a great new album by Tito Puente. The name of the album is Puente Goes Jazz. *And here's one of the songs.*
[Introduction for "That's a Puente."]

Jazz fans are gonna flip over this new album, The Touch of Tony Scott. *Listen now to Tony Scott and His Orchestra playing "Rock Me, But Don't Roll Me." Boy, that's a crazy title.*

The first trumpet lesson, 1956.

Here's a song from another album that your gang is really gonna like. It's the new one by the Three Suns called "Easy Listening."
[Introduction for "Happy Face Baby."]

The final number in our Perfect for Parties *preview is from a wonderful, swingin' selection of dance tunes. It's RCA Victor's great new album,* Jazz Goes Dancing, *by Dave Pell's Octet.*
[Introduction for "Prom to Prom."]

Remember to ask your RCA Victor dealer for the Perfect for Parties *albums today. Now this is Elvis saying goodbye and thanks for listening.*

OCTOBER 28, 1956

EVENT: *Random comments made during the second* Ed Sullivan Show *appearance.*
LOCATION: *New York, New York.*
SOURCE: *Videotape.*

Thank you very much Mr. [Ed] Sullivan. Friends, we'd like to do a number for you from our new album [Elvis]. It was just released by

RCA Victor this week. With the help of the Jordanaires, friends, we'd like to do one called "Love Me."

Ladies and gentlemen, could I have your attention please. I'd like to tell you we're gonna do a sad song for ya. This song here is one of the saddest songs we've ever heard. It really tells the story, friends. Beautiful lyrics. It goes something like this [sings "Hound Dog"].

Ladies and gentlemen, I'd like to tell you, friends…I'd like to tell you, please. Ladies and gentlemen, I'd like to tell you that on Thanksgiving Day [November 22] I think that our new picture [Love Me Tender] is to be released, and also we'll be back with Mr. Ed Sullivan in January [6, 1957]. We'd like to thank all the millions of wonderful people that are watching in tonight, friends. And I'd like to say this. Until we meet you again, may God bless you as he's blessed me. Thank you very much.

OCTOBER 1956

ITEM: *Typewritten letter from Elvis Presley, on the set of* Love Me Tender *(Hollywood, California) to Mr. Laboe.*
SOURCE: *Original document.*
  [Exact date not known.]

Hello Mr. Laboe,
Colonel Parker just brought a tape recorder out on location where I'm completing my first picture for 20th Century-Fox, "Love Me Tender." I wanted to call you by phone; however, with my schedule of getting to the studio at five a.m., and completing the day's shooting at eight p.m., I have just been unable to do so. I hope you understand, and I want to thank my many friends for being so patient with me. I appreciate everything you have done for me. This is my first picture and a great

deal of work. Perhaps at some future time I'll have the pleasure of meeting you in person.
  [Unsigned.]

OCTOBER 1956

ITEM: *Typewritten letter from Elvis Presley, on the set of* Love Me Tender *(Hollywood, California) to Mr. Marshall (New York, New York).*
SOURCE: *Original document.*
  [Exact date not known.]

Hello Mr. Marshall,
Colonel Parker just brought a tape recorder out on location where I'm completing my first picture for 20th Century-Fox, "Love Me Tender." I wanted to call you by phone; however, with my schedule of getting to the studio at five a.m., and completing the day's shooting at eight p.m., and then into a series of interviews, I really don't have much time, hence the tape. Want to thank you for all the wonderful support you've given my records and hope to see you while I'm in New York October 28 for the Ed Sullivan Show.
  [Unsigned.]

OCTOBER 1956

ITEM: *Typewritten letter from Elvis Presley, on the set of* Love Me Tender *(Hollywood, California) for Bill Williams' restaurants.*
SOURCE: *Original document.*
  [Exact date not known.]

Hello Friends,
This is Elvis Presley, adding my congratulations to the thousands of customers of my friend Bill Williams' many fine restaurants, upon the opening of his latest and newest in this fabulous chain.

And the next time you're eating fried chicken in any Bill Williams restaurant, look closely at everybody eating that delicious chicken because it might be me.

[Unsigned.]

OCTOBER 1956

ITEM: *Typewritten letter from Elvis Presley, on the set of* Love Me Tender *(Hollywood, California) to General David Sarnoff, RCA Victor president.*

SOURCE: *Original document.*

[Exact date not known.]

This is Elvis Presley.
General Sarnoff,
It would have been one of the great honors of my life if Col. Parker and I could have been at your fiftieth anniversary dinner tonight, but we are making a picture at 20th Century-Fox, in Beverly Hills, however here is a little song for you:
Happy anniversary to you.
Happy anniversary to you.
Happy anniversary dear General
Happy anniversary to you.
I would like to dedicate a verse of my new song to Mrs. Sarnoff, "Love Me Tender."

[Unsigned.]

NOVEMBER 9, 1956

ITEM: *Telegram from Elvis Presley (Green River, Wyoming) to Col. Tom Parker (Madison, Tennessee).*

SOURCE: *Original document.*

[Elvis was traveling west by train. Green River, Wyoming, is about 150 miles northeast of Salt Lake City, Utah.]

Trip so far has been comfortable. Expect to be in Los Angeles Sunday afternoon for my appointment Monday morning. Am

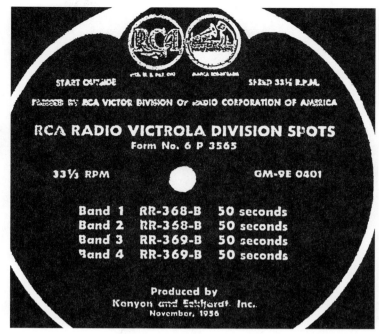

stopping over in Las Vegas for a few hours. Hope the dee jay convention [Nashville, Tennessee] is going well. Wish I could have made it as I did last year. Please express my sincere wishes to all for a successful convention.

Elvis Presley

On this LP, made for radio station use, Elvis is the uncredited spokesman for his signature model record players, 1956.

NOVEMBER 1956

EVENT: *Recording of* RCA Radio Victrola Division Spots.

SOURCE: RCA Radio Victrola Division Spots *(LP)*.

[Exact date not known. Elvis recorded two 50-second radio commercials for RCA's Elvis Presley Autograph Model Victrolas, as well as for the bonus SPD-22 and SPD-23 EPs. Each track is intended to be preceded by an Elvis song.]

Spot No. 1

Hello friends, this is Elvis Presley. And that was only one of twelve of my records that RCA Victor has put out in two great forty-five extended play albums. There's also "Blue Suede Shoes," "Hound Dog," and lots of others.

And you people can have 'em absolutely free. All you gotta do is buy one of RCA

89

Victor's great new record players, made especially for you. They call 'em Elvis Presley Autograph Models, with my name stamped on top.

One of 'em plays all four speeds. It's a portable. It's only $32.95, including eight of my records.

Then there's another portable—an automatic—just push a button an [plays segment of "Don't Be Cruel"].

This one's only $44.95, and with this you get all twelve songs free.

But hurry while this great offer lasts, friends. Just buy one of RCA Victor's Elvis Presley Record Players.

See you in the movies, when Love Me Tender comes to town.

Spot No. 2

Thank you very much. But did you know that's only one of twelve of my records that RCA Victor has put out in two great forty-five extended play albums. There's also "Blue Suede Shoes," "Hound Dog," and lots of others.

And I'd like to tell you how you can get either one of these albums absolutely free. All you gotta do is get one of RCA Victor's new record players—a Elvis Presley Autograph Model. They aren't hard to take, either. They're finished in blue denim with my name stamped on top.

One of 'em plays all four speeds. It's a portable. It's only $32.95, and you get eight of my records absolutely free.

Then there's another portable—an automatic—just push a button an [plays segment of "Tutti Frutti"]. This one's only $44.95, with all twelve songs free.

But hurry while this great offer lasts, friends. Just get one of RCA Victor Elvis Presley Record Players, and you get all the records free.

See you in the movies, when Love Me Tender comes to town.

LOCATION: *Sun Recording Studio, Memphis, Tennessee.*

SOURCE: The Million Dollar Quartet *(CD).*

About "Don't Forbid Me"

Have you heard Pat Boone's new record, "Don'ta Forbid Me"? That som'bitch sat around. It was written for me and it was sent to me and it stayed over at my house for ages, man, I never did even see it. You know I got so much junk around.

About Seeing Billy Ward and His Dominoes in Las Vegas

I heard this guy in Las Vegas [with] Billy Ward and the Dominoes. There's a guy out there that was doing a take-off on me, "Don't Be Cruel."

He tried so hard, until he got much better, boy. Much better than that record of mine.

Wait, wait now. It's this way. He was real slender. He was a colored guy. He got up there and he said. He had it a little slower than me...He was hittin' it, boy. He grabbed that microphone and on that last note went all the way down to the floor, man, lookin' straight up at the ceiling.

I was under the table when he got through singing.

He had his feet turned in like this. And all the time he was singin' them feet was goin' in and out, both ways sliding like this.

[He's] just a member of Ward's Dominoes. He'd already done "Hound Dog," and another one or two and he didn't do too well, you know. He was tryin' too hard. But he done that "Don't Be Cruel" he was tryin' so hard that he got better, boy. Whoo! Man he sung that song. That quartet standing in the background you know, "ba-da ba-da, ba-da ba-da." He was out there cuttin' it, man, and all of 'em goin' way up in the air.

I went back four nights straight, man. I

went back four nights straight and heard that guy do that.

Boy, he sung the hell out of that song. Man, I was under the table lookin' at him: "get him off, get him off."

He got a big hand on that too, boy.

That's the way I thought about recording it, after it done come out. I thought about doing "Paralyzed" the same way he done "Don't Be Cruel"…slower you know. [Little did Elvis realize at the time, the singer he so admired in Las Vegas was likely Jackie Wilson, later to become one of Elvis' favorite entertainers. In 1958, Wilson began a very successful solo career.]

About "Is It So Strange"

Ol' Faron Young wrote this song and sent it to me to record. He didn't want to give me none of it…he wanted it all (laughs), called "Is It So Strange." Ol' Faron wrote that.

About "That's When Your Heartaches Begin"

This song I was telling you about is called "That's When Your Heartaches Begin." I recorded the son-of-a-bitch and lost the dub on it. When I come in here and made that little record when I first started out. That's the one I recorded.

If somebody could sing it right and have a guy with a real deep voice talking it off, I think it would sell.

About Jam Sessions

That's why I hate to get started in these jam sessions. I'm always the last one to leave, always.

DECEMBER 1956

ITEM: *Generic typewritten reply letter from Elvis Presley (Hollywood, California), copies of which were sent to fans.*
SOURCE: *Original documents.*

[Exact date not known.]

Hi Friend!

Thanks for your very nice fan letter. Gosh it's exciting to have so many wonderful people write me. I wish it were possible to shake hands with all my friends and tell 'em how much I really do appreciate it. But between the movies, records, TV, and personal appearances, they've got me hopping around like a jack rabbit being chased by a hound dog. That's why I'm writing you this short note to tell you how nice it is to have you as one of my friends. Please accept this membership card to my fan club. Enclosed with this letter, you will find "The Elvis Presley Story," which I hope will answer any questions you may have asked about me. In addition, you will read about some fine souvenirs which are available to my friends. I know you will enjoy having some of them. A million thanks.

Sincerely yours,
Elvis Presley

1956

EVENT: *Telephone interview between Elvis and a radio announcer known to us only as "Buddy."*
SOURCE: *Audiotape.*

[Exact date not known.]

[Buddy] Hello there, Elvis?
Yeah, hello. How are ya?

[Buddy] Oh boy, this is really wonderful, Elvis.
(Laughs.) Well, thank you very much, and I want to thank you for calling up and to invite me to call you.

[Buddy] Elvis, they've given me some questions here to ask you, and I know you don't have a lot of time. When is your birthday, Elvis?
The eighth of January.

[Buddy] Happy birthday [in advance for] next January.

Actually I wish I was sixteen years old again (laughs).

[Buddy] Bet you do.

I'd give anything if I was. But all through high school, well I always had sideburns and long hair, you know.

[Buddy] Uh-huh.

Not to be different from anybody but it's just that I always wanted to have hair to comb, you know. So, everybody to their own taste. Everybody is allowed to like what they like. Some people like crew cuts, some like long hair, different things, you know. But me, I always thought I looked a little more mature or some-thin'...I mean I must have been nuts but (laughs) anyway, I got stuck with it and I can't get rid of it right now.

[Buddy] You always do tell the truth and... Well.

[Buddy]...in any interviews or anything, you're always very frank and honest, and that's one reason that the fans like you. Not only because of your music but because of the way you talk, and your own personality.

Well thank you. I feel that you have to because if you lie about something or if you fake, well, it'll come back to you. I mean, the truth will come out sooner or later and the only thing you've done is make an idiot out of yourself, so it's best just to come clean from the beginning.

[Buddy] What is your favorite song among the songs that you have recorded?

The ones that I have recorded?

[Buddy] Yes, what is your favorite?

Well I guess I would have to say "Don't Be Cruel."

[Buddy] If you could have anything in the world, what would it be?

Yeah, well, it's a logical question.

[Buddy] Uh-huh.

I suppose the most important thing in a person's life is happiness. I mean, not worldly things because, gee whiz, I mean, you can have cars, you can have money, you can have a fabulous home, you can have everything. If you're not happy, what have you got?

[Buddy] That's right.

So I suppose if I can just continue to make other people's life enjoyable and to make my own life happy, well then that's all I could expect out of life.

[Buddy] How do you like making pictures?

They wanted to put me in a movie real quick. Love Me Tender, the first one, almost finished me off in the business (laughs).

[Buddy] Uh-oh, why? Why?

Well it almost killed me, I mean, it was a rushed deal, they rushed me in the thing to get my name...

[Buddy] Uh-huh.

You know...on the...on the [marquee].

[Buddy] Uh-huh.

So they did. And the picture wasn't all that good of a picture.

[Buddy] Uh-huh.

It was a Western...it was an old, old picture, I mean storywise, and I shouldn't have been in it from the beginning. And I started tryin' to act in it.

[Buddy] Uh-huh.

In other words I was tryin' to act in it, and the minute you start tryin' to act on the screen, you're dead.

[Buddy] Yeah.

If you can play yourself, well then you're much better off. Like Jimmy [James] Dean played himself, Marlon Brando plays himself.

[Buddy] Yes.

All the top guys in the business play themselves. They don't try to act.

[Buddy] Uh-huh.

Well in Love Me Tender *I couldn't play myself because this character that I was portraying was so far from me till it wasn't even funny.*

[Buddy] Yes, I noticed that.

Course, I am about half crazy sometimes.

[Buddy] Uh-huh.

I mean, I get things in my mind and I and you know, I start thinkin' about things and I get a little confused and about half mad.

[Buddy] Uh-huh.

But that's human nature, like people get in moods sometime.

[Buddy] Uh-huh.

You get in moods sometime where you're very happy, you get in moods where you're very sad, where everything looks dark and gloomy and it looks like there's nothing for ya in life. I guess everybody feels that way. It's human nature.

[Buddy] Yes, and on that song "Old Shep" that you do, I suppose that you were feeling that when you were singing about "Old Shep."

Yes, because I had a dog that the same thing happened to.

[Buddy] What was your dog's name?

My dog was named Tex. But he had mange real bad and they had to kill him.

[Buddy] Oh boy. And you thought about that when you were singin' "Old Shep," I'll bet.

Yeah. And I'd like to say somethin' else. Every once in awhile I like to talk to somebody and, get things off my chest (laughs).

[Buddy] 'Cause they'll be glad to hear it.

Because it's very seldom that I have an opportunity to talk to anybody, really.

[Buddy] Yes.

The kind of life I lead, it moves very fast, like I said before, and you don't have much time to sit around, you know. I stay on the move about half the time. Well Buddy, I'm gonna have to run. This is the longest I've talked to anybody but it does you good to talk to people every once in awhile. I wanna thank everybody down there for all the support and everything they've given me, and I hope I can continue to record good songs and everything. After all, the minute I stop pleasin' them, I'm dead.

EVENT: *"1957 March of Dimes" 30 Second Radio Spot.*

SOURCE: 1957 March of Dimes Galaxy of Stars—Discs for Dimes *(LP).*

Hey kids, could I talk to you for about thirty seconds? Ah, this is Elvis Presley. If you believe polio is beaten, I ask you to listen:

[Young boy] Remember me.

Now that's the voice of thousands who know the fight against polio is just as tough as it ever was. They're crippled and the Salk vaccine can't help them recover. But you can. Remember polio victims. Join the 1957 March of Dimes today. Now here's a song.

Elvis offers support to the 1957 March of Dimes campaign.

EVENT: *"1957 March of Dimes" open-end interview. Responses by Elvis to prepared questions.*

SOURCE: 1957 March of Dimes Galaxy of Stars—Disc Jockey Interviews *(LP).*

[When issued on a special, promotional 16-inch disc, a "Script and Instructions" packet was provided to deejays as a script of sorts to follow, "giving the impression that Elvis is in the studio with you." Only Elvis' responses are transcribed here.]

(Laughs.) Well, there's one thing I'd like to know right away. What's so controversial about me?

Well, no offense meant, but alright I'll answer it. Some people seem to have the idea I'm a controversial influence on the young folks. Whatever I do, I always want to do my best for the teenagers. I certainly never wanna do anything that would be a wrong influence. When I sing, I just... I just sing from my heart.

Well, now you're putting me on the spot. Some people say it's because I'm offering folks a new kind of rhythm. I really don't know about that though. Actually, my kind of rhythm is really about as old as music itself.

(Laughs.) Yeah, I'll buy it. But that's one thing I'd like to say, and that's this: As long as I live, I'll never stop being grateful to the American people for giving me this big break.

Yeah, that's right. And that kind of leads me into the reason for being here. You know, so many kids and adults too have gotten one of the roughest breaks that can happen to a person. I'm talking about polio. Sure, we're on the way to conquering it, thanks to the Salk vaccine. But take it from me, it sure isn't licked yet. Right now, some eighty thousand polio victims need help. Some of them are paralyzed so they can't even move a finger. Others can't do the simplest,

everyday things that we take so much for granted. But the situation isn't hopeless. We can help these people, and the way to do it is this: Join the 1957 March of Dimes. Please. It's very urgent. Give every dime and dollar you can to this great cause.

Ah, well we'll do "Love Me Tender" for 'em.

This is Elvis Presley again. Don't forget, folks, give a break to a polio sufferer. The need is urgent. Join the 1957 March of Dimes. Thanks.

EVENT: *Random comments made during the* third *Ed Sullivan Show appearance.*
LOCATION: *New York, New York.*
SOURCE: *Videotape.*

[Ed Sullivan] Now ladies and gentlemen, as you probably know, after he leaves here tonight with Colonel Tom Parker, who's done such a magnificent job as his manager, Elvis Presley goes out to Hollywood to do his new Paramount picture *Running Wild* [*Loving You*] for Hal Wallis. While he's out there, while he's out there, he's gonna do a big Hungarian Relief show. But because he feels so keenly—this young man feels so keenly about Hungarian Relief—he urges all of us through the country to remember that immediate aid is needed, so long before his benefit show is put on, he wants to remind you to send in your checks to your various churches, Red Cross, etc. And now he's gonna sing a song. He feels that this is sort of in the mood that he'd like to create. "Peace in the Valley." Here is Elvis Presley.

[For a time, Running Wild *was the working title of the film* Loving You. *It is not clear where Ed Sullivan came up with the information about Elvis doing a Hungarian Relief benefit show. Elvis made no such appearance.]*

[E.S.] Elvis. Ladies and gentlemen, in as much as he goes to the coast now for his new picture,

this will be the last time we'll run into each other for a while, but I wanted to say to Elvis Presley and the country that this is a real decent, fine boy. And wherever you go, Elvis, all of your group here and the guys that accompany you over there, we wanna say that we've never had a pleasanter experience on our show with a big name than we've had with you. You're thoroughly all right. So now, let's have a tremendous hand for a very nice person. C'mon if you're gonna let him here it!

*Thank you very much. Here's a song from my album [*Elvis*] friends. Before we do this song I'd like to tell everybody that they made this the best Christmas that we've ever had. We'd like to thank everybody for the wonderful Christmas presents and Christmas cards, and birthday presents that came in. I got exactly two hundred and eighty-two teddy bears over the Christmas holidays. We've have the walls lined with them. I'd like to tell you that we deeply appreciate it. We're sorry we couldn't give each one of you a new Lincoln, but they wouldn't sell us that many.*

We'd like to do the song that was my very biggest record last year. I mean, it was no bigger than the rest of 'em...but it sold a few more. And we'd like to tell you, to all the people watching, and all you people that are here tonight, that we really are thankful for all the success that you made us have, and everything. This is my biggest rack...record, and it goes something like this [sings "Don't Be Cruel"].

JANUARY 11, 1957

LOCATION: *Union Station, Los Angeles, California.*
INTERVIEWER: *Ivan Smith (ABC-TV).*
SOURCE: This Is Elvis *(Video).*

[Ivan Smith] Here at Union [train] Station, in spite of all the secrecy, Elvis Presley, being mobbed by teenagers, is coming up to the...Elvis Presley, how are you?
Fine sir, how are you.

[I.S.] Ivan Smith, representing ABC. Which

With Lou Costello, Ferlin Husky, and Jane Russell, Hollywood, 1957.

song do you think is the biggest right now?
"Don't Be Cruel" is the biggest.

[I.S.] "Don't Be Cruel"? How about "Teddy Bear"? How's it doing?
It's about two million.

[I.S.] We have a bunch of teenagers up on the other side of the studio waiting to see you and as you can see, in spite of all this secrecy and little devious plan, that a lot of it's leaked out.
Yes, it always does. It always does, but I don't mind it. In fact, if you come into a place and there's nobody there to meet you, you start wondering, you know. It's very nice talking to you, sir, we're gonna have to run.

[I.S.] Alright, thank you very much.

JANUARY 13, 1957

LOCATION: *Radio Recorders Studio, Hollywood, California.*
SOURCE: Elvis As Recorded in Stereo '57, Vol. 2 *(CD).*

Comments Made Between "Peace in the Valley" Takes:

(Laughs.) Next song! Who do you think I am...[Jordanaire] Hoyt Hawkins?
It's easy, see I can sing this song all day.

FEBRUARY 27, 1957

ITEM: *Telegram from Elvis Presley (Hollywood, California) to Alan White, Manager, Radio Station KLUB (Haynesville, Louisiana).*
SOURCE: *Original document.*

Dear Mr. White,
Your wire sincerely appreciated. Am deeply grateful for concern of your listeners regarding me here in Hollywood during recent storm and earthquake. Disturbance very minor. In fact, some of my friends didn't know about such an event until

they read it in the newspaper here. Working very hard on new picture, "Loving You." Please convey my sincere thanks and best wishes to all your listeners and your staff.

Sincerely,
Elvis Presley

MARCH 25, 1957

ITEM: *Telegram from Elvis Presley (Memphis, Tennessee) to PFC Herschel Nixon (Millington, Tennessee).*
SOURCE: *Original document.*

PFC Herschell Nixon
Naval Air Technical Training Center
I read in the paper that you wanted an apology and I am willing to give you an apology. In fact I think we owe each other one. The whole thing is kind of uncalled for. I'm sorry that it happened but Heaven knows it was all strictly uncalled for. I would like to straighten out another rumor that started out there a few months ago. Somebody started the rumor that I didn't like Marines or Sailors and it was for a while that every time I got out, there was some Marine or Sailor that tried to cause trouble with me. And also somebody started a rumor in Mexico that I didn't like Mexicans and a lot of Mexicans got mad at me. And then here in Memphis the rumor got out that I didn't like colored people and God knows I have never said that I didn't like anybody. It's just that rumors like that get started and there is nothing I can do about it. The Marines and the Navy and the Army and the Air Force protect our country and they have been around for a long time protecting us so who am I to say that I don't like anybody because God created everybody

equal and I would never say that I didn't like anybody. I'm not saying this because I am afraid for Heaven knows I am not in the least bit afraid but I just don't want anybody thinking I said things like that when I never even thought about it. I got a lucky break in life and I am very thankful for it but there are a few people who want to take shots at me. The majority of the people all over the world are very nice but there are a few who want to prove something. I have talked my way out of trouble so many times that I couldn't even count them. Not because I was afraid but just because I was always the type of person that I never did believe in fighting and all that kind of stuff unless I thought it was absolutely necessary. And about the instance the other night and about the gun. The gun is a Hollywood prop gun and I brought it home because a lot of people ask me about how movies are made and about the guns and so on. I had about six of those guns with me and I was just showing them to some people and you

called me over there. Many times there have been people who came up to me and stick out their hands to shake hands with me and they hit me, or I have had guys to come up and ask for autographs and hit me and then take off, for no reason at all. I have never laid eyes of [on] them before. I said many, actually there were very few, but I have had it happen to me. So when you and your friends called me off [over] the other night and you started that stuff about me bumping into your wife I didn't know what you were going to do. I'm just like you. If a guy can do something to protect himself he should do it. Again I say I am sorry the whole thing came up. I hope you have the best of luck in the future and I would like to add that some of my best friends are Marines and some are Sailors and [in] the Army and the Air Force and so on and I think they are all great outfits because if it wasn't for them and if it wasn't for God where would our country be. So long.

Elvis Presley

Meeting the Philadelphia media, 1957.

LOCATION: *Detroit, Michigan.*
EVENT: *Press Conference. Questions by numerous media representatives.*
SOURCE: Southern Gentleman *(CD).*

[Media] How much sleep did you get last night?
Sleep? What's that? I slept for about five hours. We got in at about six o'clock this morning about four o'clock this morning. I'm kinda used to it. I'm trying to get used to it. If you get sleep, it scares you.

[Media] Could I have your autograph?
We got a lot of people here wantin' interviews…I got to get to those guys.

[Media] Let me have your attention! We're not gonna have autographs now, please. There's a lot of people wantin' to have interviews with him. They want to ask him some questions for papers, so no more autographs right now, please.

[Media] Will you be in Special Services?
Well sir, I'll be honest. I'm not gonna ask for it. If they put me in Special Services, okay, if they don't want to it's still okay. In other words, just whatever they want me to do I'll try to do the best I can.

[Media] Would you like to be sent overseas?
I wouldn't say that [but] I wouldn't mind goin' over there.

[Media] Will the Army let you have long hair?
I'm gonna get my hair cut before I go in.

[Media] What is your next film?
My next movie role is a prison picture.

[Media] Is there a name for that, Elvis?
The Hard Way.

[Media] *The Hard Way.*
Yes sir.

[As a film title, The Hard Way *would, within days after this interview, give way to* Jailhouse Rock.*]*

[Media] Were any fans waiting for you when you arrived?
I came in about four o'clock and there was nobody there. Then I came out a back way.

[Media] Where is it, at the Sheraton?
Cadillac Sheraton. Might as well tell you, everybody knows it anyway. Don't tell anybody though (laughs).

[Media] After this tour, do you go to Hollywood for the picture?
After this tour I go back home, then I go to Hollywood.

[Media] I see. Is this the last stop on your tour?
No sir, we wind up in Philadelphia.

[Media] Next Saturday, I think.
It'll be about a month.

[Media] Where is your new house?
It's just in the suburbs of Memphis.

[Media] Pillars on the front?
Yes sir, there's big posts in front.

[Media] Is there a lot of land?
Eighteen acres.

[Media] Eighteen acres. You got eight cars and a four-car garage. What do you do about that?
We're gonna have to build another garage (laughs). Yes sir.

LOCATION: *Ottawa, Canada.*
INTERVIEWER: *Mac Lipson (of CKOY).*
SOURCE: When All Was Kool *(CD).*

[Mac Lipson] I did manage to corral Elvis Presley in a back room of Ottawa's Auditorium. I found someone that I didn't expect. I found a twenty-two-year-old boy who doesn't drink,

With bodyguard Billy "Whipper" Watson, Toronto, 1957.

doesn't smoke, who is better looking than most of his pictures, and who handled himself in front of a battery of reporters without show, without ostentation, and with no attempt at being smart. He was a quiet sort of boy who gave straight answers. He just finished an interview with the newspaper boys when I moved in and asked him if big money in such a short space of time has changed him in any way.
Nah, it hasn't changed me. It's (laughs) like I said earlier, it's just that I can afford things that I never would have gotten otherwise, if I hadn't gotten lucky in life.

[M.L.] **What are some of the big things you've done with your money? Some of the things you've always wanted to do, and suddenly you've got the money to do them with?**
Well I've got a nice home, which is I guess it's a desire of everybody to have a nice home. And I got cars and everything I've always wanted. When I was small, I used to see cars, you know, real shiny cars and everything, and I said if I ever had any money I was gonna get my fill of cars.

[M.L.] **How many cars have you got now, Elvis?**
Eight.

[M.L.] **Are they all Cadillacs?**
Nah sir, four of 'em's Cadillacs, one of 'em is a Lincoln Continental, and I got three little sports cars.

[M.L.] **Now do you mind my asking how much money you've grossed last year?**
About a million, two hundred thousand dollars.

[M.L.] **Have you any plans for getting married? With all that sort of money I imagine a lot of girls would be…on the chase.**
I have no plans for getting married. Besides, if the girl is on the chase for that well she's on a wild-goose chase, because I can usually sense whether or not that's what they're after or not.

[M.L.] **Here in Ottawa, there's a situation which you've probably experienced elsewhere in your travels across the continent. The separate school board recently, unanimously passed a motion in which they were going to encour-**

age the parents and teachers to stay away from your show because they thought your singing was vulgar. No doubt you've run across these situations before and what is your answer?
Well yes I've run across 'em before. I just wish the people would stop judging a tree by its bark—something they've heard or something they've read or something. They should come out to the show and judge it for themselves. And then if they still think it, well just let 'em think it because that's all I can do. I certainly don't mean to be vulgar or suggestive and I don't think I am.

[M.L.] That's all part of your performance, your technique.
That's just my way of expressing songs. You have to put on a show for people. You can't stand there like a statue.

[M.L.] Well Elvis, you've watched teenagers when they've been pretty excited. You've seen a lot of them when they've been very excited. What's your opinion of teenagers in North America? Ah, have they lost a lot of their morals or are they just the same as they've been lots of other times?
No, they haven't. They're growing up, you know, and they're having a nice time and nobody's gonna stop that. I mean the only way they gonna stop that is for the United States to turn communist. And I don't think that'll ever happen.

[M.L.] But you…
You're not gonna stop a group of kids and young people and everything from having a nice time, because they only grow up once. And they're gonna have a ball while they're growin' up. I know I don't blame 'em and I don't see why anybody else should.

[M.L.] A lot of your publicity, Elvis…I wouldn't say a lot of it, but some of it…has been adverse. I mean people and educationists are saying it's no good and it's vulgar and it's no good for the children and they go crazy. Have

Meeting the San Francisco media, 1957.

you had any nice things said about you from adult groups in the States or in Canada?
Yes sir, I've had quite a bit. But not as much as I have the bad stuff though, I gotta admit.

[M.L.] Your feeling is that your show is entertainment and you go on to give 'em a show.
That's true. Well there are people that like you, there are people that don't like you regardless of what field you're in, and regardless of what you do, there're gonna be people that don't like you. I mean, even if you're perfect, I mean I'm not saying, you know, that I'm perfect, because no man is perfect. But there was only one perfect man and that was Jesus Christ…and people didn't like him. You know they killed him. And he couldn't understand why. I mean, if everybody liked the same thing, we'd all be drivin' the same car and married to the same woman and it wouldn't work out (laughs).

[M.L.] How 'bout this question, do you really think you have got a good voice or do you think you've been successful primarily because of your stage technique?
(Laughs.) It's a pretty tough question there. I

have never thought I had a good voice, I just, well, I enjoy what I'm doing. I put my heart, soul, and body into it. But I guess one of the reasons that the people have liked it is because it was a little something different.

[M.L.] Well thank you, Elvis. It's a pleasure to have met the real thing.
Thank you very much, sir.

APRIL 3, 1957

LOCATION: *Ottawa, Canada.*
INTERVIEWER: *Gord Atkinson (of CFRA).*
SOURCE: *Document transcription.*

[Gord Atkinson] Elvis, is this the first time you've been to Canada?
Yes, it's my very first trip to Canada.

[G.A.] [Though it is too] soon for any impressions, do you have any?
No. Yes. Well, I do. I was in Toronto last night [Maple Leaf Gardens concert] and I was very much surprised by how wonderful the people

are. How friendly, you know, in this part of the country.

[G.A.] They have certainly been waiting for you for a long, long time.
I have been wanting to come up here. In fact, when I started looking at the tour, I said: "By all means. I want to go to Canada." About a year ago, I tried to get them to book a tour up here but I wasn't well enough known. A year and a half ago, everybody didn't know me well enough.

[G.A.] Sounds almost unbelievable.
So they figured I wouldn't make enough money.

[G.A.] No doubt about that now. Elvis, you've certainly even topped the popularity Frank Sinatra had in his heyday. This may seem like a foolish question for a Presley fan to ask—it seems like an obvious answer—but have you, yourself, given any thought to what it is about you that has made you the phenomenal show business personality that you are?
I sure have, only I don't like to figure it out

Meeting the
Canadian
media, 1957.

because I'm afraid if I find out what it is, I might lose it. So I just keep guessing myself.

[G.A.] You just recently built a home?
Well, I didn't build it, I just bought it. It's an estate [Graceland]. It's about ten miles from where I live now [Audubon Drive]. We had to have a larger place because I have accumulated so much junk in the last two years, I just don't know where to put it.

[G.A.] Will you be living with your parents?
Yes.

[G.A.] You are an only child, aren't you?
Yes sir.

[G.A.] Do you have a girlfriend, may I ask?
I don't have a special [girl]. I mean, when I'm home I date a few different girls in Memphis, but I don't have a particular one.

[G.A.] Have you given any thought to the fact that some day you might meet a certain someone and decide that you'd like to get married?
I probably will.

[G.A.] Do you think this would hurt your popularity?
It probably will. I have no plans for marriage [soon]. I haven't met anybody yet.

[G.A.] What about your singing style? Would you say that you are an outgrowth of country music, or the pop field? Or a combination of both?
I guess I kind of like 'em both—more rock and roll than anything else. Rock and roll is actually, you see, what put me over.

[G.A.] There are many people waiting to talk to you and I want to thank you so much. I have something here to present to you. It's a scroll from our program, called *Campus Corner*. It is a show that is presented each Saturday. It's a teenage show, if you can imagine. We had a popularity poll, with the boys and girls on the station voting. And for the past year and a half you have been number one.**
Oh, that's great. Thank you very much.

[G.A.] Elvis, I wonder if you'd like to say something to all those fans right now?
I would like to tell them how I deeply appreciate this. I guess I've gotten more mail from Toronto, Ottawa, and Montreal than any other place. I've gotten more fan mail from right around this area than I have from anywhere in the United States.

[G.A.] That's wonderful.
I am not telling that to you [just] because I am here, but it is very true. That is one of the reasons why I always wanted to come up here, because I've gotten more letters from Canada than I can count.

[G.A.] That should make your fans here very happy. It has been a sincere pleasure talking to you, Elvis Presley.
Thank you very much.

LOCATION: *Vancouver, Canada.*
INTERVIEWER: *Red Robinson and other media representatives*
SOURCE: The Elvis Tapes *(CD).*

[Media] Have you got any [songs] coming out that we haven't heard yet?
Yes, the theme song from my next picture will be out about the middle of next month.

[Media] What is the picture?
Jailhouse Rock.

[Media] That's a single 45?
Yes.

[Media] How did you find Hal Wallis as a producer/director?
He's a very…very…very fine gentleman.

[Media] Did he help you out, or who was the

big help or aid in your show "Loving You"?

Well, there's nobody that helps you out. They have a director and a producer. They just…as far as the acting and as far as singing and all, you're on your own. I mean, nobody tells you how to do that. You have to learn it yourself.

[Media] How do you rate yourself as an actor?

Pretty bad. I mean that's something you learn through experience. I think that maybe I might accomplish something at it through the years.

[Media] Do you think it's just for the sake of acting natural? Don't you do that? In your last two pictures I'd say you had.

In some scenes I was pretty natural. In others I was tryin' to act and when you start tryin' to act, you're dead.

[Media] Uh-huh. Would you say the Jordanaires helped ya a lot in your career with your songs, backing you up?

Well, ah.

[Media] I mean, do you think the assist itself…

The boys have done a very fine job, the Jordanaires have, but actually there's a lot of groups, you know. There's a lot of very fine groups that back different people up on their records.

[Media] They are under contract with Capitol, aren't they?

Yes.

[Media] Now I know you're under terrific strain after a show. How do you taper down? What relaxes your nerves after a big show like tonight?

Well take for instance last night. We had a show in Vancouver [the August 30 show was actually in Spokane, Washington] and I didn't sleep any until about ten o'clock today. I just get all keyed up and it's just tough to relax.

[Media] What do you do before a show to help defer some of the excitement, or the tension?

I just walk around and swallow and (laughs) clench my fist.

[Media] What did you pay for your guitar?

About five hundred dollars.

[Media] Is it specially constructed or just a standard model?

No, it's a standard guitar. I have a leather cover over it. I had that made.

[Media] Ladies next. Do you find that touring is much more harder on you than making movies and doing TV shows?

Well, touring is the roughest part. It's really rough, because you're in a town and you do a show, you come off, you ride in a car, you're gone to the next town.

[Media] Would you prefer more to be making movies and doing TV or would you rather just stick to movies and records?

I think every performer likes to work to a live audience.

[Media] How's the Pacific Northwest struck you, what you've seen of it?

Oh it's terrific. It's really, really beautiful country up here.

[Media] How was the weather down in Memphis when you left? Or were you in Memphis before coming to the Northwest?

Yes, I was home. It was beautiful weather.

[Media] Why did you have the Great Northern train stop two miles out of town. Planning? Is it because you knew the fans were waiting for you?

Usually I can't get in (laughs). You see I have to prepare for a show that night.

[Media] Not only that, he wants to be around for it, right?

Yes, and therefore I have to rest and we have rehearsals in the afternoon. So I don't have too much time. I'm actually pressed for time. It's not

that I'm trying to avoid them, because that's certainly not it. It's just that I'm rushed for time and I have to make every moment count when I'm on the road.

[Media] Can you make faster time in a town in your Cadillac than you can by the train?
I beg your pardon.

[Media] Can you make faster time in a town in your Cadillac than you can by the train?
Actually, you're trying to trap me now. I don't know what to say (laughs). Next?

[Media] Everybody stops all of a sudden. Have you ever been thrown by a question, Elvis? You've been through a lot of interviews. What question do you dislike the most?
I don't know. Like I said, I've been asked everything. If they're too rough…

[Media] If they're too rough…

…if they're too rough I just can't answer 'em, naturally.

[Media] How do you feel about being asked questions about your personal life? Do you think an entertainer should be asked myriad of questions about marriage and what girls he's going with and so forth? How does that strike you personally?
Well let's face the facts, anybody that's in the public eye, their life is never private. I mean, everything you do the public knows about it and that's the way it's always been, that's the way it'll always be.

[Media] Elvis, you've been on the road for a long, long time and it's about time you had a nice big rest, because you deserve it. Where would you like to go for a holiday somewhere?
Africa (laughs).

With Natalie Wood and Dewey Phillips at Sun studio, Memphis, 1956.

[Media] Why (laughing)?
No, I don't know. There's a lot of places I'd like to go.

[Media] Have you considered a holiday? I mean you've been on the go for, what, two years now? Just about? About a year and a half anyway.
About four years now.

[Media] Well this throws a different light on things altogether. What happened four years ago? Did you get your start four years ago?
Yes.

[Media] Where?
In Memphis.

[Media] Is that when the first record came out?
Yeah.

[Media] What was it, "That's All Right, Mama," or something else?
Yeah, that's the name of it.

[Media] 1953?
Actually I wasn't known at all until Colonel Parker started managing me, you see, and I got on RCA Victor and on television. Then I started being known.

[Media] Before that time, you were recording on the Sun label…
Yes.

[Media]…for Sam Phillips down in Memphis?
Yes sir. I was known in certain sections, but I wasn't known all over.

[Media] Was it Dewey [Phillips] that played the first one? Is he related to the other Phillips [Sam] in any way?
No. They're no kin.

[Media] Just a coincidence.
He says he was the first to play it. I don't know.

[Media] Do you want to go abroad someday, Elvis?
I beg your pardon.

[Media] Do you want to go overseas someday?
Yes, I would like to. (Sudden crashing noise.) I would like to. (Laughs.) That wasn't me folks, it's these guys clashing these mikes.

[Media] (Laughter.) What are your thoughts on permanent retirement?
I'd like to (laughs).

[Media] Voluntary…of your own free will.
Retirement?

[Media] Yeah, what do you think about it? Just quitting. When?
I'll put it like this, I'll never quit as long as I'm doing okay.

[Media] You'll never quit…what do you consider doing okay?
It's the public…as long as you're pleasing the people, you'd be foolish to quit.

[Media] Elvis, we're running a marathon right after this interview here tonight, from eleven until whatever time it takes tomorrow morning. Would you like to say somethin' to everybody out there tonight listening in to this show? Would you like to say look for your new release or anything, or just say "hi" to them all?

I sure would. I'd like to tell everybody…

[Media]…to see *Jailhouse Rock* (laughs).
Sure. Get in a plug. Nah, I would like to tell everybody how very much I appreciate it…the listening to my records and everything, and…

[Media] Well I can say this much.
…and I'll do my best to continue to please them, put out songs and movies that they like.

[Media] Well, thank you very kindly. Elvis, when you get caught in a mob or something, have you ever been seriously hurt by the girls?
Yes, I've been scratched and bitten and everything (laughs).

[Media] What do you think about being scratched and bitten?
I've been scratched and bitten and everything (laughs). I just accept it with a broad mind because actually they don't intend to hurt you, I mean it's not that. It's just they want…they want pieces of you for souvenirs is all (laughs). A crowd of people can hurt you and not even realize they're doing it, you know.

[Media] Elvis, you got a crowd out here tonight. What do you consider your best crowd…the best show that you've ever had? I mean every entertainer feels like, well in this town here I had a terrific time and everybody was wonderful. What do you consider your favorite place?
Well I have no favorite place.

[Media] No, but the one that stands out in your memory, shall we say?
Probably the biggest crowd was in Dallas, Texas, last year.

[Media] Was that a good crowd?
Yes. I played the Cotton Bowl. I had thirty-two thousand people there.

[Media] Wow! What is that stone on the beautiful ring on your left hand?

That's star sapphire. There was a girl [Judy Spreckles] gave that to me in California.

[Media] Elvis, you haven't much of a private life right now, have you?
No sir, I haven't.

[Media] Where do you go for a quiet cup of coffee nowadays?
When I'm traveling around, I don't go anywhere. I just eat in the room.

[Media] When do you head out to the Army, Elvis?
The Army?

[Media] Yeah. Are you going into the Army, or military service at all?
I haven't heard from them so I don't know yet.

[Media] You haven't heard anything from them at all?
No I haven't. [Elvis' draft notice arrived in December 1957.]

[Media] So you weren't linked to *Confidential* magazine, but what do you think of the *Confidential* magazine trial?
Well, I don't know what to think about it. It's just so I don't get involved in it, that's all I worry about. It doesn't matter much.

[Media] How do you like the motion picture field, Elvis?
I think it's great. In fact, I like it better than any phase of the business other than the public appearances.

[Media] You'd rather be in movies than sing, shall we say?
Well no, I'm not gonna say that.

[Media] You don't wanna commit yourself there, eh?
No, because singing…

[Media] Why don't we see more of you on television, seeing that you can command such big fees?
(Laughs.) I don't know. I guess Colonel Parker

In front of the TV camera, 1956.

could probably answer that if he's here. He's not here, is he?

[Media] We'll speak to him later, Elvis. And what about your trip. What's the reaction been of girls across different sections of the country? Are they all the same?

Well, the crowds have…young people are pretty well the same all over the country, I found out.

[Media] Well Canadians are supposed to be a little more subdued. Have you found that with Canadian girls?

(Laughs.)

[Media] I don't think you've answered my question. Are Canadian girls more enthusiastic girls?

Actually, I'd rather not compare them because it's like I said before, a group of young girls and young boys are pretty much the same all over.

[Media] Don't you get tired of newsmen and cameramen all the time, Elvis?

Nah, I don't mind 'em.

[Media] Really?

I really don't.

[Media] Do you think the rock and roll craze is dyin', Elvis?

No sir, I don't think it's dying. I'm not sayin' that it won't die out, but I don't think it is right now.

[Media] Elvis, who would you say is responsible for your greatest success in the music field, I mean getting your start away? Where did you get your start? Was it in western music that you got your start? How did Hank Snow fit into the picture, if he did?

Well at the time that I started singing, Colonel Tom Parker was managing Hank Snow.

[Media] I see.

And that's how we got connected. I don't know why Hank and my name were linked together so much 'cause actually we wasn't connected in any way in business.

[Media] You…

I just worked on some of Hank's personal appearances.

[Media] Do you know his son at all?

Yeah. Jimmy Rodgers Snow. Yes I know him.

[Media] Did you ever pal around with him or anything?

Yes…yes, quite a bit.

[Media] Did you go to school with him down in Memphis?

No, I never went to school with him.

[Media] Do you know Dewey Phillips down in Memphis?

Very well.

[Media] He said to say hello to ya. I just talked to him on the phone this afternoon.

Good deal.

[Media] Elvis, is your first love western music?

No sir, it's not. My first I would say would be spiritual music.

[Media] Like "Peace in the Valley," or that?

Not exactly that. I mean some of the old colored spirituals, you know, from years back.

[Media] Elvis, your actions make quite a reaction in the audience. What is your opinion of the audience?

What is my appearance…mmm…mmm. Would you say that again (laughs)?

[Media] What is your opinion of the people who a…?

Oh…opinion of…of the audience! Well, I mean I would look pretty funny out there without one, but (laughs) actually, I suppose you are talking about all the yelling and everything. Actually it's good because it covers up my mistakes, you see. I mean, whenever I hit a sour note, nobody knows it but me.

[Media] What's this new flame…Anita is it…Anita Wood.

Anita Wood. Well she's a…

[Media] She's what, Elvis?

(Laughs.) Oh incidentally, she won a beauty contest last night where she gets a seven-year

contract for…for Paramount Pictures. She called me last night.

[Media] While we're firing questions right and left here, let me fire on at ya. If everything folded up tomorrow, which it isn't gonna by the looks of things, what would you do? What would you do?

Go back to drivin' a truck (laughs).

[Media] You like drivin' a truck?

Nah, I don't know what I would do. That's counting your chickens before they hatch. Actually, I'd like to learn a lot about acting, unless something…

[Media] Who's your favorite actor on the screen, Elvis?

I have quite a few.

[Media] How about James Dean? Did you like him?

Yes.

[Media] You really do.

And Yul Brynner and Marlon Brando and quite a few of 'em.

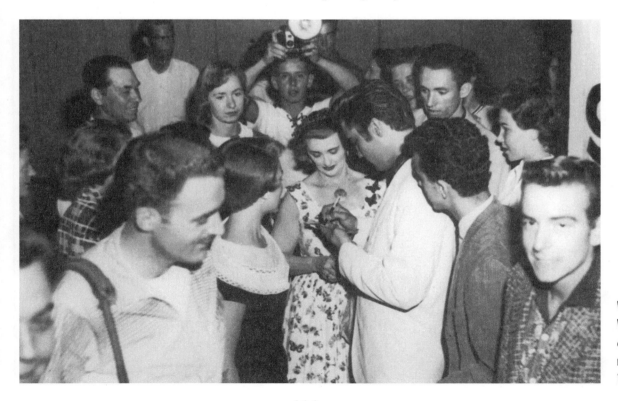

With Anita Wood (black dress), meeting fans, 1956.

Meeting the Philadelphia media, 1957.

[Media] Any plans for more motion pictures?

Yes, I have contracts for about eight more.

[Media] What about TV appearances? We don't see you too often on TV except on the *Ed Sullivan Show* occasionally.

Well I have no control over that, you see. I have an agent, a manager that takes care of that for me. I don't even...

[Media] Were you happier now or when you were driving a truck and could have a quiet cup of coffee?

I'm happier now in a lot of ways. And in some ways, I was having a lot of fun then.

[Media] What do you think of TV? I mean compared to the movies. You've worked in both of them. What do you think of TV? I mean, not that you're slamming 'it.

I like movies better than I do TV work.

[Media] Because you've got more time to do things right?

Yeah, well, if you goof in movies you can just go back and take it over. In [live] TV you just goofed.

[Media] I see what you mean. There's no time to repair the mistakes.

There's no goin' back and takin' it over, that's right.

[Media] Elvis, how are you fixed for the future? I know the contract with Victor is good in future years, but what are your plans for the future, financially?

I have quite a few things. I have two music firms. And then I have, like I said, a seven-year contract with Paramount Pictures, whereas each year it amounts to more money.

[Media] When you see things sold on the street, some of them saying "I Like Elvis," and others saying other things.

"I Hate Elvis." (Laughs.)

[Media] Do you get money for each kind? Do you get a percentage when they sell an "I Hate Elvis" button?

To be truthful, I really don't know.

[Media] It's hard to keep track.

Yes, it is. I don't know who sells an "I Hate Elvis" button (laughs).

[Media] **Well, it's the same man who sells the "I Like." (Laughter.)**
He's a communist (laughs).

[Media] **Elvis, you've come in for a lot of criticism on your wiggling on the stage. Some people have called it suggestive, but do you mean it to be suggestive?**
No, I've never thought of it as being suggestive. That's just my way of expressing the song, that's all.

[Media] **Well you seem to be popular enough on your singing and appearance alone, would you stop the wiggling if criticism grew too fast?**
No sir, I can't…because it's…

[Media] **It's a part of you. Would you consider toning it down?**
Toning it down?

[Media] **Like two songs I recall, "Love Me Tender" and "Love Me," that you play.**
To be truthful, I can't do ballads nearly as well as I can the other kind because I don't have the voice for it.

[Media] **Do you think disc jockeys made you?**
Definitely yes (laughs). I mean, if disc jockeys didn't play it, the people couldn't hear it, so they wouldn't know what was happening, you know. So, I contribute it to a little bit of everything. I contribute it largely to the people who've accepted me, and then the disc jockeys and then the good handling that I've had…the management and everything.

[Media] **Gettin' back to religious songs. If you could put an album out, say an extended play, what songs would you put on it? I mean, have you ever considered any of them, some of the ones you maybe know?**
Are you talkin' about religious…songs?

[Media] **Religious songs, yes.**

Oh, I know practically every religious song that's ever been written.

[Media] **Is that right? What do you think of Pat Boone?**
I think he's undoubtedly the finest voice out now, especially on slow songs. I mean, I'm not sayin' that to make me look good, I actually think that. I mean I thought that—you know Boone was recording before I was—and I bought his records even back then.

[Media] **What chance do you think the female vocalist has of getting in the limelight, or on the Top Ten nowadays?**
You talkin' about any female vocalist?

[Media] **No, just female vocalists in general.**
Oh well (laughs), I don't know.

[Media] **I mean, do you like their singing?**
Yes. I would imagine it's just according to the songs they sing.

[Media] **I see.**
In other words, your material can make you or break ya. If you sing a good song, well naturally it'll sell. If you sing a bad one it won't.

[Media] **What is your favorite female singer right now?**
Patti Page and Kay Starr.

[Media] **What's your favorite of the songs you've recorded?**
"Don't Be Cruel."

[Media] **"Don't Be Cruel" is your favorite. I've got a good one here—why do all the good artists come from Tennessee (laughs)?**
(Laughs.) I don't know.

[Media] **Is it real rhythm crazy down there? People real happy for the music? 'Cause that's the way it sounds on record.**
Yes it is. I don't know. I suppose you're speaking of Pat Boone and couple of the others.

[Media] **And yourself.**

I don't know.

[Media] Elvis, are there any plans in the immediate future for marriage?
No sir. None whatsoever. None that I know of.

[Media] How are your mom and dad? Where are they now?
They're in Memphis. They're at home. I talked to them this afternoon.

[Media] Well, how do they feel about you being on the road all the time? I mean, doesn't it bother them, and they like to see their son once in awhile, I imagine.
Well it's my life, you know, and they don't say too much about it.

[Media] They accept it otherwise.
Yeah.

[Media] One thing that's got a big plug lately is that if you went into the Army you'd have to have your hair cut. How do you feel on that?
I…

[Media] There's been an awful lot of newspaper publicity on it.
Well I…

[Media] Would it bother you to?
No, I don't care.

[Media] It doesn't bother you?
It'll grow back. I mean, if it was a case of cutting it off and never having any more, then I would grumble (laughs).

[Media] What about the sideburns trademark?
Well I'm stuck with 'em. I had 'em [since] I was old enough to grow 'em, about sixteen years old I think.

[Media] No particular reason?
I just got stuck with 'em. I can't get rid of 'em now (laughs).

[Media] What's your age, Elvis?
Twenty-two.

[Media] How does it feel to be right at the top of the entertainment world? Are there any drawbacks to it?
A few (laughs).

[Media] What are they?
Well, you…

[Media] Besides a million women (laughs).
I guess it has its advantages and its disadvantages.

[Media] Don't you seek out privacy all the time? Isn't that it?
Yes. Well, that is the main thing. Naturally you can't go places like other people. You can't go to ball games. You can't go to the local theater and things like that. Like back at home…whenever I wanna see a movie, I have the theater manager show it to me after the movie…after the theater closes up at night. We have a fairgrounds there and I rent the fairground there after it closes up. Sometime and I use it…

[Media] How has your success affected your mom and dad?
In a lot of different ways. They're just like they've always been, I mean as far as being

themselves. But it it's a kind of a strain on them because you know, people never leave 'em alone, I mean to be truthful about it.

[Media] Have they moved into your home at Graceland?
Yes.

[Media] Elvis, we've heard newspaper accounts about a few scuffles you've been in, where the other fellow seemed to get the end of your fist. What about these newspaper reports? Are they accurate?
Yes sir, I would imagine.

[Media] What happened? Did you lose your temper?
Well, it's just a case of get them or be got (laughs).

[Media] What started the incidents most of the time?
Somebody hittin' me or tryin' to hit me. I mean I can take ridicule and slander, and I've been called names, you know, right to my face and everything. That I can take. But I've had a few guys that tried to take a swing at me and naturally you can't just stand there. You have to do something.

[Media] What's your favorite sport, Elvis?
Football.

[Media] You like playing football?
Yes.

[Media] Where were those pictures taken in that fan mag there, with you playing football?
That was taken at a park near my house.

[Media] That's down in Memphis?
Yeah.

[Media] It's been said that your only extravagance, or extravagances, have been your cars. Would that be accurate?
Yes it's accurate. I'm just now realizing how extravagant it was. But because I have too many…nobody drives 'em. They set up and they

get stale (laughs), the tires go down on 'em. Actually, I have no need for 'em. I just went ape…I just went crazy when I (whistles, laughs).

[Media] What about shirts, Elvis? Elvis, I just love your shirts. You got a fad for shirts, have you?
I'll tell you what I did the other day. I had a German-made Messerschmitt, a little car, and there's a guy there in town that has been wanting that Messerschmitt for the last year. And so he owns a clothing store—one of the top clothing stores in Memphis. So I went up there the other day and I told him…I said you been wantin' that car so bad, I'll make a deal with you. He said okay, and I said…you let me pick out all the clothes in here that I want, you can have the car. So I was up there for about two hours and a half. The store was a wreck when I left (laughs).

[Media] What do you think of serious music? Do you ever listen to it, Elvis?
Serious music?

[Media] Like opera…symphony.
Truthfully, I don't understand it. And I'm not

Meeting the press on the USS *Matsonia*, Hawaii, 1957.

Love notes to Anita Wood, 1957.

gonna knock it, I just don't understand it. It's like I don't understand jazz.

[Media] What do you think of young actresses that you date? How do they compare with the girls back home that you dated before you were a star?
Well they're just like everybody else. They just got a lucky break in life. They're just like other girls.

[Media] How 'bout your fabulous collection of teddy bears? What started that?
Oh, it got started from a rumor. It was an article came out that I collected stuffed animals, and I was swamped with 'em. Actually, I mean naturally I keep 'em because the people give 'em to me, but I never even thought of collecting stuffed animals in my life.

[Media] Do you appreciate them now you have them or do you just save them?
Yeah, yeah. I keep 'em. I have 'em all over the

walls and in the base[ment] and in the chairs, and everywhere else.

SEPTEMBER 2, 1957

LOCATION: *Portland, Oregon.*
INTERVIEWER: *Unknown.*
SOURCE: In Days Gone By *(EP).*

[Media] For your concert tonight, how long a duration will it be?
The entire show will be about two and one-half hours. I think I'm on for about forty minutes.

[Media] What songs are you going to hit?
I'll do practically all of my songs.

[Media] Which song do you think is the biggest right now?
"Don't Be Cruel" is the biggest. Yes.

[Media] How about "[Let Me Be Your] Teddy Bear"? How's it doing?
It's at about two million now.

[Media] There are a bunch of teenagers up the other side of the studio waiting to see you and as you can see, in spite of all the secrecy and this little devious plan, that a lot of it's leaked out.
It always does (laughs). It always does. But I don't mind it. In fact, if you come into a place, there's nobody there to meet ya, you start wondering (laughs).

[Media] Surely. Are you going to allow film tonight at your press conference during your show?
Am I going to do what, sir?

[Media] Allow film, movie film.
Oh yes.

[Gene Smith] No, not movie film.

[Media] Not movie film?

[G.S.] I'll explain it at the conference tonight.

[Media] Well, that won't do us a great deal of good you know.

Excuse me! I said yes, he says no. I don't know.

[G.S.] Well I'll explain to you tonight.
Very nice talkin' with you, sir. We're gonna have to run here.

[Media] Thank you very much, sir.

Bye-bye.
Gene!

[Media] So Elvis Presley leaves in his official car, with motorcycle escort, and headed now for his hotel. All these youngsters and people have come down to see him and no one even knew where his car was going to be. But, in spite of all the secrecy, here they are. And I can imagine the pandemonium going on right now in Union Station.

DECEMBER 31, 1957

ITEM: *Typewritten letter from Elvis Presley (Memphis, Tennessee), copies of which were sent, along with checks, to numerous Memphis-based charities.*
SOURCE: *Original documents.*

Gentlemen,
Please accept the enclosed check, as a small contribution to the great work your organization is doing for our city and country
Yours very sincerely,

Elvis Presley

1957

LOCATION: *Memphis, Tennessee.*
ITEM: *Handwritten love notes on two photographs given to Anita Wood.*
SOURCE: *Document photocopy.*
[Exact date not known. According to Anita Wood, "During the time Elvis and I dated, his pet name for me was 'Little.' He referred to himself as 'The Thing.'"]

I love you, love you, love you, you Little.
  Love you always.
From "The Thing."
To Little, with all my love.

E.P.
Elvis Presley

1958

ITEM: *Telegram from Elvis Presley (Madison, Tennessee) to Wanda L. Grubb, Elvis Presley Fan Club (Bradford, Ohio).*

SOURCE: *Original document.*

[Many Presley fan clubs received this generic telegram message, actually sent by Col. Parker's staff.]

Hello Fans,

Just a word before I leave. I am about to embark on a new career of which I am very proud. Of course you know it is an honor and a privilege to serve our country. Glancing backward once more, I am overcome with the loyalty and with all of the little thoughtful deeds which you, my fans, have displayed toward me in the past two years. What has touched me most of all is the wonderful things you have done in my name to aid and build up faith in the human race. It has been fun and I love every one of you. Be good. Do your very best in everything you undertake and before you know it I will be back with you once again. I am looking forward to this with great anticipation. Let's just say so long.

Loving you always,
Elvis

With Sophia Loren, Paramount Studios, Hollywood, 1958.

LOCATION: *Memphis Draft Board, Memphis, Tennessee.*

EVENT: *Swearing-in as a Member of U.S. Army, directed by Major Elbert Turner.*

SOURCE: This Is Elvis *(LP).*

[Elbert Turner] Gentlemen, repeat after me.

[E.T.] I [your name]
I, Elvis Presley.

[E.T.] Do solemnly swear.
Do solemnly swear.

[E.T.] That I will bear true faith and allegiance.
That I will bear true faith and allegience.

[E.T.] To the United States of America.
To the United States of America.

[E.T.] Congratulations! You are now in the Army. You are all privates. That's the way you'll be addressed from now on. Private Presley, you'll be in charge of the group.

LOCATION: *Waco, Texas (at the home of Eddie Fadal).*

SOURCE: Home Recorded *(LP).*

[Exact date not known. During basic training at Fort Hood, Texas, Elvis frequently spent his weekend leave time at the Fadal home in Waco. On this occasion, Elvis, who is playing the piano, is joined in songs and conversation by his girlfriend Anita Wood, and Eddie Fadal.]

[Eddie Fadal] Anita, you sing one. Sing one.

[Anita Wood] Oh no, no.

[E.F.] Man, you've got to! We've gotta have a premiere of your upcoming record.

[A.W.] I just like listening to you all sing.
I want her to do "I Can't Help It [If I'm Still in Love with You]" for some reason.

[E.F.] Oh man, I wanna hear that one.

[A.W.] I can never do that one. When I start it I can't hit the right key, ever (laughs).
Well we'll find it, c'mon.

[A.W.] Where is it you played it last time?
I don't remember.

[A.W.] B-flat is my key but you changed it. B or C.
That's it. Alright.
[After song.] Isn't that pretty?

[E.F.] Boy, Anita, that is tremendous.

[A.W.] Oh thank you. That's a beautiful song.

[E.F.] I can't wait until your first record comes out.
I hope it does.
It better be a good one. I wish they'd let me pick it.

[E.F.] I do too. Do you have one in mind?
You could put her on a song like that one ["I Can't Help It (If I'm Still in Love with You)"] or "Happy, Happy Birthday Baby."

[E.F.] Oh, I wish you'd record that. I wish you'd [Elvis] record that one too.
Or "Cold, Cold [Heart]," you know, something with "heart" in it. What I'm afraid of is they're gonna put her on somethin' a little too modern…a little too popular. You know what I mean?

[E.F.] It'd just die too quick.
Well, no.

[E.F.] It'll catch on and then fade.
No, I'm talkin' about…they're gonna give her some music, I'm afraid, that's more of a Julie London type. They gotta give her somethin' like Connie Francis sings. Somethin' with some guts to it.

[A.W.] What is that new one of her's…Connie Francis?

[E.F.] Did you play the new one ["I'm Sorry I Made You Cry"] I sent you?
I don't care for it.

On leave in Waco, Texas, with Anita Wood, 1958.

[E.F.] You don't like it?
I'm sorry dear, so sorry dear…I don't care to much for that.

[E.F.] Do you know "Blue Moon"?
I did that…one of my first records, "Blue Moon."

[E.F.] Do you like [Lavern Baker's] "Tomorrow Night"?
Oh yeah.
   [Surprisingly, Elvis makes no mention whatsoever—as he did with "Blue Moon"—that he had also recorded "Tomorrow Night," while at Sun Records.]

[E.F.] Lavern Baker, you like her?
Oh yeah. That's a good hi-fi set.

[E.F.] "Little Darlin'" is what you wanted?
Yeah. Hey, how about "Just a Closer Walk with Thee"?

AUGUST 1958

ITEM: *"Thank you" card from Vernon and Elvis Presley (Memphis, Tennessee), signed by a member of the Presley staff. Mailed to those who sent expressions of sympathy to the Presleys for the loss of Gladys.*

With Sammy Davis Jr. on *King Creole* set, 1958.

SOURCE: *Original document.*
Your kind expression of sympathy is deeply appreciated and gratefully acknowledged.
Vernon and Elvis Presley

SEPTEMBER 22, 1958

EVENT: *Press Conference. Questions by media representatives.*
LOCATION: *Brooklyn, New York.*
SOURCE: This Is Elvis *(Video).*

[Media] Elvis, did the other soldiers give you a rough time because you're famous?
No sir, I was very surprised. I've never met a better group of boys in my life. They probably would have if it'd been like everybody thought. I mean, everybody thought I wouldn't…I wouldn't have to work, and I would be given special treatment and this and that. But when they looked around and saw I was on K.P. and I was pulling guard and everything, just like they were, well they figured well, he's just like us.

[Media] Elvis, what do you think about going to Germany?
Well sir, I'm kinda lookin' forward to it, I mean,

just before I came in the Army we were planning a tour of Europe. And I get quite a bit of mail from over there and everything, you know, and I'm kinda lookin' forward to it, really.

SEPTEMBER 22, 1958

LOCATION: *Brooklyn, New York.*
EVENT: *Press Conference. Questions by numerous media representatives.*
SOURCE: The Complete '50s Masters *(CD).*

[Media] Here at the Brooklyn P.O.E. where Elvis Presley, Private Elvis Presley of the United States Army, is due to embark for Germany today. And let me tell you a little of what the hub-hub is like here. We've been, as I say, waiting for the past two hours for Presley to come in. There was some delay with his train…and he has just stepped off the elevator, which has brought him up from the lower level where many of his fellow embarkees have been preparing to go aboard the *General Randall,* the ship that he will take over to Germany.

[Media] Now Elvis moves over and is going to sit down behind the desk. The microphones

will be brought in. More pictures will be taken. Elvis apparently enjoying the whole thing very much, he's been in smiles since he walked into the room.
Ma'am.

[Media] What are your medals for?
Is it all right to stand up, sir? These medals right here, ma'am, are for expert with a carbine rifle and also tank weapons.

[Media] What?
Tank weapon. That's a ninety-millimeter gun. And this one right here, I didn't do quite as well. It's the pistol. I got a sharpshooter over there [pointing to another soldier].

[Media] A forty-five?
Yes sir, that's right.

[Media] Elvis, what do you think about going to Germany?
Well, sir, I'm kind lookin' forward to it.

[Media] Do you speak any German at all?
No ma'am, I don't.

[Media] Are you planning to learn a little bit?
I'll probably have to in order to survive in Germany.

[Media] What does the "A" in your name stand for?
Aron.

[Media] Who was the author of the book you were carrying when you got off the train?
I had just gotten the book, sir. I don't know.

[Media] Where'd you get it? Somebody gave it to you as a gift?
One of the boys gave it to me on the train. The title of the book was [A. L. Alexander's] Poems That Touch the Heart.

[Media] Did any of them touch your heart?
(Laughs.)

[Media] Have you had a chance to read it?
Yes ma'am, I read a couple poems in it. I read one in particular called "Should You Go First," which is a beautiful poem.

[Media] Do you prefer poetry to short stories?
Yes ma'am, I do.

[Media] Do you know by whom the poem was?
The author was unknown in the poem. That's right.

[Media] Elvis, is your dad going to Germany shortly after or at the same time you do?
Yes ma'am, he is supposed to leave, I think, on the twenty-sixth.

[Media] Is anybody else going with you?
My grandmother and one of the boys that used to work for us is going too.

[Media] Do you like to go to Germany? I know you have no choice, but ah…
(Laughs.) Yes sir. I'm looking forward to it. In fact, before I came in the Army we were planning a tour of Europe. I've never been out of the States except to Honolulu. Rock and roll music is very big over in Europe, in Germany, and all over Europe. It's very big.

[Media] Do they have still very active groups that you hear about, even though you're in service?
Yes sir. In fact, I think my fan club, my fan clubs, probably doubled.

[Media] Since you been in?
Yes sir.

[Media] That's amazing.
And the mail almost drove everybody crazy at Fort Hood.

[Media] What happened to all that mail?
It was all sent to Colonel Parker to be answered, in Nashville.

[Media] How many fan letters do you get each day now?
Well sir, I suppose I get…probably fifteen thousand letters a week.

[Media] Fifteen thousand a week?
Yes sir.

[Media] Do you expect to get a chance to sing over in Germany at all?
Well sir, I don't know. I really don't.

[Media] Do you hope to?
Actually it's a pretty tough question. So far I've just been soldiering, and I've been doing very well at it. So I don't know exactly what they have planned for me.

[Media] March 24, 1960?
Yes sir.

[Media] To keep your career going while you're in the Army, will you have to give sort of press conferences, you know, as a Paramount star and all that, while you're in Europe?
I would imagine that there will be quite a few people from the press over there. I really don't know. I don't know how it's gonna be handled over there.

[Media] Elvis, at the time you entered the service, I think it was Colonel Parker who said that the federal government was going to lose money by taking you into the service, meaning of course income taxes. Did you share that sentiment with him?
(Laughs.) Well, I'll put it like this. I've paid a lot of income tax, I know that. Although the government has a lot of money...I hope.

[Media] Can we see your haircut?
Ma'am, it'd be out of uniform, ma'am, I can't take my hat off.

[Media] Did you have a rougher time in the first day at camp or later? What comments did the other soldiers have?
Some of 'em wouldn't look good in print, sir.

[Media] Elvis, most people have a song that is sort of special to them. Do you have a favorite song?
My favorite song is a song called "Padre." Are you familiar with it, by Toni Arden? And also, "You'll Never Walk Alone" was always one of my very favorites.

[Media] Elvis, do you think your high school R.O.T.C. did you any good in the Army?
Yes ma'am, it definitely did. I knew my left leg from my right one and it helped quite a bit (laughs).

[Media] Did that color guard that you outfitted at Humes High School in Memphis give you any going away presents?
Yes ma'am, they gave me an old musket—one of the old rifles, you know, you had to pack the powder in the end of it.

[Media] From the Civil War or before that?
I think it was the Civil War.

[Media] Your family's been here a long time. Were any of your ancestors in the Civil War, or the Revolutionary War?
Ah, let me see. On which side, let's see? (laughs).

[Media] Do you still have your four Cadillacs?
Three now, sir. I traded one for a Lincoln, sir.

[Media] Are you going to take any of your cars with you?
No ma'am. I'll get a German...when in Germany, do as the Germans do. I'll probably get a German car.

[Media] Don't you have one...a Messerschmitt?
I had one. I gave it away, sir.

[Media] How is it possible that you're not in Special Services?
Ma'am, I don't know.

[Media] It's not your choice? I mean no one asked you?
I haven't said anything. I mean I guess the Army knows what's best for me.

[Media] What kind of work do they have you doing? What kind of work do you do generally?
Well, for about eighteen weeks I was in the

tanks. *I was a tank commander. And then the last few weeks I was there I was a truck driver. I drove a truck.*

[Media] **Elvis, should rock and roll die out between now and the time you get out of the service…**
…I'll starve to death, sir (laughs)…I beg your pardon, sir.

[Media]**…What do you think you might do?**
If rock and roll music were to die out—which I don't think it will—I would try something else. I would probably try…I would really probably go in for the movies then and I would try to make it as an actor, which is very tough 'cause you got a lot of competition.

[Media] **Elvis, are you surprised that you're as big a success and as lasting a success as you are now? Did you think it was gonna turn out this well?**
I didn't know, sir. I was hoping, but uh, I just took every day as it come along. I didn't anticipate that I was gonna, I was gonna do well, or I didn't anticipate I was gonna die out.

[Media] **How many Gold Records do you have, incidentally?**
Twenty-five, sir.

[Media] **Twenty-five? That's tops, isn't it, in the business? Paramount says eight.**
Eight? Sir, they're behind time.

[Media] **Twenty-five?**
I have twenty-five million-sellers and two albums that have sold a million each. In fact, the RCA Victor men are here. They can verify that. Isn't that right?

[Col. Tom Parker] **Mr. Sholes is right there.**
They've all disappeared, sir. Isn't that right, Mr. Sholes?

[Media] **Steve Sholes?**

[T.P.] **The gentleman with the red badge over there.**

[Media] **Do you plan to make any records while you're on furlough in Germany? I understand that's a privilege of all Army personnel.**
I beg your pardon, sir.

[Media] **Do you plan to make any records while you're on furlough in Germany? I understand that's a privilege of all Army personnel.**
No sir, I don't. I don't think so.

[Media] **On the rock and roll, Elvis, do you think there's a sort of developing form of music? In other words, will it stay like it is or do you think it may change its form? Well, there's been criticism of the wiggling there. Do you think it's gonna straighten out or something like that? Do you know what I mean?**
Sir, the wiggle can't straighten out (laughs). If you do, you're finished. It's like a guy down in Fort Hood…one of the sergeants one day…I was…I was sitting down on my foot locker and my left leg was shaking. I mean just unconsciously. He said, "Presley, I wish you'd quit shaking that leg." I said, "Sarge, when that leg quits shaking I'm finished."

[Media] **You've probably seen that your fans brought down the ceiling in London when *King Creole* was showing last week. Do you plan to go to England at all on furlough from Germany?**
I would like to, if I can make it on a three-day pass.

[Media] **Elvis, what would you like to do the most on your first leave in Europe?**
I'd like to go to Paris…and look up Brigitte Bardot (laughter).

[Media] **Elvis, do you have anything you want to say to your many admirers before going overseas…any farewell word?**
Yes sir, I would. I'd like to say that I'm gonna do my best to keep putting out the records and everything that they enjoy, and that I'll be looking forward to coming back and entertaining them again.

[Media] Do you have any records cut that are not released?
Yes ma'am, I do.

[Media] How many?
I have two...or is it three. I don't know. He [Col. Tom Parker] says it's four.

[Media] Could you tell me what you think of [Dean Martin's] "Volare," and the Italian singers that have come along?
I think it's great. I went out and bought the record when I first heard it.

[Media] Do you think you might record something like that?
Me record an Italian song? I don't know if I could cut the mustard (laughs).

[Media] While you're in the service, do you plan to take advantage of any of the educational benefits given by the armed services?
Well, I have thought a lot about the different types of schooling the Army has to offer. And I do know for a fact that a lot of fellows have gone through the service and benefited out in civilian life, after they come out of the service. A lot of guys that had nothing prior to the time they went in, and they go in service and they take some kind of schooling for maybe a year or two years and when they come out of the Army, well they're qualified for a good job. Now, it doesn't hurt for anybody to have a profession to turn to in case something did happen to the entertainment business, or something happen to me. I don't know exactly yet what kind of a school that I would like to go to.

[Media] Elvis, on the trip here, on the trip here on the train from wherever you took off from...
Fort Hood, sir...

[Media] Fort Hood to here in Brooklyn, you must have had some time to yourself. What did you think about?
Well, there were three hundred and fifty guys on the train with me. They didn't give me much time to think. You know, the boys come around and they talk. They want to know about Hollywood and different things. They want to know about making movies and things. We pretty well kept occupied. I don't like to sit alone too much and think.

[Media] Have you formed any real close buddies in the service, friendships since you been in?
Yes sir, I've got quite a few buddies in there.

[Media] Elvis, are you sorry you never got to college?
Right at the time, we didn't have enough money to go to college. I would have liked to have gone.

[Media] Would you like to go back at some point?
Well it's according to what the future holds for me.

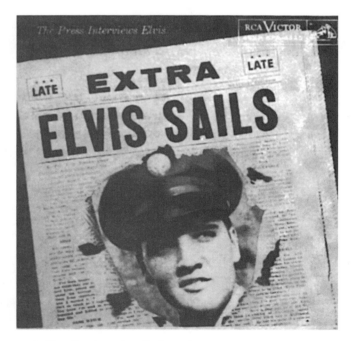

An EP collection of media interviews made just before Elvis shipped out for Germany, 1958.

LOCATION: *Brooklyn, New York.*
EVENT: *Press Conference, titled "Press Interview with Elvis Presley." Questions by numerous media representatives.*
SOURCE: Elvis Sails *(EP).*

[Media] Elvis, do you feel that your fans have been pretty loyal to you since you been in service?
Yes sir, I certainly do.

[Media] What about the presents? What are you going to do with them?
All the presents…the majority of the presents consists of cookies, cakes, and all of that. And whenever you get a box of cookies or cakes or anything, when you're livin' in the barracks…you don't even see the box, you know.

[Media] (Laughter.) Do you have any plans for after you get out of service, Elvis? What do you want to do?
Yes sir. When I get out of service, I plan to pick up where I left off, if possible.

[Media] You interested in movies more than ever now?
Yes sir. I'd like to become a good actor. That's my ambition right now.

[Media] When do you get out, Elvis?
Scheduled for March 24, 1960, sir.

[Media] Was Miss [Anita] Wood the only girl you know well who saw you off at Fort Hood?
No ma'am, there was quite a few others down there (laughs).

[Media] (Laughter.) Are there some here to say goodbye today?
I beg your pardon.

[Media] Are some here to say goodbye today?
I don't know. I haven't seen any.

[Media] Why is that?
Well…umm…it's school…school's going on.

[Media] (Laughter.)
I beg your pardon, ma'am.

[Media] Did you have a rough time…a rougher time than most soldiers because you were a celebrity?
No ma'am, everything was just straight down the middle. I was treated no better or any worse than any of the other boys.

[Media] What about…
…and that's the way I wanted it because I had to live with the other boys, you know.

[Media] Well, not by the Army. I mean by the other boys. Did the boys treat you roughly?
Oh no sir, not at all. I kind of expected it because out in civilian life I get harassed a little bit by a few people, you know. And I was expecting it in there, but when those guys looked around and they saw me pulling K.P. and marching with a pack on my back, and every-thing, well they figured, well, he's just like we are. So I got along very well with them and they're all a good bunch of boys.

[Media] Have the other G.I.s a nickname they've given you?
Quite a few (laughs).

[Media] (Laughter.) Elvis, what's your idea of the ideal girl?
Female, sir (laughs).

[Media] (Laughter.)
No sir, I (laughs)…excuse me. I really don't know. I like a lot of different types. Ah, I sup-pose I'll know if I ever find someone that I really fall in love with.

[Media] If you found someone while you were in service that you thought you were in love with, would you get married in service?
I don't think so, sir. Because the way I look at it, if you find someone you're in love with and she's in love with you, she will understand about my career, and she will…she wouldn't want to do

anything to hurt it. So she wouldn't rush me (laughs), in other words.

[Media] Do you think you could ever be satisfied with a girl that was also in show business?
Oh well sir, actually I don't think that would make much difference—whether she's in show business or driving a truck.

[Media] (Laughter.) A lot of young people are interested in your views on marriage, you were mentioning, you know, earlier on. Now, do you have in your mind a sort of ideal age for a guy to marry? Have you got a target age, or for kids in general, what do you say?
Well, as you're growing up, a lot of times you think you're in love with somebody and you want to get married, and then later on in your life you find out you were wrong. That actually you didn't love 'em, you only thought you did. And I was no different several times as I was growing up I would've probably married had my mother and dad not talked to me and said, "You better wait and find out if this is what you want." And I did, and I'm glad that I did.

[Media] When was the last time you thought you were in love?
Oh, many times, ma'am. I don't know. Ah, I suppose the closest that I ever came to getting married was just before I started singing. In fact, my first record saved my neck (laughs).

[Media] (Laughter.) Elvis, the readers of our magazine asked me to pass along their sympathies to you on the recent death of your mother. And I wondered if you'd like to say a few words of tribute to the way she's helped you in your life.
Yes sir, I certainly would. My mother…I suppose since I was an only child that we might've been a little closer than…I mean everyone loves their mother, but I was an only child and mother was always right with me all my life. And it wasn't only like losing a mother, it was like losing a friend, a companion, someone to talk to. I could wake her up any hour of the night and if I was worried or troubled by something, well she'd get up and try to help me. I used to get very angry at her when I was growing up. It's a natural thing when a young person wants to go somewhere or do something and your mother won't let you, you think, "why what's wrong with you?" But then later on in the years you find out, you know, that she was right. That she was only doing it to protect you, to keep you from getting in any trouble or getting hurt. And I'm very happy that she was kinda strict on me, very happy that it worked out the way it did.

[Col. Tom Parker] Thank you, ladies and gentlemen. Time has run out.

SEPTEMBER 22, 1958

LOCATION: *Brooklyn, New York.*
EVENT: *Press Conference, titled "Elvis Presley's Newsreel Interview." Questions by numerous media representatives.*
SOURCE: Elvis Sails *(EP).*

[Media] Elvis, you've got quite a reception here, but there is quite a group of people who don't sort of approve of the thing you do.
Yes.

[Media] They seem to think it contributes to juvenile delinquency and all sorts of things. Do you have any thoughts to the unpopular side of your audience?
Yes sir, I have. I've tried to figure it out. I don't see how they can think that it would contribute to juvenile delinquency, someone's only singing and dancing. I don't see that. Because, if there's anything I've tried to do, I've tried to live a straight clean life and not set any kind of a bad example. I will say that there are people that are gonna like you and people that don't like you regardless of what…what business you're in or what you do. You cannot please everyone.

[Media] Do you feel that rock and roll...the popularity of rock and roll will diminish in any way while you're in the Army?

That's hard to tell. The only thing I can say is I hope not.

[Media] Is it a relief to get away from all the autograph hounds and the hysterical females?

No sir, it is not. Once you get used to it if nobody comes up and asks for an autograph, or no one bothers you, well then you start worrying (laughs). As long as they come around and everything, you know that they still like you and it makes you feel good.

[Media] If you think rock and roll won't diminish in popularity, what do you think sustains its popularity? What quality of it do you think makes it popular?

Well sir, rock and roll has been around for many years. It used to be called rhythm and blues, and as far back as I can remember it's been very big, although in the last five years it's gotten much bigger. I personally don't think it will ever die completely out, because they're gonna have to get something mighty good to take its place as far as the young people are concerned.

[Media] What about maybe taking the wiggle out of it?

Rock and roll music, if you like it and if you feel it, you can't help but move to it. That's what happens to me. I can't help it. I mean I have to move around. I can't stand still. I've tried it and I can't do it.

[Media] Well, do you feel that you've been very lucky, or do you feel that you do have a talent that most of the other people you meet don't have?

Well sir, I've been very lucky. I've been very lucky, and I happened to come along at a time in the music business where there was no trend. I was lucky, I mean the people were looking for something different and I was lucky. I came along just in time.

LOCATION: *Brooklyn, New York.*
EVENT: *Interview, titled "Pat Hernon Interviews Elvis Presley in the Library of the U.S.S. Randall at Sailing."*
SOURCE: Elvis Sails *(EP).*

[Pat Hernon] We've now moved down into the library of the U.S.S. *Randall*, and we are now only minutes away from sailing time. And Elvis Presley will shortly be on his way to Germany, and a return to the United States...well, who knows. It'll be some time anyway. Elvis, we have just a small group and a few moments to talk about things. I know you're a pretty tired fellow. You've had a busy couple of days getting here to the Brooklyn Port and getting ready to leave, haven't you?

Yes sir, that's right.

[P.H.] Well now, how long has it been, for example, since you've had a chance to eat today?

Well I ate breakfast this morning and haven't eaten since. Course it's...

[P.H.] Now it's almost two o'clock in the afternoon.

I don't feel like that I could eat anything right now (laughs).

[P.H.] Elvis, since we're so close to sailing time, and we're getting pretty close to the last thoughts that you have here in the country before you go overseas in your stint of duty, what do you think about? How do you feel?

Well I'm gonna be very honest about it. I'm looking forward to Germany. I'm looking forward to seein' the country, meeting a lot of the people, but at the same time, I'm looking forward to coming back here.

[P.H.] Now, as I say, we're getting closer and closer to the time that they're gonna pull that gangplank away, and you'll be on your way.

Pvt. Presley meets press upon arrival in Germany, 1958.

Since this is probably the last chance that you'll have to say something to your fans, do you have any particular message that you'd like to pass on to them.

Yes I would. I'd like to say that in spite of the fact that I am going away and I'll be out of their eyes for some time, I hope that I'm not out of their minds. And I'll be lookin' forward to the time when I can come back and entertain again like I did. And...

[P.H.] All we can do is wish you a wonderful trip and all the best luck in the world, and come home soon.

Thank you very much. I'll do my very best.

OCTOBER 1, 1958

LOCATION: *Bad Homberg, Germany.*
INTERVIEWER: *Unknown.*
SOURCE: Welcome in Germany *(CD).*

[Media] Okay, we're rolling.

Thank you very much. I would just like to say, ladies and gentlemen, that it's really a privilege to be in Europe. It's something that I've looked forward to for some time. I consider it a privilege to be assigned to such a fine outfit as the 3rd Armored Division. And I hope that I can live up

to everybody's expectations of me, and I will do my very best to. I only regret that I can't do some shows and different things while I'm here. But I will be looking forward when my Army hitch is over. I would like very much to come back on a regular tour. I was very surprised at the reception. I wasn't expecting anything quite that big. And I only regret that I didn't have more time to stay there with them. But maybe someday I can come back, when my Army tour is up, as an entertainer, and then I'll have more time and maybe I'll have an opportunity to kind of make myself at home over here. Arrivederci! No, that's Italian, isn't it? (Laughs.)

[Media] Thank you very much, Mr. Presley, and we wish you a pleasant stay in Germany.
Thank you very much.

OCTOBER 1, 1958

LOCATION: *Friedberg, Germany.*
INTERVIEWER: *Unknown.*
SOURCE: Conversations with the King *(Audiotape) and* All the King's Men *(Video).*

[Media] Welcome to Germany, Elvis!
Hello. I'm happy to be here...I'm happy to be here...I'm happy to be here, sir...I'm very happy to be here, thank you, sir. Ah, sir, I don't think they want me to say anything right now, sir. I'm sorry.

[Media] Mr. Presley, your flowers.
Flowers are where, ma'am?...I better not, sir, really...This ring? Can you have my ring? Okay, honey, it's a gift [gives his ring to a fan].

[Media] Do you miss the singing career very much or are you enjoying this Army life?
I miss my singing career very much. But at the same time, the Army's a pretty good deal too.

OCTOBER 28, 1958

ITEM: *Three-page letter handwritten by Elvis*

(Bad Nauheim, Germany), sent to Anita Wood.
SOURCE: *Document photocopy.*

[Letter, on Hotel Grunwald stationery, is undated. According to Anita Wood, "During the time Elvis and I dated, his pet name for me was 'Little.'" This is Elvis' first letter to Anita from Europe.]

For the first time in a hundred years I am writing a letter. You can see why I don't like to write, the reason being I can't write worth a ??? I just thought of so many things I wanted to say to you and I couldn't say them on the phone. You'll never know how much I miss you baby, and how much I want to pet you and call you "Widdle Bitty." Your little picture is by my bed and every night before I go to sleep I always say "goodnight little Pee Pee." The people over here are very nice and friendly although they are living about 30 years behind us. Don't quote me. *I haven't dated a single girl since I have been here, the reason being I don't have time and everytime I get out of the hotel [Grunwald] I get mobbed. Also I haven't seen a girl yet that could speak English. You say hello to one and she says "Luben Slich Ein EP skep skep skep Von Heimer Bull Shit." I want to explain something to you and you have got to trust me and believe me because I am very sincere when I say it. I will tell you this much. I have never and never will again love any one like I love you sweetheart. Also I guarantee that when I marry, it will be Miss "Little 'Presley' Wood." There is a lot you have to understand though. Only God knows when the time will be right. So you have got to consider this and love me, trust me and keep yourself clean and wholesome because that is the big thing that can determine our lives and happiness together. If you*

believe me and trust me you will wait for me and our future will be filled with happiness. With God's help it will work itself out and you will understand and be patient. I worked so hard to build up my career and everything, and if you truly love me you would not want anything to happen to it and cause me to be unhappy. No matter what I'm doing, whether it be the army, making movies, traveling or singing, I will be thinking of the time when we have our first "Little Elvis Presley." So keep this in mind and don't get discouraged and lonely. Just remember this is a guy that loves you with all his heart and wants to marry you. One more thing, honey, for goodness sake please don't let anyone read this and don't say a word about this letter to anyone. You know how I hate that so be careful baby. If you love me and you are sincere you wouldn't want to let anyone know our intimate secrets. I better go for now love, so be happy and remember down in your little heart that I love you, love you, love you. Keep writing.

Yours *Alone and Forever*
E.P.

P.S. I love you

Pvt. Presley meets press upon arrival in Germany, 1958.

My Dearest "Little" Darling,

I just received your letters and I can judge by the last 3 that you are a little disappointed. Well I can't blame you, especially since all that mess was written about "little puppy" and all that "horse shit". Well I don't know where they got the information but the girl they speak of was a photographers model and she was brought over by some newsman the first week I was here. I have seen her one time since then. She doesn't speak a word of [...] I have not been dating [...] not say all that stuff [...] her 4 or five times and 5[...] to keep anything from [...]

that was really played up big because the papers figured it was good for German, American relationships. Do you understand? But don't you dare ever mention it to a soul because if you do, I am finished in Germany. Just keep it inside of you and regardless of what you read or what obstacles come up in our way, please remember that I am yours my darling, your yours, yours, yours, yours. No one will ever take the place of "my little" in my life. Baby you will never know how lonesome and miserable I am. I will be so thankful to God when once again I am free,

Letter to Anita Wood from Elvis in Germany, 1958.
Top right: Anita and Elvis, 1956.

ITEM: *Four-page letter handwritten by Elvis in Friedberg, Germany, sent to Anita Wood in Oceanside, New York.*

SOURCE: *Original document.*

[Envelope has a November 14 postmark by the "U.S. Army-Air Force Postal Service." Letter is undated.]

My Dearest Little Darling,

I just received your letters and I can judge by the last three that you are a little disappointed. Well I can't blame you, especially since that mess was written about "little puppy" and all that "horse shit." Well I don't know where they got the information but the girl they speak of was a photographers model and she was brought over by some newsman the first week I was here. I have seen her one time since then. She doesn't speak a word of English and I have not been dating her and I did not say all that stuff about seeing her five times and I have not tried to keep anything from you.

You see that was really played up big because the papers figured it was good for German, American relationship. Do you understand? But don't you dare ever mention it to a soul because if you do I am finished in Germany. Just keep it inside of you and regardless of what you read or what obstacles come up in our way, please remember that I am yours my darling, yours, yours, yours, yours, yours. No one will ever take the place of my "Little" [pet name for Anita] in my life. Baby you will never know how lonesome and miserable I am. I will be so thankful to God when once again I am free, free to return back to singing, making movies, and above all returning to your little arms and lips.

Every night I lay in my bunk, I see your little eyes and your little nose, and it's almost like you are here, like you are pressed up close to me. I can feel your little hair on the side of my face and sometimes I get so excited and want you so bad I start sweating. "WOW"

Well so much for that. Listen my Love never doubt my love for you, always trust me and believe me when I say that I love you.

It sure is going to be a blue Christmas this year. But in 15 short months it'll be over and as General [Douglas] MacArthur said, "I shall return." Have a Merry Christmas Darling and rem[em]ber there is a lonely little boy 5,000 miles away that is counting the hours till he returns to your arms.

If you get a chance try to locate a record called "Soldier Boy" [by the Four Fellows]. Play it and think of me. By the way our song from now on is "[Please] Love Me Forever" by Tommy Edwards. Every night I play it just for you.

Always loving and wanting you.
Yours alone Darling,
Elvis Presley

P.S. No one ever reads this, o.k.!

ITEM: *Two-page letter handwritten by Elvis in Friedberg, Germany, sent to "M/Sgt. Bill Norwood," in Killeen, Texas.*

SOURCE: *Original document*

[Envelope has a November 28 postmark by the "U.S. Army-Air Force Postal Service." Letter is undated. Note underlined emphisis of "PFC" designation. Elvis was clearly proud of his November 27, 1958, promotion to Private First Class.]

Dear Sgt. Norwood and Family,

Well I am writing a letter for the first time in years. I received your letter and was glad to hear everything is o.k. I am in a

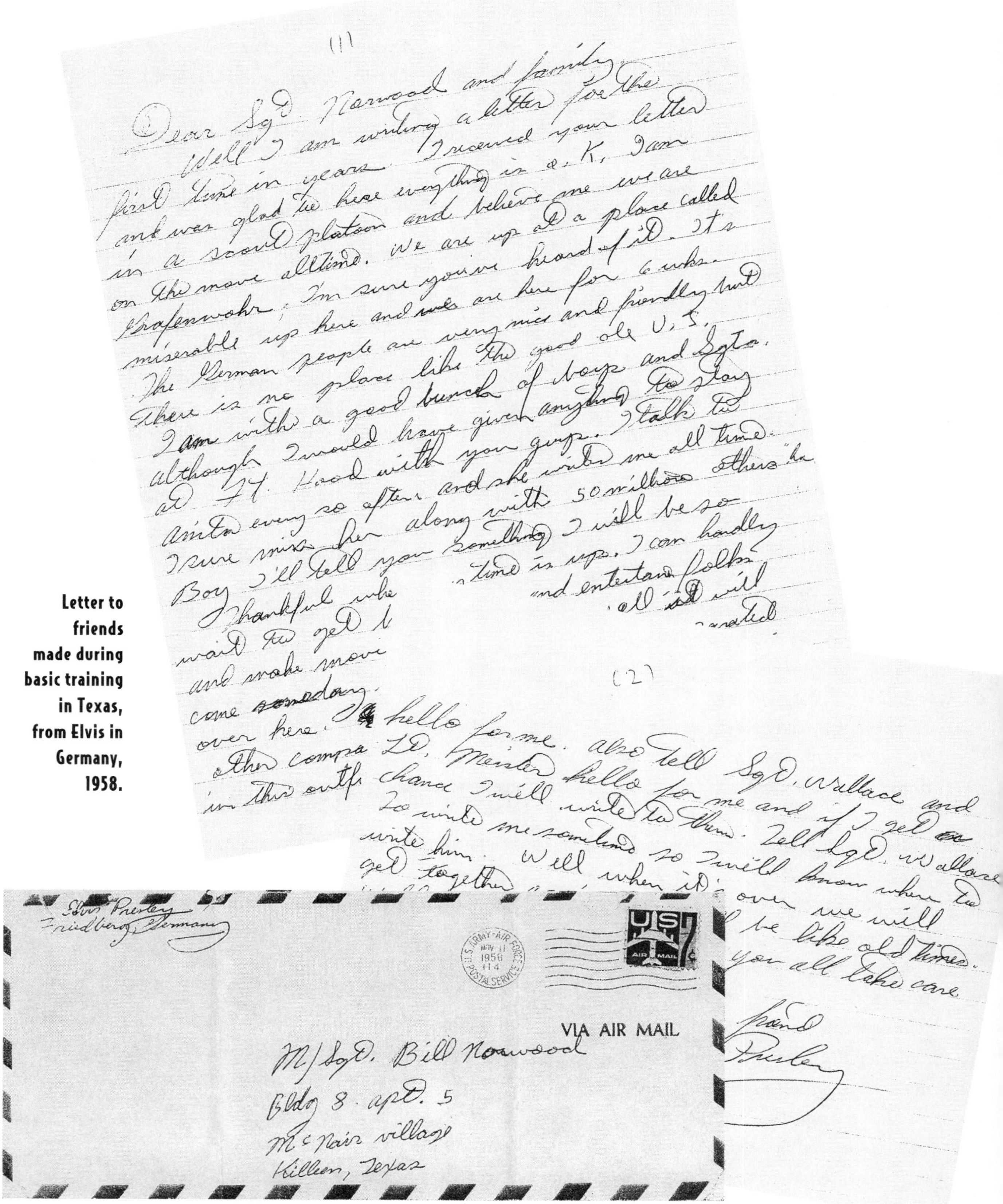

Letter to friends made during basic training in Texas, from Elvis in Germany, 1958.

(1)

Dear Sgt. Norwood and family,

Well I am writing a letter for the first time in years. I received your letter and was glad to hear everything is o.k. I am in a scout platoon and believe me we are on the move all time. We are up at a place called Grafenwohr; I'm sure you've heard of it. It's miserable up here and we are here for 6 wks. The German people are very nice and friendly but there is no place like the good ole U.S. I am with a good bunch of boys and Sgts. although I would have given anything to stay at Ft. Hood with you guys. I talk to Anita every so often and she writes me all time. I sure miss her along with 50 million others. ha Boy I'll tell you something I will be so thankful when time is up. I can hardly wait to get back and entertain folks and make movies. Well it will come someday. _____ other compa _____ in this outfit _____

(2)

hello for me. Also Tell Sgt. Wallace and Sgt. Meister hello for me and if I get a chance I'll write to them. Tell Sgt. Wallace to write me sometime so I will know where to write him. Well when it's over we will get together again it'll be like old times. You all take care.

Friend
Presley

Elvis Presley
Friedberg, Germany

VIA AIR MAIL

M/Sgt. Bill Norwood
Bldg 8. apt. 5
McNair village
Killeen, Texas

130

scout platoon and believe me we are on the move alltime [all the time]. We are up at a place called Grafenwohr [Grafenwör]. I'm sure you've heard of it. It's miserable up here and we are here for 6 weeks.

The German people are very nice and friendly but there is no place like the good ole U.S.

I am with a good bunch of boys and Sgts., although I would have given anything to stay at Ft. Hood [Texas] with you guys. I talk to Anita [Wood] every so often, and she writes me all the time. I sure miss her along with 50 million others. Ha.

Boy I'll tell you something. I will be so thankful when my time is up. I can hardly wait to get back home and entertain folks and make movies and everything. Well it will come someday soon. All of us were separated over here. [William R.] Norvell and [Donald R. "Rex"] Mansfield are in other companies, but there is a lot of good boys in this outfit. Well tell Olley [Mrs. Norwood] and the kids hello for me. Also tell Sgt Wallace and Lt. [Melvin E.] Meister hello for me and if I get a chance I will write to them. Tell Sgt. Wallace to write me sometime so I will know where to write him. Well when it's over we will get together again and it'll be like old times. Well I have to go now so you all take care and write again.

Your friend,
PFC Elvis Presley

NOVEMBER 1958

ITEM: *Two-page letter handwritten by Elvis in Grafenwohr, Germany, posted in Friedberg and sent to Alan "Hog Ears" Fortas, in Memphis, Tennessee.*

SOURCE: *Original document.*

[Exact date not known.]

Dear Hog Ears,

Got your letter and was glad to hear from you. Well you know I am bound to be pretty lonely or I wouldn't be writing a letter. We are up at a training area for 50 days, and believe me it's miserable. It's cold and there is nothing at all to do up here. I am about 200 miles from Friedberg and won't be back until the 20th of December. It will sure be a great Christmas this year. Ha!

I would give almost anything to be home. You know it will be March of 1960 before I return to the States. Man I hate to think about it. Of course don't say anything about it because a miracle may happen.

Boy it will be great getting out. I will probably scream so loud they'll make me stay two more years. Ha! I can hardly wait to start singing, traveling, making movies, and above all seeing the old gang and old Graceland. All I do is sit and count the days. Well it'll be over in about 15 months and as Gen. [Douglas] MacArthur said, "I shall return." Tell D.J. [deejay George Klein], uh, and Lewis [sic] [Louis Harris] I said hello and to hold down the fort till I get back. If you see cous [cousin Gene Smith] tell him I said ep skep skep skep. I have been dating this little German "Chuckaloid" by the name of Margrit [sic] [pinup model Margit Buergin]. She looks a lot like B.B. [Brigitte Bardot]. It's Grind City [a steamy affair]. Well I gotta go wade in the mud.

Your Pal,
Elvis Presley
"Eri Viar Ditchi" [Arrivederci]

Dear Hog Ears (1)
Got your letter and was good to hear from you. Well you know I was bound to be pretty lonely or I wouldn't be writing a letter. We are up at a training area for 50 days and believe me it's miserable. It's cold and there is nothing at all to do up here. I am about 200 miles from Friedberg and won't be back until the 20th of Dec. It will sure be a _great_ Christmas this year. I would give almost anything to be home. You know it will be March of 1960 before I return to the States. Man I hate to think about it. Of course don't say anything about it because a miracle may happen. Boy it will be great getting out. I will

probably scream make me stay. I can hardly wait (travel) making Movies, all seeing the old gang and old Graceland. All I do is sit and count the days. Well it'll be over in about 15 months and as Gen. MacArthur said, "I shall return". Tell D.J. uh, and Lewis I said hello and to hold down the fort till I get back. If you see cousin, tell him I said go ship shep. I have been dating this little German "Chuckaloid" by the name of Margrit. She looks alot like B.B. 20 1/2 _Mine City_. Well I gotta go wade in the mud.
"over"
Yours Pal, Elvis Presley

EVENT: *Phone call from Keith Sherriff in Memphis to Elvis in Bad Nauheim, Germany.*
SOURCE: *Transcript.*

[Keith Sherriff] Elvis, how are you?
I just got in from work. I still got my fatigues on.

[K.S.] Are you concerned about your popularity fading while you're overseas?
Well I don't really know 'bout that. I have no way of telling. And I'm in no position to worry about it right now. It's pretty hard to say about somethin' like that. I've got so much on my mind all the time... if I'd worry 'bout everythin' I would go nuts.

[K.S.] Along those lines, how many songs did you record before you left the States?
Not very many.

[K.S.] Do you have any plans to record in Germany?
I don't plan to, but that would all be handled in the States. I really don't know what they're gonna do.

[K.S.] Do you miss Memphis, and your home?
I would give my neck to be back home. I am homesick all the time...you just don't know. I'm happy to do my part in the Army, but you'll never know how much I want to get back home...back in the entertainment business. I guess I'll stay in the entertainment business one way or another the rest of my life...whether playing or as a stagehand. You will never know how wonderful old Memphis is until you've been away for a while.

[K.S.] There was one story that said you might sell Graceland. Is that true?
That's strictly a rumor. I would never sell Graceland! Not at no price to nobody, as long as I can hang on to it. Besides it would be foolish to sell now that I've got it completed. And, uh, I don't think my mother would like it if I did.

[K.S.] Some people saying you wrote your latest hit "I Got Stung." Did you, Elvis?
No. I never wrote a song myself. I probably could've if I sat down and tried hard enough, but I never had the urge.

[K.S.] Has there been any talk of you being put in Special Services, to possibly entertain troops and so forth?
Well, I don't know just what they're gonna do with me, you know what I mean.

[K.S.] Do you have to say "yes sir"?
You better believe it.

[K.S.] The papers carried a story about you and a German girl. Anything to that report?
About the German girl, there is nothing to it but a lot of...publicity. That's all it is. Don't get me wrong, she's a cute little girl and all of that, but it's mostly a lot of publicity.

Pvt. Presley visits with German friends, 1958.

EVENT: *Phone call from Tom Moffet in Honolulu, Hawaii, to Elvis in Bad Nauheim, Germany.*
SOURCE: The Elvis Presley Interview Record *(LP).*

[Tom Moffet] What do you do, Elvis, primarily, in your spare time?
Well I don't have too much spare time but what time off I have I usually just stay around home, read mail, try to answer mail, and I usually try to practice things.

[T.M.] Your fan mail keeping up to its usual capacity?
Yeah, it's pretty good. It keeps us all pretty busy. I have a couple secretaries and it keeps everybody pretty busy.

MARCH 1959

EVENT: *Phone call from Dick Clark in the United States to Elvis in Friedberg, Germany.*
SOURCE: *Audiotape.*
  [Exact date not known.]

[Dick Clark] Hello, Elvis.
Hello, Dick. How are you?

[D.C.] Fine, thank you. Where on earth are you at this minute?
Oh, I'm in a little place called Germany.

[D.C.] Yeah, so I've heard. What is the name of the town, Elvis?
The town that I'm in is Friedberg, Germany; however, I live in a place called Bad Nauheim, just north of Friedberg.

[D.C.] Oh yeah, that was when we got around to putting the call through. You know, it's an amazing thing, you sound a little far away you could very well be around the block somewhere.
It does sound like you're very close although you're about two thousand miles away.

[D.C.] Tell me a little bit about your activities. What did you do, say, today?
Mostly classroom work.

[D.C.] What are you studying?
Map reading and then how to grease my Jeep. Just the regular things.

[D.C.] Sounds like they're keeping you kinda busy.
Oh yeah. Army life's got a habit of keepin' people busy.

[D.C.] Does it agree with you?
It's not bad, Dick. It's really not bad at all.

[D.C.] Do you have any time for music anymore?
Only at night. You see, I get off work at five o'clock in the afternoon, and I have a guitar up here in the room and I sit around up here. I don't want to get out of practice, if I can help it.

[D.C.] I should hope not. Let me tell you some good news. I know you know by now why we're calling, they sent you the cablegram and so forth. In the annual American Bandstand Popularity Poll you walked away once again with a couple of honors this year. The Favorite Male Vocalist Award and the Favorite Record of 1958 Award. The kids voted you top man all around.
Well that's sure tremendous, Dick. It's really great, boy.

[D.C.] I know that you, down home, have a place for trophies and Gold Records and so forth. We, of course, have that silver record award. Suppose I send them along to Colonel Tom [Parker]?
Oh, that'd be great. I'll have to wait 'til I get home to see them.

[D.C.] Speaking of that, do you have any idea when you'll be traveling back home?
No I don't, Dick. I wish I did know.

[D.C.] How about it, do you miss home?
Oh boy, I can't hardly talk.

[D.C.] That's kind of a silly question on my part, I guess. How's it been now that you've been stationed in Germany?

I've been in Germany now about five months. And I've been in the army a little over ten months.

[D.C.] Now, your full term will run how long?

The full term, it's supposedly twenty-four months. Which means I'll have about fourteen more months to go.

[D.C.] Well Elvis, there's one thing, and I guess maybe our poll is an indication of it, I remember hearing your parting comments the other day, on the record *Elvis Sails*. The folks at home certainly haven't forgotten you. If anything, they're more and more interested in your activities, the things that you're doing, and anxiously await your return.

Well that's really great, Dick. That, believe me, that is the big thing that I'm looking forward to. You'll never know how happy I'll be. I mean, I'm glad that I could come in the Army and do my part, but you'll never know how happy I'll be, boy, when I can return to the entertainment world, because once you get a taste of show business, there's nothin' like it.

[D.C.] You know it. Elvis, thank you ever so much for talking to us. We look forward to your return. We'll see you just as quick as we can all get together.

Well thank you very much. I'd like to say one more thing before you go.

[D.C.] Sure. Please do.

Boy, I'm so excited I can hardly talk.

[D.C.] Take your time. We got all the time in the world.

I'd just like to tell all those wonderful kids that they'll never know how happy they made me, and I'm just longing for the time when I can come back out and entertain them again, travel around and make movies, records, and things like that.

With producer Hal Wallis, Germany, 1959.

[D.C.] Fine! Wonderful!

I wanna thank you very much for everything. That's about it.

[D.C.] That's it.

JUNE 19, 1959

LOCATION: *Munich, Germany.*
INTERVIEWER: *Unknown.*
SOURCE: *Audiotape and* Perfect for Parties *(CD).*

[Media] Elvis Presley was for a few days on a visit to Munich. He came to Munich to go from here incognito on a fourteen-day vacation in Paris. Having a little something to drink in his hotel while waiting for the train to leave, I found him to make an interview.

[The preceding introduction—made later for a radio broadcast—as well as the first question below, are translated by us from the German language. These words are spoken in German only, whereas the remaining questions are by the same woman but spoken in English.]

[Media] Elvis, what is your favorite music?

I like many different kinds of music—some classical. There's some that I understand, some that I do not understand. But my, naturally my…my best is rock and roll.

[Media] What do you think is your best song you ever sing?

"Don't."

[Media] "Don't"?

A song called "Don't."

[Media] Uh-huh.

Yeah.

[Media] Elvis, the teenagers wonder why you don't give any concert during your staying here…in Germany.

Well I will try to explain it to you. I was sent over here by the Army, as a soldier. You understand? And it would not be fair to the other boys in the Army if I were traveling around and singing. I cannot be treated any different from the other boys. Do you understand?

[Media] Yes (laughs).

And I'm very sorry that I am not over here as an entertainer…as a singer. But maybe—I hope—when I'm out of the Army, someday, I can come back to Europe on a tour, and then I will travel around and…

[Media] And?

As an entertainer…in eight…eight or nine more months.

JUNE 19, 1959

ITEM: *Telegram from Elvis Presley (Bad Nauheim, Germany) to Col. Tom Parker (New York, New York).*

SOURCE: *Document photocopy.*

Dear Colonel:

While in New York on business would appreciate it if you can work out something with RCA folks where I can get a message to the fans. I want to be able to thank them not only for buying my records

Telegram from Germany to Col. Parker, 1959.

TO ALL THE WORLD · TO SHIPS AT SEA

CLASS OF SERVICE

FULL RATE
LETTER TELEGRAM (LT)
PRESS

FULL RATE UNLESS OTHERWISE MARKED

FAST **RCA** DIRECT

RADIOGRAM

NUMBER

CHECK

TIME

SENDER'S NAME AND ADDRESS   ELVIS   BADNAUHEIM 152 19 1300 PAGE 1/50   1959 JUN 19 AM 8 08

TO   COLONEL TOM PARKER CO RCA VICTOR RECORDS 155 E. 24TH NEWYORKNY

DEAR COLONEL WHILE IN NEWYORK ON BUSINESS WOULD APPRECIATE IF YOU CAN WORK OUT SOMETHING WITH RCA VICTOR FOLKS WHERE I CAN GET A MESSAGE TO THE FANS. I WANT TO BE ABLE TO THANK THEM NOT ONLY FOR BUYING MY RECORDS AND FOR THEIR LOYALTY TO ME BUT ALSO FOR THE HELP THEY HAVE GIVEN ME IN DECIDING THE KIND OF SONGS TO SING FOR IN TALKING WITH THEM AND READING THEIR LETTERS I WAS ABLE TO GET SOME IDEA OF WHAT THEY LIKED . I AM DEEPLY GRATEFUL TO THEM AND I WANT THEM TO KNOW IT . WHEN I AM OUT OF THE ARMY AND RECORDING AGAIN I WILL ALWAYS LISTEN TO THEIR IDEAS JUST AS BEFORE . JUST WANTED TO LET MY FANS KNOW HOW I FEEL .

SINCERELY

ELVIS

RCA COMMUNICATIONS, INC., A SERVICE OF RADIO CORPORATION OF AMERICA

and for their loyalty to me but also for the help they have given me in deciding the kind of songs to sing. For in talking with them and reading their letters I was able to get some idea of what they liked. I am deeply grateful to them and I want them to know it. When I am out of the army and recording again I will always listen to their ideas just as before. Just wanted to let my fans know how I feel.

Sincerely,
Elvis

JULY 1959

EVENT: *Phone call from Don Owens (WARL) in Arlington, Texas, to Elvis in Bad Nauheim, Germany.*
SOURCE: Hey Baby, Let's Rock It *(CD).*
   [Exact date not known.]

[Don Owens] Hello, Elvis?
Yes sir.

[D.O.] This is Don Owens at WARL in Arlington.
Oh, how're you doin', Mr. Owens?

[D.O.] How are you today?
Oh I'm…living.

[D.O.] (Laughs.) You know, we're having a country music spectacular here on the Fourth of July?
Yeah.

[D.O.] And we wanted to kinda get your comments on country music. You've been in the semi-country and rock and roll fields and we kinda wanted to get your impression of what country and country-style songs mean to you.
Well, I'll give you my honest opinion. I think that it'll always be around, really. I mean, I think country music, it's probably the oldest music in the world, you know.

[D.O.] Uh-huh.

And I think it'll be around a long time to come.

[D.O.] Elvis, let me ask you somethin' else about country music. How do you feel about the kind of music you do? Do you feel that it's exclusively rock and roll or that it touches on some of the other types of music?
I don't think I understand the question.

[D.O.] In other words, they call you a rock and roll singer but suppose you do a song, for instance, like "[Now and Then There's] A Fool Such As I," which was a country song. Do you consider it completely rock and roll just because you put a little beat to it?
Well, I wouldn't say it was completely rock and roll because it was written as a country song, you know.

[D.O.] Um-mm.
But I kinda changed the beat around a little bit. And I did it the only way that I can do it, that's with a kind of a rock and roll feeling to it, you know.

[D.O.] Elvis, what do you think's gonna happen when you get back to this country? I was talkin' to Gene Autry about you the other day.
Uh-huh.

[D.O.] And he kinda feels that when you come back you're gonna be doin' greater than ever. How…how do you think you're gonna affect the public when you come back from Germany?
Well I'll tell ya, Mr. Owens, [or would] you rather me call you Don?

[D.O.] Uh-huh, go ahead, go ahead.
Actually I don't know.

[D.O.] Uh-huh.
I wish I knew.

[D.O.] Uh-huh.
I'm over here in Germany and I'm in the Army and the only thing I can do is just sit and wait.

[D.O.] Uh-huh.

And read letters people send me. That's about it.

[D.O.] Well, Elvis, that's real great and I'm sure that a lot of good things are gonna happen to you when you return to the United States, and I know all the folks down in Memphis is thinkin' about you and all over this country, and your popularity continues.

I'm certainly thinkin' about them too. Actually, I don't know what's gonna happen to me in the future. I mean I don't like to make predictions because a lot of times you can be wrong.

[D.O.] (Laughs.) Well I think you'd be right, Elvis. And it's a pleasure talkin' to ya here on the program today.

Thank you very much.

[D.O.] Elvis.

You tell everybody hello for me, and I'll see 'em again someday.

AUGUST 1959

EVENT: *Phone call from Dick Clark in the United States to Elvis in Bad Nauheim, Germany.*
SOURCE: Got a Lot o' Livin to Do *(LP).*
[Exact date not known.]

[Dick Clark] Hello, Elvis?
Hello, Dick, how are you?

[D.C.] Fine to talk to you. We've had a little trouble getting through to Germany. But finally glad that we could make it.
I guess the lines were…were kind of busy, uh?

[D.C.] I imagine so, and I would imagine they've got you kind of busy these days, don't they?
Oh yeah, well we're gettin' ready for a big inspection. A new inspection, so we've been workin' pretty hard for that.

[D.C.] Elvis, so many of us here are interested in your activities and I think probably the big question on most people's minds these days are

when and if and everything goes right, you're out in February, what will be your plans?
Well as you know I have a contract with ABC.

[D.C.] Uh-huh, the ABC Television Network.
Yes, that's true…for some television. I don't know exactly what it will consist of yet. I don't know what Colonel Parker has arranged.

[D.C.] Um-mm.
Or what kind of program [it] will be. And then I have the three pictures to make; one for Mr. [Hal] Wallis, and then the other two for Twentieth Century-Fox.

[D.C.] Those are the three motion pictures?
Yes, uh-huh.

[D.C.] Elvis, I've got some good news. I imagine by now they've passed the word along to you. With the latest RCA Victor recording out, "[A Big] Hunk O' Love" and "My Wish Came True," you got yourself another Gold Record to add to the collection.
That's great, Dick. That sure is nice. I was surprised to hear it, really.

[D.C.] I'll tell you what. We're gonna show it to the folks here on *American Bandstand*, and then I'll forward it down to Colonel Tom Parker, and he can save it for you when you come back.
Okay, that'll be fine.

[D.C.] Elvis, do you have any idea of how many Gold Records you have now in your collection?
To my knowledge, Dick…this one will make thirty-one, I think.

[D.C.] Boy, that is a fantastic record. There's no getting away from it.
I'll ask my daddy to go down and (laughs) and recount them to make sure (laughs).

[D.C.] (Laughs.) Well alright, we'll get the latest count then.
Yeah.

[D.C.] Elvis, one more quick question that might interest the gals in this country. I know probably you don't have too much to yourself but when you go out amongst the German people, what is the thing that strikes you as most interesting? Are they very different than the people back home?

No. The main difference is naturally the language barrier there. It's kinda hard to talk to most of 'em, especially older ones because a lot of 'em don't speak English at all and I don't speak any German.

[D.C.] How do you find the reaction of young people toward you...mainly the girls? Do they know who you are and so forth?

Well it's, ah (laughs), that's kind of a hard question.

[D.C.] That's real difficult. It's a leading question, Elvis, because I know, of course as I guess everybody else does, that they go pretty crazy for you. Do you get along well with them?

Yeah, I get along real well. Every day when I finish work and I come in, well there's always a lot of people at the gate, from all over Germany, you know.

[D.C.] Uh-huh.

And they bring their families. Especially on weekends, I have a lot of visitors here from all over Germany...all over Europe in fact. They come here and bring pictures and take pictures and everything.

[D.C.] Must be a fairly exciting thing that's happened.

Yeah it is. It's kind of exciting trying to keep up with that life plus the Army life too, you know (laughs).

[D.C.] I imagine. You're kind of a man torn between two careers, both of which are very, very important. Elvis, I did want to thank you very much for calling on this day. As you probably know, this is our special anniversary day.

Oh, well congratulations! How many years it make, Dick?

[D.C.] And many, many thanks and we all look forward to your return.

Thank you very much. You don't know how I'm looking forward to my return.

[D.C.] Elvis again, thank you for calling...and bye-bye.

Bye-bye, Dick.

SEPTEMBER 1959

EVENT: *Phone call from Wink Martindale on his* Dance Party *show on KHJ-TV (Los Angeles, California) to Elvis in Friedberg, Germany.*

SOURCE: That Was Elvis to Me *by Wink Martindale (CD).*

[Exact date not known.]

[Wink Martindale] Elvis, where are you stationed?

I'm in Friedberg, Germany.

With Wink Martindale on *G.I. Blues* set, 1960.

[W.M.] How is life in the service, Elvis? What do you do in your spare time?

Well, if I don't have to work late, I usually have some people over here at the house, and we get to wake all the neighbors up, play music and try to pass the time away. It's nice over here, Wink. I mean, I've met a lot of nice people and I've seen a little of the country, not too much. I went to Paris and a few places. But I'd like to come back over here someday as an entertainer, you know. I'd like to come back and have a chance to travel around all over Europe.

[W.M.] Listen, we're hearing a lot of rumors in the States these days about a certain Elvis and a certain German girl. Any truth to those rumors, and how do the girls over there compare to American girls?

Well, I couldn't give you any comparison, Wink. The only thing I can tell you is that I find that the girls here are a lot like the ones in the States. The only thing is the language difference. I've been reading a lot…I've been getting a lot of articles through the mail that people have sent me about this little German girl that's a movie actress, Vera [Tschecowa]. And according to a lot of the articles in the magazines, we're almost ready to get married. Actually, I haven't seen her since the first of the year [March]. It's funny,

I get a lot of mail, people asking me about it and things. And there's no chance of marriage, over here, over there, or anywhere for a while, Wink. I will get married someday if nothing happens. First of all, I'm not ready for it. I've got a lot of things I would like to accomplish first. Like in the movie industry, I'd like to learn to act. That's where I got my head put on right now.

[W.M.] I gotta tell you that we receive nothing but glowing reports here of how you're conducting yourself in the service, Elvis. Anything you want to say to everybody back here at home, while we got you on the telephone?
Well, the only thing I can think of, Wink, is that for the people that have stood by me during the time I've been in the Army, and everything, I owe everything to them and I can't thank 'em enough, really. Because I've tried to play it straight in the Army, you know. It's the only way it could be. In other words, I couldn't do any entertaining or…I couldn't be or do except just what the other boys do. And that's the only way it could be. And I'm glad that it turned out the way it has because I've made a lot of friends, in the Army among the men that I would have never made before. And I'm glad of this. I would just like to say that, to all the people that have stood by me and written to me and so forth, it really helped me go through it better.

[W.M.] Elvis, I want you to know that I speak for everybody here. We all miss you very much. And I also want you to know how much I appreciate personally you taking time from your busy schedule to talk to us as we kick off our new *Dance Party* show. And we look forward to your return home.
Okay, well that's good. And best of luck to you on your new show, Wink. And I'll see you when I get back.

[W.M.] Thanks again, Elvis.
Okay, well good luck boy! Yeah, bye-bye.

ITEM: *Four-page letter handwritten by Elvis (Wildflecken, Germany), sent to Anita Wood (Memphis, Tennessee).*
SOURCE: *Original document.*

[Envelope has a November 6 postmark by the "U.S. Army & Air Force Postal Service," and the return address, "Sp 4 Elvis Presley, US-53-310-761, HQ Co 1st M.T.B, 32 Armor, APO 39, N.Y. New York." Letter is undated. According to Anita Wood: "During the time Elvis and I dated, his pet name for me was 'Little.'"]

My Dearest Darling 'Little',
Well here I am. Back out in the field for 30 days again and believe me it's miserable. There is only one consolation, and that is the fact that it's almost over, and I will come home to my career, fiends, and most of all you my darling. Anita there are many things I can't tell you over the phone so I will try to tell you now. First of all I don't really know how you feel about me now because after all 2 years is a long time in a young girl's life. But I want you to know that in spite of our being apart I have developed a love for you that cannot be equaled or surpassed by anyone. My every thought is you my darling, every song I hear, every sunset reminds me of the happy and wonderful times we've spent together. I tell you this because I want you to know my feelings toward you have not changed, but instead has grown stronger that I ever thought it could. I have hurt you sometimes because I was mad at some of the things you did or I thought you did, but everytime these things happened I thought that maybe you only liked me for what I am, and didn't really love me for myself. These things happen in life baby, misunderstandings, heartbreaks and

---

141

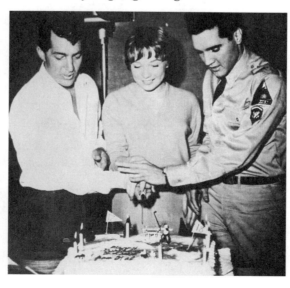

Telegram to Dean Martin, 1959.

WESTERN UNION TELEGRAM

PD Charge:13SZ484 COL. PARKER BOX 417 MADISON TENN.

MR DEAN MARTIN   FRIARS CLUB 326 NORTH RODEO DRIVE BEVERLY HILLS CAL.

DEAR DEAN : CONGRATULATIONS AND GOOD ROCKING TONIGHT -- WITH
SO MANY FRIENDS LOVING YOU -- AND FEELING LIKE A TEDDY BEAR--
WE KNOW THAT YOU MUST BE ALL SHOOK UP -- SO DON'T, I BEG OF
YOU, DON'T BE CRUEL, I'M COUNTING ON YOU NOT TO GET ON JAILHOUSE
ROCK, TREAT ME NICE OR YOU'RE NOTHING BUT A HOUND DOG.

          YOUR PALS ELVIS AND THE COLONEL

STRAIGHT WIRE, MUST BE
DELIVERED BY 8 p.m.

Dean Martin, Shirley MacLaine, and Elvis, cutting Dean's birthday cake. Hollywood, 1960.

lonliness [sic], but the fact remains, if it's really love Anita, if we really love each other it will last, and these things will be something of the past, although things will come up in the future that will hurt us both. They are to be expected. I have had feelings that in the last few months something has happened as far as you're concerned, not only because you haven't written but by the sound of your voice when I talk to you. The warmth and love seems to have dimmed.

It may be my imagination but you seem as though you have something to tell me but yet you're not sure. I hope I'm wrong. You know after going through what I have in the last 18 months you sometimes wonder if anyone really cares. Please believe me when I tell you it's you and only you my darling. But I think that you will keep your word, and tell me if you had grown to care for someone else and vice versa. I have been sleeping out on the ground, and I have a fever and tonsillitis again. I am listening to the radio and all the guys are sitting around with sad looks on their faces. Do you remember when you used to bounce for me and I would laugh so hard. Darling I pray that you haven't let your lonliness [sic], passions, and desires make you do something that would hurt me. If you have it is better you tell me now. I can't believe you have or would. Well we are all counting the days until we come home. The reason I didn't want you there on the first night because in spite of the fact that I love my friends and relatives, when we first lay eyes on each other we will cling to each other like a vine. So I think some other people might get their feelings hurt. So please understand honey. You have surprised me at how understanding you are. So darling if you still feel the same and if you love me and me alone we will have a great life together even though you hear things and read things. Just think as you said, everyone knows how I feel about you. I can't explain to you how I crave you and desire your lips and your body under me darling. I can feel it now. The things we did and the desire we had for each other's body!!! Remember darling, 'True love holds its laurels through the ages no mater how loud the clamor of denial.' That which deserves to live—lives.

Yours alone,

EP

NOVEMBER 8, 1959

ITEM: *Telegram from Elvis Presley and Col. Tom Parker (Madison, Tennessee) to Dean Martin (Beverly Hills, California).*
SOURCE: *Original document.*

> *[On this evening, at the Beverly Hilton Hotel, the Friars Club honored Dino by presenting "The Dean Martin Testimonial Dinner."]*

Dear Dean,

Congratulations and Good Rocking Tonight—with so many friends Loving You—and feeling like a Teddy Bear—we know that you must be All Shook Up—so Don't, I Beg of You, Don't Be Cruel, I'm Counting on You not to get on Jailhouse Rock, Treat Me Nice or you're nothing but a Hound Dog.

> *Your pals,*
> *Elvis and the Colonel*

1959

LOCATION: *Germany.*
SOURCE: Greetings from Germany *(CD).*

> *[Exact date not known.]*

Hey, listen to this:

> *(Singing.) When I was just a little pup*
> *I asked my mommy what will I be*
> *Will I be hound dog, will I be mutt*
> *She told me tenderly…you ain't nothin' but a hound dog!*

(Laughs.) I'm gonna do that on stage. That'd be cute, wouldn't it?

1959

LOCATION: *Germany.*
INTERVIEWERS: *Unknown.*
SOURCE: From the Bottom of My Heart *(LP).*

> *[Exact date not known.]*

[Media] Elvis, professionally speaking, when did you start to sing and play the guitar?
1954.

[Media] In 1954?
That's right.

[Media] Elvis, would you tell us who else in the family is musical? Where did you inherit the talent from?
No one in the family was…is musical. I don't know. I guess I just loved music so much and so

I decided to try to make a career out of it.

[Media] Which did you try first, to sing or to play the guitar? Or did they both come together?
I imagine I was singing first, if you wanna call it singing. I was about three or four and I would sing in a church choir. And actually all I was doing was yelling (laughs). Some people still think that's what I do.

[Media] Which record of your own do you like the best?
I don't think I have a favorite one.

[Media] Uh-huh.
Some of them I like okay. Some I don't even like to listen to (laughs).

[Media] (Laughs.) That happens to all of us. Do you play any other instruments?
I play the piano a little bit.

[Media] Uh-huh.
Not very much.

Above and right: Meeting the press and fans before leaving Germany, 1960.

[Media] I think I remember a very pretty record that you did where you played piano. Wasn't it "Old Shep"?

Yes sir. That's correct.

[Media] Are you a sports man in any way?

To a certain extent. Football is my favorite.

[Media] Which band do you like best? Apart from the boys that play for you, the Jordanaires.

Well I think one of the finest instrumental groups that is making records today is Billy Vaughn and His Orchestra.

[Media] Now a very important question—this is for the girls—which do you like: blondes, brunettes, or redheads? Or do you like them in all colors?

All colors (laughs). And I'm gonna get a haircut. I haven't had an opportunity yet but I am. I wish that I could understand German, then I would know what you said, you know.

[Reporter is translating Elvis' answers for the German-speaking audience.]

And I find the people very, very friendly here. I am living for and looking forward to the time when I can return here as an entertainer.

[Media] Uh-huh. Thank you very much *und Auf Wiedersehn.*

Thank you very much. "I" Wiedersehn.

1959

EVENT: *Telephone interview between Elvis (Germany) and WBPM (Kingston) radio.*
SOURCE: *Audiotape.*

[Exact date not known.]

Well, I have three movies to make in 1960, plus a television show. I think I've got a lot of work to do but I'm willing to try.

[WBPM] Elvis, we don't want to keep you away from your duties too much longer for Uncle Sam. It's certainly been a pleasure chatting with you for these few minutes, all the way from Germany. And your fans here, we would just like to tell you, Elvis, are more loyal than ever. I think this is true.

Well, I certainly appreciate that and I'll do my best to live up to it, and I'm looking forward to coming back and everything.

[WBPM] One more note. We've had more requests for this question than, I think, for any other. Elvis, when you get out of the Army are you going to keep your crew cut, or are you going to let your hair grow long?

Am I going to do what?

[WBPM] Are you going to let your hair grow long?

Oh! To a certain extent, yes.

JANUARY 8, 1960

EVENT: *Phone call from Dick Clark in the United States to Elvis in Bad Nauheim, Germany.*

SOURCE: Got a Lot o' Livin to Do *(LP).*

[Dick Clark] This is his birthday. As a matter of fact, we've always had kind of a tradition where we put through a call to Bad Nauheim, Germany, as best we can, and you have to listen carefully because the lines sometimes are not the clearest, and I'd like to talk to him on his birthday. Al, could you…could you put through the overseas telephone call, please?

[D.C.] Hello, Elvis?
Hello.

[D.C.] Hi. We had no idea we could catch a-hold of you today.
Oh, yeah, well I just came in the door, Dick.

[D.C.] What were you doing?
Well, I just came in from the day's work. It's about five-thirty here.

Media meeting with Tom Diskin and friend, 1956.

[D.C.] Five-thirty in the evening.
In the evening, yeah.

[D.C.] You know, Elvis, I called Colonel Tom and had words with his assistant [Tom Diskin] and say, gee, do you suppose there's any chance we could talk to Elvis on his birthday, and they seemed to think you might be off on maneuvers. Have you been pretty busy?
Yeah, we've been pretty busy. I don't go on maneuvers until the twenty-second, or the twenty-fourth.

[D.C.] Oh, I see. What is the situation regarding your release from the Army? Do you have any word on it?
The only thing definite, Dick, as far as the way it stands now, I leave Germany somewhere between the twentieth of February and the second of March. That's as far as I know right now.

[D.C.] That's as much information as you have. When you come back, I understand you've got a television show with Frank Sinatra and a few movies to make. How are you gonna squeeze 'em all in?
Well (laughs), I'm told that Colonel Parker will have everything arranged. I know the first picture is for Mr. Wallis. It's called G.I. Blues, *I think. The other two's at Twentieth Century-Fox, and I don't know exactly when the television show will be. In fact, I don't even know what's gonna happen, really.*

[D.C.] Elvis, what is your general feeling about doing your first television show upon your return with Frank Sinatra? You two fellows have sort of different musical stylings. Do you have any thoughts on that?
Well, I really do. I consider it an honor, really, Dick, because this man…he's proven himself.

[D.C.] He's somewhat of a legend, I guess.
He is, and admire him very much, and I really am honored.

[D.C.] Let me ask you about your Christmas and New Year's. How did you celebrate the holidays?

We had a Christmas party here. I had a lot of guys from all over the post, you know. I had as many of the boys here as possible at my house…try to make 'em feel at home around Christmastime.

[D.C.] Uh-huh.

And we had a little Christmas party. Then on New Year's night we had another little party. This one was pretty nice, but it was better last year.

[D.C.] Elvis, I want to thank you very, very much for taking the time out from your busy schedule, to reassure you once again that we're all awaiting your arrival back home and on this day to wish you happy birthday.

Thank you very much, Dick, and I'm kinda lookin' forward to it. Yeah, there's still a lot of stuff in print about my getting out early and all that stuff.

[D.C.] It's not true, as far as you know, uh?

Well it's been in print and I had a lot of people ask me about it, just from that. The only time I heard anything about it is when I read it.

[D.C.] (Laughs.) That happens more than once, I guarantee.

It is news to me.

[D.C.] Elvis, all the best. We'll see you on your return.

Okay, thanks a lot, Dick, and tell everybody hello for me.

[D.C.] Will do. Bye-bye.

JANUARY 1960

ITEM: *Generic typewritten letter specifically for European fans, signed by a member of the Presley staff. Includes handwritten note from Elvis. From "Elvis A. Presley" (Bad Nauheim,*

Autographs and photos for fans in Germany, 1960.

Germany) to Karin Konrad (Oberhousen-Sterkade, Germany).

SOURCE: *Document photocopy.*
[Exact date not known.]

Dear Friend:
Thanks a lot for writing in. It's nice to know you care.
I thank you for the [Holiday] greetings, they were most welcomed.
I'm already preparing my return to the States and therefor [sic] I am very busy!!
I've found many new friends during my stay in Germany and you are one of them. I appreciate your support over this period of time!!
Ask your local DJ to play my songs—and remember that I'll be singing them for nobody else but you!!!
I will finish my duty by March this year, so please mail future correspondance [sic] to:
RCA
C/o Elvis Presley
30 Rockefeller Plaza
New York City 228, N.Y.
U.S.A.

*Again, thank you for your interest and taking
the time to write! Best of luck and I hope
that this new year will bring success and
happiness to you!!*

*Your friend,
Elvis Presley*

*Dear Karin,
May you have a very happy 11th birthday,
and a lot of "Teddy Bears."
Your friend,*

Elvis

LOCATION: *Ray Barracks, Friedberg, Germany.*
EVENT: *Armed Forces Radio and Television
Services Network interview.*
INTERVIEWER: *Johnny Paris.*
SOURCE: Elvis Army Interviews *(CD).*

**[Johnny Paris] We are speaking to you from
Frankfurt, Germany, and our very special guest
on the scene is Sergeant Elvis Presley. Elvis, it's
nice to see you.**

*Thank you very much, Johnny, it's nice to be
here.*

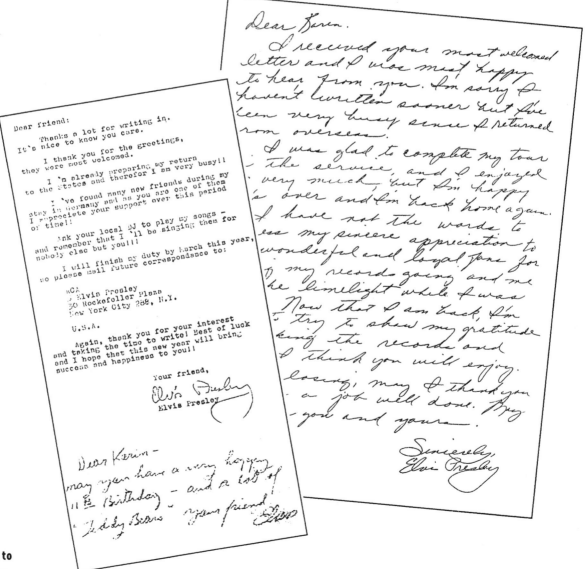

**Letters to
fans.**

[J.P.] Elvis, what are you plans now that you are about to leave the Army?

Well the first thing I plan to do, naturally, is to go home. And then after that I have a television show with Frank Sinatra, sometime latter part of April. And then I start work on the picture G.I. Blues *for Paramount…Mr. Wallis. And then after that I have two pictures with 20th Century-Fox. And after that, heaven knows…I don't (laughs).*

[J.P.] Well we'll talk about *G.I. Blues* a little later on. How are you going home, Elvis?

I believe I'm flying, from [Frankfurt airport] Rhein-Main.

[J.P.] Are you going home with some of your buddies here that you met in Germany, or have perhaps come over with?

Yes, I believe the same group that I came over here with.

[J.P.] The same group?

Yes, the same group. In fact, all the boys who came in in Memphis the same time I did, well we're all going back together.

[J.P.] Have you recorded while you were in the service?

No I haven't.

[J.P.] Not one tune?

No. I was home on leave at the end of basic training and I made two records. But since that time I've done nothing. Nothing at all in the line of show business.

[J.P.] Elvis, what about here in Europe. Where did you spend most of your leave time?

In Paris.

[J.P.] Uh-huh.

I went there twice.

[J.P.] Oh yeah.

Yeah, I was in Paris twice, once for ten days and another time for six days.

[J.P.] What do you remember most about those trips?

(Whistles, laughs). Well, I'll tell you, it's a gay town. I mean if you like nightlife and everything. I went over there to see some of the shows and, you know, to get a touch of the old life a little bit.

[J.P.] Elvis, how much time have you spent while in the service on maneuvers?

Oh, I couldn't give you an exact number of days, but I would imagine about half the time we were over here.

Left to right: Meeting the press before leaving Germany, 1960.

[J.P.] While you were in the field, were you troubled at any time by reporters?

No, not really. The Army P.I.O. [Public Information Officer] came out and took some, you know, training shots.

[J.P.] Well, did you have any unfavorable encounters with any disguised reporters?

Ah, (laughs) maybe yes, I don't know. If there were reporters I didn't know it.

[J.P.] I see. Elvis, do press conferences bother you at all?

No, they don't bother you. They (laughs)…it's pretty interesting. I get a big thrill out of 'em, a press conference, because you have all these different people there with different questions you know, and they're poppin' them to you like a district attorney. And you're sittin' there like you were on trial for something. They ask you "Is it true on the night of so-and-so you were in so-and-so?" "Is it true that this girl did that and you did this?" (Laughs.) And actually, it's a…it makes me stutter (laughs) because I have to think on all the questions in order to give 'em a halfway sensible answer…I have to think, and when they're poppin' them to you so fast, well I'm just

goin' ah-ah-ah-ah-ah, like that, you know (laughs).

[J.P.] Do they upset you?

Oh no. You get used to it after a while.

[J.P.] Many American artists have entertained, Elvis, as you know, behind the Iron Curtain, with the help of the Exchange Program.

Uh-huh.

[J.P.] Do you feel that you would like to do something like this?

Well, if certain people think I should then I would have no objections at all. To give a try… I don't think I'm very well liked over there. They possibly think I'm a bad influence on their youth or something of that nature. And, uh, for that reason, I'm not very well liked over there. But if it were decided that I should go, then I would go.

[J.P.] You would go?

I would go. There's no doubt.

[J.P.] Elvis, you've sold some forty-five million records. Is that right?

Yes sir, all totaled.

[J.P.] And while you've been in the service, the record market has changed some, hasn't it?

You mean the styles of music?

[J.P.] Yes indeed.

That I couldn't tell you. I won't know until I can get back. I've heard reports. I've read reports about the record industry…about what's happening to the music and this is dying out, that's dying out, this is finished. But actually, I don't know. I was reading the same thing in 1955, and that was the big beginning of the whole thing.

[J.P.] What are your plans…to sell another forty-five million records, Elvis?

(Laughs.) I never make a statement like that, to tell you the truth, because I don't know.

[J.P.] Um-mm.

In the entertainment business the future is very uncertain. You never know. You can only try.

[J.P.] Um-mmm.

So I'm only gonna say I'll try to continue to please the people enough that they, you know, that they keep liking me and keep interested. As far as actually knowing what the future holds for me, I've got no idea.

[J.P.] Getting to recording, do you approve all of the tunes before they're cut?

Ah, yes.

[J.P.] All of 'em.

I choose my own songs.

[J.P.] You do?

Yes.

[J.P.] Well, do you feel that you have a feel for the material that you select?

Yes. I don't think there's anybody who can decide what I can do best, better than me.

[J.P.] Um-mm.

And I think it would be a bad mistake if I had someone else tellin' me what to record, or how to

record it, because I work strictly on instinct and impulse. I don't read music. My taste might be a little different because I choose songs with the public in mind. I try to visualize it as though I'm buying the record myself. Would I like it? And I try to please the public, and I don't think anybody could choose 'em for me like I can.

[J.P.] Are you doing anything to try and attract an older audience?

Ah (laughs). My type of music—I say my type of music, I mean the kind of records that I have been making—they don't seem to appeal to the older people like they do the young people. But you'd be surprised at the older people who do like that type of music. And as far as making more of them like me, it's almost impossible to make everybody like you. You can't please 'em all, regardless if I change my style and started singing something that maybe would appeal to the older people, then I might lose something else. So you have to let time take care of itself.

[J.P.] Then I take it you are not planning to change your style.

I'd be foolish to change my style unless I was told to do so by the public themselves. In other words, if I just took it on my own and said well I'm gonna change my style, I think I'd be makin' a bad mistake. If the people become disinterested in you or they get tired of whatever you're doing…

[J.P.] Um-mm

…they'll let you know.

[J.P.] Earlier, Elvis, you mentioned the movie *G.I. Blues*, that you'll be doing soon. When do you do the film?

Well, I can't give you an official date.

[J.P.] Alright.

It's after the Sinatra show, which is sometime around the first of May.

[J.P.] And who'll be in it?

I don't think they've picked a co-star yet.

[J.P.] Um-mm.

Not to my knowledge they haven't.

[J.P.] Do you know what part you'll play?

Ah (laughs), no I don't. I haven't seen the script yet.

Right and opposite: Meeting the press before leaving Germany, 1960.

[J.P.] Oh, I see. So you then perhaps have not had an opportunity to contribute any of your own ideas.

No, not yet. You do that at the filming of the picture.

[J.P.] Elvis, are you perhaps planning a European tour sometime in sixty or sixty-one?

Oh yes. I don't think it will be sixty. Maybe in sixty-one. I'm not saying yes or no. Actually that's not my end of the business. That's my manager's end of it. But I would like to very much because this is all a new market over here, you know, for me. The people over here have only read a few things and they've heard a few records and everything, but you can never actually become established until the people can see you in person and physically. And I'd like to come over here and do a complete tour of Europe someday.

[J.P.] Elvis Presley, do you feel that the Army did anything for you?

Yes I certainly do. In a lot of ways it's been a good experience. I made a lot of friends I never would have made otherwise.

[J.P.] You have no regrets.

I have no regrets of the whole thing. The only thing I can say is that for people to ask me what effects [it] would have on my career, I can't say. Again, because I don't know. The only thing that I can say is that I like it better this way than if maybe I had taken an easy way out, or so-called pulled strings—that's what a lot of people said, you know—and had something staring me in the face rest of my life that I always would regret.

[J.P.] You would rather be out in the field with the boys than perhaps entertaining in a Service Club somewhere.

Oh yeah, sure. I was in a funny position. Actually, that's the only way it could be. People were expecting me to mess up (laughs), to goof up in one way or another. They thought I couldn't take it and so forth, and I was determined to go to any limits to prove otherwise, not only to the people who were wondering, but to myself.

[J.P.] You turned out to be one of America's finest soldiers, Elvis Presley.
Thank you.

MARCH 1, 1960

LOCATION: *Ray Barracks, Friedberg, Germany.*
INTERVIEWERS: *Unknown, from* Screen Digest *magazine.*
SOURCE: In Days Gone By *(EP).*

[Media] Has your military experience been beneficial to you in any way?
It's been a big help in both my career and my personal life, because I learned a lot, I made a lot of friends that I never would have made otherwise, and I've had a lot of good experiences…and some bad ones, naturally. It's good to rough it, to put yourself to a test, to see if you can take it, to see if you can stand it.

[Media] Another thing we hear a lot about in the Army, especially here, is that we are not only soldiers but goodwill ambassadors. How do you feel about that?
Well that definitely stands to reason because we are in a foreign country and what we do here will reflect on America and our way of life.

MARCH 3, 1960

LOCATION: *Fort Dix, New Jersey.*
INTERVIEWER: *Unknown.*
SOURCE: Elvis Army Interviews *(CD) and* From Introduction to Demob *(Video)*

[Media] Elvis, if I may ask you just a few questions: Would you like to spend more time in the Army?
Would I like to spend more time in the Army.

Like I said, I was anxious to get back to show business. I'll answer that by saying I'm glad I served the two years and that it worked out as well as it did, but I'm very happy to get back into what I was doing.

[Media] There's a rumor floating around, Elvis, that you plan to get married soon. Is that true?
No sir. I don't expect to be a bachelor, sir, I just…I think it's all according to the individual when they want to get married. I'll know when I want to.

[Media] In other words, it's just a rumor. You haven't set a date.
I haven't set a date, I haven't found anyone yet that I wanna marry. But when I do, it doesn't make any difference if I'm twenty-five or forty-five or seventy.

[Media] Very good. What do you think the Army has done for you, Elvis?
I think I have a little better understanding of life, I met a lot of friends, like I said. I just think it's been a big help in many ways.

[Media] Do you have any immediate plans?

Happy to be leaving snowy Germany, 1960.

Go home for a while and then I'll be makin' some records. And then I'll be doing the television show with Frank Sinatra for ABC, then the picture G.I. Blues *for Mr. [Hal] Wallis, then after that, I think, two pictures for Twentieth Century-Fox.*

[Media] Now that you're about to be discharged from the Army, Elvis, have two years of sobering Army life changed your mind about rock and roll?

Sobering Army life? No it hasn't. It hasn't changed my mind, because I was in tanks for a long time, and they rock and roll quite a bit.

[Media] Elvis, you have some screaming fans out there. Do you still like screaming girls?

(Laughs.) If it wasn't for them, I'd have to re-up in the Army, sir, I'll tell ya.

[Media] Elvis, there's a report that you liked the Army so much that you wanted to write a book about it. Did you ever think of reenlisting?

(Laughs.) No sir, I never thought of (laughs)… I never thought of reenlisting, but maybe someday I will write a book about my experiences in the Army, you know.

[Media] Elvis, are you glad to be getting back to normal, or don't you think your life could ever be normal?

Sir, if my life ever gets normal, I'll have to start drivin' a truck again (laughs).

[Media] Elvis, do you feel that you're a little old for the teenagers now?

That's the first time I've been asked that one (laughs). I don't know. I don't feel too old. I can still move around pretty good.

[Media] Are you apprehensive about what must be a comeback?
Yes I am. I mean I have my doubts. I'm not gonna commit myself in saying I'm gonna do this or I'm gonna do that because I don't know, actually. The only thing I can say is that I'm gonna try. I'll be in there fighting.

[Media] A woman said in an interview that you were the sexiest man she'd ever seen. What's your reaction to that?
(Whistles.) Are we on television?

[Media] What can you tell us about the two girls, one on each arm?
They're both female, sir. That's all I have to tell you.

[Media] Did you meet any Russian girls over there?
No sir. I beg your pardon, I believe I met one Russian girl.

[Media] What did she look like?
Pretty shapely, I mean (laughs).

MARCH 7, 1960

LOCATION: *Onboard interview, conducted while arriving by train in Memphis, Tennessee.*
INTERVIEWER: *Bill E. Burk; possibly others.*
SOURCE: *Transcript.*

[Media] Elvis, you look a little tired.
I couldn't sleep any last night.

[Media] What did you do?
We just talked and kidded around most of the night. I guess it will take awhile for me to realize I am out of the service. I'm still tense inside. If I act nervous it's because I am.

[Media] Did you do any reading in Germany? What did you read?
I read Mad magazine a lot. Other than that, I read Western novels and some magazines.

No movie magazines though.

[Media] You look a little thin. What's your weight now?
I'm down to one hundred and seventy pounds and want to stay about that weight. I weighed one eighty-two when I went in. Guess it was the Army life and it's not a bad life.

[Media] What have you missed most about being away from Memphis?
Everything! I mean that. Everything.

[Media] What's the first thing you want to do?
I want to get home, and I may stay right at home for a couple of days. Then I want to get around and meet some of the old gang. It's been nearly two years since I've seen any of them. That's a long time.

[Media] Are you anxious to get out of the [Army] uniform?
No. I don't have to be wearing it now. I sorta like this uniform.
    [Looking at his wristwatch.] I've been out of the Army forty-two hours now. Yeah, forty-two hours.

Nancy Sinatra with a gift from Frank Sinatra, Fort Dix, N.J., 1960.

On the train from Memphis to Miami, 1960.

[Regarding a German tailor who mistakenly added four stripes—indicating a staff sergeant—when three would have been proper for a sergeant, Presley's rank upon discharge.] I'll probably get put in jail about that. It was a tailor's mistake in Germany. We had a rush job on it the last day I was there. I called and told him to sew on sergeant's stripes, and he added a fourth stripe.

[Media] Do you plan to take off the bottom stripe?
I haven't thought much about it. I don't suppose they would send me to jail for having it.

[Media] Since you didn't make any personal appearances while in the service, have you kept up with your singing?
I sure have. I had plenty of time for it when I was off duty. I would play records and sing. I guess I got in more singing than I would if I had been working on it.

[Media] What are your plans for the movies?
Well, my ambition is to develop as an actor. I am looking forward in some ways to the Frank Sinatra show. It will be my first appearance on TV in over two years. I know I will have butterflies when I go on. I've been gone a long time…a long time.

[Media] It's been reported that you have stated that you want to pattern your movie career after Frank Sinatra. It that true?
I have great respect for Mr. Sinatra as an actor. However, I've never made that statement, that I want to pattern my career after Mr. Sinatra. I want to do it my own way, but it will take time and experience.

[Media] Do you plan to wiggle your hips when you return to singing?
I'm gonna sing and I'll let the shaking come naturally. If I had to stand still and sing I'd be lost. I can't get any feeling that way.

[Media] Any special plans for romance when you get home?
I don't know who I'll go with in Memphis. I've been gone a long time. I guess I'll just let nature take its course. Eighteen months out of this country is a long time. It has been a good experience in many ways. I have learned quite a bit. But I'm glad to be back. I really don't know what's ahead. I'm not exactly worried, but I'm not sure of myself either.

MARCH 7, 1960

LOCATION: *Graceland, Memphis, Tennessee.*
EVENT: *Press Conference Rehearsal. Questions by numerous media representatives.*
SOURCE: Elvis Army Interviews *(CD).*

[This interview has widely been reported as taking place on March 8, 1960; however, it occurred the day before. A likely explanation for the mistake is that Memphis newspapers actually reported the event in their March 8 editions. Not included here are questions and answers identical to those found in the broadcast press conference, the transcription of which follows.]
Now gentlemen, I have called you here to discuss a very important matter (laughs).

[Media] What can you tell us about your upcoming movies?

I have three pictures in a row to do. I hope they won't be rock and roll pictures 'cause I have made four already and you can only get away with that for so long. I'm thinking in terms of, I'd like to do a little more of a serious role. Because my ambition is to progress as an actor, which takes a long time and a lot of experience.

[Media] What is your favorite style of music?
My first, I would say, would be spiritual music. Some of the old colored spirituals. Why I know practically every religious song that's ever been written.

MARCH 7, 1960

LOCATION: *Graceland, Memphis, Tennessee.*
EVENT: *Press Conference. Questions by numerous media representatives.*
SOURCE: *Videotape.*

> *[Excerpted portions of both March 7 meetings with the press have been edited mercilessly for use in numerous audio and video projects over the years. The following transcription is taken directly from an original, unedited videotape of the event. It is accurate and complete.]*

[Media] Ready to go?
Ready. Ready when you are.

[Media] All set?
I'm always ready (laughs).

[Media] Okay, we're gonna start it. This is not part of the questioning, but did you get the black-eyed peas when you got home?
I haven't eaten anything yet.

[Media] Haven't eaten anything?
No (laughs). I've just been lookin' around, more or less, since I been back.

[Media] Now, to get down to the serious side of it, Elvis, now that the Army's part of the past, can you give us in detail some of your future plans?
Well, the first thing I have to do is to cut some records. And then after that I have the television

show with Frank Sinatra. And then I have the picture with Mr. [Hal] Wallis. And then after that I have two for Twentieth Century-Fox. And after that, heaven knows. I don't (laughs). I suppose that'll keep me busy for the rest of this year, you know. After that, I don't know.

[Media] Well, Elvis, now you're really at home. How does it feel?
It's pretty hard to describe. I'll tell you, it's hard to get used to it. I mean, I've been lookin' forward to it for two years and all of a sudden here it is. It's not easy to adjust to it.

[Media] Now that you are back, as you look back on your two years in the service, what was the most important thing that happened to you during your two years—whether it was overseas or here in the States?
There were a number of things that happened. I had quite a few interesting experiences...slept out in the snow (laughs)...ate c-rations, you know, all the regular things. But I suppose the biggest thing of all is the fact that I did make it. I made it just like everybody...I mean I tried to play it straight, like everybody else. And I made a lot of friends that I never would have made otherwise. And all-in-all it's been a pretty good experience, you know.

[Media] Elvis, you still have time to serve now for Uncle Sam. Have you given any thought as to where you're going to serve your Reserve training?
Well, sir, I will be on the Reserve status here in Memphis, at the Reserve Center here. But, they have a clause which covers people with traveling jobs. If you have a traveling job or if you live too far away from a Reserve Center, they put you on standby. Whereas you don't have to make their meetings but you are subject to be called in any emergency or anything of that nature.

[Media] Now that the Army's part of the past,

can you give us in detail some of your future plans?

Well, the first thing I have to do is to cut some records. And then after that I have the television show with Frank Sinatra.

[Media] Elvis, one of your future commitments, as you mentioned, is the Frank Sinatra show on the ABC Television Network. Do you have any idea when this will be aired?

I really don't know the exact date. I would imagine it's somewhere around the first of May.

[Media] If you'll forgive me, I have one other part to my question.

Okay.

We understand, speaking of Frank Sinatra, that there has been some rumor about Nancy Sinatra and yourself. Is there a romance in the making here?

(Laughs.) Ah, no sir, I'm afraid not. I only met her at Fort Dix, and she gave me a gift from Frank. And it was very brief. I think she's

Back home in Memphis, 1960.

engaged to Tommy Sands. I don't think he'd appreciate that too much (laughs).

[Media] Thank you very much. Elvis, do you think the music has changed since you've been out of the service? I mean, since you've been *in* the service.

Possibly yes. I can't say really. I haven't been here long enough to even know. Excuse me.

Go ahead.

The only thing I can say is that if it has changed, well, I would be foolish not to try to change with it. But, as of now, I have no reason to change anything.

[Media] As to your acting, you have stated you would like to be a more serious actor. And do you plan to possibly go to some school, or some dramatic school?

Well it wouldn't hurt me any to go to school, but I learn best by experience. I never was very good in school is the thing (laughs). And it's gonna take me a long time, and a lot of experience.

[Media] But that is your ultimate ambition?

But at the present time, it really is. That's what I wanna do.

[Media] Elvis, you were asked about Nancy Sinatra. How about any romance…did you leave any hearts, shall we say, in Germany?

(Laughs.) Not any special one, no. There was a little girl that I was seeing quite often over there that…her father was in the Air Force. Actually they only got over there about two months before I left. I was seeing her and she was at the train…at the airport when I left. And there were some pictures made of her (laughs). But it was no big…it was no big romance. I mean the stories came out "The Girl He Left Behind" (laughs), and all that. It wasn't like that, I mean (laughs). I have to be careful when I answer a question like that (laughs).

[Media] Elvis, in your service life, which did you find the most difficult, when you went in for basic training, or when you got over into Germany, over with the experienced soldiers? Which gave you the hardest time?

Well, basic training wasn't hard for me at all. It was harder afterwards, after I had gotten into a regular outfit. Not the service itself, but the surroundings, and I was in a strange land, and the outfit I was in, they had quite a bit of field duty. We stayed in the field six months out of the year. And it gets cold in Germany (laughs). It snows quite a bit and it was pretty hard to adjust to.

[Media] One thing further on that, do you have any advice for the boys your age who are now going to have to put in a certain amount of duty with…in the service?

The only thing I can say is to play it straight, and to do your best because you can't fight 'em (laughs). They never lost yet (laughs). And you can't fight 'em. So you can make it easy or you can make it hard on yourself. I mean, if you play it straight and get the people on your side, let 'em know you're trying, you, as the Army would say, you've got it made. And if you're going to try to be an individual or try to be different, you're gonna go through two years of…misery (laughs).

[Media] Elvis, when do you think you'll record again? And when you do, do you think you'll lean toward the ballad-type music or the more upbeat sounds?

As far as when I'll record, I really don't know. Possibly this week or next week. And what I'll record, I don't know yet. I've got quite a few songs to choose from, I've collected over two years. I don't know exactly what type or what instruments I'll use, whether it'd be the Firestone Orchestra or Mantovani, or what (laughs). I really don't know yet. Shoot.

[Media] You said, at the train, that you wanted

On the train from Memphis to Miami, 1960.

to get back to what you were doing. And of course that is singing and entertaining. And I take it from that, that you really enjoy what you're doing, or what you were doing before you went in the service.

Oh yes, sir, I do. In fact that was the hardest part of the entire military service, being away from…

[Media]…Being away from the fans?

Just being away from show business altogether. That was the hardest part of all. It wasn't the Army. It wasn't the other men. It was that. It stayed on my mind. I kept thinking about the past all the time, contemplating the future, and that was the hardest part.

[Media] Elvis, we know your family status has changed since you went in the service. Are you going to keep Graceland? Do you have plans of moving away from Memphis? Or what?

No sir, I have no plans for leaving Memphis.

[Media] Are you going to keep Graceland?

I'm going to keep Graceland as long as I possibly can (laughs).

[Media] Well Elvis, was this Christmas tree a surprise?

Since it's March, I was a little surprised (laughs). That's the tree we used in 1957.

[Media] If we can leave the Christmas tree long enough, about your tonsils and the tonsilectomy that you were contemplating while you were in the service, did you deliberately ask that it be held off until you could get to the United States, and a local doctor?

No sir.

[Media] Or did they improve that much?

I didn't ask that. They don't like to perform surgery of any kind in Europe. They don't like to. If it's an emergency they will. But I took penicillin and wonder drugs, or whatever they're called.

[Media] You had no recurrence?

I had two attacks of tonsillitis when I was there.

[Media] Elvis, did you like the food over there, outside of the Army? When you would go out, did you like that type food?

I never went out (laughs).

[Media] You never went out to a restaurant?

I never ate in a restaurant the entire time I was in Germany. It's funny. I either ate in the mess hall or at home, one of the two. I never…in fact I never went anywhere while I was in Europe except to Paris. I went to Paris on a leave and that was all.

[Media] Now how did the fans respond to you over there, as compared to here in the States?

Rehearsal with Frank Sinatra, Miami, 1960.

It's a pretty difficult question to answer because anything I'll say, it might sound a little like I'm bragging (laughs), but it was pretty much the same there as here.

[Media] They had seen a lot of your movies?

And the records, and so forth. I'd like to go back on a tour over there someday, all of Europe. All of Europe, because the only thing they know about me is what they've read, the records and the movies and so forth.

[Media] Elvis, this is not in the form of a question, but I'd like to take this opportunity to welcome you home, for everybody in Memphis and the South.

Thank you. You'll never know how happy I am to be here. Someone asked me this morning "what did I miss about Memphis?" and I said "everything."

[Media] I asked that question on the train this morning and we used it several times and you said anything you mention about Memphis that I missed, I missed that much.

Well sir, I was here…I've been here for quite a while—about fourteen or fifteen years now—I pretty well know Memphis. Or I thought I did 'til I drove home (laughs).

[Col. Tom Parker] Gentlemen, if you get any more now and I'll have to start chargin' you.

[Media] Hey Elvis, how'd it feel to come all the way into the station on the train for the first time?

Huh?

[Media] How's it feel to come all the way to your destination on the train?

Ah…

[Media] You normally get off.

I couldn't believe it. I couldn't…oh yeah, I know what you're talkin' about now. Escape and evasion they call it in the Army. But I don't know. I mean, I was hopin' there'd be some, you know, people there at the station. And I knew there'd be a lot of my friends there, my personal friends, and I wanted to come into the station. I wouldn't have gotten off anywhere else. This time it's different.

[Media] **If we'd only known that yesterday.** *(Laughs.)*

[Media] **How long do you think you'll be back in Memphis recuperating or getting adjusted back to civilian life?**
I would say a couple weeks. That's about all.

[Media] **Okay, is that all? Everybody got enough?**
Thank you, gentlemen.

MARCH 26, 1960

LOCATION: *Miami, Florida.*
EVENT: *Taping of* The Frank Sinatra Timex Show.
SOURCE: The Frank Sinatra Timex Show *(Video).*

[The frequently seen video clip of the show's opening begins with Elvis walking on stage and singing the first line of "It's Nice to Go Traveling." Before Presley enters, however, the following lines are performed by the other stars. We feature them here because they are interesting and relevant.]

[Frank Sinatra] **It's very nice to go traveling, to join the Army and roam.**
   It's very nice to go traveling, but it's so much nicer, yes, it's so much nicer to come home.

[Nancy Sinatra] **It's very nice to play hostess, to read a "welcome back" poem.**
   It's very nice to help Daddy, when he's telling Elvis that it's very nice to have him home.

[Joey Bishop] **I am Joey Bishop, and I'm here to bring you some news.**

[F.S.] **But I tell you folks that no jokes he**

Jammin' on drums with Boots Randolph, Nashville, 1960.

brings will get half the laughs he gets whenever he sings.

[J.B.] **A lot you know about singing.**

[Sammy Davis Jr.] **I wasn't there when they told him [Elvis] that he'd have to go 'cross the foam.**
   I wasn't there when they told him, he would have to give up his guitar, his fancy car and comb.

[Tom Hansen Dancers] **If you're seeking answers, we're the Tom Hansen Dancers.**

[F.S.] **And they're all fancy prancers. Take my word, 'cause I know him [Tom Hansen].**

[Group] **It's very nice to go traveling, but it's oh so nice to come home.**
   The Fontainbleau [Hotel] is a gasser, it's known from Norway to Nome [Alaska].
   Miami Beach has the weather, which we much prefer to Paris, London, yes and even Rome.
   Let the drums start drummin', the guitars start strummin', look and see who's comin'.
   His smile could glitter like chrome [Elvis enters].

[F.S.] **There he is, folks!**

[S.D.] **Elvis, could I have your autograph?**
   [Following "Fame and Fortune" (abbreviated

version) and "Stuck on You," the following dialogue takes place.]

[F.S.] Elvis, I'll tell you somethin', it was great. It was great, and I'm glad to see the Army hasn't changed you. Wasn't it great?

[J.B.] It's the first time I've ever heard a woman screaming at a male singer.

[F.S.] Don't you remember me there, Charlie?

[J.B.] Elvis, excuse me, sir. Mr. Presley, would you think it presumptuous of Frank to join you in a duet?

[F.S.] Yeah, that would be great, yeah.
Well, I would…I would consider it quite an

honor. I'll tell ya…I'd like to do one of your songs.

[F.S.] Alright.
I mean, you know, with you.

[F.S.] Fine, fine. You know, I was wondering, as a matter of fact while you were singing, Elvis, I thought to myself, I wonder what would have happened if I had recorded "Love Me Tender," instead of you. I wonder if it'd a made any difference.

[J.B.] I think it would. About two million records less.
[Pointing to Joey Bishop.] He said that!

[F.S.] You smarty pants. Alright, I'll tell ya what

With Bobby Darin and George Burns, Las Vegas, 1960.

we'll do. We'll do…you do "Witchcraft," okay, and I'll do one of the other ones. Okay? We work it the same way, only in different areas.

[As with the opening, the frequently seen video clip of the show does not include the reprised ending. Here Elvis and Frank again sing the "Love Me Tender" ending, but this time instead of Frank saying "Man, that's pretty," the following is said.] It gets prettier all the time, Frank.

[F.S.] It sure does, buddy.
    Thank you, Elvis.
    Hey, uh, Nancy…Nancy…Nancy, you've met Mr. Presley, haven't you?

[N.S.] Of course, how are you, Mr. Presley? *You can call me Elvis.*

[N.S.] Oh, thank you.

[F.S.] You call him Mr. Presley on account of she's been spoken for [engaged to Tommy Sands].
That's the way the cookie crumbles.

[F.S.] That's the way the cookie crumbles.
    [Elvis makes a final, nonspeaking appearance at the end of the show, as all guests are thanked by Frank Sinatra. Though recorded March 26, this show—titled It's Nice to Go Traveling *or* Welcome Home Elvis—*did not air until May 12, 1960.]*

APRIL 1960

EVENT: *Telephone interview with Elvis. We have only his side of the conversation.*
SOURCE: *Audiotape.*
    [Exact date not known.]

How It Feels to Be Home

I'm just now beginning to realize that I am out, believe it or not. Because when I first came home it was a little strange for the first few weeks. I kept expecting somebody to come in and say "well, it's time to go," you know. I couldn't realize where I was going or exactly

what I was doing. Believe it or not, after two years like that you become adjusted to that type life and you become used to it and all of a sudden overnight it changes again, it's pretty hard just to go right back into things and feel your old self, you know.

Army Life Is Quite an Experience

Army life was quite an experience for me. I had a difficult time adjusting. Many nights I would lie awake in my bunk most of the night, unable to sleep. After I got used to Army life, I would awaken at five every morning, no matter if I didn't go to bed until four. But that will change I guess. I will be working at night, playing at night and living at night. So I guess I will soon be changing schedules. Right now I just want to rest.

Not Much of a Dancer

I can't dance to rock and roll music. I can slow dance, but I never learned to bop.

Letter in response to a music publishing question, 1960.

Right and opposite: Letters to fans, 1960.

About Recording a German Song

There were some German songs I liked, but I never thought of recording one.

And His Favorite Singer Is

I can't say. There are so many that it wouldn't be fair to name one and overlook others.

ITEM: *Handwritten letter. Written and signed by a member of the Presley staff. Sent to Karen Reed (Pierre, South Dakota).*
SOURCE: *Document photocopy.*

Dear Karen,
I received your most welcomed letter and I was most happy to hear from you. I'm sorry I haven't written sooner but I've been very busy since I returned from overseas.
I was glad to complete my tour in the service, and I enjoyed it very much, but I'm happy it's over and I'm back home again.
I have not the words to express my sincere appreciation to you wonderful and loyal fans for keeping my records going and me in the limelight while I was away. Now that I'm back, I'm going to try to show my gratitude by making the records and movies that I think you will enjoy.
In closing, may I thank you again for a job well done. May God bless you and yours.
Sincerely,
Elvis Presley

ITEM: *Handwritten letter. Written and signed by a member of the Presley staff. Sent to Karen Reed (Pierre, South Dakota).*
SOURCE: *Document photocopy.*
[Letter appears to be in response to an inquiry from one who may have written a song, hoping Elvis would record it.]

Dear Miss Reed:
I appreciated your interest in me, but we are unable to handle music here. You may, however, refer it to: Elvis Presley Music, Inc., 1619 Broadway, New York, N.Y. Attn: Mr. Freddy Bienstock.
Sincerely,
Elvis Presley

ITEM: *Handwritten letter. Written and signed by a member of the Presley staff (Hollywood, California). Sent to "June" (last name and location not known).*
SOURCE: *Document photocopy.*
[Exact date not known.]

Dear June,
Thank you for the nice note. I'm doing "G.I. Blues," so I can't come to the meeting. Sorry.
Elvis Presley

Dear Tommy,
I recieved your most welcomed letter, I am very sorry I haven't written sooner but I've been busy getting re-adjusted to civilian life again, I was proud to do my tour in the service, but now that its over I am truly proud to be back with all my fans and friends, And in the entertainment field,
I sincerely want to thank you fans for your loyalty and devotion to me while I was away.
I shall try to show my sincerest appreciation by trying to give you the songs and movies you enjoy most.
Thanking you again And May God Bless you And Yours
Sincerely,
Elvis Presley

JUNE 2, 1960

ITEM: *Handwritten letter. Written and signed by a member of the Presley staff (Memphis, Tennessee). Sent to Lucille Lingerfelt (New Orleans, Louisiana).*

SOURCE: *Document photocopy.*

Congratulations on your forthcoming graduation! May you always be happy in the future.
       Sincerely,
       Elvis Presley

JULY 20, 1960

ITEM: *Handwritten generic thank-you letter from, and signed by, Elvis Presley (Memphis, Tennessee), to fans who had written to him.*

SOURCE: *Document photocopies.*

Dear [Name of Recipient]
I received your nice letter a few days ago and thought I'd drop a line to say hello. I just finished "G.I. Blues" and am at home resting. I want you to know how much I appreciate you and all the rest of my friends for remembering me while I was away. May God bless you and yours.
       Loving You,
       Elvis Presley

AUGUST 19, 1960

ITEM: *Handwritten letter. Written and signed by a member of the Presley staff (Memphis, Tennessee), to Catherine Stokes (Houston, Texas).*

SOURCE: *Document photocopy.*

Dear Catherine,
I received your nice letter and thought I drop you a line. I just finished "G.I. Blues" which will be released around Thanksgiving. I Hope you will get to see it. May God bless you and yours. *Sincerely,*
       Elvis Presley

P.S. Write again soon.

ITEM: *Handwritten letter. Written and signed by a member of the Presley staff (Memphis, Tennessee), to "Hendrick and Members" (of the Danish Fan Club).*
SOURCE: *Document photocopy.*

Dear Hendrick and Members:
Hello there! How's everything with you? I've been doing quite a bit of horseback riding lately and it's really keeping me in shape. As you probably know, I'm just now completing my newest movie entitled "Black Star" [soon retitled Flaming Star] *which will be in Technicolor. Dolores Del Rio plays my mother in the film. My newest record album will be released in the near future. The songs are taken from the movie "G.I. Blues." I certainly hope you like it as much as my last album, "Elvis Is Back." I want you to know how much I appreciate everything you're doing for me,*

Car shopping in Memphis with Anita Wood, 1960.

and I hope I can repay you with the movies and records I'm making now. I'd better close for now. May God bless you.
Loving You,
Elvis Presley

ITEM: *Handwritten generic letter. Written and signed by a member of the Presley staff (Memphis, Tennessee). Sent in response to fans who had written.*
SOURCE: *Document photocopies.*
[Exact date not known.]

Dear Friend [or name],
How've you been? I suppose you've heard about my accident while playing football [October 16, 1960]. It was only a broken finger which won't take long to heal.
I'm at home now resting here at Graceland, but I'll be heading back to the coast in a couple of weeks to start working on another movie. There's not much I can do with my right hand in a cast. Naturally I enjoy going skating with a group of friends or maybe practicing on my karate, but just being home with loved ones and receiving all your nice cards and letters is very encouraging. I'd love to be able to spend more time at home, but with the way my schedule is, it is almost impossible.
I guess I'd better sign off for now—maybe next time I'll have more news for you. May God bless you. Write soon!
Elvis Presley

LOCATION: *Hollywood, California.*
EVENT: *Radio Spot for* G.I. Blues *film. Features two unidentified females.*

166

SOURCE: Southern Gentleman *(CD).*

[Exact date not known.]

[Girl 1] Gee, I want to see Elvis in his new picture.

[Girl 2] Gee, I wouldn't miss it. It's Elvis' first since he came out of the army.

[Girl 1] Gee, I can hardly wait.

[Girl 2] What's the name of the picture?

[Girl 1] Gee, I...wait a minute. I'll ask Elvis. G.I. Blues. *Gee, I hope you like it.*

1960

ITEM: *Handwritten letter. Written and signed by a member of the Presley staff. Sent to "Tommy."*

SOURCE: *Document photocopy.*

[Letter is not dated but is presumed to have been written in late 1960.]

Dear Tommy,

I received your most welcomed letter. I am very sorry I haven't written sooner but I've been busy getting readjusted to civilian life again.

I was proud to do my tour in the service, but now that its over I am truly proud to be back with all my fans and friends, and in the entertainment field.

I sincerely want to thank you fans for your loyalty and devotion to me while I was away.

I shall try to show my sincerest appreciation by trying to give you the songs and movies you enjoy most.

Thanking you again and may God bless you and yours.

Sincerely,
Elvis Presley

LOCATION: *Claridge Hotel, Memphis, Tennessee.*

EVENT: *Press Conference, in conjunction with Elvis' benefit concerts. Questions by numerous media representatives.*

SOURCE: Elvis, Exclusive Live Press Conference *(LP).*

I guess you're wondering why I called you here. Okay, shoot.

[Media] Elvis.
Yes sir.

[Media] I'll have to apologize to you for this first question, but everybody wants to know… how is your love life?
(Laughs.) Well it hasn't progressed any. It's about like it was. Nothin' serious. I'll let you know if anything comes of it. Couldn't hide it anyway (laughs).

[Media] Do you think your career may make you wind up bein' a bachelor at seventy?
It's hard to say, really. I wouldn't think so. It's just that I'm not ready for marriage yet, that's all. And until I am, I'm not gonna attempt it. But, it wouldn't be because of a career. It's just that I just am not ready for it and I haven't found anybody that I cared that much about really.

[Media] Has your personal taste changed from rock and roll to what we call a little more commercial, better music? Do you think your own personal taste has changed any?
No it hasn't changed. I've always liked all kinds of music. I mean, I don't just like rock and roll. I appreciate all types of music. But I have to do what I can do best and so I do the rock stuff.

[Media] What caused your cousin's [Carroll "Junior" Smith] death in bed?
Nobody knows, ma'am.

[Media] No one knows?

[The reported cause of death of 29-year-old Junior Smith (February 4, 1961) is a heart attack.]
No.

[Media] Are you planning on going back to Hollywood soon?
I got another picture starting about the twenty-fifth of March.

[Media] What kind of picture is it?
It's a kind of a drama. It's called Blue Hawaii. *That's all I know about it right now.*

[Media] What is your favorite record, of the records you've done?
My favorite record, of the ones I've recorded, is "[It's] Now or Never." Simply [because] it sold more than anything else…next to "Don't Be Cruel." "Don't Be Cruel" is still my biggest seller to date.

[Media] "Don't Be Cruel" sold more than "It's Now or Never"?
It sold more… "Now or Never" went over four million, I think.

[Media] How many's "Don't Be Cruel" sold?
Around six million. Next?

[Media] I understand you've sold some seventy-five million records. Isn't that some sort of record for the record business?
I wouldn't know, really. I think that includes everything. All the albums…everything combined.

[Media] Is that all for RCA Victor?
Right. All for Victor. But I don't know anything about it settin' any kind of record.

[Media] What type role do you enjoy playing in the movies the most? A Western role, or some type of dramatic role? Which type do you enjoy?
I would like to play a dramatic role, but I'm not ready for that either, really. I haven't had enough experience in acting. And again, until I'm ready for it, it would be foolish to undertake something very dramatic.

[Media] What about your musicals, like *Loving You*? That was one of my favorites.

Well probably so, honey. It's up to the studio, mostly. But you can rest assured that there'd be music in almost all of 'em. There has to be.

[Media] When will *Wild in the Country* be released?

May or June.

[Media] Elvis, have you filled out your income tax?

(Laughs.) I think my accountant has, Mr. [Bill] Fisher, he takes care of that.

[Media] Has your eating habit changed since you went into the Army?

No ma'am.

[Media] When you came back, did you eat the starchy and fatty foods that you did before?

I still eat pretty much the same thing. Kinda got used to it, it's hard to change over.

[Media] What songs have you recorded for *Blue Hawaii*?

I haven't made it yet.

[Media] Have you recorded any?

I haven't recorded it yet. I couldn't tell you anything.

[Media] They haven't released a soundtrack from *Flaming Star*, either on an EP or on a single.

I don't know. I think they felt that it wasn't quite commercial enough to release. I don't know really. That's left up to RCA Victor.

[Media] Elvis, are you going to move to Hollywood eventually, or are you gonna stay here?

No sir, I'll stay here.

[Media] (Applause!)

I've got a house leased out there, but it'd be back and forth. But I'll always keep my home here, as long as I can.

[Media] Elvis, I remember your enthusiasm, last time we talked, about karate. How about now?

I still practice it quite a bit.

[Media] Do you have any new enthusiasms?

No sir, nothing new's come along. I don't have much time, really, for…

[Media] Are you still skating, or doing that sort of thing, or have you slowed down on that?

Speaking at benefit show for Memphis charities, 1961.

Hollywood, 1960.

Well, we still skate a little…break boards (laughs).

[Media] What about ice skating? Have you ever tried to ice skate?
No ma'am, I never tried ice skating. But I still do pretty much the same thing. I don't do it as much. Because, since I been out of the Army I haven't had much time, you know, I been pretty busy. Been going from picture to picture.

[Media] Well, you just bought this place on the lake, or your father has. You planning to go there with your family?
I'd like to. We're thinkin' about either building a little cabin up there or gettin' a house trailer, one of the two. I'm not sure which one yet.

[Media] Which one of your movies do you think you did the best job of acting?
King Creole.

[Media] Which one?
King Creole.

[Media] Elvis, why aren't you on TV more?
[Bump!] What am I hittin' here? Because of the movie contracts I have, I'm pretty tied up in movies right now and too much television kind of hurts movies a little bit.

[Media] Do you like personal appearances, movies, or TV the best?

Well, I like personal appearances best. Although I don't know about today, because (laughs) haven't been on stage in a little over three years. I've almost forgotten a lot of the words to the songs I used to do. And I haven't had much of a chance to rehearse with the band.

[Media] You're going from here out to Hawaii in March to do a picture and also a benefit of some sort.

Right. We're doing a benefit for the battleship Arizona.

[Media] You haven't been on stage for three years, are you a little bit nervous?

Yes sir. I don't mind admittin' I am. But when I did the Frank Sinatra show, in Florida, I wasn't nervous…I was petrified! I was scared stiff. (Laughter.)

[Media] When you released your first record, did you think you'd have such a successful career as you had?

Nah, I don't think anybody did, did we, Mr. [Sam] Phillips? (Laughs.) I don't think so. Nobody had any idea, really.

[Media] Did the Frank Sinatra…to get back to that…did those people on Frank Sinatra Productions…did they give you an ample opportunity to perform there, do you think?

Oh yeah, sure. But the moving and shaking I done on that show wasn't from moving. It was from being scared (laughs). But they gave me plenty of time, you know. Yes sir, they were very nice.

[Media] Didn't they give you just six minutes of an hour?

Well, it'd been alright with me if I'd just walked out and walked off. Is there anything else I can't answer?

[Media] Still like the cheeseburgers?

I don't eat many cheeseburgers anymore.

[Media] Elvis, have you smoked yet?

No sir. I smoked a cigar every once in a while. That is when the Colonel gives me a cigar… that's very unusual.

[Media] (Laughter.) How 'bout the drinks?

No. No.

[Media] How long will you be in Memphis?

I'll be leaving sometime around the eighteenth of March, Mr. [Robert] Johnson, as far as I know.

[Media] How many Gold Records have you received in all?

I've got thirty-four…thirty-four Gold Records.

[Media] That's more than your nearest rival. Does it make you happy that you've got more Gold Records than anyone else?

Yeah, it makes me and the government very happy.

[Media] Elvis, we've been knowing your career since its inception, and wonderin' now what's in your mind about the enthusiasm to perform the kind of music you have not yet recorded. Is there something special in your mind that you'd like to do?

There definitely is, but I don't like to press my luck too far. I don't like to take chances, you know. As long as I'm doing okay now I don't want…I mean, why change it until I got reason to change it. If what I'm doing now…if it doesn't go over anymore, then I'll have to change or do something.

[Media] Are you hard to please with respect to the selection of your wardrobe, since you tend to wear things that are different?

Not especially. Not especially 'cause I don't know that much about clothes. It doesn't make a difference, really.

[Media] Elvis, you have become a little bit more conservative.

Well, I'm gettin' a little older, you know.

[Media] (Laughter.)
That's like the sideburns. They were okay for a while but you outgrow 'em.

[Media] Don't you miss 'em?
The sideburns? Not especially, no.

[Media] (Laughter.)
The Army took care of those.

[Media] What actress, that you've performed with, is your favorite?
If I answered that I'd lose a lot of friends.

[Media] (Laughter.) How about the rumor about Nancy Sharp?
Anita [Wood] around here anywhere? No. I don't know. It's just one little deal, you know. I just dated her for a time. It's kind of funny. You go out with a girl a couple times and it's a big romance. They had me married a couple times. I was down on Wilshire Boulevard one night…I was in the lobby of a theater…and some people said "I thought you were in Mexico City on your honeymoon." Come to find out, it was in a Mexican paper that I was eloped and was com-

ing there to get married. And they had a hotel suite reserved and all that stuff. And I didn't even know the girl I was supposed to be married to. Things like that happen.

[Media] Elvis, most show people have superstitions. Do you have any particular superstitions?
I'm pretty superstitious. About certain…are you talkin' about black cats, things like that?

[Media] Any one particular superstition?
No, just little things. Like breaking mirrors, things like that. (Laughter.) Photographers. (Laughter.) You said that…that's your line.

[Media] Elvis, do you still consider Anita Wood just a friend?
Well, yeah. I mean, I see her quite a bit, but it's nothing really, really serious. I see a lot of people quite a bit. These photographers are takin' pictures of each other now.

[Media] (Laughter.) Elvis, do you do much thinking of fear?
Quite a bit.

[Media] What do you think your place in the entertainment world two years from now will be?
I'll tell you, Mr. [Robert] Johnson, I wouldn't say because the entertainment world is so unpredictable, and people change and times change. It would be hard to say, really. I wouldn't try to answer that. The only thing I can say is that I'm trying to make it acting, and it takes a long time and a lot of work and a lot of experience. But I'm trying to make it that way. If I can get established that way, I'm okay. But I don't know how long the music end of it will last. I don't know how long I'll last. I got no idea, really.

[Media] Now you only have two personal appearances since you returned.
Right.

[Media] Do you plan to go barnstorming again anytime soon?
Well, the Colonel could probably answer that better than I. There's nothing planned right now. I know that eventually we've got to do a European tour…to all these countries like…that presented these awards and things, you know. But I don't know exactly.

* [Asks Colonel Parker.] Are we gonna be doing any?*

[Col. Tom Parker] We're waiting for a good offer.

[Media] (Laughter.)
He said that, I didn't.

[Media] What's your weight now, Elvis?
A hundred and eighty.

[Media] What was it when you came out of the service?
One seventy-five when I came out. I've gained about five pounds.

[Media] Elvis, you lead such a hectic life, I can imagine. Do you ever wish you could just take your money and get away from it all for about a year?
They won't let me take my money and get away from it all. The government won't let me take my money and get away from it all.

[Media] (Laughter.)
No, I enjoy it. Anytime I want to be alone, I can be, you know.

[Media] Well I know it must be pretty hectic, trying to get up for all you've done.
But these are the type things you take advantage of while they last. You take advantage of it because you might not have it later, and you'll miss it. You'd miss the people. You'd miss all the razzle-dazzle, and so forth. But I have a pretty good time, and so forth.

[Memphis Mayor Henry Loeb] Always feel home when you come back to Memphis?
Yes sir, it does.

[Media] Good. That's what we wanna hear.
Sure does. That's one reason that I keep a home here. I like California. I like to work there, [but] when a picture's over I look forward to gettin' out of there and comin' back home. And also, I'm

Hollywood, 1962.

right near Tupelo and I know a lot of people down there. The same old crowd I was raised up with still live there in the same houses. I was down there about three weeks ago. And the wind had blown the sign down…at that [Elvis Presley] Youth Center being built, they got a big sign up and the wind had blown it down. We tried to put it back up. It fell on us…there were three of us tried to lift it back up. But the sign fell on us.

[Media] Do you anticipate the Youth Center work will be completed soon?
I couldn't tell you. It's gonna take a lot of money. But it will be eventually. I couldn't say when.

[Media] Has your animal population increased any recently? (Laughter.)
Well, we got a couple a little mules.

[Media] I'll bet the hound too.
He's still there.

[Media] That was the hound…the basset hound we saw you with on TV?

[Media] That was Frank Sinatra's dog.

No, that was Frank Sinatra's dog (laughs). She's giving me answers.

[Media] How many cars you got, Elvis?
Ah, four.

[Media] Four?
Yes sir. Two of 'em are new. One of 'em—the pink car—was the one that my mother liked above all. That's why I've kept it. And another one…

[Media] Is that a Cadillac?
Yes sir. It's the first one I ever owned.

[Media] Elvis, do you still like sports cars?
No sir. Not especially. I had one in Germany and they can get you in a lot of trouble. Especially if you're in the Army. Did you run out of tape?

[Media] How many songs are you gonna sing this afternoon [first of two charity shows at Ellis Auditorium]?
I believe around twenty. Yes. I just do the biggest ones, you know. The older ones and the new. If I can remember the words to 'em (laughs).

Addressing Tennessee State Legislature in Nashville, 1961.

[Media] What has been your greatest thrill in show business, Elvis?

Well it's hard to say. I've had quite a few things happen, but I can't name any one instant that stands out, really.

[Media] How about signing your first movie contract?

I would imagine when I got the first Gold Record, 'cause that's something I never thought would ever happen.

[Media] What was your first, "Don't Be Cruel"?
"Heartbreak Hotel."

MARCH 8, 1961

LOCATION: *Nashville, Tennessee. Senate Chamber, Session of the Tennessee State Legislature.*
EVENT: *Presentation of awards to Elvis.*
SOURCE: *Audiotape.*

[Lieutenant Governor William Baird] Ladies and gentlemen, for this most auspicious occasion, and for making the introduction of the guest who is appearing here today, it is my pleasure to introduce to you our most distinguished Tennessean, a friend of everyone here and a friend of all people in all walks of life in the state of Tennessee, his excellency, the governor of the state of Tennessee, the Honorable Buford Ellington.

[Governor Ellington] Thank you. Lieutenant Governor Baird, Mr. Speaker [James Lafayette] Bomar. Let's have order in the Senate Chamber. Is there a Sergeant of Arms up in the upper gallery? You know, after battling this crowd up here, I feel like that I'm nothin' but a hound dog. Last week I had the great pleasure of introducing to you a distinguished Tennessean that all people in Tennessee and throughout America and throughout the world…we're very proud to call him a Tennessean.

I have that same privilege again today. I have known this young man for a good many years, personally. I don't believe I ever knew a young man that has attained fame…that I think is a sound[er] man than our guest here today. I want to thank the Shelby County delegation for asking him to come and visit with us on this occasion. But before I introduce him personally, there's another group here that I called and invited up because I knew that our guest would like to have them. They have backed him up on all of his recordings and, incidentally, I'm authorized to say to the speakers of both houses that these men are from Nashville, and if you should so desire next week, if you're not too busy they'd be happy to come back and sing for ya one day. But they have…they have been with our guest today—our honored guest—I don't know how many of ya stopped to think, and maybe I'm not exactly right but at least I'm not overestimating what has been done. But our guest with these men performing in the background have sold over seventy-five million records here in the United States. That doesn't count those that have been sold abroad. A great group, a great bunch of young fellows, them that I'm happy to call my personal friends, and they too have been a credit to our state…I'd like to ask the Jordanaires if they'd stand, please.

Now they don't look as good as our guest, but they're good, I'll tell you that.

You know, during the campaign when I was runnin' for governor, a lot of people said something about me not bein' a native Tennessean, well my answer was that sometimes an adopted child loves his adopted parents so very much, and sometimes more than the natural children love their parents. And I meant that because Tennessee is my adopted state. But no man could love Tennessee any more than I do. We hear that our guest this morning once was a truck driver. Well it's the truth. He came from a humble home from the same state where

Dear Charlotte:

I wanted to drop you a line before I head back to the coast, which will be sometime this week. I'm going to start working on my new movie "Blue Hawaii" very soon, which will be filmed on the Hawaiian Islands.

I've been vacationing here at Graceland with my family and friends since completing "Wild In the Country", which should be released sometime around Easter. I've really enjoyed being at home and wish I could spend more time here, but my busy schedule just doesn't permit it. I want to thank you for the Valentine card; it means so much to hear from friends on those special days.

I guess I'd better sign off for now because I have a lot to do before I leave. Have a happy Easter! May God bless you.

Elvis Presley

P.S. Sorry. I don't have any photo's right now; I'll send you one as soon as I receive them.
You can write to this address at Graceland while I am in Hawaii, and I'll get your letter when I come back home, which, I hope is soon.

Letter to a fan, 1961.

I'm—I'm not gonna say reared because I was jerked up—but after he had reached the top in the entertainment field, there hasn't been a change. His sincerity, his great purpose in life, not only to entertain but to help others, was proven back in his hometown of Tupelo not too long ago. And just last Saturday, a week ago, when he personally made such a great contribution to his adopted state and his home town of Memphis. When he gave of his time and his talent in order that he might help the needy.

I know this man to be that type of man, unaffected by fame, the great popularity, but with a sincere desire in his heart to help all that he comes in contact with. So what more could I say after I say we're proud of him, that we're happy to call you a Tennessean, and the great contribution that you've made to Tennessee, and to say we're happy to have you with us this morning, Elvis. And if you'll come up here I have a presentation to make. Elvis Presley, the greatest honor…the greatest honor that the governor of Tennessee can bestow upon a man is to ask you and present to you this certificate of Colonelship on the governor's staff. I do it with pride and with pleasure and tell you that not only the governor of the state, but every citizen of Tennessee, is very, very proud of you.

Thank you, sir. Mr. Governor, ladies and gentlemen…ladies and gentlemen, and those of you that have skipped school (laughs). I'd like to thank you very much for coming out today, and I'd like to thank you wonderful people for inviting me up here. It came as kind of a surprise to me. I was out in Hollywood about three weeks ago finishing up a picture and I got a letter from Senator [J. Lewis] Taliaferro, I think that's how you pronounce it, Taliaferro. And he invited me to come up here. And my daddy read it to me over the telephone and he said that they wanted me to come to Nashville to be made an honorary senator (laughs). So I didn't really know what to expect.

I'd like to tell you first of all, I'm not allowed to sing, really, I would like to but I'm not allowed to. And second of all, I'm not as funny as Tennessee Ernie, except when I had sideburns I was pretty funny (laughs).

And so we drove up to Nashville not knowing exactly what to expect and found all this waiting for us. And I'd like to say it's one of the greatest honors, really, that I've had in my entire career. I thought when I got my first Gold Record that it was exciting…and it was because I was makin' a little money. But truthfully this is one of the nicest things that has ever happened to me in my entire career. And I'd like to thank you very, very much. I don't have any kind of a speech and I'm not very good at speech-making, really, but I want to thank you sincerely and I'd like to say that I'm very proud to be from the state of Tennessee and I'll always (applause)…thank you.

I will always call this my home. I have people to ask me all the time "are you going to move to Hollywood?" or "do you think you'll ever live out in Hollywood?" And my answer is "definitely not" because it's nice to go out there and play around, I mean work (laughs), but it's always great to get out and come back to good ol' Tennessee again. And so I don't have very much to say, ladies and gentlemen. Again, I'd like to thank you from the bottom of my heart and I hope I can live up to this honor…and I'll do my very best to…and I'd like to say God bless all of you as He's blessed me, and guided me through my career and so forth. Thank you very much. Thank you.

[Governor Ellington] (Applause.) I think most of us know that Colonel Parker, from out at Madison [Tennessee], is Elvis' manager. Colonel Parker has done so many wonderful things here in Nashville in a charity way. I know because I've had the privilege of working with him. Colonel Parker couldn't be here this morning, he's in Hawaii. But I wanted to make this announcement now, Elvis. Colonel Parker is no longer the number-one Colonel, it's Colonel Presley.

[Speaker Bomar] (Applause.) Hold it! Come to order. This time the chair recognizes the gentleman from Shelby County, Senator Taliaferro.

[Senator Taliaferro] Thank you, Mr. Speaker, Governor Ellington, Ann Ellington, distinguished guests, colleagues of the Eighty-second General Assembly, I'd like first of all, before I say anything further, to recognize these gentlemen who are on the staff for Elvis Presley, who accompanied him up here this morning. I'd like them to stand and be recognized: Alan Fortas, Joe Esposito, and Sonny West. Let's give 'em a hand.

(Applause.) We down in the mud flats of Shelby County are not gonna let representatives and senators over those majestic mountain peaks to the east get ahead of us. Seriously, I have here a framed copy of Senate Joint Resolution Number Fifty-two. We had planned to have Elvis up the last week in February, before his big charity show in Memphis. His schedule prohibited him from coming. We're glad that he's able to come now. The reason why we wanted to have Elvis up is twofold: First, we wanted to recognize him as a Memphian and a Tennessean, for having climbed to great heights in the entertainment world. He only has one more notch to go to become the all-time great in the record business. He has already exceeded the seventy-five million mark, and only one other entertainer is above that mark, that's Bing Crosby.

We further wanted to recognize him for having served his country in the armed forces, and additionally we wanted to cite him for being a generous individual. A man who has demonstrated a benevolence and a charitable spirit on more than one occasion. He has a state charity show, which he sponsored, in Memphis on Saturday night, February the sixth, for the benefit of thirty-eight charities in that city—and I'm reading from the "Commercial-Appeal" now: "Elvis Presley probably raised more money for charity in a day's work Saturday than any other entertainer in the history of show business." Elvis is an outstanding personality, a great citizen of our city and our country, our state and the nation. He probably is more widely known internationally than any other man in the state of Tennessee.

It is therefore with great pleasure and pride, and with a lot of joy that I present this framed copy of Senate…Senate Joint Resolution Number Fifty-two to him to hang alongside of his Colonel's Certificate. Elvis, we're mighty proud of you.

Thank you, sir. Thank you.

Meeting the press in Honolulu, 1961.

[Speaker Bomar] (Applause.) Mr. Presley, on behalf of the members of the General Assembly, we'd like to thank you for taking time off from a busy schedule and bein' with us on this occasion. Just a minute. Just one second. There is a person here, a guest this morning, that I would like to have the opportunity of presenting to ya. She is the beautiful daughter of Governor Ellington, Miss Ann Ellington. Miss Ann, would you stand up?

(Applause.) Mister…will the Sergeant of Arms clear the rear doors of the gallery chambers for just a minute? Well…Mister Sergeant of Arms, would you clear these aisles here and will everybody remain seated until you have escorted the governor and our distinguished guest and his staff from the House chambers?

MARCH 17, 1961

ITEM: *Handwritten letter. Written and signed by a member of the Presley staff (Memphis,* *Tennessee). Sent to Charlotte Boyd (Brookeland, Texas).*
SOURCE: *Document photocopy.*

Dear Charlotte,
I wanted to drop you a line before I head back to the coast, which will be sometime this week. I'm going to start working on my new movie "Blue Hawaii" very soon, which will be filmed on the Hawaiian Islands.
I've been vacationing here at Graceland with my family and friends since completing "Wild in the Country," which should be released sometime around Easter. I've really enjoyed being at home and wish I could spend more time here, but my busy schedule just doesn't permit it. I want to thank you for the Valentine card; it means so much to hear from friends on those special days.

I guess I better sign off for now because I have a lot to do before I leave. Have a Happy Easter! May God bless you.

Elvis Presley

P.S. Sorry I don't have any photo's [sic] right now; I'll send you one as soon as I receive them. You can write to the address at Graceland while I am in Hawaii, and I'll get your letter when I come back home, which I hope is soon.

MARCH 25, 1961

LOCATION: *Honolulu, Hawaii (Honolulu Airport).*

INTERVIEWER: *Unknown.*

SOURCE: This Is Elvis *(Video).*

[Media] **What are you going to do today, Elvis, after this is all over? You gonna sneak out on the beach and get some sun?**

I'm gonna take these leis off of my neck so I can walk.

[Media] **It's kind of hard to concentrate this morning.**

You're not kidding. It's hard for me to concentrate any time.

MARCH 25, 1961

LOCATION: *Honolulu, Hawaii.*

EVENT: *Presentation of awards to Elvis.*

SOURCE: Elvis Aron Presley *(LP).*

[Media] **Ladies and gentlemen, for just a moment, I would like to inject a rather serious note into this gathering. Because, after all, what Elvis is doing here is for a very great cause. Now, Elvis, we have three items that we want to present to you. First of all, here is an Honor Certificate, signed by Admiral [Chester William] Nimitz, expressing appreciation to you for what you are doing tonight. Then there's a second certificate from the Pacific War**

Memorial Commission. We're asking that you serve as an honorary member of that group. And lastly, Elvis, we have a plaque. The folks here will recognize this as the outline of the Coat of Arms of Hawaii. I will read it: "U.S.S. Arizona Award of Honor, Elvis Presley, Pacific War Memorial Commission, March 25th, 1961, Pearl Harbor, Hawaii." So we present these to you, sir, and with these go our sincere…most sincere appreciation.

Thank you, sir. I appreciate this.

[Media] **(Applause.)**

Thank you very much, sir.

MARCH 25, 1961

LOCATION: *Honolulu, Hawaii (Hawaiian Village Hotel).*

SOURCE: *Audiotape.*

I would like to thank everybody again for all the support and would like to say I got all the letters and so forth when I was in the Army. It helped me a lot. I really looked forward to coming back here.

[Media] **Usually when we chat, Elvis, whether it be in Germany, Hollywood, or here in Honolulu, we ask you to select your favorite song of all your recordings. The current favorite of yours?**

I think…"It's Now or Never."

MARCH 25, 1961

LOCATION: *Honolulu, Hawaii.*

SOURCE: Elvis Aron Presley *(LP).*

Before we go any further, ladies and gentlemen, I'd like to introduce you to the members of my gang…ah, band, the Unwashables. I'm sure you've already met the fellows that do all my recording on all my records, the Jordanaires. And the fellow in the back, from Nashville,

Tennessee, this is his first appearance with us. Bobby Moore. And the fellow on drums, he's been with me ever since I started out in this racket...business, Mr. D. J. Fontana, ladies and gentlemen. On saxophone, I think you've already met Boots Randolph. On guitar—we also started out together—Scotty Moore. And on the other guitar, one of the finest guitar players anywhere in the country, ladies and gentlemen, Hank Garland. And that...no wait...[on piano] Mr. Floyd Cramer.

APRIL 22, 1961

ITEM: *Telegram from Elvis Presley and Col. Tom Parker (Madison, Tennessee) to Vice-President Lyndon B. Johnson (Washington D.C.).*
SOURCE: *Original document.*

Dear Mr. Johnson,
We have just completed raising more than sixty-two thousand dollars for the U.S.S. Arizona Memorial Fund at Pearl Harbor. Now, more than ever, we feel it proper to let you know that we are willing, able, and available to serve in any way we can, our country and our President, in any capacity, whether it is to use our talents or help load the trucks.

Sincerely,
Your friends,
Elvis and the Colonel

MAY 11, 1961

ITEM: *Handwritten letter. Written and signed by a member of the Presley staff (Honolulu, Hawaii/Memphis, Tennessee). Sent to Gertye Rogers (Seattle, Washington).*
SOURCE: *Document photocopy.*

[Envelope has a May 11 postmark from Memphis, where it was actually mailed. Letter is not dated but was probably written in April 1961.]

Dear Gertye,
I just boarded the airplane here in Honolulu to head back to Hollywood and thought you might be interested to know what I've been doing lately.
For the past month we have been filming "Blue Hawaii" over on the Hawaiian Islands. The scenery there is just gorgeous. The weather was always nice and everyone was so friendly, I really enjoyed working there. After completing the rest of the film in Hollywood, I will return home—to Memphis around the first of June. I see the stewardess serving dinner, so I'd better sign off for now.
Take good care of yourself and write soon!

Sincerely,
Elvis Presley

DECEMBER 8, 1961

ITEM: *Telegram from Elvis Presley (Bel Air, California) to* Top 10 Dance Party, *Television Channel 13 (Memphis, Tennessee).*
SOURCE: *Original document.*

Dear Friends,
Just heard you are having the special [Elvis] Dance Party, and want to say thanks and to take this opportunity to send my best wishes for a Merry Christmas and Happy New Year, and hope you have a real wonderful time today.

Sincerely,
Elvis

ITEM: *Handwritten letter. Written and signed by a member of the Presley staff. Sent in response to letters from fans.*

SOURCE: *Document photocopy.*

Happy New Year!

It's been awhile since I've answered any of your letters. But this one is to "Thank You" for your lovely cards and gifts I received during Xmas.

And I hope you and yours had a lovely Xmas and have a joyous New Year.

I didn't get home for Xmas myself as my movie "Kid Galahad" wasn't completed but I'm looking forward to a long visit this time, perhaps till early spring. I am glad you enjoyed "Blue Hawaii" and I hope you'll enjoy my two recent ones as well. Again let me say "Thanks" for a good year in '61 and I hope '62 will be as fine. Keep writting [sic]. I enjoy your letters and will answer when I have a few spare moments.

Sincerely,
Elvis

ITEM: *Handwritten note. Written and signed by a member of the Presley staff (Memphis, Tennessee). Sent to Bobbie Lynn Burchfield, Dixieland Rock & Rollers (Miami, Florida), in response to a birthday telegram from the fan club.*

SOURCE: *Document photocopy.*

Dear Bobbie

This is a brief note of thanks for the thoughtful telegram I received on my birthday. I am always delighted to hear from you. Take care and keep writing.

Sincerely,
Elvis Presley

ITEM: *Telegram from Elvis Presley to L. J. [Lou] Finske, president Florida State Theaters, Inc. (Ocala, Florida).*

SOURCE: *Original document.*

Dear Lou,

Congratulations to you and to the entire staff of Florida State Theater organization on the world premier of "Follow That

Filming *It Happened at the World's Fair,* on location in Seattle, 1962.

Dream." Our sincere appreciation to all the folks in Ocala and Florida for their wonderful cooperation while the picture was being made in the great state of Florida. Give our best to Mark Dupree and Ezra Kimbrell. We hope that all our fans and friends will enjoy the picture.

Kindest regards,
Elvis and the Colonel

APRIL 2, 1962

ITEM: *Telegram from Elvis Presley to Joe Taylor, Tampa Theater (Tampa, Florida).*
SOURCE: *Original document.*

Dear Joe,

Our best wishes with the opening of "Follow That Dream" at the Tampa Theater. We sincerely hope that you will have them standing in line. Many thanks for your fine cooperation to you and the staff while we made the picture in Florida. Our best also to Bob Harris, Frankie Connors, and all our friends in Tampa.

Sincerely,
Elvis and the Colonel

JUNE 7, 1962

ITEM: *Telegram from Col. Tom Parker, Elvis Presley, and Mrs. [Marie] Parker (Madison, Tennessee) to Dean Martin (Beverly Hills, California).*
SOURCE: *Original document.*

Dear Dean,

As always, congratulations on behalf of Mrs. Parker, Elvis and myself on your birthday [June 7]. We miss seeing you and Lieutenant Colonel Gray. Your big picture is hanging in the conference room, and we will give it a special greeting on your birthday.

Your pal,
The Colonel

JUNE 13, 1962

ITEM: *Telegram from Col. Tom Parker and Elvis Presley (Madison, Tennessee) to Sammy Davis Jr. (Lake Tahoe, Nevada).*
SOURCE: *Original document.*

Dear Sammy,

On behalf of Elvis and myself, as always, the best of luck and standing room only.

Your pal,
The Colonel

JULY 6, 1962

ITEM: *Handwritten letter. Written and signed by a member of the Presley staff (Memphis, Tennessee). Sent to Bobbie Lynn Burchfield (Miami, Florida).*
SOURCE: *Document photocopy.*

Dear Bobbie

Another year has gone by and the Fourth of July is here again. Once again I'd like to extend my appreciation to you for your support this year and I wish you and yours a very happy Fourth of July, but be careful with fireworks.

I've had a pretty busy year making movies and haven't had any time to do personal appearances. I hope you like my new album called "Pot Luck." I just finished a new movie called "Girls Girls Girls." I hope to be home in Memphis by the Fourth of July; as for now I'm going to stand by for wardrobe for my new picture. Part of it will be filmed at the Seattle World's Fair.

Keep writing your wonderful letters. I appreciate hearing from you. God bless you until I can write again.

Sincerely,
Your friend I hope to remain.
Elvis Presley

Gladys Presley holding mike for Elvis, Memphis, 1956.

LOCATION: *Hollywood, California.*
INTERVIEWER: *Lloyd Shearer.*
SOURCE: Face to Face with Elvis *(CD).*

[Exact date not known. Portions of this inter-view exist on at least two other albums; however, they have numerous differences in both content and presentation. On Elvis Aron Presley, *some excerpts are presented as an "Elvis Monologue," with no questions asked and no interviewer heard. On* Elvis Presley Interview Record—An Audio Self-Portrait, *we do hear some questions being asked, though they are neither the actual ones—properly worded—from 1962, nor are they by the original interviewer. Also, many of Elvis' responses are unmercifully edited.]*

[Lloyd Shearer] Elvis, people's opinion of you seems to have changed since back in the old days. Now everybody thinks you're a model fellow…you know, you're a good guy…epitome of a young man. Now I'm just wondering, is it by accident or by design? What do you think it is? You know, you're a…
Well, I've tried to be the same all through this thing. Naturally, you learn a lot about people, and you're involved in a lot of different situations. But I've tried to be the same, I mean the

way I was brought up. And I always considered other people's feelings. I've neve…in other words, I didn't kick anybody on the way (laughs). And I've always treated people just like that I would like to be treated myself. And I consider other people's feelings. I don't assume the attitude of "get these people out of here," like I have heard of being done, because those people are sincere in their feelings. And if they want autographs and pictures and things like that, I don't just sign the autographs and the pictures and so forth to help my popularity or to make them like me. I do it because I know that they're sincere. And they see ya and they want an auto-graph to take home. They got an autograph book, or they've got their little camera and everything, so you have to know that. And if you don't do it, well you make them mad at you, they don't understand, you hurt their feelings and you make a lot of enemies that way. And for no reason, because it's as simple as this.

Once you get involved in this racket…er, business (laughs), your life is public. Regardless of what anybody says…my private life is my own. Well it is to a certain extent. I mean, everybody has to have a certain amount of pri-vacy. But once you get involved in this business and you're doing a public service, you're trying to entertain people, your life is not your own. Because people are gonna wanna know what you are doing, where you are, what you wear, what you eat. These things are natural, or normal, and you have to consider that. You consider that these people are sincere. They don't know the kind of life you lead. They don't know what kind of person you are. And so I try to remember that, that's all. It's simple. It's no problem. It's no big effort that I put forth.

I don't have any plans or anything. I just, I just act on my own initiative. It's the way I feel that is the right way, like I have with everything else. Thank God I been pretty fortunate. I haven't made any bad, bad decisions…and everything. But, it's the way I was brought up you know. My surroundings, my mother and my father and the whole family. We're always considerate of other people's feelings.

[L.S.] Yeah, that Gladys was ah, she was a sweet, sweet woman. I got some great pictures of you two. I think I'll make a setup centerpiece.
Good.

[L.S.] She really was a sweet woman.
Yes she was.

[L.S.] Like, I can see it, you know.
I, ah…

[L.S.] Calm, and underplayed everything. But really sweet. I mean, underneath it all.
Funny, she never really wanted anything, you know, anything fancy. She just stayed the same, all the way through the whole thing. I wish…there's a lot of things happened since she passed away that I wish she could have been around to see. It would have made her very happy and very proud. But that's life and I can't…can't have her.

[L.S.] You know, about six years ago, Elvis, the girls loved you…of course the girls always love you…that'd be a big mistake, kids loved you, let's face it.

(Laughs.)

[L.S.] But the guys hated you. I'm sure they were jealous of you, people hate anybody who's getting ahead is about what it comes to. I was talking to the Colonel this morning and the image has changed, you know. The guys like you now. Of course, if they don't like you, they certainly don't dislike you. You know it's kinda like a thing Gable had going for him. All the dames loved him and all the guys liked him, you know. And this has been a change, 'cause the guys used to hate you. But now, now they like you. How do you think that came to be? Do you think it was the Army stint?
It contributed a lot to it, probably. It's pretty hard for me to analyze it because I don't know, really. But I would say the Army had a lot to do with it…and also the fact that there's never anything about my, being an egomaniac or thinking that I'm a lover or a ladies' man or something like that. Because it's amusing…it's a compliment to me but it's…it's amusing. I've never looked at, or thought of myself, as being a lady killer or anything like that. And I've never shown it, that I know of. I've never tried to…I guess the fellows, over a period of time…they figure, well (laughs) he's taken it all with a grain of salt.

[L.S.] Elvis, what do you think of yourself as?
I beg your pardon.

[L.S.] What do you think of yourself as?
You mean as an entertainer or an individual or an artist?

[L.S.] Both.
Well, I can sum it up fairly easily. I have a lot that I'd like to do, a lot that I'd like to accomplish in time, but I feel that it takes time to accomplish certain things. You can't overstep your bounds.

[L.S.] What would you like to do?
I'd like to improve in an awful lot of ways,

especially in the entertainment business. Well, for one thing, the acting thing. And naturally I try to try to get better songs and sing a little better. Things like that. But, what I look at myself as not being…not really playing everything down, but, as a human being, really, who's been very extremely fortunate in so many ways, although I have had and still have some very lonely…there are times when I really don't know (laughs)…it feels like…I don't know what I'm gonna do next. But I've experienced a lot of the different phases in life. I've experienced happiness and loneliness, and the wealthy side of life, the average side of life, not having anything…but not knowing what it's like to have anything, so. And tragedy.

[L.S.] In what sense?
Such as like like losing my mother while I was in the Army, and although I think that things like that—as tragic as they are—tend to make you a little better human being, really. 'Cause you…you learn more about yourself. It gives you a better understanding of yourself as well as other people. And it can only help. But I think that I like the business I'm in. I like to entertain people. The money or the financial end of it is not the greatest aspect as far as I'm concerned. It can't be, because if it was it would show. And I wouldn't care about the other people, I wouldn't care about a performance that I gave. I would, you know of course, I mean it's great if you can get in a position to have things. But I like to entertain people. That's why I pick all my records and try to pick the best songs possible. I try to do the best I can in the movies, with the experience that I've gotten, and everything. But I look at myself strictly as a human being who's, like I said, has been very lucky, but whose life…I have blood running through my veins…and can be snuffed out in just a matter of seconds, and not as anything supernatural or better than any other human being.

[L.S.] Do you like yourself?
Sometimes (laughs).

[L.S.] No, generally.
No, what I mean by liking myself, I'm proud of the way I was brought up to believe and to treat people, and to have respect for people. When I am pushed to a certain point, I have a very bad temper, an extremely bad temper. So much to the point I have no idea what I'm doing, you know.

[L.S.] Do you blow up often?
Not very often. Not very often. In fact, I could probably count the times. But when I have, it's always been pretty bad (laughs). But that doesn't happen very often. Of course everybody has a temper. And then I don't like myself later.

[L.S.] Looking back at it all, would you do anything differently? Like choice of clothes…or is there anything you'd change?
I wanted to go to college, I wanted to play football. I have a great ambition to play football. I have had, and I still have, believe it or not. And I've got a touch league, a touch football league back home. And I like rugged sports. I'm not knocking people who like golf and tennis and the other things, but I like rugged sports. I like some where you can take [it] as a man, such as boxing, football and karate, and things like that.

[L.S.] Do you have an outside interest, you know, other than dames, you know, which we all have, but I mean is there anything you like other than the movies?
I would say right now, really, all kidding aside, that my big…the thing I keep up with most is professional football. I know all the players. I know all their numbers, who they play for. I've had people quiz me on it, just in games when we got nothin' to do. And that's a big thing with me right now. I watch all the games that I can. I get the films from the teams themselves if I can. But next to the entertainment thing, and music, that, I guess, would be the biggest [interest].

With cousin Gene Smith, buckaroos at Mid-South Fair, Memphis, 1953.

[L.S.] What kind of life do you lead? Where do ya live up in Bel Air [California]? On Bellagio Road?

Yeah, I live on Bellagio Road.

[L.S.] What kind of a house do you have? Do you rent it?

I lease it by the year, yeah.

[L.S.] What kind of a house is it? Whose house was it?

I don't know who it belonged to.

[L.S.] Where is it, Elvis?

It's on Bellagio Road. It's near the Beverly…oh, let's see, what's the name of the hotel in Bel Air there?

[L.S.] The Bel Air Hotel.

Yeah, yeah, that's right, a little bit…the Bel Air Hotel.

[L.S.] What number? I know all those houses.

What's the number of the house Gene [Smith]?

[Gene Smith] 10539.

10539 Bellagio Road.

[L.S.] Is that the one Mrs. Owens used to rent?

Mrs. Owens still owns it. She's the one we lease from. It's the third…I think it's the third largest house there. It's a Spanish tile thing with the little balconies and so forth. It's a very, very nice house.

[L.S.] Good. Do you know…

I have to run right now. I'll talk to you a few minutes later on.

[L.S.] There's a very important thing that's been taken up in the United Nations right now.

Gene, what in the hell did you tell for? You know I'm gonna have everybody in the South on my ass.

[This last interviewer's question—itself an enigma—and the totally unrelated reply are obviously disjointed. However, this is as much as is preserved on the tape.]

[L.S.] What style of life do you lead? You got eight guys living with you in Bel Air…seven guys. How many guys are there now?

No, let me see, I've actually got a bookkeeper, a guy who…

[L.S.] Can we put the guy's name with it?

Just a second. Sure you can, why not. I have a bookkeeper. His name is Joe Esposito. He's from Chicago…Chicago [Illinois]. And I met him in the Army. He was a bookkeeper before. And then Gene [Smith], who takes care of the cars, the maintenance of the cars, you know, maintaining the cars. And another boy, Alan Fortas, is from Memphis, Tennessee. F-o-r-t-a-s, A-l-a-n, Alan Fortas. And another guy named Ray Sitton, S-i-t-t-o-n. I've actually only got five guys. And they take care, he and Billy, who's my little cousin. He's a little guy and he had quit school early. He had to quit school early to get a job, and he had a hard time finding a job because of his size, so I gave him a job, and he…

[L.S.] What's his name?

His name's Billy Smith. And he's one of my mother's relatives. He does little odd jobs. But each one of 'em has different jobs they do. They take care of the clothes and the packing and unpacking and business phone calls. They answer fan mail and things like that, and for the companionship of traveling. I couldn't travel alone. There's actually only five. And I have other people that come in from time to time and stay a little while, but they're not employees. They're just buddies or visitors.

[L.S.] A Dodge mobile, and a Rolls?
Yeah, it's a Dodge mobile homes trailer, like a trailer, that we travel in. That and a Chrysler station wagon. That's what we go back and forth across country in.

[L.S.] And you have a Rolls?
Yeah, I've got a Rolls. It stays here [California] though. I never take it anywhere.

[L.S.] Do you have a Volkswagen?
No, I don't have a Volkswagen.

[L.S.] Any others?
That's all I've got here, with the exception of that customized job, the white Cadillac limousine, a sixty model limousine that I had customized. Back home [Memphis] I've got a sixty-one Cadillac limousine and a nineteen fifty-six Lincoln Continental Mark II. And that's all, with the exception of the stuff they use there, like the truck that they haul groceries in.

[L.S.] Do you have a staff full time at Graceland?
I have three gate guards, you know, they pull eight-hour shifts, and two maids.

[L.S.] Are they [the maids] colored?
They're colored, yes. And my father takes care of all my personal…he's employed…I mean he's just like on a salary but he takes care of all the personal business, banking and any business transactions, he handles it all.

[L.S.] Are you with Spain and Fisher? Are they the accountants?
Spain and Fisher are the accountants, yeah. They have quite a job (laughs), you know.

[L.S.] Have you bought anything other than Graceland? I mean…

I bought some ten acres right across from Graceland not too long ago. There was a lady that we tried to buy it [from] one time before 'cause it's in a good spot. It's right near a shopping center. And we tried to buy it and the lady didn't want to sell it at the time. And then all of a sudden she needed money and so we bought that. But that's all right now.

    [The property referred to here is where the Lisa Marie Airplane exhibit and the Graceland Visitor's Parking Lot are now found.]

[L.S.] Do you have any time to read?
Oh I read quite a bit.

[L.S.] What do you read?
I don't read any…I'm gonna tell you what I do. I mean (laughs), very, very few people know it. But I keep up with modern medicine, medical science, medical discoveries, different diseases. Nobody knows that, and I've been doing it for a long, long time. I get doctor's handbooks, the PDR, which is the Physician's Desk Reference, and it's pretty interesting. At one time, when I got outta school, I thought I wanted to be a doctor, or something in the medical profession.

With cousin Billy Smith and Col. Parker on *Frankie & Johnny* set, 1965.

That's what I thought I wanted to be, but I didn't have money to go to college, but I got interested in it and it's pretty interesting. But I don't read any of the [best-selling] books much that other people read.

[L.S.] Have you read [the book title is not audible]?
Well, that I read, yes, and I read a lot of philosophy, and some poetry. Have you ever heard of a book called Leaves of Gold?

[L.S.] Who's it by?
It's by different people. It's different men's philosophy on life and death, and everything else. Well that type stuff interests me, to get these different people's opinions on different things.

[L.S.] You've probably dated a thousand girls. Easy. At least a hundred.
(Laughs.)

[L.S.] If you don't think it's too personal, you'll be twenty-eight in January, six years older than your daddy was when he got married.
Well, I can only answer you by saying I'd like to get married. I'd like to have a family. It's true, it's definitely true. Well, it's a normal thing to do, I mean who wants to grow old and be alone, you know what I mean?

[L.S.] Right, you are never going to be alone…come on now.
Well that may be true. I can't say that it's not. But it's pretty lonely when you, ah…

[L.S.] You're never lonely, you know that. You got 'bout seven thousand dames up there. But, ah…
Yeah, but still, they can't live with you all the time, and there are times when you have to be alone in a room and you need somebody with you. But, I mean, I'm in no big hurry. I have to…

[L.S.] You have Gene [Smith].
I have Gene? Thanks! (Laughs.)

[L.S.] (Laughs.) You got cross-eyed there.
But I'd like to someday, but I mean I'm in no big, big rush. I can't be, I have to take it easy and know for sure, you know what I mean?

[L.S.] If you had it to do all over again, would you do anything differently?
No, I don't think so.

[L.S.] What do you think [about] dating many girls?
Well, naturally you like to date. Of course, I used to date a lot more than I do now. I think the older you get, the more you look for other things other than just dating a different girl every night. You'd like a little more companionship instead of dating a different girl every night.

[L.S.] Is it a handicap, dating girls in show business?
Not necessarily, no. Ah, of course I don't make it a point to date girls in show business. It's just according to the girl herself.

[L.S.] Do those in show business stay in contact locally when they really have ulterior motives?
Well, it's a pretty tough…I mean, I can answer you…there's some of 'em that are. They have motives, you know, and some of 'em, they just wanna date for the fun of it…for the fun of dating. But as far as what you said earlier about being a handicap for one girl, still I think it would be better to find that (laughs), to find that one girl sometime. It's a thing that you can't rush. It's a thing that a lot of people think if they're not married by a certain age that they are losing out. I don't think so, myself. Of course I'm not talking about everybody, because everybody's life maybe is a little different.

But, for me, I couldn't have rushed into a marriage and I still can't. I have to be completely sure. I have to be able to trust them completely. I have to. I look for a lot of things now that I used to wouldn't have looked for. I used

On the set of *Fun in Acapulco*, Hollywood, 1963.

to...well just certain characteristics, a sense of humor, their taste for different things, just a lot of things, their understanding of me and my way of thinking. It takes a while. I mean it takes a while to find someone or to get to trust somebody like that.

[L.S.] What kind of men do you like?
I've never really thought about it.

[L.S.] That's why it's a good question. You have to think.
There are men who they don't in so many words, they're not phony. There are men who knock you behind your back and then they they're your buddy to your face, you know what I mean? I like a man who's pretty much the

same all the time, is pretty straight. He's himself to a certain extent.

[L.S.] You can never tell with many actors in this business I have found that failed to surround themselves with intellectual equals or intellectual superiors, so that there's nobody from whom they can learn, actually. They have guys on the payroll and so forth. And I wonder if this isn't true of you.
I don't think so because I've thought of this question before, and I've thought of this situation before and I have my own way of learning, just as I always have, and I learn in my own way. I don't use these fellows to learn anything from. They're all different, they got their own

little kicks going (laughs), they got their own lives to lead. But they're not dummies, by no means. And I don't have them around because they're idiots. They're pretty smart boys, and they've learned a lot just being around this industry, and around traveling. But now you can surround yourself with intellectuals or people of your so-called equal, and you can have dissension. You can be jealous of…there can be a jealousy there, and that's bad. The only thing you can learn there is to become bitter, and envy and everything else. I have my own way of learning, and I learn from people. I learn from the people I work with. I learn from everyday life itself, being connected with a lot of different people.

Now my private and personal life, I'm not tryin' to impress anybody by having a group of intellectuals around. It's not that I'm knocking [those] people. But now, you can be fooled by having a group of people around you think you're learning something from and you're not learning a damn thing. You're not benefiting anything from it. That's it. I don't think I'm makin' a mistake in that way. I have had this said to me before, "don't make the mistake." I had a girl say to me one night, "Don't make the mistake, Elvis, of surrounding yourself with people you can't learn something from." And the girl never caught it, but I got up and walked away from her. I smiled and walked away. I never said a word. But in so many words I was saying I can't learn a thing from you (laughs). So you know, you can't fool yourself.

I have my own ways of learning things. I have my own way of thinking, and nobody else, regardless of their intelligence or their belief can change me or make me think a certain way if I don't feel that it's right. There's not an intellectual son-of-a-gun walkin' the face of this earth that could make me believe a certain thing or something unless I really thought it. So I don't try to surround myself with a group of intellec-

tuals. It's more important to try to surround yourself with people who can give you a little happiness, because you only pass through this life once, Jack. You don't come back for an encore. And I learn. Little by little I gain experience, and I've had a pretty good lesson in human nature, you know.

[L.S.] What would you say, Elvis, is kind of a basic lesson you've learned from living so far?
I'll tell you, what I've learned might not apply to other people who are not in the same [business], who are not living the way of life that I am. So it'd be pretty hard to say.

[L.S.] I mean, what have you learned yourself that's capable of…
Because of my age now and the things that I've been through, the people and situations that I've been exposed to, I've learned a lot about about people, about life, about situations. It's been very…it's been very beneficial to me in that I've been able to help a few other people. And I have seen people in so many different situations. Such as—to give you an example—a woman going through the change of life thinks she's the only one who's going through the change of life…or ever has (laughs).

[L.S.] Uh-huh.
And it comes to work on her mentally, that she thinks that she's the only one…there's never been anybody else.

[L.S.] Suppose you were a fly…
And if you've seen other people and you know it's a normal phase of life that everybody goes through. Like a lot of girls between the ages of eighteen, twenty-two, twenty-three, twenty-four, a lot of them, if they're not married by then, it seems as though some of 'em go through a stage of uncertainty. They're searching for something and they don't really know what it is. Because a girl has reached a lot of maturity at that age, more so than a man. And they're

searching for something, and a lot of 'em are miserable, they're lonely and they're depressed a lot and they try different things. They go to other cities and that don't work out, then they want to go home, and then this and that. And if you realize that it's only a phase of life that you go through.

[L.S.] Do you have goals? Do you like what you're doing?

I wouldn't like to say in the same vein that…I mean, I wouldn't like to be at a standstill. I'd like to progress. I'd like to do a lot of things but I realize that it takes time. You can't bite off more than you can chew in this racket. You can't… you can't go out of your capabilities…your limitations. You have to know your capabilities.

[L.S.] What do you think yours are?

Like I have people to say to me all the time, "Why don't you do an artistic picture, why don't you do this picture and that picture, why don't you do something…?" Well that's fine. I would like to. I'd like to do something someday where I feel that I've really done a good job, you know, as an actor in a certain type role. But, I feel that it comes with time and a little living and a few years behind you. I think that, really. And I think that it will come eventually. That's my goal. You have to have something. But, in the meantime, if I can entertain people with the things I'm doing, well I'd be a fool to tamper with it, to try to change it. I can't…it's ridiculous to take it on your own and say "Well, I'm gonna some…I'm gonna change. I'm gonna apply…I'm gonna try to appeal to a different type audience, I'm gonna…" because you might not…you might not. And if you goof a few times, you don't get many more chances in this business. That's the sad part about it. So, you're better off if what you're doing is doing okay, you're better off stickin' with it until time itself changes things. I mean that's the way I believe.

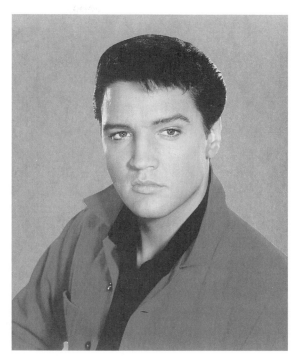

Studio portrait, 1963.

[L.S.] Do you like to work?

Yeah, I like to work. But I like to have a little time off too, where I don't have to do anything, which I've had very little of since I been out of the Army. But these are obligations and things I had to do.

[L.S.] Well, it seems you take good care of yourself, eating better, and your weight. What are you, one seventy now?

One seventy-four.

[L.S.] Do you watch your food? Do you watch your diet?

Yeah, I…

[L.S.] How do you do it? Do you use health foods?

I eat health foods and just try to use a little willpower, you know, I don't stuff, you know. Because, in this business, especially in the movies, [extra] weight can be very bad for you. It can, you know.

[L.S.] Do you smoke cigars? Do you smoke much?

Oh yeah, but I don't inhale. I don't even know how to inhale. It's just something to do with my *hands, really, it's kind of…instead of bitin' my fingernails. It's nervous energy. I mean, I'm not nervous in the way that I get scared or shook up, it's just that I've got a lot of nervous energy. I like to be doing something active.*

[L.S.] Do you drink much? How much sleep do you get?

I don't sleep. I guess I maybe get four hours a night, somethin' like that…if I'm lucky (laughs). And I don't drink at all, any alcohol.

[L.S.] That'll make you fat.

Oh yeah, that puts a belly on ya (laughs).

[L.S.] Look, if you had to entertain now, starting out, would you do anything differently?

If I had to entertain with what?

[L.S.] Well, I mean, you know, playing with the guitar, would you swivel those hips or would you do things differently?

I would do exactly what I feel or what I felt. I wouldn't make it a point to do something…do a certain thing. I've got to do just like I've always done, hence going by impulse and just what I feel on the spur of the moment. That's the only way I can op…that's the only way I can do…operate.

[L.S.] Do you think you've changed much?

As an entertainer or as a person?

[L.S.] As a person.

Well, naturally I was nineteen years old when I started out, so you get a little older, you learn a little more, you see things a little differently, and you see people a little differently, you know, usual things.

[L.S.] This is the last question, but a good one. If you were a father, and you had a son, which I have, and you had to give him one lesson: "Listen [son], I want to tell you something, just between you and I…"—just think for a minute, it might take a minute—what would you tell him? Just one thing.

If I had a son?

[L.S.] Yeah, you know, [something] that you've learned. What would you tell him?

Well, uh, not having a son and not having a child and not knowing what it's like, I don't know exactly, but I think my biggest thing would be consideration for other people, the thing I was talking [about earlier]…consideration for other people's feelings. Because anything that [you can do to] keep yourself from becoming hardened, therefore making you, I think, a better human being.

[L.S.] Thank you.

ITEM: *Typewritten generic thank-you letter from, and signed by, Elvis Presley (Memphis, Tennessee).*

SOURCE: *Original document.*

> *Dear Friends,*
>
> *This is a brief note of "Thanks" for your lovely cards and gifts I received for my birthday. I am always delighted to hear from you. Take care of yourselves and keep writing.*
>
> *Elvis Presley*

With Paul and Ann Anka on *Viva Las Vegas* set, 1963.

> *In regard to the sixteen millimeter print of "Fun in Acapulco," which was presented to me by Mr. [Hal] Wallis and Mr. [Harold] Hazen, as a personal gift, I hereby agree that the film will be for my personal use only at my home and I will not use it any way commercially or for profit.*
>
> *Elvis Presley*

ITEM: *Telegram from Elvis Presley and Col. Tom Parker (Madison, Tennessee) to Frank Sinatra (Lake Tahoe, Nevada).*

SOURCE: *Original document*

> *Dear Frank,*
>
> *Happy Father's Day. Enough said?*
>
> *Elvis and the Colonel*

ITEM: *Typewritten agreement letter from, and signed by, Elvis Presley (Hollywood, California).*

SOURCE: *Original document.*

> *[Elvis received a complimentary, boxed 16mm copy of each of his films, for which he was required to sign an agreement similar to this one.]*

With Ann-Margret on *Viva Las Vegas* set, 1963.

1964

ITEM: *Telegram from Elvis Presley and Col. Tom Parker (Madison, Tennessee) to John Lennon, George Harrison, Paul McCartney, Ringo Starr (The Beatles), in care of Ed Sullivan (New York, New York).*
SOURCE: *Original document.*

> *Congratulations on your appearance on the Ed Sullivan Show and your visit to America. We hope your engagement will be a successful one and your visit pleasant. Give our best to Mr. Sullivan.*
>
> *Sincerely,*
> *Elvis and the Colonel*

FEBRUARY 14, 1964

LOCATION: *Long Beach, California*
EVENT: *Presentation of the U.S.S.* Potomac *to Danny Thomas, to benefit St. Jude Hospital in Memphis.*
SOURCE: *Audiotape.*
I'd like to present you with a bill of sale…

[Col. Tom Parker] Take it, Danny.

Presenting the USS *Potomac* to Danny Thomas, 1964.

…to St. Jude Hospital. I'd like to tell you that we're more than happy to be able to do this, really. I'm glad that we're the ones that are able to do it.

[Danny Thomas] Well thank you, Elvis. I really can't understand why anybody wouldn't want this very beautiful and historical vessel. I wish I could afford to buy it myself for my own use and maintain it but, naturally, I'm not that financially fixed. But on behalf of St. Jude Hospital of Memphis, Tennessee, our hometown…
Our hometown!

[D.T.] You bet'cha…the children's research center there thanks you very much.
You're very welcome.

[D.T.] The diseases that are being fought there—leukemia, muscular dystrophy, sickle cell anemia, and all the horrible diseases killing our children. I mean the scientists that fight these diseases.
Well, I'm happy that we're the ones to be able to do it for you.

[D.T.] Well, now that St. Jude Hospital has taken over this vessel, we naturally plan to try to sell it or sell it as soon as is humanly possible because we're not interested in a commercial venture of any kind, or a sightseeing vessel. Although it certainly should be enshrined. I'm surprised that it hasn't been.
It certainly should.

[Media] Will we have another auction out here with people bidding like we had before?

> *[At auction, about two weeks earlier, Elvis won the U.S.S.* Potomac—*once President Franklin D. Roosevelt's personal yacht—with a winning bid of $55,000.]*

[D.T.] I don't know. We have several private buyers already interested. I don't think that we will go through the hassle of an auction, ah.
I don't think so either.

[D.T.] We will just discuss it with the interested parties and give it to…

If they do [auction it], we'll come buy it again.

[D.T.] Yeah, we'll come and buy it again.

[Media] Mr. Presley, what did you think when the March of Dimes said they weren't interested in it? What transpired there?

Well, I could understand their reason for it, really. I was a little surprised but I could understand their reason for it.

[Media] Were you ever afraid you might not be able to get rid of it?

Well that wasn't the case, because that was the reason for it was the March of Dimes.

[D.T.] No, frankly I happen to know, and I know Elvis is a little too modest to talk about it, but immediately after he purchased it, he could have sold it, at a personal profit to himself. But that isn't why he bought it. He bought it with charity in mind, and he was there and he felt that he could outbid the highest bidder, and he did…but his primary thinking and still his thinking was to turn it over to some worthy charity. His first thought was the March of Dimes, on a national basis. And they couldn't handle it. Well I can understand that too. Only volunteer (cough)…excuse me. Only volunteer organizations can handle a matter like this because, you see, volunteers work much harder than paid people, by far. And all of our people are volunteers and I know we have a half a dozen men who can handle this ship and handle it well.

Well, like I said, I can understand it.

[Media] Would you try to get more than fifty-five thousand dollars for the boat?

[D.T.] I wouldn't *try* to get any figure. I would try to get the best figure. Ah, we can use the money, we need it very badly. We still owe about six hundred and fifty thousand dollars on a six-million-dollar building, which isn't bad.

It's only two years old. And it takes a million three hundred thousand…it took that last year…to run St. Jude's. Next year it'll be a million and a half. And each year the cost of running it goes up and up and up. So we will do the best we can, get whatever we can.

[Media] Danny, what's your direct relationship with St. Jude?

[D.T.] I am the founder of St. Jude Children's Research Hospital, Memphis, Tennessee.

[Media] Is it primarily a children's hospital?

[D.T.] It is a children's research center.

[Media] Well, that's all diseases?

[D.T.] Ah, catastrophic diseases in children. At the present time there are thirteen different research projects going on.

I did a walk-on for you, didn't I?

[D.T.] Yes.

[Media] Any money derived from the sale eventually then will go toward more research, right?

[D.T.] More research, yes.

[Media] How did you first find out about St. Jude's Foundation and the ALSAC Foundation?

[Founded by Fred Gattas, ALSAC, the American Lebanese Syrian Associated Charities, is the fund-raising arm of St. Jude Children's Research Hospital.]

I did a walk on for Mr. Thomas in 1956, I believe it was.

[D.T.] Yes, at the Chicks ballpark.
Right.

[D.T.] At the Memphis Chicks baseball team ballpark.
And they built a hospital where my house used to be.

[D.T.] Yeah we did. We built a hospital right where his house used to be. His old, old house. *Like I said, we can understand about the March of Dimes, but we're just as happy to be able to give it to this organization.*

[Media] What happened to the Coast Guard Auxiliary?
I beg your pardon.

[Media] What happened to the Coast Guard Auxiliary?
Oh, I don't know (laughs). I really couldn't answer that.

[D.T.] I believe I think that was kind of an embarrassing situation. After all, the Coast Guard, you know, is United States government, and I think that somebody thought that it not in proper taste for the Coast Guard to take it and use as proceeds for some officer's club or something like that.

> *[After the unsuccessful attempt to give the U.S.S.* Potomac *to the March of Dimes, Elvis offered it to the Coast Guard—a proposition that the Coast Guard politely declined.]*

[Media] Wasn't there a story on the wire, Danny, relative to overruling by the wives of the Coast Guard Auxiliary? [That] was my impression.

[D.T.] I never heard that. I was not under the impression that the wives of the Coast Guard were running it. They might be. My wife runs me, I know that.

[Media] Will you make an effort to sell it as a shrine to President Roosevelt?

[D.T.] I will make an effort to sell it. I would prefer that the [boat] be enshrined or preserved as a shrine to F.D.R. How quickly we forget in this world. It's a strange thing, very, very strange that this vessel…
Very true.

[D.T.]…should be embroiled in any kind of

controversy or a ring around the rosie. They're playing ping-pong with ah, a momento of the history in the United States of America.

[Media] In this connection, whether the vessel really gets to be preserved as a shrine is then up to the next owner.

[D.T.] That is right. We certainly can't tell the next owner what to do with the vessel.
We might have trouble with that.

[D.T.] No, we won't, but I hope it…I hope they will preserve it as a shrine.

[Media] Mr. Presley, why did you not buy it and use it for yourself?
Well sir, I didn't buy it for myself. Like I said, the reason why we bought it was for the March of Dimes, and they couldn't accept it. I can understand that. I didn't buy it for myself.

[Media] Could you afford to keep it for yourself?
Could I afford to keep it for myself? Any answer I gave you would sound [awkward].

[Media] I wonder if we could just talk about another topic, one that's quite vague here. What about the Beatles?
The who? I knew this was gonna happen (laughs), I knew it!

[D.T.] What do we think about 'em?

[Media] Why sure.
Go ahead, Mr. Thomas.

[D.T.] I think it's absolutely wonderful that a new outfit comes along in show business to excite the imagination of those whose imagination needs exciting. I think they're fine… just fine.

[Media] How about you, Mr. Presley? Ah, Elvis?
Ah, well I've heard of 'em, about a year before. The first time I saw them was on the Ed Sullivan Show *[February 9, 1964] and the*

Colonel and I wished them the best of luck over here. Because if these young people can come over here and do well, regardless of what crowd they impress, well more power to them, really.

[D.T.] Well, many of us have gone to England and have…
Sure.

[D.T.]…taken a lot of their money. Why shouldn't the English come over here and take some of ours?
You bet.

[Media] As long as they don't take any of your fans.

[D.T.] They can't take our fans. There isn't any one of us, in any media of show business—any of the media—that's got *all* the fans. Nobody owns a hundred-and-eighty-some million people in this country.
That's true.

[D.T.] It takes a lot of us to please them all. We've all got our niche and we're all making a living and we're all very happy in our business and we don't mind newcomers coming along who excite the imagination. I think when one place does business it's good for the other place too, you know. Competition is great.

[Media] Thank you both very much.

[Media] Elvis?
Yes ma'am.

[Media] You're one of the few actors to not have a boat for your personal pleasure. So have you ever thought of buyin' a boat just to, you know, cruise around in when you're off to yourself?
Well in Memphis there's no…

[Media] How about the river?
Except the Mississippi River.

[D.T.] I think anybody…
I don't have that much time, really.

[D.T.] No, and besides any actor who made good since 1945 can't afford a yacht.

[Media] I know a lot of 'em got 'em.

[D.T.] You haven't heard about taxes, ma'am.

With actor
Nick Adams
and friend,
1956.

You're like my wife. She never heard of them either. She reads in the paper how much I make. That's how much she spends.

[Media] Elvis, ah…
About the Beatles (laughs).

[D.T.] They're no competition to you, Elvis.
Naw, well I…

[D.T.] Good gosh, you're a motion picture star.
I don't even think I am in competition.

[D.T.] Why certainly not. Certainly not.
Well that's been true about any young performer…anybody in show business. I mean, if somebody can come up and make it, well more power to them. Because I'm only glad of the success that I have had. And I couldn't be envious of some other young, or new, guy that's trying to make it too. Because as the old saying goes, I been down that road before.

[Media] Elvis, will you hand him the keys to the boat [posing for a picture]?

[D.T.] Are these the keys to the boat? With this key I thee wed.
Which bank do these fit? Which bank is your safety deposit box at?

[D.T.] Thank you very much, Elvis.
If I seem to be a little nervous, gentlemen, it's because I am (laughs).

[Media] Give him a kiss, Danny.

[D.T.] I don't know about this kissing stuff. That's a brotherly kiss, pal. There we are, there's the keys, there's the bill of sale.

[Media] Elvis, did you use the yacht at all?
I beg your pardon.

[Media] Did you use the yacht at all?
No sir, it took all the time to get it cleaned up. We worked all night last night to get it cleaned up for today.

[Media] Take us for a ride.

[D.T.] Nobody's gonna ride on it.

[Media] Danny, I want, ah…

[D.T.] Go ahead, Al.

[Al Wiman] I thought maybe Elvis might have heard some of the Dean Martin promos that are running on KFWB.
He [Danny Thomas] was tellin' me about this.

[D.T.] Yes, the teenagers march is conducted in the greater Los Angeles area by KFWB and Al Wiman of KFWB is our chairman and he's done a great job over there with [Jim] Hawthorne and Joe Drelling, all the fellows and all the deejays.

[A.W.] I was wondering if maybe you heard some of the promos during the December campaign we were having and that might have had something to do with your giving the yacht to ALSAC today.
No I wasn't here. It's been about three months since I been in town. But he was telling me downstairs about it.

[D.T.] We were talkin' about it, Al, he was out of town during the campaign, you know.
About how much help that they have been.

[D.T.] Took in sixty-three thousand dollars.
All kidding aside, I wish them the best of luck with it. And I hope they do very well. 'Cause I don't think like that. I been too lucky myself. I been too busy myself. I wish them the best of luck. I sincerely mean that, really. Them and anybody else in this business.

[A.W.] I wanted to ask you another question, a inside question about KFWB. I wanted to know if you were aware of the fact that we ran a special report on you called "The Elvis Presley Mystery." Did you hear anything about that?
I did.

[A.W.] Did you get any response or fan mail from it?

Yes I did (laughs). I didn't know exactly what it was. I tried to figure it out myself.

[A.W.] We did a special report. We had interviews with all kinds of people that knew you, and what we tried to do is give the public an idea of what Elvis Presley was really like. We had interviews with Nick Adams, and people that had worked with you in the past when you were on your way to the top. I just wondered if you had heard about it, and if you did whether or not you had any response from the fans that you have, to the program?

Well I got response at my home, and people were calling up and asking what it was and what is going on, and everything. And then I went back to Memphis and I got letters from people in L.A.

[A.W.] Do you think that it all came from the fact that we were running this special report called "The Elvis Presley Mystery"?

I'm pretty sure that it did (laughs). In fact, it was a mystery to me for a long time too. It still is.

Studio portrait, 1964.

APRIL 26, 1964

LOCATION: *New Musical Express Poll Concert, Wembley's Empire Pool, England.*
ITEM: *Specially recorded message from Elvis to his U.K. fans.*
SOURCE: Black Star *(LP).*

Well hello everybody, this is Elvis. I'm sorry I can't be with you all for the New Musical Express Poll Concert. But I'd like to congratulate all the winners, and I'd like to thank you for including me.

I'm especially proud of all my friends in Great Britain and I hope to be able to bring you the kind of songs and pictures that you like.

So again, thanks from the bottom of my heart. I send my best wishes for your good health and happiness always.

It was very nice seeing Jimmy Saville while he was visiting over here.

I'd like to wish the Beatles much continued success, as well as the other great recording artists in England. Thank you.

OCTOBER 14, 1964

ITEM: *Telegram from Col. Tom Parker and Elvis Presley (Madison, Tennessee) to Sammy Davis Jr. (New York, New York).*
SOURCE: *Original document.*

Dear Sammy,
Sy Marsh will tell you about my aching back. On behalf of Mrs. [Marie] Parker, Elvis and myself, congratulations again on "Golden Boy." Can rent you Elvis' gold suit—all the money in advance. Sy Marsh and Potentate Lastfogel [of William Morris Agency] will be there.

Regards,
The Colonel

LOCATION: *Honolulu, Hawaii.*
INTERVIEWERS: *Peter Noone of Herman's Hermits, deejay Tom Moffet.*
SOURCE: Cadillac Elvis *(LP).*

[Tom Moffet] On the set of Elvis' latest motion picture, being filmed in Hawaii. Elvis, come over here. I'd like you to meet a young man who's an admirer of yours, and has been for many years. Elvis Presley, this is Peter Noone.
Hi Peter.

[Peter Noone] How'dya do?
It's a pleasure.

[P.N.] Nice to meet you.

[T.M.] I thought for a change—we've talked to Elvis many times and also talked to Peter on this recent trip—maybe you'd like to ask each other some questions.

[P.N.] Yeah, when are you coming to England?
Ah, coming to where? Ah, excuse me. Coming to England... I don't know. Maybe in a year or so.

[P.N.] Great! Everyone keeps saying, you know, "Well, when's Elvis coming over to England?" It's headlines in the newspaper

With Peter Noone, of Herman's Hermits, Honolulu, 1965.

every week, when you coming, but you never seem to come.
Yeah, well Colonel Parker has a bad back, and so forth.

[Col. Tom Parker] Yes sir! Yes sir!
And (laughs), and as soon as he starts feeling better, we'll probably come over.

[P.N.] Good. Someone else ask a question now.

[T.M.] Anything you'd like to know about Elvis that you don't know already?

[P.N.] How come you made it without long hair?

(Everyone laughing.)

[T.M.] Herman's asking, Elvis, how come you made it without long hair. It used to be quite a bit longer, didn't it?
Flashback. Nah, the sideburns did it, I think.

[P.N.] Pardon.
The sideburns did it.

[P.N.] Oh I see, sideburns.
Yeah. You remember those, don't ya?

[P.N.] (Everyone laughing.) Yeah, everyone's laughing now, they are.
We just can't help it, we're all crazy.

[P.N.] The sun, is it?
We sit here in the sun, I guess it gets to your head (laughs). Your head, your hair. Tom, that's probably the best interview you've ever had.

[P.N.] Thanks a lot.

[T.M.] Pretty casual. I'll let you guys do the work.

[P.N.] This guy, in the hot sun. You work in the hot sun all day?
How'd your show go, Peter?

[P.N.] Who's your favorite group, after the Beatles?
Well, after the Beatles I would have to say

(laughs) Boston Pops, okay. (Laughing.) Okay, and then the Boston Symphony. (Laughing.) No, nah, I would say your group, Rolling Stones.

[P.N.] Awwwww.
You should know that I studied, obviously. Your group, the Rolling Stones. Your group before the Rolling Stones, right? Then, uh…

[Marty Lacker] L.A. Police Department?
Nah, no, no Marty.

[T.P.] Yes sir! Yes sir!

(Everyone laughing.)

[P.N.] What is filming like? Do you have to get up at six o'clock?
Yeah about five-thirty.

[P.N.] You start at six?
Yeah.

[P.N.] Nice weather anyway. What happens when it rains?
Six, seven, eight. Huh?

[P.N.] What happens every time it rains here?
We have to stop and come inside. Every time a little rain cloud comes over, we [cut!]. That's why we do a [cut!]. No, we stop and come inside.

[P.N.] Go on.

[M.L.] We let our brains cool off.

Yeah, when it rains, we let our brains cool off awhile.
How'd your show go over here?

[P.N.] Pardon.
How did the show go here?

[P.N.] I'm sorry, I can't understand everything. It went fabulous, the show went. You know, some of the language I can't pick up. Can you understand me?
Yes, very well.

[Marty Lacker] Yes sir!

(Everyone laughing.)

[T.P.] Yes sir. I gave 'em all the gifts, Elvis.

[P.N.] Oh yeah, thanks for all them doofers.
Oh, you're very welcome…all those what?

[P.N.] Doofers.
Doofers?

[P.N.] Things, you know. Doofers, things.
Okay. I'd like to wish you the best of luck.

[P.N.] Thank you very much. All the best.
Thank you. All the best to you.

[P.N.] Thank you.

SEPTEMBER 14, 1965

ITEM: *Telegram from Elvis Presley and Col. Tom Parker (Madison, Tennessee) to Ringo Starr, in care of Brian Epstein (London, England).*
SOURCE: *Original document.*

> *Dear Ringo,*
> *Congratulations to you and the Mrs. on the new member of your family [son, Zachary]. If Col. Epstein is not interested in signing this new artist, ship tape with voice track.*
> *Regards,*
> *Elvis and the Colonel*

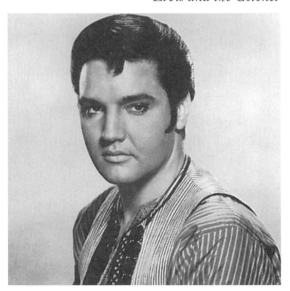

In costume, on the set of *Harum Scarum*, 1965.

APRIL 20, 1966

ITEM: *Typewritten agreement letter from, and signed by, Elvis Presley (Hollywood, California) to United Artists Corporation and Admiral Pictures Inc. (Hollywood, California).*
SOURCE: *Original document.*

[Elvis received a complimentary, boxed 16mm copy of each of his films, for which he was required to sign an agreement similar to this one.]

Re: "Frankie and Johnny"
Gentlemen,
This will acknowledge my receipt this date, from United Artists Corporation of one sixteen millimeter color print of the motion picture "Frankie and Johnny," for which I rendered my services as an actor. In consideration of your furnishing me with this print, I agree that said print will be used by me only for my personal library purposes, will not be exhibited outside my home at any time unless I am personally present at such exhibition, and that the print will not be exhibited at any time whatsoever for any public exhibition or at any exhibition for which an admission charge is made.

Very truly yours,
Elvis Presley

JUNE 15, 1966

ITEM: *Typewritten letter from, and signed by, Elvis Presley (Memphis, Tennessee) to Felton Jarvis (Nashville, Tennessee).*
SOURCE: *Original document.*

[The following note is in reference to Elvis' May 1966 Nashville sessions.]

Dear Felton,
Please convey how much I deeply appreciate the cooperation and consideration shown to me and my associates during my last two trips to Nashville.
I would like to thank you, the engineers, musicians, singers and everyone connected with the sessions.
Please see that every one of them know my feelings. And as General McCarther (sic) once said, "I Shall Return."

SEPTEMBER 21, 1966

ITEM: *Typewritten letter from, and signed by, Elvis Presley (Memphis, Tennessee) to Sheila Leyden (Merton Park, England)*
SOURCE: *Original document.*

[Letter is dated September 21, envelope is postmarked September 22.]

Dear Sheila,
This is just a short note thanking you for the nice gift which you sent me. I certainly do appreciate your thoughtfulness in remembering me and I always enjoy hearing from each of my fans.
Best wishes to you and yours

Sincerely,
Elvis Presley

1966

ITEM: *Telegram from Elvis Presley and Col. Tom Parker (Madison, Tennessee) to Roy Orbison (Culver City, California).*
SOURCE: *Original document.*

[Exact date not known.]

Dear Roy,
Congratulations on the start of your picture [The Fastest Guitar Alive], with our good friend, [producer] Sam Katzman.
Your pals,
Elvis and the Colonel

MARCH 24, 1967

ITEM: *Typewritten postcard, signed by Elvis (Memphis, Tennessee), to Jerry Jay [Osborne], KYOS Radio (Merced, California).*
SOURCE: *Original document.*

["Jerry Jay" was, at that time, a radio air name for author Jerry Osborne.]

Dear Jerry:
Thank you for the tape and for doing the special show on my birthday. I really appreciate it. I am also glad you feature some sacred music on your show, since its [sic] always meant a lot to me.
Best wishes always and may God bless you and yours this Easter.

Elvis Presley

MARCH 24, 1967

ITEM: *Typewritten postcard from Elvis (Memphis, Tennessee) to Jerry Jay [Osborne], KYOS Radio (Merced, California).*
SOURCE: *Original document.*

["Jerry Jay" was, at that time, a radio air name for author Jerry Osborne. Aside from the message,

this card differs from one above in that it is not personally addressed. Both were sent the same day.]

May your hearts and homes be filled with Peace and Happiness on this very special day, and may each day that follows be filled with God's blessings.

Elvis

> <u>This Space For Message</u>
>
> *May your hearts and homes be filled with Peace and Happiness on this very special day, and may each day that follows be filled with God's blessings.*
>
> *Happy Easter to you and yours*
> *Elvis*

1
9
6
7

> <u>This Space For Message</u>
>
> Dear Jerry:
>
> Thank you for the tape and for doing the special show on my birthday. I really do appreciate it. I am also glad you feature some sacred music on your show, since its always meant a lot to me.
>
> Best wishes always and may God bless you and yours this Easter.

MEMPHIS
MAR 24 '67
TENN

U.S. POSTAGE
.04

Jerry Jay
KYOS Radio
Merced, Calif.

Postcards from Elvis in Memphis.

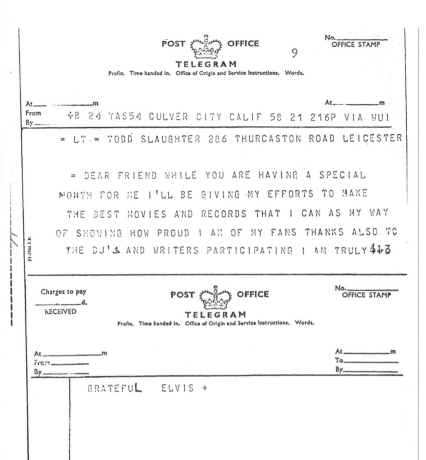

POST OFFICE TELEGRAM

9

Prefix. Time handed in. Office of Origin and Service Instructions. Words.

At_____m
From
By_____

VB 24 TAS54 CULVER CITY CALIF 58 21 216P VIA WUI

= LT = TODD SLAUGHTER 286 THURCASTON ROAD LEICESTER

= DEAR FRIEND WHILE YOU ARE HAVING A SPECIAL
MONTH FOR ME I'LL BE GIVING MY EFFORTS TO MAKE
THE BEST MOVIES AND RECORDS THAT I CAN AS MY WAY
OF SHOWING HOW PROUD I AM OF MY FANS THANKS ALSO TO
THE DJ'S AND WRITERS PARTICIPATING I AM TRULY

Charges to pay
_____d.
RECEIVED

POST OFFICE TELEGRAM

Prefix. Time handed in. Office of Origin and Service Instructions. Words.

GRATEFUL ELVIS +

+ COL 286 DJ'J + + ☆   BM 501

IQUIRY" or call, with this form
form, and, if possible, the envelope.

Above and opposite: Telegrams to British fan clubs, 1967 and 1968.

With Lee Majors on *Clambake* set, 1967.

ITEM: *Telegram from Elvis Presley (Culver City, California) to Todd Slaughter (Leicester, England).*
SOURCE: *Document photocopy.*
[*Exact date not known.*]

Dear Friend,
While you are having a special month for me I'll be giving my efforts to make the best movies and records that I can, as my way of showing how proud I am of my fans. Thanks also to the D.J.s and writers participating. I am truly grateful.
Elvis

JUNE 4, 1967

ITEM: *Telegram from Elvis Presley (Memphis, Tennessee) to Col. Tom Parker (Palm Springs, California).*
SOURCE: *Original document.*
Dear Colonel,
Congratulations to you on your twenty-fifth anniversary with RCA. Wish I could be there to join in the celebration. It's been a happy association for me too, with you and with RCA. Look forward to the many more wonderful years ahead. Please give my best to Mrs. [Marie] Parker and all there.
Sincerely,
Elvis

DECEMBER 3, 1967

ITEM: *Prerecorded Christmas program.*
SOURCE: *"Special Christmas Programming" (Reel-to-Reel Tape).*
[*A self-contained thirty-minute radio program containing ten songs and this four-second spoken greeting by Elvis.*]

Thank you for listening. I'd like to wish you a Merry Christmas and a wonderful New Year.

JANUARY 8, 1968

ITEM: *Cabled telegram from Elvis Presley (Nashville, Tennessee) to Albert Hand (Derbyshire, England).*
SOURCE: *Document photocopy.*

> *Dear Friends,*
>
> *It is an especially warming thought to know you are gathered today to celebrate my birthday. It makes this day very meaningful for me. I only hope you can have the same wonderful feeling that you have given to me and I send my thanks and sincerest wishes for the happiness and well being of each and every one of you.*
>
> *Elvis Presley*

JANUARY 17, 1968

LOCATION: *Unknown, though Elvis spent most of December and January in Memphis.*
EVENT: *Press Conference. Questions by one or more media representatives.*
SOURCE: *Document transcription.*

> *[Exact date not known.]*

Elvis, what is your reason for doing a TV show?
We figured it was about time. Besides, I thought I'd better do it before I get too old.

[Col. Tom Parker] We also got a very good deal.

Are you acting as well as singing in this special?
I'm going to sing almost exclusively in it, and I'm going to sing the songs I'm known for.

[Col. Tom Parker] If he sang the songs he's known for, that would take a couple of hours.

Elvis, do you think your audience has changed?
Well, they don't move as fast as they used to.

Why did you decide to make it a TV special?

[Col. Tom Parker] As you know, we have another mouth to feed next month [Lisa Marie due] and we need the extra income.

JUNE 27, 1968

EVENT: *Random comments made during the filming of the 6 P.M. "Arena" segment for the NBC-TV special ("Elvis").*
LOCATION: *NBC-TV Studios, Burbank, California.*

```
BM062 CT NHA228 NASHVILLE TENN 71 8 1033A


ALBERT HAND

41 DERBY ROAD HEANORDERBYSHIRE


DEAR FRIENDS IT IS AN ESPECIALLY WARMING THOUGHT TO KNOW YOU

ARE GATHERED TODAY TO CELEBRATE MY BIRTHDAY IT MAKES THIS DAY

VERY MEANTINGFUL FOR ME I ONLY HOPE YOU CAN HAVE THE SAME WONDERFUL

FEELING THAT YOU HAVE GIVEN TO ME AND

I SEND MY THANKS AND SINCEREST WISHES FOR THE HAPPINESS AND

WELL BEING OF EACH AND EVERY ONE OF YOU

    ELVIS PRESLEY


(41)
```

WESTERN UNION CABLES *via* CABLE

With Steve Binder and Bob Finkel, announcing the 1968 TV special.

SOURCE: *Videotape.*

[Two shows—at 6 P.M. and 8 P.M.—took place on this date. The song selection is the same and the patter nearly identical. The most noticeable difference is the camera angles. For the early show, Presley is shown mostly close-up. In the late show, the camera pulls back, permitting more scenes of the whole group. Elvis is accompanied on these shows by Scotty Moore, D. J. Fontana, Charlie Hodge, Alan Fortas, and Lance LeGault.]

[Entering stage] Okay. Well, goodnight!

[D. J. Fontana] It's been a long show.

[Charlie Hodge] It's been a long show.

Let's see, what do I do now, folks? First of all, we'd like to thank you for coming out here tonight, to the show. This is supposed to be like an informal section of the show where we…faint, or do whatever we're wanna do.

[C.H.] We're gonna have to call a plumber.

We don't have our…we don't have our full band here tonight, but we'd like to…we'd like to give you an…give you an idea of how I started out about fourteen years ago, and the sound that we had back then. And the guy over here on my left is the guy that played guitar for me when I first

started out in nineteen-twelve…er, nine-teen…nineteen, when did I start out, man?

[D.F.] It's been a long time.

Fifty-six. Nineteen fifty-six.

[C.H.] I was just a little bitty kid.

You're still just a little bitty kid. This is Scotty Moore, my guitar player. And this is my drummer, he's from Shreveport, Louisiana. I met him about ten years ago, D. J. Fontana.

[D.F.] What do we do now?

We just sit here, that's it, man.

The first thing that we recorded, the very first thing was an old rhythm and blues type song…and if I fall asleep here just…is an old rhythm and blues type song called "That's All Right Little Mama." And we only had two or three instruments at the time. We had a guitar [Scotty Moore], and bass [Bill Black], and another guitar [Elvis]. And it went like this.

Are we on television?

[C.H.] No, we're on a train bound for Tulsa [Oklahoma].

Give me that piece of paper, man. Let me see what I'm supposed to do next here.

[C.H.] No fair lookin' at the script.

It says here, "Elvis will talk about first record."

[D.F.] We're late.

A little late, all right. "And how things started happening after that."

[C.H.] Tell me, Elvis, what did happen after that?

Wait a minute. "Elvis will talk about shooting from the waist down, and not being able to touch hands with body…er, body with hands." We just got this show off the air, boy I'll tell ya. "Talk about Chrithmas song." Christmas, yeah Christmas.

[C.H.] Chrithmas. That's Southern for Christmas.

Anyway. Yeah, that's Southern for Christmas. I'd like to talk a little bit about music…very little. There's been a big change in the music field in the last ten or twelve years. You like that, uh? And I think everything's improved. The sounds have improved. The musicians have improved. The engineers have certainly improved. I like a lot of the new groups, the Beatles, and the Beards, and the…whoever. But I really like a lot of the new music. But a lot of it is basically…our music is basically…rock and roll music is basically gospel or rhythm and blues, or it sprang from that, and its people have been adding to it, adding instruments to it, experimenting with it. But it all boils down to just…I don't know what I'm talkin' about. I'm just mumblin', man. They told me to talk, so I'm talking. So I told 'em, I said look, man, you can do anything you want to do. You can do anything you want to do, baby [sings "Blue Suede Shoes"].

There's something wrong with my lip, man. No, wait a minute, wait a minute. There's something wrong with my lip [curls lip].

Hey, you remember that, don't ya?

I got news for you, baby, I did twenty-nine pictures like that.

[D.F.] Hey Elvis, the [little] finger.
That's all I could move in Florida.

[D.F.] Yeah, that's right.
The police filmed the show one time in Florida. Because the P.T.A., the Y.M.C.A., or somebody, they thought I was…something. They said, "Man, he's gotta be crazy." So the police came out and they filmed the show. So I couldn't move. I had to stand still. The only thing I could move was my little finger [wiggling finger], like that. "You ain't nothin' but a hound dog, cryin' all the time," for the whole show.

[Alan Fortas] How about the little old hound dog on stage?

We won't talk about that.

That's one thing about this TV special I'm doing. They're gonna let me do what I wanna do, which is just sit down, really. Not really. But…but…I'll think of something, just give me time.

[D.F.] How about San Antonio?
You tell 'em about San Antonio. Man I don't know nothin'…

[C.H.] We never really had any trouble, like the time this girl got in the house and got on the intercom and said, "I'm in the house, where's Elvis?"
I told her…I said, "If you're lookin' for trouble, you came to the right place."

[Scotty Moore] Would you sing me that song? I got to hear it.

[C.H.] First time in twelve years he's said anything on stage, man.
Twelve years, man, he played guitar for me and he never said anything. The other night he leaned over and said, dead serious, he said, "Would you sing that 'Lawdy, Miss Clawdy' one time, man? First time in twelve years. I told him, 'No, forget it!'" [Sings "Lawdy, Miss Clawdy."]

[S.M.] I won't say anything for the next twelve years.
Man, you talk about somethin' hot, baby, this leather [suit] is tough.

JUNE 29, 1968

EVENT: *Random comments made during the filming of the "Guitar Man with Road" [8 P.M.] segment for the NBC-TV Special.*
LOCATION: *NBC Studios, Burbank, California.*
SOURCE: *Videotape.*

[Two shows—at 6 P.M. and 8 P.M.—took place on this date. Elvis is assisted by Lance LeGault.]

Do I have any sound? Steve [Binder], I don't have the guitar on "Trouble." You know what I'm talkin' about?

[Steve Binder] Yes sir. Elvis, what I would like to do is . . . at the very end is use the guitar. It's in the "Evil" segment, not the opening "Trouble" one. It starts out in a nightclub and ends up here. You have a guitar. You don't use one but you just have one on your shoulder, in other words.
Okay. Oh yeah.

[S.B.] Okay gang, remember what I said. Here we go. If you want, Elvis, you can pick it up [guitar]. You can just be down on the platform and when you finish the song and start to leave [arena] you can just pick it up.
I'll be where . . . what?

[S.B.] It'll be right on the floor, and just pick it up as you leave and walk down the road. Lance [LeGault] can hand it to you.
Alright.

[S.B.] Okay, are we ready?
No, but we'll try it.

[S.B.] Let's get it. Let's rock and roll.
[Speaking, not singing] Well I come a long way from the car wash, got to where I said I'd get, u-mmm, u-mmm [laughs]. I'd like to do that first show [6 P.M.] over again [applause].

[S.B.] Who's that strange man [stagehand] out there, Elvis?
He's gonna do the song with me. We'll both go strolling on up the road.
I don't know what I'm doing.
[Off mike] Should I be on the microphone here?

[S.B.] Yeah!
Oh! Dummy [me]! Wait a minute, I stripped my tape [holding jacket together]. Wait a minute. Okay, sock it to me.
Hold it! Hold it man. Hold it! I got my lip [curled]. You remember that don't ya? You know that . . . I did twenty-nine pictures like that. Okay. Ready when you are.

With Edward G. Robinson and French star Line Renaud at her Revue in Las Vegas, 1968.

[S.B.] Probably do twenty-nine more too.
I hope so. Okay.

Just a second. We better do another one, I got hung up with the guitar over here [put the guitar on backwards].

[S.B.] I love it!
How long am I gonna be standing here? Are we ready?

[S.B.] Just recuing right now.
'Cause otherwise I gotta go into a soft shoe, man, you know. [Dances and sings pieces of "Tip-toe Through the Tulips" and "MacArthur Park."]

My boy, my boy. They're gonna put me away some day. It's gettin' embarrassing standing out here, Steve, I gotta do something.

[Fan says] You're still king!
Thank you. You know, with no more time than I got in this part, it's hard to get really into it. No, but it really is. Fifteen minutes.

Thank you, goodnight. Thank you very much. Goodnight.

JUNE 1968

LOCATION: *NBC-TV Studios, Burbank, California.*
EVENT: *Rehearsal for NBC-TV special ("Elvis").*
INTERVIEWER: *Unknown.*
SOURCE: From Burbank to Vegas *(CD).*
> *[Mid-to-late June, though exact date is not known.]*

[Media] Are you gonna play that guitar? Are you gonna play that kind of guitar?
We might. It's better with a rhythm [acoustic guitar]. If you get another electric one you're gonna get mixed up a little bit.

[Media] Play the hell out of it.
You know that stuff you're doing, Chris, like on that saxophone, and bass trombone that Bob's

doing and everything. That's the kind of stuff...I wasn't thinkin' about it really (laughs)...that's the kind of stuff you add to it, man. It's just basic stuff.

JULY 21, 1968

ITEM: *Filmed greeting from Elvis Presley (Los Angeles, California) to fans gathered in Leicester, England.*
SOURCE: *Document transcription.*
> *My Dear Friends,*
> *Wish I could be there to share this day with you. Mr. Todd Slaughter and his fine staff deserve credit for making possible a day that is unforgettable for me, as I hope it will be for you.*
> *To all of you who have come from far and near, we hope this meeting brings you personal happiness and many newfound friendships.*
> *Our thanks to MGM for making available "Speedway" for this special showing. And I am also highly pleased to know that the Guide Dogs for the Blind Association will benefit from your meeting.*
> *I am truly honored by this tribute.*
>
> > *Sincerely,*
> > *Elvis*

DECEMBER 14, 1968

ITEM: *Typewritten postcard from "Elvis and the Colonel" (Nashville, Tennessee) to Jerry Jay [Osborne] (Modesto, California).*
SOURCE: *Original document.*
> *["Jerry Jay" was, at that time, a radio air name for author Jerry Osborne.]*
> *Jerry,*
> *Merry Christmas and a very Happy New Year to you and yours.*
> *Thanks for all the spins and support.*
> > *Elvis and the Colonel.*

JANUARY 8, 1969

ITEM: *Telegram from Elvis Presley (Memphis, Tennessee) to Albert Hand (Derbyshire, England).*
SOURCE: *Document photocopy.*

Albert, Phylis and Son,
Dear folks, allow me to express my deep and
sincere appreciation for your celebrating
my birthday in England.
Would appreciate if you would pass on the
gratitude to all the fans in England who
participate in this celebration.
Many many thanks. Anxiously looking
forward to the time when I can visit all of
you over there.

Sincerely,
Your friend, I beg to remain,
Elvis Presley

JANUARY 1969

EVENT: *Phone call from Arlene Cogan in Chicago, Illinois, to Elvis in Memphis.*
SOURCE: Make the World Go Away *(CD).*
[Exact date not known.]

Hello

[Arlene Cogan] Elvis?
Yeah.

[A.C.] How are you?
Hello, how are you?

[A.C.] Just fine.
Good.

[A.C.] I tried to get you for your birthday but I missed you.
Oh, you know it's kind of hectic around here.

[A.C.] How have you been?
Well, pretty good. How have you been?

[A.C.] Oh just fine.
Haven't seen you in a long time.

[A.C.] I know it. Oh, I haven't forgotten you. I never would.
You what?

[A.C.] I haven't forgotten you.
(Laughs.)

[A.C.] I hear you have a beautiful daughter.
Yeah.

[A.C.] I'd just love to see her sometime.
Yeah, well maybe you can. What are you doing?

[A.C.] Nothing. I'm back in Chicago right now.
Yeah.

Telegram to British fan club, 1969.

ALBERT HAND
41 DERBY RD HEANOR DERBYSHIRE

ALBERT PHYLIS AND SON DEAR FOLKS ALLOW ME TO EXPRESS MY DEEP
AND SINCERE APPRECIATION FOR YOUR CELEBRATING MY BIRTHDAY IN
ENGLAND WOULD APPRECIATE IF YOU WOULD PASS ON THE GRATITUDE
TO ALL THE FANS IN ENGLAND WHO PARTICIPATE IN THIS CELEBRATION
MANY MANY THANKS ANXIOUSLY LOOKING FORWARD TO THE TIME WHEN
I CAN VISIT ALL OF YOU OVER THERE SINCERELY YOUR FRIEND I
BEG TO REMAIN

ELVIS PRESLEY

[A.C.] And, well, I'm getting a divorce.
Are you really?

[A.C.] I'd hoped it wouldn't be that, but for three years I knew, you know, it was coming.
Yeah. Well, it happens some times.

[A.C.] But anyway I'm glad to hear you're doing real good.
Yeah, I'm doing okay.

[A.C.] Yeah, I know. Oh, by the way, Gene Drew wanted me to ask you a question before I forget. He wants to know if you're going on tour?
Yeah. Yes, I don't know exactly when yet but I am going.

[A.C.] Are you really?
Yeah.

[A.C.] Will you be coming up this way?
I don't know. I don't know exactly the places or the schedule yet, you know, but I do know I am going.

[A.C.] Oh. Well I'm glad to hear that.
Oh you are?

[A.C.] Yeah.
Well that's good. Maybe I'll see you.

[A.C.] Okay. And, do you ever see any of the gang?
Uh?

[A.C.] Do you ever see any of the old gang?
Yeah, I see some of 'em. They're still around. A lot of 'em are out in Hollywood.

[A.C.] Darlene is living out there.
Yeah.

[A.C.] Do you ever get to see her?
No. I don't think so. It's been quite a while, I think.

[A.C.] Yeah, I know it. How are all the boys? Are they okay?
Yeah.

Studio portrait, 1968.

[A.C.] All of 'em married?
Yeah.

[A.C.] Well, you know, I didn't realize how long it was until I called the first time and Joe [Esposito] had to stop and think who I was, you know.
(Laughs.)

[A.C.] That's when I realized how long it has been.
Yeah, it's been a while. The time has gone by pretty fast.

[A.C.] It has. It really has. Oh, did you get that package that I sent?
Huh?

[A.C.] Did you get the package I sent for Christmas?
Yeah, I sure did, honey. Thank you very much.

[A.C.] Okay. I really didn't know what to send, but I hoped you like it anyway.
Well then, maybe I'll see you sometime.

[A.C.] Okay Elvis. Take care. Say hello to Priscilla for me.
Nice talking to you. Thanks for calling.

[A.C.] Okay.
Bye-bye.

Elvis with Vernon Presley, meeting the press in Las Vegas, 1969.

APRIL/MAY 1969

LOCATION: *Unknown.*
EVENT: *Press conference. Questions by one or more media representatives.*
SOURCE: *Document transcription.*
   [Exact date not known.]

[Media] How did it feel to get back to performing live again?
It felt really great. I just can't describe it.

[Media] Why has it taken so long for you to perform live again?
During the last few years I've been tied up in movies, so I was too busy to do live shows.

[Media] How did it feel to appear on TV again?
It felt terrific. But it has been so long since I last appeared, I think it was the Frank Sinatra show way back in 1960, when I came out of the Army.

[Media] Were you a little nervous?
Very much so. In fact, I was more than that. I will go as far as to say I was petrified. You could tell that at the start of the show. As soon as I got hold of the mike, my hands were shaking.

[Media] If this show is a success, will you do more live shows?

Yes, I sure will. I know it's been such a long time—too long—and I feel a bit rusty. But I'll get better as I go on. I know that I've almost certainly got the feel back for live shows.

[Media] Will you do more TV?
I sure hope so.

[Media] What about other live shows, and touring?
Yes, I want to do more live shows, and I want to tour again very much.

[Media] How about a world tour?
Yes, I would like that. I would like to go and do a European tour and visit England. But I would like to tour the States again first, just to get my feel back.

[Media] Whose idea was it to do a TV special?
Well, that's a long story. We all had a say in it, but we all felt it was about time. We decided to do it before it was too late and I got too old.

[Media] Originally, wasn't the show going to be a Christmas special?
Yes it was. But after some serious thought we decided to change that. I'm so glad we did.

[Media] How do you judge your life now, being a married man and a father? Has it changed you at all?
Well I suppose it has, in a certain way, being married and having a child. I feel a kind of responsibility. I've got everything to work for. But, believe me, I wouldn't change anything for the world.

[Media] Do you want to do more movies in the future?
I would like to do more, but only if the script is good. I don't want to sing in them anymore. I'd still like to develop into a serious actor, while there is still time.

[Media] Your recent movie *Charro* was a good role for you. You did a good job acting in that.
Yes, I really enjoyed making Charro. *It was the*

best film I've done since Flaming Star. *The story was good and so was the cast. I would like to do more films like this in the future.*

[Media] Is it true that Clint Eastwood turned it down?

He did, but I'm glad. The role was just right for me. It was good to be in a film with no singing in it.

[Media] What about the song "If I Can Dream"? Is it a change of style for you?

I agree, it's a great song. Steve Binder and Bones Howe told Earl Brown to write a great song for the TV show, and he did just that. This is what he came up with. What a song! I don't think that it is a change of style for me. I try to do all types of songs. This was too good, I just couldn't turn it down.

[Media] What do you think of the song "MacArthur Park"?

I think it's a great song. If Richard Harris hadn't recorded it, and they had given it to me, I would have done it.

[Media] How does it feel to have been on stage again?

Frightening. Scary. But fabulous. I will do more live shows.

AUGUST 1, 1969

LOCATION: *International Hotel, Las Vegas.*
EVENT: *Press Conference. Questions by various media representatives.*
SOURCE: *Document transcription.*
   [*This 12:30 A.M. gathering followed Elvis' opening night show, July 31.*]

[Media] Did you enjoy performing live again?
Yes! This has been one of the most exciting nights of my life.

[Media] Did you feel nervous during the show?
For the first three songs or so, before I loosened up. Then I thought, "What the heck. Get with it, man, or you might be out of a job tomorrow."

[Media] Do you have a share in the [International] Hotel?
No, I have not.

[Media] Why did you choose a Negro backup group [Sweet Inspirations]?
They help me get a feeling and get to my soul.

[Media] Have you ever seen England's top singer, Cliff Richard?

Yes, I met him in Germany a long time ago.

[Media] Mr. Presley, I've been sent to the press conference to offer you one million pounds Sterling to make one appearance at the Wembley Empire Stadium in England, for two concerts.

[Pointing to Col. Parker.] You'll have to ask him about that.

[Col. Tom Parker] Just put down the deposit.

[Media] Why have you led such a secluded life?

It's not secluded. I'm just sneaky.

AUGUST 1, 1969

LOCATION: *International Hotel, Las Vegas.*
SOURCE: Opening Night 1969 *(CD).*

About Funky Angels

I'd like to welcome you to the big freaky International Hotel (laughs). I just wanna…you know these little freaky dolls on the wall they got, man. Little funky angels up here. A funky angel, boy.

On stage, explaining "desert throat," Las Vegas, 1969.

About First Appearance

I'd like to thank you for coming out. This is my first appearance, first live appearance in nine years. (Applause.) Thank you. Appeared dead a few times, but this is…but I really like it and I hope you do too.

About Vegas Throat

Could I have some wa-wa? That's Southern for water. Thank you. It's very dry here in Las Vegas, ladies and gentlemen, and a lot of singers have a problem—course I was never a singer so I don't have that problem. But lot of singers have trouble with what they call…somebody applauded in the back (laughs)…a lot of singers have a problem with what they call a Vegas throat. It's either too dry or you swallowed too many chips. I don't know what it is, but a lot of people have that problem, so you have to drink a lot of water during these shows to keep going. So if I stop, and everything, just watch me and look at my…little red things in my pants, the belt, and then talk about "is that him?" He's got his name on his guitar. I thought he was bigger than that, man. Hair flying everywhere, he's gotta be a weirdo, man, I'll tell you. Stone cold natural freak, man. That's why he ain't been in public nine years…they put me away, boy. Get him outta here. Oh, Lord have mercy.

About His Career

I'd like to tell you a little bit about how I started and when I started and all that stuff because a lot of it has been so inaccurate. A lot of people haven't really known what really happened.

I'd just gotten out of high school, and I was driving a truck…and I was…I was studying to be an electrician. And I got wired the wrong way, man, or somethin'. But, I was studying to be an electrician and one day I was driving my truck and I had a lunch break, and I went into a little record shop and I made a record for a guy, a little demonstration record. Well the guy put the record out in Memphis. Memphis…Memphis. That's my hometown. You gotta be loose when you say it. Where're you from, boy? Memphis. If I get any looser, I'll just fall apart.

Anyway, the guy put the record out and it became pretty big in Memphis, and all over the South…certain parts…but nobody ever really heard of me, so I was working for about a year and a half in nightclubs and football fields, barns, Louisiana Hayride, yes sir. They threw me off the Grand Ole Opry. I went to the Grand Ole Opry, man, they gave me six dollars and said: "Look, go home, man."

I went to the Arthur Godfrey Show, *auditioned for the* Arthur Godfrey Show. *He said: "Nah, nah, he's bad, vulgar, bad." So (laughs) I didn't get on there either. And then I met Colonel Sanders…ah, Parker. And so they arranged to put me on television…they put me on television, and then somewhere in 1956 or something. And I did four shows on the* Jackie Gleason Show. *I did three or four shows on the* Ed Sullivan Show. *I did the* Steve Allen Show. *And they had me dress in a tuxedo on the* Steve Allen Show, *and stand perfectly still. I couldn't move, I was standing like this and they had me singin' to a dog, man, there was a dog here. And I'm singing: "You ain't nothin' but a hound dog." And the dog's lookin' at me like: "What are you doin,' callin' me names or what?" And they photographed me from here up, and so forth, you know. It was pretty hairy back then.*

[As most students of Presley history know, Elvis made six appearances on Jackie Gleason's Stage Show, starring Tommy and Jimmy Dorsey, two on the Milton Berle Show, one on the Steve Allen Show and four on the Ed Sullivan Show.]

With Jeannie C. Riley, Las Vegas, 1969.

So anyway, I went into the Army in 1958. I got drafted and went in the Army for two years. I came out in 1960. Then I made some movies, G.I. Blues, Blue Hawaii, *and several pictures that did very well for me (applause). Thank you.*

But as the years went by, I really missed the people, the audience contact. I really was gettin' bugged. I was doing so many movies and I couldn't really do what I could do. They would say "Action!" and I'd go: "What? What? Uh? Memphis!" They'd say: "That ain't what you're supposed to say," and I'd say: "Uh?"

So anyway, it all kept going and I really wanted to come back and so this is…that's why I'm here tonight and I just wanted to give you a brief [history].

And I'll tell you what. If you think long hair and sideburns are freaky now, fourteen years ago, man, I couldn't walk down the street. Some guy would say: "Hey, are you Elvis Presley?" I'd say "Yeah." Pow! I'd go: Uh? Uh? Memphis!"

So anyway, you didn't know you were comin' to see a crazy man, did ya? Let's see, I got a list of two hundred and twenty-eight

With Nancy Sinatra on *Speedway* set, 1967.

songs on it, and I can only do two hundred, so I gotta drop the twenty-eight.

Unusual Introduction

Before anything else, I'd like to introduce the members of my band.

Charlie [Hodge], this is Jerry [Scheff].

Now that they know each other, we can go on with the show now.

About Hung Cord

Hey Charlie. I got my cord hung on your thing, man. Ya ever get your cord hung on your thing? That's bad, boy, bad.

AUGUST 6, 1969

LOCATION: *International Hotel, Las Vegas.*
SOURCE: *Audiotape. "Elvis in Days Gone By, Vol. 1" (EP)*

Home for the Silly

Thank you very much. Yeah, they're gonna put me in a home for the silly, man, I know it. A home for the silly.

It was really a problem when I started to put this show together, if I could talk to you

for a few minutes. It was really a problem deciding what songs to do. Because, over a period of years, I've done so many songs. It was hard to figure out which ones, so I try to do—I try to get my breath back is what I try to do.

I'd like to play this thing [guitar] a little bit. Contrary to a lot of beliefs, I can play a little bit...very little bit.

About His Career

I'd like to tell you a little bit about how I got in this business, and how I got started, and where, when, and so forth, because it's been written up so many times, but people don't even really know the true story.

And it happened when I just got out of high school, I just graduated high school and I was driving a truck.

[Fan shouts.] "Tupelo?"

No, not Tupelo. Memphis...Memphis! And, I was driving a truck and I was training to be an electrician. And I got wired the wrong way somewheres along the line. I went into a recording studio one day and I made a record for a guy, named Sam Phillips, he owned Sun Records. And he put the record out in about a week. And I went back to drivin' a truck and just forgot about it, man.

The record came out and it went over real big in Memphis. They started playing it and it got real big. It scared the devil out of me, you know. Ah-ha-aaaa! In fact, that's what I did on the record: Ah-ha-aaaa!

But they put the record out and it got pretty big in the South. And I still held my job. I was drivin' a truck in the daytime and I was workin' nightclubs at night...little barns and fairs...things like that.

And in 1956, I met Colonel Sanders...Parker. And they arranged to put...to have me go on television, so they put me on television, and all hell broke loose, boy, I'll tell you for sure.

I did the Ed Sullivan Show *four times, and I did the* Steve Allen Show, *I did the* Jackie Gleason Show. *I mean, they filmed me from here up. [They said] "You stand still...stand still!" then said "Where you from, boy?" Memphis...Memphis! [They said] "He's a dummy, put him in the back, you know." So, I went on television and...I gotta tell you, first I went to Arthur Godfrey's, his talent show. They turned me down. They said, "Man, get him outta here. Get him out."*

So I went to that other cat...what's his name? Ted Mack, yeah. Anyway, they turned me down and took Pat Boone. Which is alright. He did okay with the white shoes and stuff.

Then later on they sent me to Hollywood to make movies. It was all new to me. I was twenty-one, twenty-two years old. And they yelled, "Action" I didn't know what to do. I said, "Memphis!" They said, "That's all we can get out of him, you know."

**Just pickin',
1968.**

217

With Shelley Fabares on *Girl Happy* set, 1964.

So then in 1958…I made four movies…then in 1958 I got drafted. And I went into the Army and stayed a couple of years, and that was loads of fun. You know, they made a big deal outta cuttin' all my hair and all that jazz, you know. [They said] "Soldier!" "Memphis…Memphis!"

Then I came out of service and I went back and made a picture called G.I. Blues, which I thought I was still in the Army see, and then I did a few good pictures that did very well for me, like Blue Hawaii and stuff.

Anyway, it kinda got in a routine or a rut and I really wanted to come back and work live in front of people again. I've been wanting to for a few years now, so that's why [I'm here].

I hope I didn't bore you too much, but I just wanted you to know.

AUGUST 12, 1969

LOCATION: *International Hotel, Las Vegas.*
SOURCE: *Audiotape.*

An Unusual Audience

I missed the contact with an audience. I really wanted to come back and work in front of live reptiles again.

AUGUST 15, 1969

LOCATION: *International Hotel, Las Vegas.*
SOURCE: *Audiotape.*

Wacky Memories

In 1956, I met Colonel Sanders…Parker. And they arranged to get me a bunch o' chicken! At that particular time, you didn't see people moving too much on television. They were gettin' it on in the back room.

Fourteen years ago it was weird, walkin' down the street with long hair and sideburns. So I was shakin' and jumpin'. That's how I got into this business…shakin and jumpin'.

I went to Hollywood and made several pictures. I did Love Me Tender, Loving You, *loving her, and several other people I can't tell you about.*

The guys in the Army must get very homesick…'cause they all call each other "mother." I picked it up, but you know that was only half of it (laughter). It didn't go over so good when I got back to Hollywood. Director would say "Hello Mr. Presley," I'd say "Hello there, mother…"

After G.I. Blues *and* Blue Hawaii, *I wrote an eight-millimeter picture called* Up Your Nose, *but it's not out yet. It's about a homesick little squirrel, in the winter, trying to find his nuts.*

AUGUST 16, 1969

LOCATION: *International Hotel, Las Vegas.*
SOURCE: *Audiotape.*

Introducing Harry James

I'd like you to join me in saying hello to a man that I really admire. He's been in our business for quite a while. He's a legend in his own time. He plays one heck of a trumpet, and he's a heck of a nice fellow. Mr. Harry James, ladies and gentlemen.

LOCATION: *International Hotel, Las Vegas.*
SOURCE: Superstar Outtakes *(LP).*

Introducing Tutt and Scheff

The young man on drums, he's from Dallas…Big "D"…his name is Ronnie…Ronnie Tutt.

The guy that plays a whole lot of Fender bass, his name is Jerry Scheff.

So that's Tutt and that's Scheff. That's Tutt Scheff any way you look at it, boy, I'll tell you for sure. Sure got a lot of nerve, boy.

LOCATION: *International Hotel, Las Vegas.*
SOURCE: *Audiotape.*

From Hollywood to Las Vegas

There's been a lot written and a lot said about how I got into this business, but never from my side of the story. That's 'cause I couldn't talk.

I went to Hollywood. That's how it works, you get a record and you get on television, and they take you to Hollywood to make a picture. But I wasn't ready for that town and they weren't ready for me. I was only about nineteen or twenty, and I got all excited. So, I was out there…they were sayin' "Watch him, man, he's just…he's squirrely boy." So I did the picture, Love Me Tender, *and they yelled "Action," and I was lookin' up at the sky goin' "Huhhh…huhhh?" So (laughs) I did* Love Me Tender *and I did* Loving You, *loving her, loving whoever I could get my hands on at the time,* Jailhouse Rock *and* King Creole. *I did four pictures, so I got real good and used to the movie star bit. Man, you know, I'm sittin' in the back of a Cadillac with sunglasses on and my feet propped up sayin' "I'm a movie star…I'm a som'bitch… hey, hey!" You know, eatin' hamburgers and drinkin' Pepsies, and just, you know, totally nuts man (laughs). So I was livin' it up man.*

This Space For Message

Jerry,

Merry Christmas and a very Happy New Year to you and yours.

Thanks for all the spins and support.

Elvis and the Colonel

Jerry Jay
2722 Floyd
Modesto, Calif.
95350

Holiday greetings postcard, 1968.

But then I got drafted, shafted, and everything else. So overnight it was all gone. It was like it never happened, like a dream. I made four movies and it was all gone. All the guys in the service, at first they just watched me to see what I was gonna do. But it was okay. They didn't treat me any better or any worse than any of the other guys.

But I was in a rut in Hollywood…right in the middle of Hollywood Boulevard there's a big rut.

What we're doing here tonight is recording a live album, and there's a couple of new songs I have to try. So, if we make a mistake, we may go back and do it over again. We may be here all night.

AUGUST 28, 1969

LOCATION: *International Hotel, Las Vegas.*
SOURCE: *Audiotape.*

Introducing Lightnin' and Booger

The young man on lead guitar, he's one of the finest guitar players I've ever met, ladies and gentlemen. His name is Lightnin' Hopkins…James Burton.

The guy that hands me my water and stuff up here on stage, he's a good friend of mine, I met him when I was in the Army, his name is Willie Booger. Naw, Charlie Hodge.

Guest Introductions

There's some people in the audience I'd like to say hello to tonight, ladies and gentlemen.

First of all, the young lady that opens tomorrow night. I just did a picture with her. I don't know what to say about her. I mean I really dig her. She's really fantastic. She's gonna have a fantastic show here. I'd like you to say hello to Miss Nancy Sinatra.

The guy that's sittin' at her booth is one hell of a songwriter, ladies and gentlemen. He has written some beautiful stuff, and he wrote one of my biggest records. I'd like to say hello to Mac Davis. He wrote "In the Ghetto."

There's a guy in the audience that's a fantastic comedian. I don't know if he remembers it or not but when I was in the Army, he wrote me a letter in Germany one time. I was up in the snow, on the Russian border, man. And this guy wrote me a letter and said he was takin' care of my girlfriend in Chicago. He's really fantastic. I'd like to say hello to Buddy Hackett, ladies and gentlemen.

Another guy in the audience I'd like to introduce…the only thing I can tell you about this guy is he's one of the most fantastic performers I've ever seen, ladies and gentlemen, and he's also my good friend, Thomas Jones.

I'd like to introduce a young lady that I've done three pictures with. She's one of the most lovely creatures I've ever met. She's a good actress. I'd like you to say hello to Miss Shelley Fabares.

JANUARY 26, 1970

LOCATION: *International Hotel, Las Vegas.*
SOURCES: True Love Travels on a Gravel Road *and* Electrifying *(CDs).*

About New Album

I just did an album, ladies and gentlemen, called Elvis in Memphis…Elvis in Memphis…Elvis in Memphis…*plug! In that album is a song that I'd like to do for you right now [*"True Love Travels on a Gravel Road"*], but I've forgotten the words to it. Excuse me for a second while I get some water. Don't turn your back on the audience…don't turn your back on the audience…keep the cord between your legs. Cool it, silly!*

About "Sweet Caroline"

There was a record that came out this past year by a good friend of mine [Neil Diamond], that was recorded in Memphis, my hometown…Memphis! And it was one of the biggest songs of the past year. I'd like to do it for you after I get some water. Boy, it sure gets quiet in here when I do this. Just look at the belt, suit, whatever.

FEBRUARY 1, 1970

LOCATION: *International Hotel, Las Vegas.*
SOURCE: Walk a Mile in My Shoes *(CD).*

Image in Trouble

Thank you very much. If I'd get my hair outta my eyes, I could see you out there maybe. It's blown my image, but it's been blown before (laughter). Image! Image! Say image. Well that's it, boy.

FEBRUARY 23, 1970

LOCATION: *International Hotel, Las Vegas.*
SOURCES: True Love Travels on a Gravel Road *and* Electrifying *(CDs) and Audiotape.*

The Turtle's Big Chance

Good evening, ladies and gentlemen.

Welcome to the Flamingo. Same owner [as Hilton] so I can say that. Excuse me while I get a drink of straight vodka back here. I got a turtle back here, man. I tried to get him to perform in the first show and he wouldn't do it. Man, he had his big chance and he blew it. C'mon, c'mon, c'mon, move, move, move. He won't do nothing, he's like Charlie [Hodge]. C'mon, I'll give you a little guitar, you can play it. One thing I hate is a dead turtle, man, I'll tell you.

In the Beginning…

I'd like to do a couple songs that I recorded thirty-five or forty years ago, when I was a little baby. I had little tiny sideburns, and a little bitty tiny guitar, a little shaky leg. So they put me on TV, and Ed Sullivan said "ummm, som-bitch." So I said, "thank you, Ed, that's very nice."

Anyway, I did a ballad on the Ed Sullivan Show. *You gotta stand like this to sing this song. You can't stand up straight, man, or you'll strip your gears, boy. You really will. You gotta lean over like this.*

I really don't feel like doin' this song, you know that. You don't feel like doin' it either, do you [speaking to band]? It's one of those…a lot of times I wish I was the type performer, guys that say like [singing] "Everybody Loves Somebody." But I can't do that, see. 'Cause people come in here and they say "He can't move no more." So I have to get the bod movin' whether I like it or not.

Anyway, I did a very tender love song. You get up in a girl's face and you say… "You Ain't!" And her hair goes straight back like that. [Sings "Hound Dog."]

Then about the same time as I had "Hound Dog" out…let "Hound Dog" out. Sounds funny, man, have "Hound Dog" out. Anyway, about the same time I had blah, blip, blech. It's not working! My mouth, it stopped working,

Jerry [Scheff], I can't talk no more. It just happens like that sometimes. Had out a movie, and the title song of the movie went like this. [Sings "Love Me Tender."]

Kissing Priscilla [During "Love Me Tender"]

I recognize that girl! Oh, I forgot to tell you, I got the flu.

Comical Introductions

Before we do anything else, I'd like to introduce the members of my group, ladies and gentlemen. They're doing a fantastic job for me here for four weeks. I really mean it, they've done a fantastic job because we've done two shows a night for four weeks.

And first of all, the young ladies that opened our show tonight, I'd like you to say hello to the Sweet Inspirations…Girls.

The beautiful quartet voices you hear in the back belong to the Four Aces, ladies and gentlemen…the Four Aces…The Imperials.

My favorite guitar player, on lead guitar, say hello to Chuck Berry…James Burton.

Then on rhythm guitar, he makes records for RCA Victor, his name is John Wilkinson…John.

The young man that's doing a fantastic job keeping up with me on drums, his name is Bob Lanning…Bob.

The guy on the tympany drums back there, his name is Pa Kettle…Eddie Graham.

Young man on Fender bass, his name is Jerry Scheff…Jerry.

Young man on the piano, he also arranged some of the songs for me tonight, ladies and gentlemen, say hello to Steve Allen. Steve. Thank you, Steve.

The guy that sang harmony with me on "Don't Cry Daddy," his name is Kate Smith. Kate. Take a bow, Kate, don't just stand there.

Our orchestra conductor, ladies and gentlemen, say hello to Mr. Leonard Bernstein. Leonard. Oh yeah.

And the wonderful Elmer Bernstein Orchestra, ladies and gentlemen. Bobby Morris Orchestra. Thank you, ladies and gentlemen.

His Name Change?

[After "Blueberry Hill"] I used to be known as Fats Domino…until I lost weight.

About Mopping Up

Give me a mop and I'll start moving around…and sweep up at the same time.

FEBRUARY 27, 1970

LOCATION: *Houston, Texas.*
EVENT: *Press conference.*
SOURCE: Elvis (Speaks to You) *(LP).*

Elvis, how do you like Houston?
Nice. I like it, boy. Quite a lot of space.

What made you decide to come to Texas?
To tell you the truth, I started out here in Texas. I think the first shows that I worked was down here around Houston, and all over Texas.

Do you remember what locations you worked at in Texas?
I worked Houston, I worked Corpus Christi,

every little town here, Longview, man, you name it, I've been there. Really, I've been all over Texas.

What do you think of Texas?
I like it. I like it. Really enjoy it.

Elvis, can you give us—I understand with all the big engagements like Las Vegas, etc.—the reason why you selected the Livestock Show and Rodeo this year?
Well, they asked me to do it, and I was anxious to do some live appearances. I haven't…it'd been a long time since I'd been on stage in front of anybody live, and I was anxious to do some live appearances and I thought it would be a good opportunity to get in front of the people.

Have you ever seen the inside of the [Astro] Dome before?
Never have. It scares the (laughs)…it's a big place, man.

You've been known in the past as the King of Rock and Roll. Do you think your style has changed now from the days when you were king, or do you consider that still your style?
I think the overall thing has improved. The overall sound has improved, I mean. But I think…it's according to the songs. It's just according to the songs.

Did your stage presentation still [stay] the same way it was, or did you improve on that?
I just do whatever I feel…on stage. I always did that.

Are you gonna keep making films?
I hope to (laughs).

What kind?
Well I'd like to make better films.

What do you mean by better?
Well, better than the ones I made before. (Coughs.) Excuse me, I can't take this fresh air, man. I'm used to the garbage can at the

International Hotel, man (laughs). If I can't smell some garbage, I don't feel at home, man. I'll tell ya (laughs).

Do you have any films in the making right now, or any plans?
No, there's nothing in…as far as I know of…is there, Colonel? Anything in the workings?

[Col. Tom Parker] I can't commit myself.
An eight-millimeter Walt Disney special we're doing next year, I think. I don't know.

[T.P.] We're shooting some now.

When you look at your opportunity to go and try and fill up the Astrodome?
Well, it'll be the type stuff that I do. It's a mixture of things. It's a little rock, a little country western.

Is that the same thing you do at the International Hotel?
Yeah, it's the same type of thing. A lot of different type of songs. So I just hope I can put on a good show, mainly.

What ever happened to the Jordanaires?
I can't get 'em out of Nashville. Man, they got

Receiving sales awards, Houston, 1970.

In concert, 1970.

stuck in Nashville and (laughs) they make so much money…they do so well in Nashville…you can't get 'em out of there.

Do you have any thoughts about the rising interest in country music?

I think it's fantastic. You see, country music was always a part of the influence on my type of music anyway. It's a combination of country music and gospel and rhythm and blues all combined. That's what it really was. As a child, I was influenced by all of that.

Do you consider yourself basically a country music singer then?

I would hate to say strictly country because of the fact that I liked all different types of music when I was a child. Of course the Grand Ole Opry is the first thing I ever heard, probably. But I liked the blues and I liked the gospel music…gospel quartets and all that.

Do you ever pull out any of those old records from the Sun label and listen to them at all?

(Laughs.) They sound funny, boy. (Laughs.) They got a lot of echo on 'em, man, I'll tell you. That's what I mean, I think the overall sound has improved today.

Would you think there's more gimmicks today than there was, say, fifteen years ago?

There's probably more gimmicks but I think that the engineers have improved and I think that the techniques have improved…the overall recording.

Consideration of further reevaluation of your career to get you back in front of live audiences again?

[Elvis looks understandably confused, considering this goofy question.]

In other words, you were available to the public only in films.

Yeah.

For a long period of time.

I think the most important thing is the inspiration that I got from a live audience. I was missing that.

Was it rough at the International? Was there a strain on you after not being out in front of an audience?

It was tough, but I enjoyed it. I did some…I enjoyed it…like I know I'm gonna enjoy it here because it's a live audience and that makes a world of difference.

Let me ask you one thing, what's your father up to?

He's around here somewhere, ask him. I don't know. Daddy, what are you up to?

Elvis, there's evidence of sart…

[T.P.] I'd like to introduce Elvis' father, Mr. Vernon Presley. Could he come right here and sit down? Vernon, don't sign nothing unless I check it over.

[Vernon Presley] I can't write…I never sign nothing.

(Laughter.)

(Coughs again.) It's this fresh air, man.

Elvis, there's quite an evidence of sartorial splendor. Does this indicate that the…
Of what? (Laughs.) What?

The attire is not one that we are familiar in seeing you in.
It was taken from a karate suit…just a regular karate-type outfit [a gi].
[Siren can be heard.] Are they comin' to get me? Is that it? (Laughs.)

I mean does this indicate that with your type dress and everything now, that you're changing a little bit of style, perhaps, in deference to what you did a few years ago?
I don't know. I think that you'd have to see the show. It's difficult to tell. I don't feel any different. I don't think the dress has that much to do with it. I got the idea from a karate suit because I studied karate for a long time, and I had 'em make up a couple suits like it.

What do you do for relaxation? You said you study…
Karate! (Laughs.) If you can relax doin' this [swinging his hands], I don't know. No, I read a lot and go horseback riding and stuff like that.

Do you still live principally in…
Memphis! (Laughs.) About half the time…half the time, yeah. Half the time in L.A.

In the show you have planned for the Dome, do you plan any of the old, old songs…some of the first ones?
I'd like to…

Any special ones?
…Try out a couple of 'em…just to see if they work.

How big is your band with you, Elvis?
It's a big [one]…fantastic.

Elvis, let me pin this on you. This is your official badge, and we got another…didn't wanna put your name…not that people didn't know who you were, but we's afraid they be tryin' to take it off of you for a souvenir. Pin that on ya. Mr. [Vernon] Presley, it's a real pleasure to have you down here with your son. We think we're gonna set all kinds of records down here.
I hope so. I hope I can give 'em a good show. That's the most important thing.

No question about that. You sure will.
If I can give 'em a good show, I'll feel like I've done something, man.

You will. What's the biggest live crowd you've ever performed for?
If I'm not mistaken, it was in Vancouver, Canada, wasn't it, Colonel?

[T.P.] The Cotton Bowl.
In the Cotton Bowl, in Dallas. Ah, it was about twenty-five thousand, I guess.

Would you like to do more songs about people going from poverty to the land of plenty?
I think so, if it's the right type of song. I think so, if it's the right type of material.

You've already made a couple of songs.
Yes I have.

Like "In the Ghetto."
I did "In the Ghetto." I don't know. I wouldn't like to do all that type stuff. In other words, I wouldn't like for everything to be a message, 'cause I think there's still entertainment to be considered.

JULY 14, 1970

LOCATION: *MGM Studio Recording Stage, Culver City, California.*
EVENT: *Rehearsals for Las Vegas 1970 Summer Festival, portions of which are filmed for the movie* That's the Way It Is. *Random comments are noted. (Rehearsals continued at MGM the following two days.)*
SOURCE: That's the Way It Is *and* This Is Elvis *(Videos).*

We haven't...as you can tell, we don't know these songs. We haven't rehearsed...we're just foolin' around.

"I [Just] Can't Help Believing," I need the words. I don't know the words. I think somebody ate 'em last night, man.

Do the instrumental [Glen D. Hardin]. Hit that big mother [piano] over there!

[Reading.] Here's hoping that you have a very successful opening and that you break both legs.

[Signed.] Tom Jones.

[Reading.] Best wishes for a continuing, successful Vegas show. Hope to get a raise in the next six months.

[Signed.] Joe Esposito.

[Reading.] Dear Elvis, after fifteen years we have finally learned to understand what you say on record.

Signed RCA.

Rehearsal for Las Vegas appearance, Los Angeles, 1970.

[Reading.] My God, my God. Why has Thou forsaken me?

Signed, the Pope.

This is the nitty-gritty time as far as being nervous, you know, opening night.

You should have seen me at dinner tonight. I was going [shoveling it in gesture], in tempo. I never swallowed any of it...it was all right here [in throat].

If the songs don't go over, we can do a medley of costumes.

You know, when I first started in this business, I was a little bitty guy, had a little bitty guitar, that's it, man [holding tiny toy guitar] little bitty sideburns, little shaky leg, and Ed Sullivan saw me and said "ummm, som-bitch." So anyway, they put me on TV and filmed me from the waist up. You know, I'm going [wiggles]. Anyway, MGM is doing a movie here, and so don't let these cameras throw you...and try not to throw the cameras. So those of you who have never seen me before will realize tonight that I'm totally insane, and have been for a number of years. They just haven't caught me yet.

B.J. Thomas has out a new record. And, ah, I don't particularly like it. But it's his own thing, you know. You got the words to it ["I Just Can't Help Believing"].

Keep some music going back there. Don't be afraid to play. Just play the hell out of it!

AUGUST 11, 1970

LOCATION: *International Hotel, Las Vegas.*
SOURCE: Walk a Mile in My Shoes—The Essential '70s Masters *(CD).*
Prologue to "Walk a Mile in My Shoes":

There was a guy that said one time...he said:

You never stood in that man's shoes, or saw things through his eyes.

Or stood and watched with helpless hands, while the heart inside you dies.

So help your brother along the way, no

Showing the Ade for his Gator, Las Vegas, 1970.

matter where he starts.

For the same God that made you made him too.

These men with broken hearts.

I'd like to sing a song along the same line. ["Walk a Mile in My Shoes"]

[It is not clear whether or not Elvis knew that Hank Williams is the writer of these words. Originally recorded by Hank using his pseudonym, Luke the Drifter. Among other sources, this narrative, "Men With Broken Hearts," is found on the 1955 LP Hank Williams As Luke the Drifter *(MGM E-3267).]*

AUGUST 12, 1970

LOCATION: *International Hotel, Las Vegas.*
SOURCE: Make the World Go Away *(CD).*
Only 45 Songs to Go

"I gotta explain to you something. We had to learn some fifty songs for the show. We were supposed to learn fifty songs...we only learned five. So we were short about forty-

five songs. Anyway, this is one we don't know" ["Twenty Days and Twenty Nights"].

tell ya (laughs). "You!" "We!" "Us!" What?" "You ain't!" "You ain't!" "You!" "You ain't!" (Finally begins "Hound Dog.")

AUGUST 19, 1970

LOCATION: *International Hotel, Las Vegas.*
SOURCE: *Audiotape and* The Memphis Flash Hits Vegas *(CD).*

My Name Is…

Good evening, ladies and gentlemen. Welcome to the Landmark. My name's Johnny Cash.

About Water and Sound

Thank you very much. I need water. Gimme a little wah-wah, wah-wah Charlie [Hodge], a little wah-wah. A grown man saying wah-wah. Ummm, lord, lord. Is the sound off on the stage, Bill [Porter]? We can't hear up here. Huh?

[Bill indicates the sound is not off.]

Okay, then we're deaf.

Very Lengthy Intro

And then…(singing) "and then along came Jones." About the same time I had those records out, I did a song. But you gotta stand like this to sing it because if you stand up straight, you'll strip all your gears. It's a very tender love song, and you get right up into a girl's face and you say "baby…baby…baby." She thinks you're a frog and she leaves, you know. She says "well, he's nuts." Anyway, you get up into her face and you say "you" (whispering)…no you don't do that either. "You!" (Screaming.) It blows her hair straight back, if it's that loud. "You ain't!" Is that right? Is that it? "You!" I'm gettin' tired of standing over like this, man. It's ridiculous. Gatorade ain't workin' tonight. Let's see, there's one bead of sweat…two…three…four-five-six. Three of 'em came down real fast, one after another. "You!" This was a very big record for me, really folks. It was about that big. Lord have mercy, I'm the gray ghost man, I'll

AUGUST 20, 1970

LOCATION: *Las Vegas Hilton (early show).*
SOURCE: A Dinner Date with Elvis *(CD).*

The second record that I ever recorded is a song called "Tiger Man." Not too many people have heard it. It went like this: "Spffft!" That's how a tiger goes, and then he strikes. But this is just a little bitty tiger: "Meow!" He had a bone caught in his throat.

[There is certainly no record of Elvis recording "Tiger Man" before 1968. We also hear Elvis making this same claim during numerous different shows in the early 1970s, each time saying it was his second record—which we know is "Good Rockin' Tonight"/"I Don't Care If the Sun Don't Shine" (Sun 210). Sun did have a record of "Tiger Man" out in 1953, but by Rufus Thomas (Sun 188).]

My Name Is…

Good evening, ladies and gentlemen. Welcome to the Landmark. My name's Johnny Cash.

You think I'm crazy. You really think I'm nuts, don't you? I got some Gatorade back here, to aid my gator in case he gets tired. It works twelve times faster than water.

AUGUST 20, 1970

LOCATION: *Las Vegas Hilton (late show).*
SOURCE: The Memphis Flash Hits Vegas *and* Standing Room Only *(CD).*

Welcome:

Good evening, ladies and gentlemen. Welcome to the Golden Nugget.

[Female fan screams] "Love Me Tender."

I will later, baby. If I have to go back…if I

have to go back here during the show and drink water it's because…I'm thirsty for one reason. No, it's very dry in Las Vegas and you gotta keep your whistle wet.

[Fan whistles]

That's a wet whistle! I've also got some…got some Gatorade back here. I've also got a little gator back here. Aw, let me see what we got here. Got a bunch a birds…got a laughing box…that's about the extent of my show, really, just a few little gags.

When I first started out in this business, I was a little bitty cat—not cat, I was a little kid. Had a little bitty guitar, had little bitty fingers and little bitty sideburns, a little shaky leg that went like that. I had a rough time in the Army with that. They say "Attention!" I kept tryin' to play the rifle. Anyway, I was very young and Ed Sullivan saw me and said "Ummm, sombitch." I didn't say anything back to him. Anyway, I came to Hollywood…makes sense 'cause Hollywood didn't come to me. And I made a movie called Gone with the Wind. The title song of the movie went like this: uhh-hhhh, uhhhhh, uhhhhh. No, it didn't go like that, I was just gettin' my breath.

AUGUST 21, 1970

LOCATION: *Las Vegas Hilton.*
SOURCE: From Vegas to Macon *and* The Memphis Flash Hits Vegas *(CDs).*

My Name Is…

Good evening, ladies and gentlemen. Welcome to the Golden Nugget. I'm Johnny Cash. I used to be Fats Domino but I lost a lot of weight.

There's a Reason It Wasn't Too Big

The second record that I recorded, nobody really knew who I was at the time, so it really wasn't too big. It was called "Tiger Man."
[See comment of August 20, 1970, regarding "Tiger Man."]

Introducing Neil Diamond

There's a couple people in the audience I'd like you to say hello to…"Hello couple people in the audience, how're ya'll doin?" [spoken in Butterfly McQueen–type voice]. (Laughs.) No, no, no…don't, don't, don't give me no jive, now. You know, just sit over there. Supposed to sing "Happy Birthday" to James Burton. "Happy Birth…" oh, we already done that haven't we? In the audience, ladies and gentlemen, is a great songwriter and a heck of a performer, he's a heck of a nice guy. He wrote "Sweet Caroline." He wrote "Holly Holy." I'd like you to say hello to Mr. Neil Diamond. Neil…finally found you with the spot[light], man. Thanks for comin' in. Thank you for comin' in. "Holly Holy"? (Sings a few words). Naw, he came here to enjoy the show, folks, he came here to watch the show. He's not working right now.

Introducing Grandma Minnie

What I'd like to do…I'd like to say hello to my grandmother. She's seventy-eight years old and it's her first time to ever see me on stage. And she's been with me all my life. She's out in the audience. Hello, Grandma.

SEPTEMBER 1, 1970

LOCATION: *International Hotel, Las Vegas.*
SOURCE: *Audiotape.*

My Name Is…

Good evening, ladies and gentlemen. Welcome to the Golden Nugget. My name is Johnny Cash.

SEPTEMBER 9, 1970

LOCATION: *Phoenix, Arizona.*
SOURCE: *Audiotape.*

My Name Is…

Good evening, ladies and gentlemen. My name is Glen Campbell. [Sings a line of "By the Time I Get to Phoenix."]

NOVEMBER 6, 1970

LOCATION: *Beverly Hills, California.*
ITEM: *Fire-Arm Registration, signed by Elvis Presley.*
SOURCE: *Original document.*

Date of Registration: *11-6-70.* Make of Gun: *Smith & Wesson.* Type: *Revolver.* Caliber: *.357.* Serial No.: *K688344.* Registrant: *Elvis A. Presley.* Residence: *1174 Hillcrest Dr., Beverly Hills.* Phone: *Unk[nown].* Business Address: *3764 Hwy 51. S., Memphis, Tenn.:* Phone: *Unk[nown].* Hair: *Br[ow]n.* Eyes: *Blu[e].* Height: *6-1.* Weight: *160.* Age: *35.* Date of Birth: *1-8-35.* Compl[ection]: *Fair.* Build: *Slim.* Occupation: *Singer.* Gun Used For: *Self-Protection.* Gun Obtained From: *Kerr's Sporting Goods, Beverly Hills, Calif.*

I hereby certify that I am a citizen of the United States of America and have never been convicted of a felony.

Elvis A. Presley [signed]

BEVERLY HILLS POLICE DEPARTMENT
FIRE-ARM REGISTRATION

DATE OF REGISTRATION: __11-6-70__
MAKE OF GUN: __Smith & Wesson__ TYPE: __revolver__
revolver,pistol,automatic
CALIBER: __.357__ SERIAL NO. __K688344__
REGISTRANT: __Elvis A. PRESLEY__
RESIDENCE ADDRESS: __1174 Hillcrest Dr., Bev. Hills__ PHONE __Unk.__
BUSINESS ADDRESS: __3764 Hwy. 51 S., Memphis, Tenn.__ PHONE __Unk.__
HAIR __brn__ EYES __blu__ HGHT __6-1__ WGHT __160__ AGE __35__
DATE OF BIRTH __1-8-35__ COMPL __fair__ BUILD __slim__
OCCUPATION __Singer__
GUN USED FOR: __self-protection__
GUN OBTAINED FROM: __Kerr's Sporting Goods, Beverly Hills, Calif.__

I HEREBY CERTIFY THAT I AM A CITIZEN
OF THE UNITED STATES OF AMERICA, AND
HAVE NEVER BEEN CONVICTED OF A FELONY.
SIGNATURE: *Elvis A. Presley*

- -

INVESTIGATION REPORT
DATE: __11-6-70__

Registrant is familiar with state laws and use of the above weapon.

Joseph Paul Kimble
Investigating Officer

(9/2/57)

Firearms registration form.

Date: *11-6-70.* Registrant is familiar with state laws and use of the above weapon.

Investigating Officer: *Joseph Paul Kimble [signed]*

NOVEMBER 11, 1970

LOCATION: *Portland, Oregon.*
SOURCE: One Night in Portland *(CD).*
My Name Is…

Good evening, ladies and gentlemen. My name is Johnny Cash. It's a pleasure to be here in Oakland. Naw, we were in Oakland last night, weren't we? I played this town when Tom Jones was first learning how to do this, cat.

NOVEMBER 12, 1970

LOCATION: *Seattle, Washington.*
SOURCE: *Audiotape.*
My Name Is…

*Good evening, ladies and gentlemen. My name is Johnny Cash. I did a movie here in 1912 I think it was…*It Happened at the World's Fair. *I played Seattle, Washington, when Tom Jones and [Engelbert] Humperdinck were in diapers.*
Who's on Piano?

The young man on the piano, his name is Jerry Lee Lewis. Jerry Lee, play it hard.

NOVEMBER 16, 1970

LOCATION: *Oklahoma City, Oklahoma.*
SOURCE: Go Cat Go *(CD).*
My Name Is…

Good evening, ladies and gentlemen. My name is Johnny Cash. I'd like to tell you that it's a pleasure to be back here in Oklahoma City. When I was in Oklahoma [last] [1956] I was just a baby.

LOCATION: *International Hotel, Las Vegas.*
SOURCE: *Audiotape,* Long Lost and Found Songs *(CD), and* Elvis: The Lost Performances *(Video).*

[Exact date not known.]

Introducing the Tiplers

There's somebody in the audience I'd like to say hello to, ladies and gentlemen. Before I started singing, I was driving a truck, and I was working for an electric company [Crown Electric Company, 1953]. I hauled electrical equipment. And the couple that I worked for is here tonight. I think I was just out of high school. Anyway, Mr. and Mrs [James and Gladys] Tipler, and it's her birthday so I'd like to say happy birthday to you. Thank you. Nice to see you. Thanks for the job too!

Introducing Telly Savalas

There's somebody in the audience I'd like you to meet, ladies and gentlemen. I've been a fan of this gentleman for a long time, and I know that you've seen him in many, many great movies. He's one of the finest actors in the business. Mr. Telly Savalas. Please stand up. There he is…my man. That's it. Thank you,

sir. Thank you for coming in. It's a pleasure.

Not Exactly His Way

[Sings "My Way."] That's a very good song, ladies and gentlemen, but I wouldn't want it associated with my own personal life. "Now the end is near and all that jazz." It's a nice song. It's okay for [Frank] Sinatra. I haven't even ate it up and spit it out yet…I'm still chewing on it! Naw, it's a good song.

Mission Accomplished

I've got to please the crowd…excite them…make them happy.

ITEM: *Handwritten note from Elvis Presley to Col. Tom Parker.*
SOURCE: *Original document.*

[Exact date not known.]

Hello Colonel,
I used your phone. Hope you don't mind.
Respectfully,
E.P.

P.S. Also stole your black panther. Will replace it later.

JANUARY 16, 1971

LOCATION: *Memphis Municipal Auditorium.*
EVENT: *Elvis honored by America's Jaycees as one of America's Ten Young Men of the Year.*
SOURCE: *Audiotape.*

When I was a child, ladies and gentlemen, I was a dreamer. I read comic books and I was the hero of the comic book. I saw movies and I was the hero in the movie. So every dream that I ever dreamed has come true a hundred times. And these gentlemen over here, you see these type people who care, that are dedicated. You realize that it's not possible that they might be building the kingdom of heaven. It's not too far-fetched from reality. I'd like to say that, uh, I *learned very early in life that without a song, the day would never end. Without a song, a man ain't got a friend. Without…without a song, the road would ever bend, without a song. So I'll keep singin' a song. Good night.*

JANUARY 26, 1971

LOCATION: *International Hotel, Las Vegas.*
SOURCE: All Things Are Possible *(CD).*

My Name Is…

Good evening, ladies and gentlemen. My name is Johnny Cash. I'd like to welcome you to the Frontier, er, International.

Introducing Hal Wallis

My first big movie contract was with a gen-

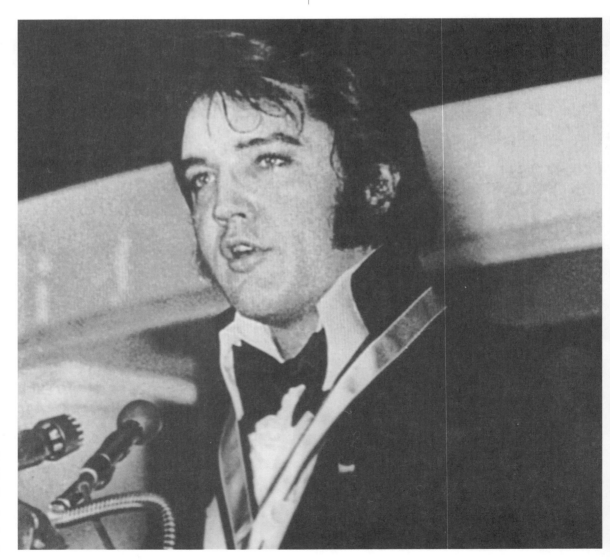

Accepting
National
Jaycees
Award,
Memphis,
1971.

Surrounded at the National Jaycees Award Dinner, Memphis, 1971.

tleman who's name is Hal Wallis. Mr. Wallis made about ten of my movies, and one we did, Blue Hawaii, *had a song in it, we usually close our show with it but we're gonna do it early. I'd like to dedicate it to Mr. Wallis because he still makes very good films. Like* Anne of a Thousand Days, True Grit. *I'd like to dedicate this to you, Mr. Wallis.*

LOCATION: *International Hotel, Las Vegas.*
SOURCE: All Things Are Possible *(CD).*

My Name Is...

Good evening, ladies and gentlemen. Welcome to the International. My name is Frankie Avalon. I'd like to tell you, those that got kissed, that I have the flu. And I'll be around in the back later. I usually make the rounds, up in the balcony, you know. I'm a lying som-bitch, ain't I?

About "Polk Salad Annie" Stage Routine

If you ever have a weight problem, just do that a couple times a night.

LOCATION: *International Hotel, Las Vegas.*
SOURCE: *Audiotape.*

The Truth Is Out

[Fan screams.] Sing "Just Pretend"!
Honey, I've been pretending for sixteen years!

LOCATION: *International Hotel, Las Vegas.*
SOURCE: Live Experience in Vegas *(LP).*
[At this time, author Jerry Osborne used the radio name "Dan Coffey." After a handshake and exchange of scarfs between the two, Elvis gave this two-word introduction so the audience would know who he was horsing around with.]

Introducing Dan Coffey

[This is] Dan Coffey.

ITEM: *Typewritten letter written and signed by Elvis Presley (Memphis, Tennessee) to John Finlator [U.S. Department of Justice/Bureau of*

Narcotics and Dangerous Drugs] (Arlington, Virginia).
SOURCE: *Original document.*

Dear Mr. Finlator,
Would you please make the credentials to read "Agent at Large," as I may be going overseas at any time on a concert tour. No one knows or respects your position more than myself. The credentials are of the utmost secrecy and importance. I will never abuse or misuse this great honor. I know I can assure you that I fully understand the importance of the bureau.
I would like you to know that I have studied drug abuse, communist psychological brainwashing techniques, etc., for ten years on my own. I want you to know that it is part of my nature, sir, that when I do something there is no middle-of-the-road, it's all the way. That is why I became interested in drug abuse, anti-American activists, radicals, S.D.S., etc. You name it, I have studied it in depth.
This country has been great to me and if I can ever help it out in some way, I will whole heartedly [sic]. I am an entertainer and I believe that entertainers should entertain and make people happy and not try to impose his personal philosophy on anyone through songs, television or through the guise of comedy.
Motion pictures and rock music are directly responsible for much of the confusion in this country, so you see I would have sincere interest as I am directly in the middle of both. But I certainly would not want them to know, as I would lose them, to say the least.
Again, I assure you of my awareness and seriousness. I will contact you from time to time to say hello. I would like to extend a personal invitation to my home in Memphis or Los Angeles to spend an evening with myself and my family.
Respectfully,
Elvis Presley
Home number in Memphis: 398-9722
Los Angeles: 278-3496

MARCH 23, 1971

ITEM: *Typewritten letter written and signed by Elvis Presley (Memphis, Tennessee) to Col. Tom Parker at MGM Studios (Culver City, California).*
SOURCE: *Original document.*

Dear Col.
Due to my present illness with eye infection, it may be a few days before I am able to return to the West Coast. Therefore, I will be unable to sign a contract on this one merchandising deal with RCA Victor. Therefore, I would like to authorize you to sign my name for me on this deal. The deal sounds fantastic. I hope to be up and back in the swing of things real soon.
Sincerely,
Elvis Presley

EARLY APRIL 1971

EVENT: *Phone call from Ron Pietrafeso in Denver to Elvis in Memphis.*
SOURCE: Moody Blue and Other Great Performances *(CD).*
[Exact date not known.]

What'cha been doin'…recording there?
Well, that's what I was doing. I was in the process of makin' an album, but that eye thing just blew everything sideways, you know.

Oh yeah?
So I gotta…I'm goin' to L.A. and spend Easter with the family.

Yeah.

But I still gotta go out and make that album. I gotta make a Christmas album, a gospel album, and a couple of singles.

Yeah.

Then after that go on a short tour. Then be back in Vegas in August…this summer.

Oh yeah, when do you think you'll be there?

I don't know, Ronnie. Either July or August.

July or August, uh?

But we're gonna go on some tour before then.

Man, I sure wanna thank you for the good time we had there in Vegas.

Well good.

We really enjoyed it.

I'm glad ya'all did.

Yeah, my wife just…that was an experience she'll never forget.

(Laughs.) You bet.

She really enjoyed it, and if you're gonna be out there again, maybe we can make it out there again.

I'll be out there August. Just let us know…let Joe know. We'll be at the same place. It's usually better in August. It's usually better for us because the crowd…it's a much more exciting crowd.

Yeah.

We get a lot of younger kids there because school's out and everything.

Yeah, get a wilder crowd.

Yeah, it's pretty exciting. It's not really wild, it's just a little more excitement.

Yeah. Tried to call your house today, and you must have had the number changed or something, uh?

Yeah, I just did. We just had it changed because they were bothering the hell out of my wife.

Yeah, that's what I figured.

Well, you know we're goin' through the process of interior decorating, and every interior decorator in the world knows about it.

Oh God.

So they're all calling. So we had to change the number.

Yeah.

Because they don't care what time of night they call.

(Laughs.)

So I had to change it for her.

Yeah, how is she and the girl?

Oh, they're all fine. She's fine. The baby's taking swimming lessons.

Good.

She's three years old, you know. She turned three while I was there in Vegas.

Yeah, I remember you talkin' about havin' to charter a plane to fly her presents back.

Yeah.

(Laughs.)

(Laughs.) That's the damn truth, man, the kid got more presents.

Hey, did you have any problems with your house in the earthquake or anything?

No, no. I'll tell you what, that International Hotel almost fell. That son-of-a-bitch was rockin' back and forth.

No kidding.

I swear to God, I went to bed at six o'clock in the morning, and Priscilla was there. I laid in bed and I thought "God almighty, what's goin' on here." The bed was movin', see.

Yeah.

So I got up and walked out in that hallway… had my flashlight and my gun in one hand.

(Laughs.)

I looked at that big chandelier hangin' over the dining room table.

Yeah.
That son-of-a-bitch was shakin', man, back and forth.

Umm.
It was the weirdest feeling I ever had in my life, Ron.

Yeah, I bet. Up there on the top of everything.
Well, I opened the door to see if the wind was blowing.

(Laughs.)
No wind blowing.

You know, I think that happened the Monday we left. Wasn't it the day that Priscilla came in?
Yeah, right.

Yeah, well see, we saw her at the airport when we were leavin'.
Yeah, yeah, that's right. It happened that day or the next day, yeah. Well it was the weirdest feeling I've ever had.

Yeah. I'll tell ya, I've sat through 'em here in Denver. Not nothin' that bad, but it's a wild feeling.
Yeah.

I've sat at the kitchen table and watched a three-foot-tall weed out in the flower bed bounce back and forth. And Ginger was outside, I walked out and asked her if she felt it…she never even felt it but it darn near shook me out of the chair.
Well I tell you what, it was the weirdest feelin' I ever had. Course that big hotel was movin' now, back and forth.

Oh yeah.
It's supposed to move and that son-of-a-bitch was doin' it, boy! I was ready to get out of that place, man. I was headin' for the elevator in my underwear.

(Laughs.)
That third show was gonna be a dilly, boy.

Yeah (laughs).
Tell 'em hello for me, would ya?

Yeah. Yeah, everybody's doin' fine.
Tell 'em I asked about 'em and I'm doin' okay. The eye thing was a little more serious than they put in the paper.

Yeah, well you never know if they're playin' it up or down.
I told 'em what to put in the paper. I told 'em to say "eye infection" 'cause that's what I want it to be. It was glaucoma.

Umm. Well I'm glad everything's coming out okay.
But it's gone. It's all cleared up. I'm out runnin' around now.

Umm. Hey, is Lamar out there with you?
No, he's in Nashville.

Really? You don't have a number where I could get hold of him, do you?
Just a second. Let me get Charlie back on. Charlie, get him a number to reach Lamar. Ron, I'm gonna take off.

Well hey, tell Joe and Sonny and everybody hello for me. Jerry and all.
I sure will. I also got another promotion. I got promoted to fourth-degree black belt in karate.

Oh no kidding?
Yeah. See, I continued it when we got back here to Memphis.

Yeah.
So I got promoted to fourth-degree black.

Good deal. Hey, that's great.
(Laughs.)

Are you at your folks' house?
Huh?

You at your folks' house? Your mom's and dad's?
At my house, yeah.

Tell them hello for me.

I sure will.

I don't know if they'll remember me.

Yeah, they'll remember. Ah, they don't live here, Ron. My grandmother lives here. It threw me when you said that.

Oh. Oh.

They live in another house on another street, right by this house.

Oh yeah.

But nobody lives here except my grandmother and my aunt.

Oh, yeah.

But I'll tell 'em that you said hello. Yeah.

Okay, good enough. Well, hey guy, it's good talkin' to you. Take care of yourself.

I'll talk to you later.

You bet.

AUGUST 10, 1971

LOCATION: *International Hotel, Las Vegas.*
SOURCE: *Audiotape and* Rockin' Against the Roarin' Falls *(CD).*

Introducing Charlie Hodge

On alcohol…is Charlie Hodge.

Introducing Charley Pride

[Here's] a young fellow that has been very successful in the recording business. He's a very good friend of mine, Charley Pride. (Sings a couple of lines of "Kaw-Liga.")

Introducing Marty Allen

There's a couple people in the audience I'd like you to say hello to. Hello, couple people in the audience! There's a good friend of mine here, and let me tell you something. When I came to Vegas, there was an eight by ten [inch] picture in my room of a guy with sideburns and a suit just like mine…and it was Marty Allen. (Sings two lines of "The Most Beautiful Girl in the World.")

[The connection between comedian Marty Allen and the Charlie Rich hit "The Most Beautiful Girl in the World" is not yet clear to us.]

Introducing Mike Stone

I keep up with the art of karate, and this guy was Grand International Champion for two years, which means he was the best in the world for two years. His name is Mike Stone. My God, he will dissect you.

AUGUST 12, 1971

LOCATION: *International Hotel, Las Vegas.*
SOURCE: *Audiotape and* The Memphis Flash Hits Vegas *(CD).*

My Name Is…

Good evening, ladies and gentlemen. My name is Johnny Cash. I'd like to welcome you to Lake Tahoe International. I'm actually killing time, my drummer just fell apart.

Introducing Richard Egan

My very first movie, ladies and gentlemen, was Love Me Tender, *and I had the privilege of working with a very fine actor—he played my older brother—and we became very good friends since making that film. His name is Richard Egan. He's here tonight. Richard. Didn't mean to knock your drinks over, it was an accident. What do you want…what do you want, honey? The belt, me, the pants, what?*

I got killed in Love Me Tender, *he [Richard Egan] got the girl.*

Introducing Sweet Inspirations and Imperials

The old ladies…young ladies that opened our show tonight, the Sweet Inspirations. The gentlemen behind the Inspirations are the Inspirations' husbands. Naw, they're the number-one gospel group in the field… which is where they should be (laughs)… oh God o'mighty…the Imperials, ladies and gentlemen.

My Name Is…

Thank you. Good evening, ladies and gentle-men. My name is Johnny Cash.

My Name Is…

Thank you. Good evening, ladies and gentle-men. My name is Johnny Cash.

Introducing Brenda Lee

There's a little girl in the audience that I met when she was only eight years old, and she

```
ZCZC UFF130 T301 NSA020

FRPA CO  UFNX

LOSANGELESCALIF 76 29 1545


ELVIS PRESLEY

CONVENTION CARE

JEAN MARC GARGIULO

PALAIS DE CONGRES DE VERSAILLES

PARISFRANCE




DEAR FRIENDS IT IS A SPECIAL PLEASURE AND HONOR FOR ME WHEN

FANS JOIN TOGETHER IN A CONVENTION IT IS GREAT PLEASURE TO KNOW

THAT YOUR MEETING TOGETHER HERE TODAY MEANS AS MUCH TO YOU AS IT




T301 NSA020 ELVIS P2


DOES TO ME THANK YOU FOR BEING HERE AND SINCEREST THANKS

TO THOSE WHOSE EFFORTS BROUGHT YOU  ALL TOGETHER I WISH

YOU ALL HAPPINESS

     ELVIS PRESLEY
```

Telegram to French fan club, 1971.

was singing back then when I first started singing. She opens at the Fremont tomorrow night...Brenda Lee. Where are you, Brenda? She's so little you can miss her. Brenda, if I get the chance I'll come over and see you.

AUGUST 30, 1971

LOCATION: *International Hotel, Las Vegas.*
SOURCE: *Audiotape.*

My Name Is...

Good evening, ladies and gentlemen. My name is Johnny Rivers. Welcome to the International.

Introducing Sweet Inspirations and Imperials

The young ladies that stood out in the sun too long, the Sweet Inspirations (laughs).

AUGUST 31, 1971

LOCATION: *International Hotel, Las Vegas.*
SOURCE: *Audiotape.*

My Name Is...

Good evening, ladies and gentlemen. My name is Jerry Lee Lewis. Welcome to the International. I don't like this room.

SEPTEMBER 6, 1971

LOCATION: *International Hotel, Las Vegas.*
SOURCE: Rockin' Against the Roarin' Falls *(CD).*

Introducing Charley Pride

There's a guy in the audience I'd like to introduce you to, country singer Charley Pride. Charley...where are you. Next...c'mon, Charley. (Sings a line of "The Easy Part's Over.")

OCTOBER 31, 1971

ITEM: *Telegram from Elvis Presley (Los Angeles) to Jean-Marc Gargiulo (Paris,*

With Brenda Lee on *Wild in the Country* set, 1960.

France), for reading to European fans gathered at Palais de Congres de Versailles.
SOURCE: *Document photocopy.*

Dear Friends,
It is a special pleasure and honor for me when fans join together in a convention. It is [a] great pleasure to know that your meeting together here today means as much to you as it does to me.
Thank you for being here and sincerest thanks to those whose efforts brought you all together. I wish you all happiness.

Elvis Presley

NOVEMBER 10, 1971

LOCATION: *Boston, Massachusetts.*
SOURCE: The Power of Zhazam *(CD).*

Introducing Tony Bruno Orchestra

The Tony Bruno Orchestra, ladies and gentlemen. That's the entire northeast members of the mafia. You guys all mafia? Tony Bruno? Don't kid me, with that name.

LOCATION: *Dallas, Texas.*
SOURCE: *Audiotape.*

My Name Is…

Good evening, ladies and gentlemen. My name is Glen Campbell.

ITEM: *Handwritten letter to President Richard M. Nixon. Five pages, written on American Airlines stationery, in-flight from Los Angeles, California, to Washington, D.C.*
SOURCE: *Document photocopy.*

[Letter is transcribed as originally written, punctuation errors and all. Even though proper punctuation would make it easier to read, no polishing or editing has been done. Portions underlined here are underlined for emphasis in the original letter.]

Dear Mr. President
First I would like to introduce myself. I am Elvis Presley and admire you and have great respect for your office. I talked to Vice-President [Spiro] Agnew in Palm Springs 3 weeks ago and expressed my concern for our country. The drug culture, the hippie elements, the SDS [Students for Democratic Society], Black Panthers, etc. do not *consider me as their enemy or as they call it the Establishment. I call it American and I love it. Sir I can and will be of any service that I can to help the country out. I have no concerns or motives other than helping the country out. So I wish not to be given a title or an appointed position. I can and will do more good if I were made a Federal Agent at Large, and I will help out by doing it my way through communications with people of all ages. First and foremost I am an entertainer but all I need is the Federal credentials. I am on this plane with Sen. George Murphy [R-California] and we have been discussing the problems that our country is faced with.*

So I am staying at the Washington Hotel room 505–506–507. I have two men who work with me by the name of Jerry Schilling and Sonny West. I am registered under the name Jon Burrows. I will be here for as long as it takes to get the credentials of a Federal Agent. I have done an in depth study of drug abuse and Communist brainwashing techniques and I am right in the middle of the whole thing, where I can and will do the most good. I am glad to help just so long as it is kept very private. You can have your staff or whomever call me anytime today tonight or tomorrow.

I was nominated this coming year one of America's Ten Most Outstanding Young Men. That will be in January 18 in my home town of Memphis Tenn.

I am sending you the short autobiography about myself so you can better understand this approach. I would love too [sic] meet you just to say hello if you're not to [sic] busy.

Respectfully
Elvis Presley

P.S. I believe that you Sir were one of the Top Ten Outstanding Men of America also.

I have a personal gift for you also which I would like to present to you and you can accept it or I will keep it for you until you can take it.

Dear Mr. President

First I would like to introduce myself. I am Elvis Presley and admire you and Have Great Respect for your Office. I talked to Vice President Agnew in Palm Springs 3 weeks ago and expressed my concern for our country. The Drug Culture, the Hippie Elements, the SDS, Black Panthers, etc. do not consider me as their enemy or as they call it the Establishment. I call it America and

I Love it. Sir I can and will be of any Service that I can to help the country out. I have no concern or Motives other than helping the country out. So I wish not to be given a title or an appointed position. I can and will do more good if I were made a Federal agent at large, and I will help out by doing it my way through my communications with people of all ages. First and Foremost I am an entertainer but all I need is the Federal credentials. I am on this Plane with

Sen. George Murphy and We have been discussing the problems that our country is faced with. So I am Staying at the Washington Hotel Room 505-506-507. I have 2 men who work with me by the name of Jerry Schilling and Sonny West. I am registered under the name of Jon Burrows. I will be here for as long as it takes to get the credentials of a Federal agent. I have done an in depth study of Drug abuse and Communist Brainwashing

Techniques and I am right in the middle of the whole thing, where I can and will do the most good. I am Glad to help just so long as it is kept very Private. You can have your staff or whomever call me anytime today tonight or Tomorrow. I was nominated this coming year one of America's Ten most outstanding young men. That will be in January 18 in my Home Town of Memphis Tenn. I am sending you the short autobiography about myself so you can better understand this

Letter to
President
Nixon.

JANUARY 26, 1972

LOCATION: *International Hotel, Las Vegas.*
SOURCE: Opening Night *(CD).*

Introducing J. D. Sumner

I'd like you to say hello to J. D. Sumner and the Stamps Quartet. This man [J. D. Sumner] is the world's lowest bass singer…in more ways than one.

Introducing Red Skelton

Mr. [Red] Skelton, we love you very much.

JANUARY 26, 1972

LOCATION: *International Hotel, Las Vegas.*
ITEM: *Engraved plaque.*

[At this time, author Jerry Osborne used the radio name "Dan Coffey." Deejays are frequently referred to as "jocks." This plaque, a joke gift from Elvis, has a bronzed jock strap, or athletic supporter, along with the following inscription:]

"Dan Coffey
My Favorite Jock
Elvis"

MARCH 30, 1972

LOCATION: *RCA Studio, Hollywood, California. Tour rehearsal.*
SOURCE: Between Takes with Elvis *(LP).*

[Joe Esposito] "Release Me" would be a good number.
Yeah. "[Media] Can't Stop Loving You" is a good stage number. I don't know if we'll get clearance or not.

[J.E.] Well we did that.

[Charlie Hodge] No we didn't, it wasn't in the film.

[J.E.] Oh, we never got clearance on it. That's the one Tom [Parker] was tryin' to get.

[C.H.] I think they got it for this one though, if

I'm not mistaken.
That's why I'm not reading it out loud.

[C.H.] "Just Pretend" is a good song but I don't know whether the bass player knows it.
No, he doesn't. There's about four hundred that we CAN do. I'm tryin' to figure out…
Why don't we do, uh…why don't we do…

[J.D. Sumner] Why don't we do that song "Kill Ed" [Enoch].
Let's kill Ed!

[J.D.] Sit down, Donnie [Sumner]. Play it, son, or I'm gonna kill ya.
Put you on the spot.
I feel those [bass] parts, if I was just low enough. I'm low enough…my voice isn't.
I was singin' bass but he [J. D. Sumner] covered me up, man. He…he wiped me out. I know how you feel, Rich [Sterban].
I got your "Melancholy Baby," you son-of-a-bitch. She's built like a melon with a face like a collie, man…we got millions of little things like that that we can't use.
"Can't Stop Loving You," did we ever clear that?
We got all the voices here, we can do "I'll Remember You." Where's the words to the son-of-a-bitch. See that. They remembered it and I don't. Have we got the words to this, Joseph? Hold it! There's no sense in wasting all that good music when I don't know what I'm doin' up here. I plan on doing it for an album. I don't know…I don't know…I just don't know. I'll remember ya'll. I'm doin' this because of Lamar [Fike]. Oh Lord, don't just look down on us…help us.

[J.E.] Elvis, did you listen to this before I throw it out?
Yeah. I just left it out…because…one reason is because I was lazy.

[J.E.] (Laughs.) How about "Burning Love"?
We've already done "Burning Love."

[J.E.] Where would you like to put it in the show?

Y-e-a-a-a-h-o shit, where would we put it? "Shoot," excuse me, sound fellow. I keep forget-tin' [you're recording this]. Doo-doo, where would we put it? (Laughs.) A thirty-seven-year-old man up here sayin' doo-doo (laughs).

Well hello there. I don't think we all knew…let's start it again. It's only fair that I tell you guys what I'm gonna do, you know (laughs). I don't know why…I never have (laughs). Well I guess I've lost my mind. Ah, we might do "How Great Thou Art" somewhere, so let's run that…see if the Stamps know it. I don't know, we might [do it].

I think the G string is broke on this thing, fel-lows. Wouldn't it be funny if I'd come on stage with this blammed thing, and play it?

[J.E.] That would be funny.

(Laughs.) Flowers flyin' all over the place.

Now that's funny, a news guy's takin' a pic-ture of a news guy (laughs).

MARCH 31, 1972

LOCATION: *RCA Studio, Hollywood, California. Tour rehearsal.*
INTERVIEWERS: *Pierre Adidge and Robert Abel.*
SOURCE: Between Takes with Elvis *(LP).*

[Pierre & Robert] Tell us a little about J. D. Sumner. Where did you know him from?

He came to Memphis to sing with a group called the Blackwood Brothers, it was the first time that I'd ever seen him.

[P&R] How did you run into him this time, just…in Vegas?

I just realized that they were available, and he'd formed a new quartet, called the Stamps. And I listened to some of their records, and they had all this power, which I liked.

[P&R] He made the Stamps, he brought them back together.

He put 'em together.

[P&R] One of them's his nephew [Donnie Sumner] and one's his son-in-law [Ed Enoch]. The other two, I don't know where they came from.

But each one of the guys, individually, are good, as you can see.

[P&R] Oh yeah, I've noticed. See, we come from a different background. We come from the Middle West or the West Coast.

You don't hear this too much.

[P&R] So we don't hear this. So we see a bunch a guys…and it has a whole different kind of level of meaning to us because it's just not part of our background. 'Cause, like, everybody comes from the same background. Or is that…that's as much to you guys as to a kid in California going out for surfing or little league baseball. It's kinda like *Roots*.

We grew up with it. From the time I was…I can remember…like two years old…I grew up with this, because my folks took me there. When I got old enough, I started to sing in church.

[P&R] That's how you got into singing?

Well it's one of the ways.

[P&R] One of the ways.

But I liked all type of music, you know. When I was in high school, I had records by Mario Lanza…and the Metropolitan Opera. I just I loved music. The Spanish…I liked the Mexican flavored songs. But this thing here—the gospel thing—is just…gospel is really what we grew up with, more than anything else.

[P&R] In choosing music too, 'cause there's a kind of…if you've seen Baptist choirs, there's a kind of intensity about it. And it's the same kind of intensity-electricity that you have on stage. It's a kind of soul—a fantastic strength that's inside. It isn't just singing notes, it's singing something that seems to come from very deep inside.

And at certain times, you push out, and you pull

in. It's just a part of you. You don't even think about it.

[P&R] When I was in London and France, about three or four years ago, doing a film on [world-class skier] Jean-Claude Killy, and I asked him just offhand who was his favorite singer. And he said, "oh," he says, "Elvis Presley. He's my man! He's my man!"
Oh really? Well, he's my favorite skier (laughs). That's nice.

[P&R] And I asked him why. But he, he did this whole thing, he says "he has soul." You know, it's hard for an American to talk to a Frenchman and understand that he understands soul better than you do. But he really, really does. He says "he sings from in here." And that was his way of describing…he had a very limited English at the time.
It's fantastic. But this…you know this is very…this is very basic. When we get through our work, what we have to do, we usually wind up doing this.

[P&R] And you're doing it because you wanna do it?
We're doing it because we wanna do it.

[P&R] In Las Vegas, after he's done two shows, everybody's so tired they're up in the suite singin'…all night, till about six or so in the morning.
We do two shows a lot of times and we will go upstairs and sing until daylight, you know, gospel songs.

[P&R] How do you do it? How do you?
Not too often (laughs), when you're workin' every night there.

[P&R] And what does it do for ya? I mean to get into this. Is it like a…
I think it more or less puts your mind at ease. It does mine. Because you've been really concentrating and everybody's been working out. So these things, we know.

[P&R] It's like old friends.
Right. And it…it puts your mind at ease.

[P&R] Takes you down and just levels things off.
Takes you down to a level, otherwise you'd go outta here and just [panting] and you couldn't sleep. There's nothing wrong with it, but I'd be ending on a real fast, uptempo song or something. We'd leave the studio, nobody can sleep for hours.

[P&R] You're right though, when you leave the stage in a place like Vegas, you're really up.
Oh yeah, sure.

[P&R] You're really flying.
It takes at least four or five hours to even begin to unwind. And we usually wind up doing this type stuff.

[P&R] Where did you find the guys? I mean we know about J.D., but like the other guys who are in the chorus? It seems like you've known 'em forever, just watchin' you around the piano and singin'…like you're like real super old friends from a long, long time.
Well like I said, I knew J.D. from back when I was fifteen, that was when he first started…when he first came to Memphis to sing with a group called the Blackwood Brothers. And I was a big gospel music fan, so they would sing all night, and I would stay there all night. And he had formed this new group himself, a couple years ago, and I just heard their records and put them together with the Inspirations and everything else that we had.

[Joe Esposito] Looked in the gutter and there they were.
Looked in the gutter, man, and dug 'em out (laughs).

[P&R] When all of that's going on on the stage it's really fantastic.
Anyway, you put it all together.

In concert, 1972.

[P&R] It seems to be kind of a relationship on stage. It's like everybody is a friend of everybody else on stage. Now that's something very rare. 'Cause we've seen a lot of groups perform and don't get that kind of feeling.

I think it's because we enjoy it. And we constantly enjoy it, which means that we do two shows a night for five weeks, but we never let it get old. Every song is like we do it for the first time and that's one of the secrets.

[P&R] Like it's not a planned thing. You don't do the same songs [in] the same sequence.

Not necessarily. We can change 'em around. But even if we do the same songs…

[P&R] It's not the…

…they're new, and the sound is. The feeling is there every time.

[P&R] But it's a different feeling each time, right?

It's a good feeling. We never let it down, 'cause

there's a new audience out there. Plus, we enjoy what we're doing.

[J. D. Sumner] Well, Elvis communicates with us, really. I mean you really do on the stage. I've sung with a lot of people but he has some way of keeping you interested and communicating between you and him.

I'm not gonna tell you how (laughs).

[P&R] You aren't gonna tell us the secrets.

Things that go on behind my back and things (laughs). Nah, but we'll keep it interested…or interesting, somehow.

[J.E.] Hopefully more interesting than it's been.

Ah, shut up (laughs). At the end show…at the end of the five weeks, it went by like that (snaps his fingers). And it seemed like a day.

[P&R] Well I don't know. For instance, this evening I know you were running through everything just for us—for the cameras and

245

what have you—which would seem like if you did the reverse on us and said, well guys, just walk around with your cameras like you normally do at a concert, would be a drag to us because it would be hard for us to get up to that level. But what's hard for us to figure out is that you can turn it on here just like you do on the stage.

Well you know why…what's interesting about…about music, and about all the people here. They find new sounds, and they do things differently themselves. So it's like a new experience every day. The guy on the guitar will find a new lick, or the guy on the piano will find something, or the voices will add something. And I hear all this and it inspires me. I like it.

[P&R] 'Cause we watch…it's new for us. We're watching things like you and the lead guitarist kinda looking…the looks that go back and forth, [while] we're lining up shots. There's like really something goin' on, some sort of magic. We know already the game that goes on with Charlie Hodges [Hodge] and the kidding back and forth, and that's part of it too. So there's a kind of a thing going on there. There's something goin' on there. I notice when your eye goes over to J.D. when the chorus comes in. Each one of 'em is like a little turn-on, you know. It's like a conversation that goes on. Each one. Are there surprises in that? It's like a feedback. Back and forth and you turn each other on.

Well, that's what I mean. I mean it…it never ceases. It goes on.

[P&R] And that's what we're looking for in the film. That's what the film has to explore totally. It's that whole electricity, you know, that's just kinda circulating back and forth.

I hope you find it (laughs).

[P&R] Hey it's not…we have to tell you, we looked and it wasn't there (laughs).

Gee thanks!

[P&R] So we're wrapping (laughs). Hey, let's call it a night. We gotta rest up for the road. We got a big…

Got a big jump, from here to…

[P&R] Buffalo. Shuffle off to Buffalo. This is a tour where I usually lose about two inches, not in here [waist] but in here [height, from shouldering video camera] (laughs), have to hang by my hands for about two weeks to get it back. Yes! All one night stands too.

But that's fun, see. It's excitement.

[P&R] Gotta figure out how to get a piano in each room for these guys to sing after the show. Well, let's go home, everybody.

I think so. I enjoyed it, fellows.

[P&R] This is only the beginning of a really enjoyable experience.

Thank you. We'll do our best.

[P&R] I know you will. We'll try and do ours…now you're supposed to say "I know you will." See, and then we're all cool.

No comment. Now we're even (laughs).

[P&R] Good night.

MARCH 31, 1972

LOCATION: *RCA Studio, Hollywood, California, and various tour sites.*
EVENT: *Interviews that provide narrative heard during film, as well as random comments.*
SOURCE: Elvis on Tour *(Video).*

[Studio interview was conducted March 31; random comments are from April tour dates.]

My dad had seen a lot of people who'd played guitar and stuff, who didn't work. So he said, "Make up your mind about either being an electrician or playing a guitar. I never saw a guitar player that was worth a damn" [laughs].

When I left the stage, they were yelling and screaming and so forth, and it scared me to death, man. I didn't know what I'd done, so [to] the manager backstage, I said, "What'd I do, what'd I do?" He said, "Well, whatever it is go back out and do it again."

I've never gotten over what they call stage fright. I go through it every, every show. I'm pretty concerned, I'm pretty much thinking about the show. I never get completely comfortable with it, and I don't let the people with me get comfortable with it, in that I remind them that it's a new crowd out there. It's a new audience and they haven't seen us before, so it's gotta be like the first time we go on.

I don't like to stay backstage too long. I've got to please the crowd. I mean, I've got to excite them, you know, or make them happy, and gear myself to doing that show. And somebody could walk up to me and say "Hey, your head just exploded." I wouldn't hear it.

First time that I appeared on stage, I mean it scared me to death. I really didn't know what the yelling was about. I didn't realize that my body was moving. It was a natural thing to me, so [to] the manager backstage, I said, "What'd I do, what'd I do?" He said, "Well, whatever it is go back out and do it again."

[Though quite similar to the second paragraph in this section, that piece is used in the movie trailer; whereas this line appears in the film itself.]

We do two shows a night for five weeks. A lot of times we'll go upstairs and sing until daylight—gospel songs. We grew up with it, from the time I was, I can remember, like two years old. It more or less puts your mind at ease. It does mine.

APRIL 11, 1972

LOCATION: *Roanoke, Virginia.*
EVENT: *Roanoke Mayor Roy Webber presents Elvis with key to the city.*
SOURCE: Elvis on Tour *(Video).*

[Roy Webber] Women been callin' me all day wantin' to know what time you'll get here.
Thank you.

[R.W.] Among the many other things.
Does the key fit the vault?

[R.W.] The vault, and it fits the jail and all the public buildings.
Okay, and the bank.

[R.W.] You gonna play "I Ain't Nothin' but a Hound Dog" tonight?
Yes sir…yes sir, I'll do it.

[R.W.] Good. That was my favorite when you's, ah…I remember…
I broke a string [on toy guitar]. I broke the whole thing.

[R.W.] That's all right. The girls down at the place just made it up to have somethin' unusual for ya. You never played a guitar they said, and they wanted you to have one. But, ah…
I played here several times.

[R.W.] You have?
Yes sir. I was in Roanoke when I first started out.

[R.W.] Now these little names are listed on it: "To Elvis from your friends…your fans."
Yes sir.

[R.W.] Is there anything I can do for ya while you're here? Is everything okay?
Well, every…everything's just fine, sir.

[R.W.] The City Manager sends his regards and the members of the Council send their regards too. They'd a liked to been here to receive ya, but we know that you have so many things to do, and your show starts at eight-thirty and you have to dress. So again, many thanks for comin' to Roanoke.
Thank you very much. I appreciate it.

[R.W.] And we'll enjoy your show tonight and any time you're through here, just let us know what you want done, we'll be right happy to do it.

Thank you, sir. Thank you. Thank you very much. Appreciate it. Thank you.
[Singing.] Carry me back to old Virginie.

LOCATION: *Greensboro, North Carolina.*
EVENT: *Comments recorded and filmed backstage for possible inclusion in the 1972 film* Elvis on Tour. *This segment did not appear in* Elvis on Tour, *but is seen in* This Is Elvis.
SOURCE: This Is Elvis *(Video).*

> *[The first transcription below is taken from the original 1981 film, as it appeared in movie theaters. Following is the cleaned-up version made for video cassette release four years later.]*

Dogs and Chicks

A-hole [asshole] family, takeoff time will be at eight-fifteen.

> *[To Jerry Shilling.] You know that girl I was with last night?*

[Jerry Shilling] That dog.
Oh man! She gave great head.

Hey Joe [Esposito]. The chick last night gave great head.

> *[The commercial VHS video of* This Is Elvis— *with over forty minutes of additional footage— dubs in Ral Donner's voice with a less explicit line.]*

[To Jerry Shilling.] You know that girl I was with last night?

[Jerry Shilling] That dog.
[Dubbed.] I'll tell you, she could raise the dead, boy.

LOCATION: *Macon, Georgia.*
INTERVIEWERS: *Pierre Adidge and Robert Abel, along with comments by various members of Elvis' entourage.*
SOURCE: Between Takes with Elvis *(LP).*

Last time I played in Macon it got pretty wild.

> *[During the afternoon show, a swarm of fans rushed the stage. After the show, this discussion centered on that event and an earlier episode.]*

[Pierre & Robert] What year is that Elvis?
It's gotta be, ah…

[P&R] Eighteen, ah…
Oh shush.

[P&R] 1943 (laughs). What was it?
Fifty-six [Actually it was May 9, 1955]. Well [tonight], we're not going to play around with the crowd, you know, like I usually do.

[P&R] No. Things got out of hand. Pretty wild scene today. You're not kidding. We left before it happened.
[It happened on the] Next to the last song.

[P&R] That's when Colonel started beatin' the stage with his cane. If you're gonna flirt with 'em, stay back.
I don't see it. I only see like isolated instances, over here…I don't see what's goin' on over there. I see people reaching up, but I don't see what's goin' on.

[P&R] So it just came like a wave, uh?
Yeah…yeah.

[P&R] He just sees the people's hands. If it'd a been a seven-foot stage, we'd a been in trouble.
So I'm not gonna be as loose tonight.

[P&R] What was it, a certain song that triggered it, or what? [General William Tecumseh] Sherman's march through Macon, backed by the Artillery, right.
Yeah, it's a…

[P&R] Sherman took Macon but Elvis stormed it.
…it's ah…when I started givin' the…the scarves out and I started shakin' hands with people. And I couldn't see that they were coming in the back.

[P&R] It's just…I guess it just takes a couple to start it, you know, to trigger the whole thing. When they see one or two get through, then they all know it's a free-for-all. There was more people up there today than…
When you're foolin' with that many people, you can't do it. It's not like Vegas or whatever.

[P&R] Two breed four and four breed eight. It must be a terrible feeling to have thousands of people want ya.
Oh yeah, it's really bad (laughs).

[Lamar Fike] They want to touch you. That's what I mean you get that many who want to touch you. I had the same problem (laughs)…continually. I did, man, I cut out. I said I don't need this (laughs).

[P&R] And there's enough of him [Lamar] to go around. He ran for thirty minutes in one spot.

[L.F.] I went out backwards. I was lookin' at the crowd on the way out. You don't want to turn your back on 'em. They'll drive you into that wall like a nail.

[P&R] Lamar has left the auditorium (laughs).
In the car, on the way here, I started sweating.

[P&R] Just thinkin' about it…plus it was hot (laughs).
Oh my. Got a bunch o' wise cracks right here. Are you gonna interview me. This is all being taped in living color, right?

[Red West] Those people that was sittin' behind the vocal group, they couldn't see the show. When he [Elvis] introduced the vocal group they booed.

[P&R] Well they were booing last night while we were shooting. They couldn't see the show.
Well I did the best I could. But the people that are behind the Stamps, when they can't see ya, they start…they yell…they get mad.

[P&R] We have that problem in every city, because they're up there and they have the seats behind where they can't see.
Especially these guys that work for me, you know. No, but it's always a problem, you know. I'm gonna have to invent a stage…a portable.

[P&R] People all the way around you, it's always a problem. People behind you…they're upset because you don't turn around.
Right.

[P&R] Well then you gotta be on a pivot, man, you gotta rotate. Just have 'em slowly turn it. Figure out a way to get the orchestra in there. Where did they do that? Where was that?
We had been on stage…

[P&R] Where was it? Was it Houston?
Will you let me say something…for a minute!

[Lamar Fike] Well you don't have to get hostile (laughs).
Our true nature's comin' out.

[P&R] It was Houston…Houston, that's right.
We had been on stage, but the vocal group was down…

[P&R]…in the pits…in the pits.

APRIL 16, 1972

LOCATION: *Jacksonville, Florida.*
INTERVIEWERS: *Pierre Adidge and Robert Abel.*
SOURCE: Between Takes with Elvis *(LP).*

There's something strange about doing a matinee.

[P&R] It's like you just got out of bed.
There's something strange about singing at three o'clock in the afternoon, in daylight. And when the show's over you come out…are you listening? That's the Colonel! Meet Colonel Parker.

[P&R] No, it's like going to a movie and gettin' out in the daylight, you know. Same type of feeling.

I got news for ya…these guys [film crew] don't miss a trick, boy. I mean they had a microphone in the air conditioning of the car. We didn't know it was on sound. I mean, we were talkin' real nice, gentlemanly.

[While traveling to and from the Coliseum, the microphone in the limousine picked up the following conversations.]

[Lamar Fike] Well, we talk that way all the time. What's different about that?

[Joe Esposito] Whew! Boy, that one girl really reached.
I'm hep, man.

[Red West] How far are we?
About five to seven minutes. There's the building back over there, Red.
Well hell, we could'a taken a boat.

[R.W.] I was gonna say, we gotta cross the bridge?

[J.E.] Good, the last matinee of the tour.

[R.W.] Just so we don't get bogged down in this muddy water.
"I washed my hands in muddy water." I started to do that last night [Macon, Georgia] but nobody ever heard…nobody heard me.

[J.E.] What? You did?
I did the first three or four lines to it, man, nobody heard me.

[R.W.] Did you tell 'em you were gonna do it?
Yeah.

[J.E.] Did you tell yourself?
Na-huh.

[J.E.] (Laughing.) You didn't tell yourself.

[R.W.] That looked like that little theater where you played before.

[J.E.] It may be. The Florida Theater, it is the place he played before [August 10, 1956]. It is the place.

[Security "Chief"] It's right down the end of this street. That's where I had him, my first security…I was a lieutenant then.
It was fifty-six.
I had you then, and then I was a captain when you came back the next time.

[R.W.] At the stadium.

[Chief] At the stadium.
Right. I played here about twice, didn't I, sir. Two or three times.

[Chief] Yeah, boy, it was pure hell back in them days with you.

[J.E.] At the Florida Theater?

[R.W.] Wait till today, Chief.

[Chief] We had to fight like hell. I had you there [Florida Theater] and then I had you at the…that's when the Colonel…
…that's when he first started to manage me, right?

[Sonny West] That's the reason the Colonel insisted that he have him when he came back here.

[Chief] The Colonel pulled me all the way from…[my fishing vacation]…all the way from my place up here.
He never forgets. He never forgets anybody.

[S.W.] He'll have you goin' fishin' over here at the [Veteran's Memorial] Coliseum (laughs).

[Chief] I said, "Colonel, I don't take any more jobs out." He said, "Well, I want you back." So he called me and…he's my old friend.

[J.E.] Yeah, he jaws.
No, he never forgets. He never forgets people. He never forgets openings, or dates, birthdays.

[J.E.] It's like Admiral Sims [Hotel].

[R.W.] Yeah, I was gonna say he never forgets them old hotels he stayed in.

[J.E.] He stayed there forty years ago and he came back to the same old hotel.

[S.W.] Admiral Sims…if it's not condemned, we'll stay there again.

[Chief] We fought 'em [wild fans] all the way from the stadium…we had escorts…we had motorcycles on him…that's when you stayed at the Roosevelt [Hotel]. And we fought 'em all night long. I mean *fought!* They threw their bras at him (laughs).

[J.E.] They did that last week.
Except they were in *them (laughs).*

[J.E.] Which is a good trick.

[S.W.] If they haven't moved those plants, you'll be walkin' through a jungle to get to the stage.
What's that?

[S.W.] A bunch o' plants back there. It's like a jungle. Potted plants.
They should put those on stage so I can hide behind them. I can do the show behind the plants.

[J.E.] There it 'tis…the Dome.
Boy that's a big…it's a big place, isn't it?

[R.W.] Well what is this over here?

[J.E.] That's the Gator Bowl.
Yeah, right.

[Chief] When he first played, that place wasn't that big. They've revised it.
Is that where we got caught that night, Chief (laughs)?…at the Gator Bowl [July 29, 1955].

[Chief] Yep.
And you guys put me through a window into a paddy wagon and took me to the hospital.

[Chief] We like to never got you out of there. That's what I said, we fought all night.

[J.E.] That was security.
Oh yeah man, splinters and all.

[Conversation continues immediately after the show.]

Off we go, into the wild blue yonder.

[J.E.] Good show! Good show!
Whew! Boy. How was the sound in that building?

[J.E.] Very good. Very, very good. Good show. Did you take this [leather wristband] off or what? Did it come off?
I took it off.

[J.E.] You did. It start to tear your wrist up.
It was cuttin' my wrist. On both sides this time. On my wound I think.

[S.W.] Was it hot out there?
It was hotter than yesterday, and I thought yesterday was hot. That stage is so slick…awful slick, man.

[J.E.] Yeah, I know it was slick. I could tell you was sliding. You know what you should do…change shoes too. I think these shoes are worn a little bit. I noticed you was sliding.
Uh-huh. Flip-flopped here. It's a hot time in Florida.

[S.W.] Boy, it is.
A rainy night in Georgia. That's a big room, you know it?

[J.E.] It is, very big.

[R.W.] What'd you do, give one scarf away?

[J.E.] No, three.
No, it was three.

[J.E.] And he gave one to that little crippled girl.

[R.W.] Looked like a spotlight goin' through that window up there where those people are in front of us.
Yeah, I didn't know what that was, man. I didn't know if it was sunlight comin' through the building or what. I thought it was awfully bright, man. Hey look they got the fountain

goin', fellows. I'd like to go out there and dive into it right now.

[J.E.] Man, I'm starving to death. I haven't had breakfast.
It took me three hours to eat…then I had breakfast (laughs).

[J.E.] That car…they got a gray-haired woman in the back…ah, man…oh it's Lamar.
I shouldn't have thrown that water on him. He might catch a cold.

APRIL 17, 1972

LOCATION: *Little Rock, Arkansas.*
SOURCE: Between Takes with Elvis *(LP).*

[Red West] Have they told you the setup?
No.

[R.W.] You go up on the stage, take a right there, take a right here…and there's people everywhere (laughs). So…
…[on the side of] the group [Stamps, Sweet Inspirations, etc.] or the piano?
     You go up on the left. There's steps goin' up by the group. Good luck!

[J.E.] We'll see you at the airport, Elvis (laughs).
Okay. I may be there first (laughs).

[R.W.] Knowing you, probably.
I have to go.

[R.W.] Joe, how's your voice tonight…'cause we'll be up there singing (laughs).

[Little Rock Promoter] I was telling you about the time Elvis played the [Little Rock] Auditorium. Next day he was playin' for me in Camden [Arkansas], and then over to Hope [Arkansas], and he missed the road from Camden to Hope, and he'd just bought a new white Cadillac. When he got there, he wasn't so worried about gettin' stuck, he wondered how he's gonna get it washed. I recommended a

place and they got the car all cleaned again. It's been a long time. I believe you was…just before that I'd seen you once before, Elvis, when you was down in Shreveport.
Yes sir.

[L.R.P.] You and Tommy Sands were back there at the same time, wasn't ya?
The first year I was in this business I was in Shreveport.

[L.R.P.] Mine and Tom Parker's days go back to the tent show, with Eddy Arnold, Minnie Pearl, and Uncle Dave Macon. Most of those people are dead now. How's the tour been, Elvis, great?
Fine sir. Yes sir, it's been great. Thank you.

[L.R.P.] We're certainly delighted, you've broke all our records here at this building [T. H. Barton Coliseum].
It's great. Thank you.

[L.R.P.] Just delighted.
What's the capacity in this building?

[L.R.P.] Ten thousand. That is with the extra seats put in. I had a call at five o'clock this afternoon from Green Hills—is that what I was tellin' you where it was—a man had chartered an airplane and said, "I'm at the airport, I've chartered an airplane for eight hundred dollars, all I need is standing room for five people." I said, well it's just impossible. Just don't come. I hate for people to fly that far—Rock Hill, South Carolina.
Well I'll be darned.

[L.R.P.] Rock Hill, South Carolina.

APRIL 18, 1972

LOCATION: *San Antonio, Texas.*
INTERVIEWERS: *Pierre Adidge and Robert Abel.*
SOURCE: Between Takes with Elvis *(LP).*

[Charlie Hodge] Okay, after the introduction,

and after you've done…what's that new song we just did.
"Burning Love." No, no, no, no. Not "Burning Love"…"For the Good Times."

[C.H.] "For the Good Times," yeah.

[Pierre & Robert] You gonna do "Burning Love" tonight?
You don't even know this one. That was funny though because they had forgotten the ending. It was "a hunka, hunka burnin' love…a hunka, hunka burning love"—twice. And a drum right there. They didn't do it. [Ronnie] Tutt went crazy, man, the [Sweet] Inspirations [did too].

Is that the key we're doing it ["Hawaiian Wedding Song"] in?

[C.H.] Yeah. Do you want the quartet to say "heart," now, in harmony [on the ending of "Hawaiian Wedding Song"].
"Heart," yeah, because they don't know the Hawaiian part. With all my, then, "he-a-a-a-a-r-t." It's held out, that long.

[P&R] I don't know which is worse—the hot weather or the cold weather.
(Laughs.) I think the hot weather.

[P&R] Yeah, it just gets to ya. It drains you.
When it's humid and hot, about halfway through the show I can feel it.

[P&R] The suit's hot too, right?
Yeah. It has to be…it has to be well built, so it's heavy.

[P&R] The suit's gotta be strong. The suit's gotta go through a lot.
I ripped ten suits out in Las Vegas on stage.

[P&R] Ten? Not this year?
No, when I first opened. Right in front of the audience. Ten of 'em, just ripped "woosh!" Mohair (laughs). The audience thought it was a part of the show, because I'd leave the stage and these guys would dress me backstage.

[R.W.] With the curtain wrapped around [him], you know, we'd be right on the stage there.

[P&R] Yeah, you have to change right away.
Yeah, you don't have time to go to the dressing room.

[R.W.] He'd introduce the group while he was changing right there on the stage.

[P&R] Now when you leave the stage tonight, a big crane is coming in with a magnet and gonna pick you right straight up through the top of the roof.
With all the metal, right?

[P&R] With all the metal.
Fellows, I wanna tell you, there's just so much I can do…stand here and sweat for ya.

[P&R] Only three hours and four minutes till the show.

[Joe Esposito] Four minutes…four minutes. Like I say, just go up the stairs.
Huh?

[J.E.] Go up the stairs and just cut through the group. Then come back off the same way. You go up these steps right here, where these plants were, that's the stage. Go right through the door.
You still gotta wave a red flag.

[J.E.] I thought I'd take a cape and just wave it as you come offstage.
Like a bull…I'd go right through the wall. If you guys do it like you did it up there in Roanoke [Virginia, April 11, 1972] you'd miss me.

[J.E.] What, Roanoke? We never did that in Roanoke.
No, it was the other place, where we jumped off [stage] and fell over the trash can.

[J.E.] That's our crack security man, Dick Grob, who knocked over the trash can.

With Vernon, meeting the media in New York, 1972.

[Dick Grob] Aw, c'mon…c'mon.

Well I have to say, it wasn't only him [sings "Only Him" to the tune of "Only You"]. Let's do the show, and we're on our way.

[C.H.] You wanna do…we haven't practiced anything like "One Night," or "Tryin' to Get to You." We haven't done anything like that.

Ah, not "Tryin' to Get to You." We might do "One Night."

[C.H.] You know another thing we haven't done in a long time is that "I Got a Woman."

We might do it.

[Lamar Fike] How far is Jackie [Kahane]?

How far's Jackie. You mean there's no intermission yet?

[J.E.] No, not yet. They're running late…he's running late.

Really?

[J.E.] Would you sign this [autograph]?

We came over too soon, didn't we?

[J.E.] There'll be a short intermission—about fifteen minutes.

To who [the autograph].

[J.E.] To Jane. I want to get dressed soon after the show tonight. Are you gonna wear that on the plane?

No, I'll put my coat on.

[L.F.] That plane holds twelve. I checked on it. It holds twelve.

Well hell, that means you and six other people.

[L.F.] I don't have to take this.

[James Burton] Either you take Lamar or you take the luggage.

[Red West] No, James, no, no, no, no, no, no, no.

We got here a little too early. I'm not sweatin'…it's cooler here…I think we'll make it alright.

[R.W.] You got a lot of friends from Memphis here. Drove over.

Can they run fast (laughs)?

APRIL 19, 1972

LOCATION: *Albuquerque, New Mexico.*
INTERVIEWERS: *Pierre Adidge and Robert Abel.*
SOURCE: Between Takes with Elvis *(LP).*

[The first segment following is the text of a quick backstage meeting between Elvis and Denise Sanchez, a then-eight-year-old terminally ill cancer patient, and Denise's companion.] The

second segment is a brief backstage greeting exchanged between Elvis, who is about to go on stage, and a Mr. Newman. Though not confirmed, Newman may be the then-International/Las Vegas Hilton casino manager.]

[Companion] Tell him what you said. She's shy. Tell him the song that you like.

[Denise Sanchez] Could you sing me a special song, please?
I sure will.

[Denise Sanchez] "Don't Cry Daddy" or "Love Me Tender" or whichever one you want.
Okay. All righty (laughs), whichever one I want, okay.

[Companion] Look over here. Look at Elvis.
Okay. I'm not gonna tell you which one I'm gonna do, okay. It'll be a surprise.
[Reportedly, Elvis sang and dedicated "You Gave Me a Mountain" to Sanchez.]

[Companion] A special one. Oooh.
Okay. Bye-bye (kisses Denise).

[Companion] Thank you so much...so much.

[Mr. Newman] I think it's been a fabulous engagement, from what the Colonel tells me. I flew in special today to catch him for his last performance.

[P&R] Do you hope to have him back?

[Newman] Oh yeah. We're just waitin' for him to come back.
How do you doin', Mr. Newman.

[Newman] Hello, Elvis. How are you?
Nice to see you. Welcome to Albuquerque.

[Newman] We miss you. Come back soon.

JUNE 9, 1972

LOCATION: *New York Hilton.*
EVENT: *Press conference. Questions by numerous media representatives.*

SOURCE: Complete Paradise Hawaiian Style Sessions, Vol. 3 *(LP).*

[Numerous variations exist of this press conference; however, nearly all are edited and have dubbed-in questions. On these, the questions usually vary from those actually posed at the event. The reason for the dubbing is because many of the media's questions are not clearly audible. The transcript here is from the actual press conference.]

[Media] Ladies and gentlemen, I have the pleasure of introducing Mr. Vernon Presley, Elvis Presley's father. Mr. Presley has a friend coming out.
Hello! Thank you. Thank you very much. How are you? Would you like me to sit down?

[Media] Yeah!
First of all, I plead innocent of all charges. Okay. Alright. Okay.

[Media] We love you, Elvis.
Thank you dear, love you too. Thank you.

[Col. Tom Parker] Will you gentlemen get down in front a little bit? You can get your pictures later, please?
(Laughs.)

[Media] Elvis, why have you waited so long to appear in New York City live?
I think...I think it was a matter of not getting the building, the proper building. We had to wait our turn in order to get the building. Couldn't get a good building in fifteen years. No, all kidding aside, we had to wait our turn to get in...into the Garden.

[Media] How do you feel about appearing there?
Oh, I like it. I enjoy it. I just hope we put on a good show for everbody.

[Media] Mr. Presley, why do you think you've outlasted every other entertainer from the fifties, and for that matter, the sixties as well?

I take Vitamin E (laughs). I was only kidding…I don't know (laughs)…I just…embarrass myself, man. Ah, I don't know, dear, I just…I enjoy the business. I like what I'm doing.

[Media] I hear from a lot of people in the press corps that you're really a shy, humble, wonderful human being. Would you agree with that?

Oh, I don't know what makes them think that…I…you know…this gold belt and the (laughs)…naw. Okay…what are you doin', woman? Ah, no.

[Media] I'm reminded of the *Ed Sullivan Show*, where they wouldn't [show you below the waist].

So am I…that's why I'm sittin' down.

[Media] Elvis, I don't know if you know it or not, but some people would like to know why you no longer have grease in your hair.

No, I stopped using that greasy kid stuff too, just like everybody else did, man.

[Media] You used to be criticized so much for your long hair and gyrations, and you seem so modest now.

Man, I was tame compared to what they do now, are you kidding (laughs). I didn't do anything but just jiggle, you know.

[Media] Show us the jiggle!

No (laughs), I can't…I can't do that. I'd just as soon save it for the show.

[Media] How do you feel about the way performers act on stage now, compared to what you did and you were criticized for?

Oh, I…I don't know. I really can't criticize anybody in the entertainment field. I think there's room for everybody. I hate to criticize another performer.

[Media] Elvis, are you…are you satisfied with the image you've established?

Well the image is one thing, and a human being is another, you know. So.

[Media] How close does it come? How close does the image come to the man you really are?

It's very hard to live up to an image. I'll put it that way.

[Media] Elvis, you're thirty-seven now. So do you disagree that anybody over thirty is finished? Is this wrong?

It's according to what you're talkin' about (laughs). Nah, I don't know. I'd like to think so.

[Media] What kind of audiences do you find you attract now, Elvis?

I beg your pardon.

[Media] What kind of audiences do you find you attract now?

Well I found that in the audiences that we have, that it's mixed. It's older people, younger people, and the very young. And all types of people, you know, which is good.

[Media] After a thirty-seven-year-old's record-breaking tour, Elvis, what are you going to do next?

Punt! (Laughs.) Nah, I, ah…I just made a movie of…of the last tour that I did [Elvis on Tour], it's the first live concert that we ever filmed, so that's my next project that's coming out.

[Media] Elvis, what made you finally decide to come out of seclusion and start making public appearances again?

I just missed it. I missed the closeness of an audience…of a live audience. So just as soon as I got out of the movie contracts, I started to do live performances again.

[Media] Will you be doing more and more of the concerts now?

I think so.

[Media] Are you recording…

I'm sorry. There's so many places that I haven't been yet. Like, I've never played New York here.

[Media] What about Britain, Elvis?

I've never been to Britain either.

[Media] Would you like to go there?
I'd like to, yes sir, very much. I'd like to go to Europe. I'd like to go to Japan and all those places. I've never been out of this country except in the service.

> *[Elvis, of course, did perform and travel out of the country—to Canada in 1957.]*

[Media] You were in the Army and were drafted. What is your opinion of war protesters? And would you today refuse to be drafted?
Honey, I'd just soon to keep my own personal views about that to myself. 'Cause I'm just an entertainer and I'd rather not say.

[Media] Do you think other entertainers should also keep their views to themselves?
No. I can't even say that.

[Media] Elvis, are you going to perform again here in New York?
I beg your pardon.

[Media] Are you going to perform again here in New York?
I might. I might. It's according.

[Media] They filmed your concert in Boston recently. Why aren't you filming in New York?
I don't know. That's a good question. Why is that, Colonel (laughs)?

[T.P.] I didn't hear that. What's the question?
She said why did they film the concert in Boston and they couldn't film it here?

[T.P.] To film it here…it could have been outlawed.

[Media] (Laughter.) Elvis, why don't you spend longer working on a film of your life or writing a biography of it?
I just don't feel that it's time yet. Maybe I will someday, but not right now.

[Media] Elvis, is there any chance New York knows that the firm has vacated to Phoenix?

> *[The meaning of this question is unclear, and the response provides no clues.]*

Who's talking, the camera? Oh, I'm sorry. What'd you say?

[Media] Do you think that your return signals the start of the return of some of…
I don't know. I didn't know they ever stopped. Did they? No, they didn't. Talkin' under the table, that guy.

[Media] Are you thinking of doing something different…like running for public office?
No sir, I don't have any other aspirations in politics or anything of that nature.

[Media] How about in acting?
Oh yeah, I'd like to do something in the way of a movie script, if I can find the right kind of a property. Like, we're looking for it now. You're talking about a nonsinging type thing. Yeah, I'd like to do that.

[Media] Elvis, why have you've gone away from the hard rock and roll that you did two, three years ago? You really don't do that hard rock anymore, like "Heartbreak Hotel."
It's very difficult to find that type of song. It's hard to find good material nowadays, for everybody…for all of us.

[Media] You were the forerunner of rock and roll, you really…you don't record hard rock anymore. Why?
It's very difficult to find any good hard rock songs, really. If I could find them I would do them.

[Media] Mr. Presley, who do you find sexy? Who are the people that you think are sexy (laughs)?
I don't know. There's a lot of people…that I like. I got out of that one, didn't I?

[Media] What with increased political activity on the part of any number of entertainers, do you plan to or are you now campaigning for, or

helping to raise campaign funds for any particular political presidential candidate?

No sir, I'm not. I'm not involved in that at all. I'm just an entertainer. Okay.

[Media] Elvis, what do you miss most about the passing of the fifties?

I don't really miss that much about it. I enjoy it just as much now or more than I did then. I would like to think that we've improved ourselves over the past fifteen years.

[Media] How about musically?

That's what I mean. I mean musically and vocally and everything. I'd like to think that I've improved over the past fifteen years.

[Media] Elvis, I'm going back to when you said you like to tour and perform in Europe. What do you think about a Far East tour?

Yeah, I'd love to go there. Yeah.

[Media] Do you ever tire of people recognizing you and asking for autographs?

No, I got used to it. I would kind of miss it if it didn't happen. If nobody saw me or if nobody recognized me or whatever, or asked for an autograph I…to me it's just part of the business, and I accept it. I think I would miss it.

[Media] Elvis, will there be a recording made of this concert?

It's possible. I don't know. They have RCA Victor's officials here, so I don't know.

[Media] Elvis, of all the records you've recorded, which is your favorite song?

"It's Now or Never," "O Solo Mio."

[Media] (Applause.) Which is your best-selling record?

That one. "O Solo Mio" was the largest selling. And then the next one too was "Don't Be Cruel," I think, then "Hound Dog"…"Heartburn Motel," whatever.

[Media] When did you arrive in New York?

I came in last night very late and I had to go to bed, because we're having a rehearsal now and I go back to rehearsal after this press conference…unless you've got something better in mind (laughs).

[Media] Go baby! Is your wife you…with you in town?

No she's not.

[Media] (Laughter.) You mentioned earlier, Elvis, the shortage of recording material. There's just been a suit filed in Nashville, Tennessee, by Nashville songwriters against the major recording companies, saying that they're not given a fair chance. In…in your estimation and in your knowledge, are the songwriters—independent songwriters—given a fair chance with major recording companies?

I don't think so. I think that there's so many companies, everybody becomes independent once they have one hit record, they form their own company. And there's so many. And also the people who write them are starting to record their own songs. And that's why I say it's very difficult to get good material.

[Media] From independent songwriters?

Yeah.

[Media] You own publishing houses yourself, do you?

Yes, I'm in a publishing firm, but I'll take songs from anywhere or from anybody if they're good. It doesn't have to be at my company. It could be just completely an unknown person or just anybody that writes a song, if they can get it to me. If it's good, I'll do it.

[Media] To your knowledge though, have recording companies favored the songwriters that work for the subsidiary publishing houses that they may own? Do they favor those songwriters?

Well, probably so. Probably so. In being honest, I would have to say yeah.

[Media] In terms of the suit that's been filed…
Honey, I'm really not aware of this particular suit that you're talkin' about, so I can't answer you accurately. I don't even know the details about it. I went to Hawaii to get a tan for New York (laughs), so I'm not aware of it, really.

[Media] You would say that the songwriters that belong to those publishing houses…
I don't think so, if they're not heard. If they got good material, if they're good songwriters, I think they should be heard. Yes definitely.

[Media] Elvis, can I have a kiss and a scarf?
I really can't sittin' down (laughs). Naw, naw, I can't do that. I'd just as soon save it for the show. I'm a…(laughs). Thank you.

[Media] Gotta watch it, fella (laughs).
Well, you know, (laughs)…watch it is right. No, I…on social comments like that. Dear, I'd just as soon not to make a comment.

[T.P.] Wouldn't it be a nice gesture if some of you people that had all these pictures…it'd be nice to step aside and let these other people take a few pictures. Please, please, step aside, please.

[Media] (Applause.)

[T.P.] Come on up with your cameras.

[Media] Elvis, what is that belt that you're wearing?
The belt…the belt is an award from…

[T.P.] Come up here. C'mon, give these guys a place, step aside will you, please. All of ya, ya'll had plenty of pictures. C'mon, bring your cameras over here. Why don'tcha give these other fellas a chance. C'mon through here.
Let's let the Colonel get through talkin' and I'll finish.

[T.P.] Come up here.
The belt is an award from the International [Hotel, Las Vegas, Nevada] for the attendance record…championship attendance record.

[Media] Come on, baby, get 'em hot.
It's like a trophy but I wear it around. It's just to show off.

[Media] May we talk to your father?
Will I talk to my father? I have to (laugh), he handles all my personal affairs.

[Media] No, could we ask your father a question or two?
Oh, sure.

[Media] Ah, the other Mr. Presley, at…at what point did you realize that your son was more than your son and now a very, very famous person?

[Vernon Presley] Well, it's kinda hard to say. You know, it happened so fast it's hard to keep up with it. It just "boom" overnight and there it was. So I'd say maybe…probably 1956, and the first television show.

[Media] Do you have any regrets?
I tried to tell him sooner, but he wouldn't listen.

[V.P.] No, I have no regrets of it. In fact, I have enjoyed it, really.
All kidding aside, it happened very fast to all of us, my mother and my father and all of us. And everything happened overnight, and so we had to adjust to a lot of things very quickly…a lot of good things.

[Media] Mr. Presley Senior, after Elvis got famous did he change in any way at all, or…?

[V.P.] No, he…no, not really. I can't tell any changes.
I sweat more.

[Media] Elvis, do you find it harder to perform yourself the old songs, while still mixing in some newer tunes, like "Bridge over Troubled

Water" and some of the newer songs. Is that conscious?

No, it's a conscious thing…I like to mix 'em up. In other words, I like to do a song like "Bridge over Troubled Water" or "[An] American Trilogy," or something. Then mix it up and do some rock and roll, some of the hard rock stuff.

[Media] Are you tired of the old songs?

No, I'm not the least bit ashamed of "Hound Dog" or "Heartbreak Hotel," or whatever those things were.

[Media] Can you see yourself retiring at all?

Not really.

[Media] No?

I've got too much energy. I don't think so. Not as long as I can [continue].

[Media] Will you have another TV special?

I think they're planning one now. They're talkin' about one now.

[Media] Elvis, are there any new groups that you like particularly?

Any what, sir?

Backstage at Bobby Darin's Sahara show, Las Vegas, 1960.

[Media] Any new groups that you like particularly?

There's a lot of 'em. I can't think of any right off hand.

[Media] Elvis…

[T.P.] I'd like to live up to my reputation of bein' a nice guy, this is it, folks.

[Media] Beautiful baby, beautiful.

I've got to go back to rehearsal, folks, thank you very much.

AUGUST 11, 1972

LOCATION: *Las Vegas Hilton.*
SOURCE: *Audiotape.*
My Name Is…

Good evening, ladies and gentlemen. I'd like to welcome you to the International. My name is…out front…and all over the place. I hope you have a good time tonight. I'm sorry to keep you waiting, but I couldn't get these clothes on, backstage.
[For this Summer Festival opening night, and in the days that followed, Elvis had difficulty adjusting to the hotel's recent name change.]

AUGUST 11, 1972

LOCATION: *Las Vegas Hilton.*
SOURCE: Elvis at Full Blast *and* Blazing into the Darkness *(CDs).*
Not Taking Requests

My first movie was called Love Me Tender. *And I didn't like it, so I'm not gonna sing it, so we can go on to something else.*

[Fan screams.] Do "Burning Love."

Nah, I don't wanna do "Burning Love." Let's do "It's Over," or somethin' like that.

[Fan screams.] "It Hurts Me!"

It does? Well honey, don't do it! Honey, I'll get to all of 'em before the night's over, really. All of 'em, man. All 400 of 'em.

AUGUST 18, 1972

LOCATION: *Las Vegas Hilton.*
SOURCE: *Audiotape.*

In the Beginning

When I first started out…I was only nine-teen and I had terminal acne.

SEPTEMBER 2, 1972

LOCATION: *Las Vegas Hilton.*
SOURCE: *Audiotape.*

My Name Is…

Thank you. I'd like to welcome you to the International Hilton Hawaiian Living Kuala Motel Inn. My name is all out front, and in the bathroom, on ceilings and floors.

Introducing David Brinkley

There's a very famous gentleman in the audience, ladies and gentlemen. Say hello to Mr. David Brinkley. Everybody knows who he is. Stand up. Thanks for coming in.

SEPTEMBER 3, 1972

LOCATION: *Las Vegas Hilton.*
SOURCE: *Audiotape.*

Introducing Bassey and Bobby

There's a couple of people that I'd like to acknowledge in the audience, ladies and gentlemen. This young lady's been in before. She's a very fine entertainer. She opens here when I close, Shirley Bassey. Are you from Wales?

Bobby Darin opens same time you do? Now, that tells me nothing. I'm just guessing. Bobby Darin.

SEPTEMBER 4, 1972

LOCATION: *Las Vegas Hilton.*
SOURCE: *Audiotape and* I'll Remember You *(CD).*

A King Without a Crown

[Fan screams.] Get it on, baby!

I'm trying to. I think the King just blew the crown.

Introducing Bobby Darin

There's a gentleman in the audience I'd like you to meet. He's a very good friend of mine. He's one of the best entertainers in the business… Bobby Darin. Bobby, stand up. Nice to see you. He opens here tomorrow night, folks. See him.

Introducing British Fan Club

I'd like to acknowledge the presence of somebody in the audience, ladies and gentlemen. There's a fan club that came all the way from England here tonight. I think there's about two hundred and fifty of them here, and I hope you enjoy the show. Thank you for coming over.

[After singing "Tiger Man."] Thank you. That was the second record I ever made.

I'd like to say something, ladies and gentlemen. You're a fantastic audience, and we've had a fantastic stay in Las Vegas. It's the best time we've had here, really. Thanks to you and all these people up here. [See comment of August 20, 1970, regarding "Tiger Man."]

SEPTEMBER 4, 1972

LOCATION: *Unknown.*
INTERVIEWER: *Tony Prince (U.K. deejay).*
SOURCE: From the Bottom of My Heart *(LP).*

[Tony Prince] Elvis, we've got a few questions the fans wanted me to ask you. Who designs your clothes these days?
A guy by the name of Bill Belew.

[T.P.] Bill Belew?
B-e-l-e-w.

[T.P.] You don't do any designing yourself?
Yeah, I dream 'em up and he writes 'em up.

[T.P.] He gets 'em together for you, huh?
Workin' together.

Announcing *Aloha from Hawaii* show, Las Vegas, 1972.

[T.P.] A lot of people want to know whether we'll ever get a full album of Elvis blues go back to rock and roll. Are you gonna get back into the blues at all?
I'm working on it.

[T.P.] Get it together…"Merry Christmas, Baby."
I just so happen to be working on a rock and roll and a blues album in Memphis.

[T.P.] Really? You're workin' on it right now?
We're gettin' the songs together.

[T.P.] Great! We'll look forward to that.
It's a coincidence that you asked me that, but it's true.

[T.P.] You only ever recorded one country-and-western album. Do you ever think of recording any more?
Oh sure.

[T.P.] Do you dig country music?
It's according to the song.

[T.P.] You wouldn't like to go out and do another full album of country sounds?
Not right now.

[T.P.] Elvis, very quickly, we've got 50 million listeners listening to an eight-hour spectacular in Europe, to your show tonight. You have any message for all the fans in Great Britain and Europe listening to your show tonight?
Just tell 'em that I really love their devotion and we gotta come see them. We got to. I've been saying it for years, but we will.

[T.P.] We pray you will, Elvis. Thank you.

SEPTEMBER 5, 1972

LOCATION: *Las Vegas Hilton.*
EVENT: *Press conference announcing* Aloha from Hawaii via Satellite *show.*

SOURCE: *Video and audiotape.*

[Comments by RCA Records President Rocco Laginestra are indicated. Other comments and questions are from unidentified media representatives.]

[Media] Are you awake?

I'm still on…I'm on stage, man.

[This press conference took place after Elvis' midnight show and he was still wired, thus the "still on stage" comment.]

[Media] The Armed Forces Network will pick it up. The Armed Forces will show it.

This is the first time that I've seen this myself.

[Media] Well it's just astounding.

I beg your pardon? Okay.

Ah, well now they shoot me all the way, see, instead of just the waist down.

[Elvis obviously intended to say "instead of just the waist up."]

Now I would like to think that I am…I have improved as an entertainer. And I like to get the rapport with an audience. 'Cause it's a give-and-take thing. If you can do that, it works. If the artist, or whoever is performing, can get that kind of rapport going with the audience, then it really pays off. It's good.

[Media] But do you feel you have more of that rapport now than you did fifteen years ago?

I couldn't answer that. I really couldn't.

[Rocco Laginestra] I really should start this conference off by congratulating Elvis because we will have two new firsts. The first "first"— new first—involves Elvis as the first performer to do a worldwide live concert via satellite, a real spectacular. And the second is that we will have a worldwide album via satellite. All of this has been made possible by the joint efforts of a lot of people, and especially including Colonel Tom Parker. Elvis, again my congratulations for this spectacular.

Thank you, sir. Thank you. Whew! It's very hard to comprehend it because I…in fifteen years, it's hard to comprehend that happening…out to all the countries all over the world via satellite, it's very difficult to comprehend. A live concert to me is exciting because of all the electricity that's generated in the crowd and on stage, but it's my favorite part of show…of the business, is the live concert.

[Media] How do you pace yourself?

Sir?

[Media] How do you pace yourself?

You mean physically or vocally, or whatever?

[Media] So you are up when you need to be up.

I just…I exercise every day. I vocalize every day, and practice if I'm working or not. So I just try to stay in shape all the time, vocally and mentally.

[Media] Which is harder?

(Laughs.) Well, both is tough. You gotta work at 'em, but I don't mind it. It's worth it.

[R.L.] I might say this about when we first approached the various countries around the world Elvis is really the only performer that could do this today. He's well known in every country that we sought, in fact, in every country in the world. And the acceptance is just fantastic. It wasn't a case of any "selling." Because you know he's been in demand for live performances around the world but you just can't do this so this is the way of approaching it. The acceptance has exceeded all of our expectations, Elvis.

Thank you very much. That's very nice, sir.

NOVEMBER 15, 1972

LOCATION: *Long Beach, California.*
SOURCE: A New Live Experience *(CD).*
About Greek Folk Songs and a Mask

Thank you very much, ladies and gentlemen…now I'd like to do a medley of Greek folk songs for ya. I got an idea. I'm gonna get a mask and put it on the back of my head, with a little silly grin on it and some hair right here.

First Introduction of Lisa Marie

My little daughter is in the audience and I dedicate this show to her. She's right down there. This is the first time she's ever seen her daddy make a fool out of himself in front of fourteen thousand people.

NOVEMBER 20, 1972

LOCATION: *Honolulu, Hawaii.*
EVENT: *Press conference announcing* Aloha from Hawaii via Satellite *show.*
SOURCE: *Audiotape.*

[Media] I'd like to ask you…
I'll try and answer you.

[Media] How do you like HIC [Honolulu International Center] for location?
There couldn't be a better place.

[Media] How can you record the sound?
Well it's not bad. We'll work on it some more.

[Media] On your worldwide telecast will you try and speak in all different languages or will you primarily stick to English?

[Media] It's a big task, Elvis.
You're not kidding. I'll probably stick to English mostly. I've done some songs in Spanish and German but I don't know yet.

[Media] Elvis, do you [think] your style has contributed anything to the new morality that we have today?

[Media] [Loud noise.] Thank you. [Laughter.] On the press release, do I read this right, at twelve-thirty A.M?
That's correct.

[Associate] That is correct. The reason for that time, twelve-thirty A.M., is because we're being beamed live around most of the world.

Australia will be picked up at seven-thirty local time, which is prime time in Japan. In Europe they will be viewing it at twelve-thirty P.M. in the afternoon. This is the reason for that particular time in Hawaii.

[Media] What time will the tickets go on sale, for donations?

[Associate 1] We will leave that up to the gentlemen over here.

[Associate 2] We will announce the details of this in the very near future. It will give you all the details.

[Media] Is this being broadcast live here? We're wondering…

[Associate] NBC has picked up the U.S. rights for the fifty states and we are currently negotiating to have it live, live here but it's still open to negotiations at this time.

[Col. Tom Parker] Mr. Roy Houston, I asked Mr. Tom Masten, the general vice president of all the hotels to give us a larger place. He couldn't do it so he wants to make up for it by [donating??] to the Kui Lee Cancer Fund, so please I had to use a little pressure but we got it.

[Media] Elvis, I have a question. Colonel Parker has intimated in the past that you might be considering retiring at the peak of your career. It seems like reaching a million and a half…a billion and a half people at one time would be considered the peak. Does this bring you any closer to retirement?
Well I…that's just a rumor because I go right into Las Vegas when I finish that.

[Col. Tom Parker] I can answer that. Did you say it's the peak of the career? We've got a long way to go yet (laughter).

[Media] How long will the concert be?

[Associate] One full hour.

[Media] Elvis, for someone that has for the past seventeen years if not [longer] dominated all the charts, country, pop, rock—if not dominated, at least had a big factor in it for seventeen years—we have seen artists and other performers come and go, people of the magnitude of the Beatles. Yet Elvis Presley is right there for seventeen years. What do you think?
A lot of praying. (Laughter.) I just…

[Media] Judging from your performance Saturday night [November 18] you have really gained and grown.
Thank you, I really like it. I enjoy live concerts.

[Media] Is that part of the reason you decided to make this a live concert, the satellite telecast? It could have been in a studio but yet you chose live or some say live. Is that part of the reason?
Yes.

[Media] How long will you be in Hawaii this time, Elvis?
I will be staying here. I don't know. I will be here about…just a few days.

[Media] I have a question. You have a project to get a Kui Lee movie out. If feasible and you are offered a part, would you consider it? I think you are a natural, having been three times in Hawaii already.
I might, 'cause everybody likes that song. I do it everywhere and everybody likes it.

[Media] Mr. Presley, do you have any intentions about coming to Japan? If so, when?
Well, I go on satellite but as far as a personal appearance I don't have any definite time. But I would like to come over there, I would like to really.

[Media] Mr. Presley, how do you think about many Japanese fans who came to Las Vegas and those in Hawaii.
I love them.

[Media] What will the format be?
It's hard to tell, it's going to be just a live show.

[Media] Are you going to capitalize on the fact you are in Hawaii?
Well, not so much as doing a good show. I mean if they are good songs.

[Media] Mr. Presley, have you bought any property in Hawaii?
No sir, I haven't.

[Media] Previously someone asked you about your morality. Have you contributed to the morality. I noticed in your movie Elvis on Tour, and also in the HIC concert, you featured a gospel tune. You highlighted it. Is this commonplace with you and is there some significance behind it?
Well, it's played a major role in my life, gospel music. I was around it and I like it. A lot of times when we do concerts, after the concert we go up to the suite and sing all night long, just for the sheer enjoyment of it.

[Media] Elvis, what kind of religious background do you have? There has been rumors that you have…you hear a lot of things.
Well, I was brought up in the Assemblies of God, but I've studied a lot of books on religion.

[Media] Elvis, how does marriage figure into your future?
There is really not that much about it, to tell you the truth. I have a little girl three years old and it's pretty hard to work the two together.

[Media question unclear]
Not enough, it's just part of the show. I throw it to one person and it usually ends up with about eight people pulling at me (laughter).

[Col. Tom Parker] Okay gentlemen, we have a few words from Elvis' friend Mr. Eddie Sherman.
I'd just like to say before anything else that it's a great privilege to do this satellite program, and

I'm gonna do my…my best and all the people that work with me, to do a good show. It's just pure entertainment, no messages and no this and that, just try to make people happy for that one hour that it comes across. If we do that then I think we've done our job.

[Eddie Sherman] I'd like to say it's a pleasure following Elvis. Highlight of my life and I want to shake his hand and thank him for everything he's done for Hawaii. For those of you who may not recall the Arizona Memorial there was a lot of publicity. It was ten years ago that Elvis and the Colonel came to Hawaii and performed at Block Arena raising over fifty thousand dollars, and as a result we got the Arizona Memorial built. I wrote a letter two months ago to Colonel Parker asking him if there was anyway he could consider helping the Kui Lee Cancer Fund since it was known that Elvis was coming to Hawaii. I was lucky enough to get the letter to him personally and when he got to Hawaii he called me and the end result is that this morning a press conference was agreed upon and it was decided [that the proceeds from] the live concert will go to the Kui Lee Cancer Fund. And all we can do is say thank you from the bottom of our hearts for the Cancer Society and the Kui Lee Cancer Fund and before I leave I would like to introduce Kui Lee's widow, Manni Lee. Manni Lee (applause). So that's it, we will be very happy to have his money stay here in Hawaii for cancer research. Thank you.

[Col. Tom Parker] I don't get the kind of money Mr. Presley gets so I don't do interviews and no pictures of the family (laughter).

DECEMBER 4, 1972

ITEM: *Typewritten letter written and signed by Elvis Presley (Memphis, Tennessee) to Col. Tom Parker at MGM Studios (Culver City, California).*

SOURCE: *Original document.*

> *Dear Colonel,*
> *As I had to leave for Memphis on short notice and was unable to meet with you to sign the contract for the worldwide satellite program from Hawaii, for RCA Record Tour's [sic], and the special agreement for the "Aloha from Hawaii" album, I would appreciate it if you would sign for me, and I hereby authorize you to do so in my behalf.*
>
> > *Thank you,*
> > *Elvis Presley*

DECEMBER 1972

ITEM: *Handwritten note written and signed by Elvis Presley (Memphis, Tennessee).*
SOURCE: *Original document.*
> *[Exact date not known. Single page from a "2001—A Space Odyssey" notepad, referencing Christmas gifts to friends at the Memphian Theater.]*
>
> *$50 Mr. Campbell Xmas gift, Memphian Theater.*
> *$50 Mr. Davis Xmas gift, Memphian Theater.*

1972

ITEM: *Handwritten note written and signed by Elvis Presley.*
SOURCE: *Original document.*
> *[Exact date not known.]*
>
> *Philosophy for a happy life.*
> *Someone to love*
> *Something to look forward to*
> *And something to do.*
> *E.P. 1972*

LOCATION: *Honolulu International Center, Honolulu, Hawaii.*

EVENT: *Random comments during rehearsal and televised* Aloha from Hawaii via Satellite *concerts.*

SOURCE: Aloha from Hawaii *and* The Alternate Aloha *(Videos and CDs).*

I'd like to thank our producer and director, ladies and gentlemen, Mr. Marty Pasetta, for putting this show together. He's really done a fantastic job, him and his staff. There's been a lot of people workin' on the show.

As you know, we're going out live [via satellite], and we're doing it for the Kui Lee Cancer Drive. We were supposed to raise five thousand dollars, er, twenty-five thousand dollars, and we raised seventy-five thousand dollars tonight. So thank you. Thank you!

One of my favorite actors is in the audience. Jack Lord—I gotta say that—Hawaii Five-O, man.

Thank you very much, ladies and gentlemen. You're really a fantastic audience, and there's a song we did in Blue Hawaii, *we did here about ten years ago, and I'd like to sing it especially for you* ["Can't Help Falling in Love"].

ITEM: *One handwritten page by Elvis, taken from "The Kahlil Gibran Diary for 1973."* Gibran's The Prophet *was one of Elvis' favorite books.*

SOURCE: *Document photocopy.*

If I wasn't tough
I wouldn't be here
[If] I wasn't gentle
I wouldn't derserve (sic) to be here
                  Elvis Presley

ITEM: *Telegram from Elvis Presley (Memphis, Tennessee) to Mrs. [Claudia "Lady Bird"] Lyndon B. Johnson (Johnson City, Texas).*

SOURCE: *Original document.*

To those of us who knew the President [Lyndon B. Johnson] as we did, the greatest tribute will be the way you carry on the Johnson tradition. To you, Lynda Bird, Lucy, and all the family, our sincere thoughts are with you.
             Elvis and the Colonel.

ITEM: *Typewritten letter, typed by "L.M." and signed by Col. Tom Parker (Las Vegas, Nevada), to Dan Coffey, KOOL-FM Radio (Phoenix, Arizona).*

SOURCE: *Original document.*

["Dan Coffey" was, at that time, a radio air name for author Jerry Osborne. The majority of the letter deals with Presley-related issues, but is irrelevant to this work. Only the following is attributed to Elvis.]

Elvis did want me to tell you how much he appreciates the charitable work you've been doing with the bus groups you are bringing to the Vegas shows. In fact, we both are grateful.

Anytime you need more giveaway records or items, just contact either myself or George Parkhill.
             Sincerely,
             The Colonel

LOCATION: *Las Vegas Hilton.*

SOURCE: The Memphis Flash Hits Vegas *(CD).*

Fight Night in Vegas

[After four drunken troublemakers, who climbed on the stage during Elvis' performance, were dispatched swiftly back into the audience by Elvis and his bodyguards.]

I'm sorry, ladies and gentlemen…I'm sorry I didn't break his goddamned neck is what [I'm sorry about]. If you wanna shake my hand, fine. If [he] wants to get tough, [I'll] whip his ass.

[Applause and standing ovation.]

FEBRUARY 23, 1973

LOCATION: *Las Vegas Hilton.*
SOURCE: Las Vegas Stage Show *(CD).*

Introducing J. D. Sumner and the Stamps Quartet

First of all, on the left, Mr. J. D. Sumner and the Stamps Quartet. I've told the story before, I'm gonna tell it again. When I was sixteen years old I was listening to him sing bass with a group called the Blackwood Brothers, in Memphis, Tennessee. And I never dreamed I'd be singing with him on stage. It's a pleasure, J. D. and the Stamps. And he is, all kidding aside, the lowest bass singer in the world. There are two bass singers in that group, one, when we do a

With Col. Parker, Lynda Johnson (President Lyndon Johnson's daughter), and George Hamilton on *Spinout* set, 1966.

song in the key of C, one bass singer [Rich Sterban] is on low C, he's [J.D.] on double low C. This little girl [Kathy Westmoreland] is on double high C, these fellows [Stamps Quartet] are in the middle. Charlie [Hodge] does something, I don't know what.

Guest Introductions

There's a lot of people in the audience I'd like you to say hello to, so many it scares me to death. But anyway, I'm glad they're here. I know you wanta meet 'em. I made a movie recently called Elvis on Tour. *It won a Golden Globe Award for Best Documentary [of 1972], and the director of that film, that put it all together, is in the audience. His name is Pierre Adidge.*

I'd like to say that up there in the balcony is a man—one man—that handles all this sound in this room. His name is Bill Porter.

The guy that I gave the belt to is a good friend of mine. His name is Ed Parker.

There's a few others, I'm not through yet. One of the astronauts is here, Buzz Aldrin. Buzz.

Mama Cass [Elliott]. You know her, Mama Cass. Stand up baby. Stand up and let 'em see you. Now stand down, make room. Okay, settle down, Mama Cass.

One of the greatest [character] actors of all time, Mr. Dane Clark.

A gentleman I've known for a long time, one of the nicest men I've ever met, and one of the finest actors, Mr. Ernest Borgnine.

Here's a good friend of mine, another actor, George Hamilton. George. That's enough, George.

The girl that opens here tomorrow night, and believe me, ladies and gentlemen (applause)…let me finish, we made a movie together called Viva Las Vegas. *Anyway, since then, she has developed one of the greatest stage acts you've ever seen. I'd like you to please say hello to Ann-Margret. Turn the light on her…you're beautiful. Put the light on her, man, I want to look at her. Thank you, dear. And I got a note here that says Col. Parker is outside selling Ann-Margret's pictures.*

APRIL 29, 1973

LOCATION: *Seattle, Washington.*
SOURCE: *Audiotape.*
Thank you very much. Good evening, ladies and gentlemen. It's a pleasure to be here in Seattle. This is really a great town for us. This is the last town that I played before I got drafted into the service, and then we did a movie here called It Happened at the World's Fair. *I was fifteen years old then.*

> [Actually, there were a half-dozen cities where Elvis performed between his September 1, 1957, Seattle show, and the end of the pre-Army concerts. His final 1957 show took place in Honolulu at Pearl Harbor, November 11.]

AUGUST 6, 1973

LOCATION: *Las Vegas Hilton.*
SOURCE: Fire in Vegas *(CD).*
Introducing Petula Clark
> *[There's some] people in the audience I'd like to say hello to, ladies and gentlemen. First of all, a very fine singer, and I don't know if I've met this young lady or not…Petula Clark. Where are you, dear? In this room…oh, back here. Stand up and let 'em take a look at you, honey.*

Introducing Guy Marks
> *And a guy that I've always thought was very funny, and I met him many, many years ago. He does this [imitating him] on the stage. His name is Guy Marks. Guy, where are you?*

Introducing Phyllis McGuire
> *And a lady…her name is Phyllis McGuire. I*

had one of my biggest fights I ever had with anybody in my entire life with her. But I still love her…Phyllis McGuire.

> [Phyllis McGuire, of the singing McGuire Sisters trio, dated Elvis for a short time. The argument he refers to took place outside the hotel in Las Vegas and involved her relationship with mob boss Sam Giancana. Their peculiar story is the subject of the 1995 film Sugartime.]

Introducing Liza Minnelli
> *And then finally, the award-winning actress, ladies and gentlemen…Lisa [Liza] Minnelli.*

AUGUST 10, 1973

LOCATION: *Las Vegas Hilton.*
SOURCE: *Audiotape.*
Audience Report Card
> *You know, we judge audiences when they come in here. We give them a C+, or a B−, whatever. You are definitely an A audience.*

But Who's Counting
> *Today is Kathy's [Westmoreland] birthday. She just turned seventeen.*

AUGUST 12, 1973

LOCATION: *Las Vegas Hilton.*
SOURCE: *Audiotape.*
Introducing Bob Conrad
> *There's a guy in the audience I'd like you to meet, a good friend of mine. He had a very successful TV series and he's a fine actor. Nice to see you. I'll tell you, he's a tough little guy, man. He was on our football team, we played the [Los Angeles] Rams, U.C.L.A., and everybody else.*

AUGUST 20, 1973

LOCATION: *Las Vegas Hilton.*
SOURCE: A Profile—The King on Stage *(CD).*

Introducing Bob Hope

There's a gentleman in the audience I'd like you to meet, ladies and gentlemen, and it's really an honor, for him to come in and see our show. He's really an American institution. He's one of the funniest men that ever lived…Mr. Bob Hope. Thank you very much for coming in.

[Then, in "Long Tall Sally," Elvis sings: "Saw Bob Hope with Long Tall Sally."]

AUGUST 26, 1973

LOCATION: *Las Vegas Hilton.*

SOURCE: *Audiotape and* Las Vegas Fever *(CD).*

Introducing Lisa Marie

I'd like to do a song for my little daughter [Lisa Marie]. She's in the audience. She's five years old. (Applause.) She gets a bigger hand than the band did, man, I'll tell ya. I'd like to tell you a little story, first, ladies and gentlemen, about the orchestra and about the members of my group up here. I can change songs on them and—we can do at least fifty songs—and I don't have to turn around and tell 'em. They can just hear it and pick it up like that. But the guys [relying] on the sheet music have heart failure…but they always catch up with me. I'd like to do a song for Lisa. This is "The First Time [Ever I Saw Your Face]."

Never Miss a Lick

I'd like to take a moment to praise my orchestra and my backup group. I kid a lot, change songs and switch around…they never miss a lick. They just catch on, and I think they're really fantastic.

We can do at least fifty songs, and I don't have to turn around and tell them. They can just hear it and pick it up. But the guys using sheet music have heart failure, but they always catch up with me.

AUGUST 28, 1973

LOCATION: *Las Vegas Hilton.*

SOURCE: Take These Chains from My Heart *(CD).*

Until It's Time for You to Go

Whoo! I like that, thank you very much. Well, it's time to go, ladies and gentlemen. They only want us to be on for a certain amount of time, like fifty-five minutes to an hour and that's all, at the Hilton. But to heck with what they say!

AUGUST 31, 1973

LOCATION: *Las Vegas Hilton.*

SOURCE: *Audiotape.*

Introducing Charlton Heston

We have a guest in the audience, ladies and gentlemen. One of the most distinguished actors of all time. He's made some of the greatest classic films ever made. I knew him from the Paramount Studios when he made The Ten Commandments *and* Ben-Hur…*Charlton Heston.*

I used to kid him a lot. We were both working at Paramount, when he was doing The Ten Commandments, *and one day it was raining. I said "Moses, make it stop raining."*

SEPTEMBER 3, 1973

LOCATION: *Las Vegas Hilton.*

SOURCE: Opening Night, Funny Side of Elvis Presley, *and* Top Act in Vegas, Vol. 4 *(CDs).*

Monkey Business

[Elvis enters with monkey doll on his back] Good evening, ladies and gentlemen and animal lovers. We hope you have a good time tonight. We're gonna sing some songs and walk around, and try to get this monkey off my back. If he has to go to the bathroom, I'm in trouble. What is this som'bitch?

Mr. Fix-It

[Referring to microphone connection.] I broke it! Just hang with me, folks, I used to be an electrician. You drove two thousand miles and paid all kinds of money to watch me screw this damn wire in.

Alternative to Tipping

Good evening, ladies and gentlemen. I hope you have a good time tonight. I'm just gonna sing some songs and walk around…kick the bellhop.

Guest Introductions

In the audience, there's a few people I'd like you to meet, as soon as I get some water. A good friend of mine, he's an actor and he's done many, many great things. I'd like you to say hello to Mister George Hamilton.

Sitting in the booth with George is my manager, Colonel Tom Parker.

This young lady is a very fine singer. She's opening at the Frontier Hotel on Thursday, Bobbie Gentry. She's good, folks, so go over and see her act. She's a lot of woman, really.

And opening tomorrow night right here, the very fine singer Shirley Bassey.

I'd like you to meet my father. He's been here awhile. Where's my dad? Here he is.

I want you to say hello to Linda [Thompson].

Tiger Man vs. Hilton

There's a guy here that works in the Italian restaurant, his name is Mario. And these people are gettin' ready to fire him as soon as I leave. And I don't want him to go. He needs the job. And I think the Hiltons are greater than that. No disrespect, I just wanna wake up Conrad [Hilton] and tell him about Mario's job. That's all. This next song [Tiger Man] is dedicated to the hierarchy—the staff—of the Hilton Hotel. "I'm the king of the jungle. They call me the Tiger Man."

LOCATION: *Home of Jimmy Velvet, Memphis, Tennessee.*

SOURCE: A Private Moment with the King *(CD).*

[Exact date not known.]

Wildlife Poetry

Did you hear the little poem that I wrote?
As I awoke this morning
When all sweet things are born
A robin perched on my windowsill
To greet the coming dawn
He sang a song so sweetly
And paused for a moment's lull
I gently raised the window
And crushed his fuckin' skull!
(Laughter.) Oh, Lord have mercy.

[Linda Thompson] Did you hear that? That was pretty bad, wasn't it? When you first told me that I thought, How beautiful, that's so pretty. I knew there was something coming up. I thought it was going to be such a pretty little poem.

Hospital Food—Not Fit for a King

[Sam Thompson] Besides Lottie [Tyson], who's the other one that works there [Graceland cooks]?

[L.T.] Nancy [Rooks], Mary [Jenkins], and Pauline [Nicholson]. Lottie.
They did all the cooking for me when I was in the hospital. They'd cook it at home and Ricky [Stanley] would bring it up there every night. I'll tell you what, they [hospital] gave us whatever we wanted, but that home cooking just really broke the monotony

[Margie Thompson, Linda's mother] That food at the hospital, it's not seasoned.
No, it's kind of bland.

1974

JANUARY 26, 1974

LOCATION: *Las Vegas Hilton.*

SOURCE: *Audiotape.*

Energy Conservation Scheme

I'd like to tell you one quick little story. My manager, Colonel Tom Parker, when he heard there was an energy crisis, he went out and bought all these signs with my name all over them. He bought this luminous-type paper, that lights up in the dark. Swear to God he did.

FEBRUARY 6, 1974

LOCATION: *Las Vegas Hilton.*

SOURCE: Checkmate in Las Vegas *(CD).*

My Name Is…

Thank you very much. Good evening, ladies and gentlemen. My name is Wayne Newton. I just work here.

Introducing the Checkmates

There's a couple people in the audience I'd like you to say hello to, ladies and gentlemen. I'd like to thank them for comin' to see our show. First of all, if you get a chance, go see the fantastic Checkmates. How're ya doin'? I used

On tour, Maryland, 1974.

to go in and see them every night…every night, you know.

Introducing Nancy Sinatra

And there's a young lady in the audience that was in a movie that we did this past week, called Speedway. *She's one of my favorite people. And she may look a little funny to you right now, I'll explain to you later. Miss Nancy Sinatra.*

FEBRUARY 9, 1974

LOCATION: *Las Vegas Hilton.*

SOURCE: *Audiotape.*

My Name Is…

Good evening, ladies and gentlemen. Welcome…welcome to the show. My name is Bill Cosby.

Introducing Sweet Analysts

The young ladies that opened our show tonight, I think they're really fantastic, the Sweet Inspirations. I call them my analysts. If anything goes wrong I go in their dressing room and I close the door and I confess everything to 'em.

Introducing Mark Lindsay

In the audience, ladies and gentlemen, there's a guy I'd like you to meet. He's with the Oakland Raiders…naw, naw, naw…Paul Revere and the Raiders. His name is Mark Lindsay. Mark, he's right there, could we get a spotlight on him. Would you stand up, please? Mark, thank you very much.

Introducing Rich Little

There's a gentleman in the audience who was in to see us last night, and he's one of the finest impressionists in the world and a very fine gentleman, Mr. Rich Little. Rich. You've got it. By jove, you've got it.

Introducing Leslie Uggams

And opening here tomorrow night, ladies and gentlemen, is a very fine singer and a very pretty lady, Miss Leslie Uggams. Leslie.

Introducing Bill Cosby

Also, a very fine comedian and a good friend of mine, Mr. Bill Cosby. Fat Albert and the whole gang's here. Thank you all, very much.

Closing Night Farewell

You're a fantastic audience, ladies and gentlemen, really. I'd like to say something. I'd like to tell you that this has been one of the most fantastic engagements we've ever had in Las Vegas. The audiences have been great and everything has been fine. Except for just a couple of microphone problems, it's been absolutely perfect. The audience and everybody on stage and everything. I really thank you. It's been really fun. Thank you.

MARCH 18, 1974

LOCATION: *Richmond, Virginia.*
SOURCE: Guaranteed to Blow Your Mind *(CD).*

Introducing John What's-His-Name

On the rhythm guitar is John Wilkerson. Wilkerson? Wilkenson? It don't matter.

MARCH 20, 1974

LOCATION: *Memphis, Tennessee.*
SOURCE: Steamroller Blues *(CD).*

Fan screams: "Elvis, turn around!"

Honey, I'll turn around as much as I can without gettin' dizzy and falling off the stage.

About Homecoming

I'd like to tell you something if I could. It's always been said that a person cannot return to their hometowns, but you have disproven that theory completely. You have really made it worthwhile.

MAY 24, 1974

LOCATION: *Sahara Tahoe, Stateline, Nevada.*

With Sammy Davis Jr. and others backstage, Las Vegas, 1970.

SOURCE: Spanish Eyes *and* Big Boss Man at Lake Tahoe *(CDs).*

My Name Is…

Thank you very much, ladies and gentlemen. Good evening. My name is Pat Boone…and we are gonna do a lot of songs tonight, old ones, new ones. Pat Boone songs.

About Sex Maniacs

I will if you will.

[Fan screams.] I will.

There's a bunch of sex maniacs in the audience.

[Reading note from fan.] I have a warm spot for you…oh yeah, honey, I'll be there. Just hang loose. Don't hang loose, just hang on. What do you want to do? You got a scarf, you got a blue one. Well I'll be doggone. [Reading note.] I can't tell you what it says, you know.

MAY 25, 1974

LOCATION: *Sahara Tahoe, Stateline, Nevada.*
SOURCE: The King for Dessert *(CDs).*

Backstage, on tour, Philadelphia, 1974.

My Name Is…

Thank you very much, ladies and gentlemen. Good evening. My name is Wayne Newton. I've got a brother named Fig. And another one that we can't mention up here.

Slightly Longer Title

This next song is our latest. It's out this week. One side of it is called "If You Talk in Your Sleep, Don't Mention My Name, and If You Walk in Your Sleep, Forget Where You Came."

[Laughter.] No, really! Written by one of my corrupt friends, Mr. Red West. On the other side is a song called "Help Me." Hope you like it.

MAY 27, 1974

LOCATION: *Sahara Tahoe, Stateline, Nevada.*
SOURCE: A Profile—The King on Stage, Vol. 2 *(CD).*

My Name Is…

Thank you very much. Good evening. My name is Sammy Davis.

Introducing Billy Eckstine

There's a gentleman in the audience I'd like you to meet. First of all, I gotta tell you a little story. When I was in school, this man was one of the biggest inspirations of my life—as far as singing. And he's performing here in town now. And it's a pleasure to introduce…I gotta tell you something else…the high collars…he originated them twenty years ago…Billy Eckstine…Billy…outta sight. Thank you for coming in. It's really a pleasure, man, thank you. [Sings a few lines of "I Apologize."]

JUNE 23, 1974

LOCATION: *Philadelphia, Pennsylvania.*
SOURCE: *Audiotape.*

My Name Is…

Thank you very much, ladies and gentlemen. My name is Frankie Avalon.

LOCATION: *Niagara Falls, New York.*
SOURCE: Rockin' Against the Roarin' Falls *(CD).*

My Name Is…

My name is Wayne Newton. We hope you have a good time this evening.

LOCATION: *Kansas City, Missouri.*
SOURCE: A Profile—The King on Stage *(CD).*

My Name Is…

Thank you very much. Good evening, ladies and gentlemen. My name is Little Richard. It's a pleasure to be here and we hope you have a good time this evening, and I hope I can get my mouth to work right, you know.

Someone Puts a Stuffed Gorilla on Stage

Don't you move, you big som'bitch. I told the Colonel to stay off the stage!

A Good Audience

You're really a good audience, ladies and gentlemen. To pay money to put up with that kind of stuff…you gotta be good.

Fun with J. D. Sumner

Let me just walk around and breathe for a few minutes. Okay with you?
How're you doin', J.D.?

[J.D. Sumner] Fine, Elvis.

Well, uh, what do ya think about the weather, J.D.?

[J.D.] Terrific, Elvis.

I think he's really that little gorilla that that girl put on stage.
I'd like to ask J.D. and the Stamps to leave the stage. Nah, I'd like to ask J.D. and the Stamps to sing one my favorite songs, "Why Me, Lord."

About Bill Baize

Bill Baize over there on the high tenor. He's

Introducing Kathy Westmoreland, Las Vegas, 1974.

higher than a cat's back, boy, I'll tell you for sure.

About Kathy Westmoreland

The little girl that does our high voice singing…is Bill Baize…no, it's Kathy Westmoreland. Why don't you wear your see-through blouse tonight, dear?

About Ronnie Tutt

On the drums, from up a tree, hardworkin' Ronnie Tutt.

About Duke Bardwell

On the Fender bass, from Lake what…red… oh, Baton Rouge. Baton Rouge? What is… Baton Rouge, Lousiana, Duke Bardwell. Explain it to me again, Duke, what is a Baton Rouge?

[Duke Bardwell] A red stick.

A red stick? Red Stick, Lousiana?

About Glen D. Hardin

On the piano from Lubbock, Texas, is Glen Campbell. Ah, Glen Hardin.

About Jimmy Dean

And be sure and buy Jimmy Dean Pure Pork Sausage, 'cause that Jimmy Dean needs the money.

About His New Record

This next song is a new record that we have

out. One side is called "If You Talk in Your Sleep" and the other side is "Make Sure You're Alone."

There Must Be Some Mistake

Singing the baritone, from Nashville, Tennessee, is Joe Esposito [Ed Hill].

LOCATION: *RCA Studio, Hollywood, California.*
SOURCE: From Sunset Blvd. to Paradise Road *(CD).*

Rehearsal (With Between-Take Comments)

["Promised Land"] Boy, that's a movin' mother.

["Softly, As I Leave You"] I think I'd rather stick with the piano and the strings, you know. I mean, the organ may be pretty but I'm not familiar with the organ sound. I can follow this [piano]. And the strings can just do some real pretty stuff in the background. No, no, no, no, no, no, no, no, no, no. I've already told you, this and the strings, just like we talked the other night. The simpler this thing is, the better. Shut up! Get out of my studio! Sound like Kang Rhee: "whooshit, booschhatt!" Be on good terms with all rednecks.

["I'm Leavin'"] I'm Leavin'! Not the song, I'm [really] leavin'.

["The First Time Ever I Saw Your Face"] The first ever I saw your friggin' face.

["If You Talk in Your Sleep"] Okay, if you talk in your sleep, don't jack around. What key are we in, Dewey? What's the intro to this son-of-a-bitch? No, it's doin' me in, vocally. Anybody got a knife, scissors, bullet, anything? That's a hard son-of-a-bitch to sing.

LOCATION: *Las Vegas Hilton.*
SOURCE: If You Talk in Your Sleep *(CD).*

My Name Is...

Good evening. My name is the NBC Peacock.

About "If You Talk in Your Sleep"

That's a weird song, you know that. That's not about me, I didn't write that song about myself because I don't do that. Charlie wrote it. No, a friend of mine, Red West, wrote it. I don't know why or what...he wrote it.

Introductions...

There's a gentleman in the audience I'd like you to meet, ladies and gentlemen. He's been with the Barnum and Bailey Circus for a long time. He's one of the greatest animal trainers in the world. I mean this cat gets in the ring with like twelve tigers and seven lions, and everything. And I sleep with that every night, but you know (laughs). No, all kidding aside, he's a very nice...good friend of mine. His name is Gunter Williams. Gunter, stand up.

There's somebody else in the audience I'd like you to meet. He's one of the coolest actors in the world, and he's been a friend of mine for a long, long time. He came on the movie set when I was doing a movie called Kid Galahad, *and that's the first time I met him. He's been in to see my show, and he's got the number-one show on television [Kojak]...Mr. Telly Savalas.*

LOCATION: *International Hotel, Las Vegas.*
SOURCE: Vegas Birthday Show *(CD).*

My Name Is...

Thank you very much, ladies and gentlemen. Good evening. My name is Wayne Newton, and we hope you have a good time here this evening. We'll do our best to entertain you, sing a lot of songs, walk around and sweat, give some scarves away, kiss some people, whatever.

I did a song in fifty-six, it's called "Heartbreak Hotel." Let me tell you, it was a little bit like the International Hotel, except it didn't have these little bitty, ugly dolls on the wall…those fat, funky angels. There's nothing worse than a fat angel except a fat, funky angel. You'd think if they're gonna put an angel up there it would be a pretty angel.

Showroom Walls Get an Unscheduled Touch-up

Let me tell you a little story. The other…put a spotlight on the wall here. You see those ugly…those weird lookin' creatures over there? The guy that directed this room…decorated this room was just, I mean, he was way out on cloud nine somewhere, he was floatin', boy. Anyway, put it back over here [spotlight]. Put it back over on this side. So, the other morning, after the last show, at four-thirty in the morning, me and some of the guys that work with me came back, there wasn't a soul here. We climbed the fence back where they keep all the paint and all the props and everything, we got a can of black paint, you know, like on Mission: Impossible. *We went out of there and stacked two tables up, and I had the paint and paintbrush…and I painted that [statue on the wall].*

[Note: Elvis tells this story again on August 27, 1974.]

Introducing Joe Guercio

Our conductor, from Tupelo, Mississippi… that's where I was born, Joe. In a little two-room shack. They got a ball park down there, or something now. Mr. Joe Guercio. Did you know that Joe is as nutty as a fruitcake? Great conductor, but offstage he's totally insane. Joe is conducting the Fantastic Weirdos.

LOCATION: *International Hotel, Las Vegas.*
SOURCE: *Audiotape.*

Introducing Kathy Westmoreland

J. D. [Sumner] is like a father figure up here, and the mother figure is the little girl that does our high voice singing, she was with the Met—Metropolitan Opera—for a year and with the vice squad in L.A. for two years, her name is Kathy Westmoreland.

Showroom Walls by El Flippo

I want to show you something about this room. Here we go. I have never liked the way this room is designed, I mean the inside of it. I'm sure the interior decorator had good intentions, but he was El Flippo. He had gone down the drain, boy. Now look over here on the left side. The other night [sings] "as I lay sleeping." Naw, the other night about four-thirty in the morning, some o' the guys that work for me—Red West and Jerry Schilling and some the other guys—came down here, and Red took off his shoes and climbed the fence, a wire, Cyclone fence, climbed it, went behind and got a bucket of black paint, tied it around his belt, climbed back over the wall, we went out here, we stacked up two tables, I had that paint and I carefully painted that statue. Ha-ha, it felt good. And then we went back to put the paint away. And we're gone. Nobody said a word about it in the hotel. I don't know if they know the difference or not, you know.

Introducing Red West

That song ["If You Talk in Your Sleep"] was written by a, one o' my longtime friends, and he works for me, runs a karate school in Memphis, he's a second-degree black belt in karate, he's a good boy, Red West. In fact, you wrote "Why Can't Everyday Be Like Christmas" ["If Everyday Was Like Christmas"], and you wrote "Separate Ways."

With Tom Jones in Las Vegas, 1967.

Introducing Kang Rhee

There's a gentleman in the audience that came from Korea to Memphis to teach the art of karate. And he has three schools in Memphis, one of the biggest in the South. And last night I had a temperature and I had to skip both shows because they advised me not to come out, it could get worse and so on. But he came in yesterday, and he and another guy, named Hank Green, made me an eighth-degree black belt. Master Kang Rhee.

You Can See It on *Hee-Haw*

[Note: The following is Elvis' response to something shouted by a woman in the audience. On our tape, she is barely audible. We certainly will not speculate on what she may have said.]

You know something. You know what in the dictionary the meaning of a nigger is? That's n-i-g-g-e-r. It says "lazy and shiftless," that's all. In that case, there are white niggers too. You don't believe it? Haven't you ever seen Hee-Haw? *What you talkin' about?*

[While his point is clear and unoffensive, it's doubtful any dictionary contains this definition of "nigger." Elvis may have confused the word with "laggard."]

Thanking Bill Cosby

I'd like to pay tribute to somebody that, when they saw I was sick last night they needed somebody to replace me in case I caught the flu real bad or something. So Bill Cosby volunteered to come down and do my shows.

AUGUST 28, 1974

LOCATION: *International Hotel, Las Vegas.*
SOURCE: *Audiotape.*

Introducing the Tom Jones

There's somebody in the audience I'd like you to meet. To me…he's my favorite singer. You know they got us as rivals and the movie magazines write all this junk, but it's not true. He's one of the greatest performers I've ever seen, and the greatest voice, Tom Jones. There he is. He's too much. Tom, you open at Caesars Palace tomorrow night, right? Folks, if you get the chance, go over and see him. He's really something. He always comes in to see my show here and I go to see his. It's a mutual respect.

AUGUST 30, 1974

LOCATION: *Las Vegas Hilton (early show).*
SOURCE: *Audiotape.*

My Name Is…

Thank you very much, ladies and gentlemen. Good evening. My name is Tom Jones. You went to the wrong place!

We hope to have a good time. We're gonna sing a lot of songs, walk around, sweat, shake hands with a few people, and kiss a few people. It's just part of the show [kisses]. It is a part of the show, and what is great about it is the guys, their attitude is so great about it. They know it's just a part of the show. And they're really great…up to a certain point.

Introducing the Wests

I'd like you to meet a friend of mine. He's

been with me a long time, written a couple of songs for me, Red West. C'mon, Red.

On the other side of the stage is another guy that works for me, he's a relative [cousin] of Red's (laughs), he's kind of shy. He's been with me for a long time, his name is Sonny West.

About Karate

I'll tell you a little bit about this thing [belt]. I've been doin' this for sixteen years. I started when I was in the Army, as a challenge. It was a challenge to me, and so I've been doing it every day of my life. Every day before we come down here for the first show, we have a two-hour class. My drummer [Ronnie Tutt] is a member, Red [West] is one of the instructors. A couple people that work here are students. We teach every day for about two hours starting at six o'clock, up in the suite where we live.

Anyway, let me tell you a little bit about this belt. There are ten degrees of black belt. This big one [stripe] stands for five degrees. I got that four years ago. Five degrees carries the title of Professor of the Art. Six, Senior Professor. [Seventh] Associate Master of the Art. Eighth degree, Master of the Art.

I hope you take it in the right perspective. It's by no means bragging. It's something that's really helped me in discipline, mind control, body control, self-confidence, and all-around. It's just good for ya. Not to hurt anybody. It's just been really great for me. I've never had to use it to hurt anybody and I hope I never would have to.

I don't want to bore you, but let me tell you what this [patches] is. This is one style of karate called [Chinese] Kenpo. This in the back is called PaSaRyu, which is the Korean version of all the karate systems into one. That explains it.

Guest Introductions

I'm gonna do something a little bit different right here, folks. I'd like to introduce you to my father. He's in the audience and I'd like to introduce him to ya. Dad, would you stand up, please. (Laughs.) He's a bigger man than I am, boy. That's where I learned all the stuff.

He's sitting with my doctor, the guy that got me over the flu, Doctor [Elias] Ghanem.

Now this little guy, he's one of my karate students. (Laughs.) He's a little shy.

My girlfriend, Sheila [Ryan]. Cool it, Sheila! See that, I get nervous when I say something like that.

What Time Is It?

How long have we been on? An hour and twenty [minutes]? Now, they don't like me to be on longer than fifty-five to fifty-eight minutes. Really, the hotel doesn't like it because they can't get the people in and out. Sometimes I go over accidentally…I don't wear a watch. We've been on a little too long, but I want to tell you something before we go, though.

The other night when I came down with…almost all of us got sick, there was something goin' around here…so I missed a couple of shows. But in my whole nineteen years of show business, I've only missed about six shows from bein' sick. I don't like to miss if I can possibly be out here, because I know people come from everywhere. Really, I'd rather be here because that's what it's all about. It's my life blood and I love it.

A guy volunteered to come down and take my place, and he's been here for two or three days now. He just volunteered—Bill Cosby. Thank you very much!

About Rings and Things

About these rings. First of all, about the suit. The suit…I usually wear the jumpsuits,

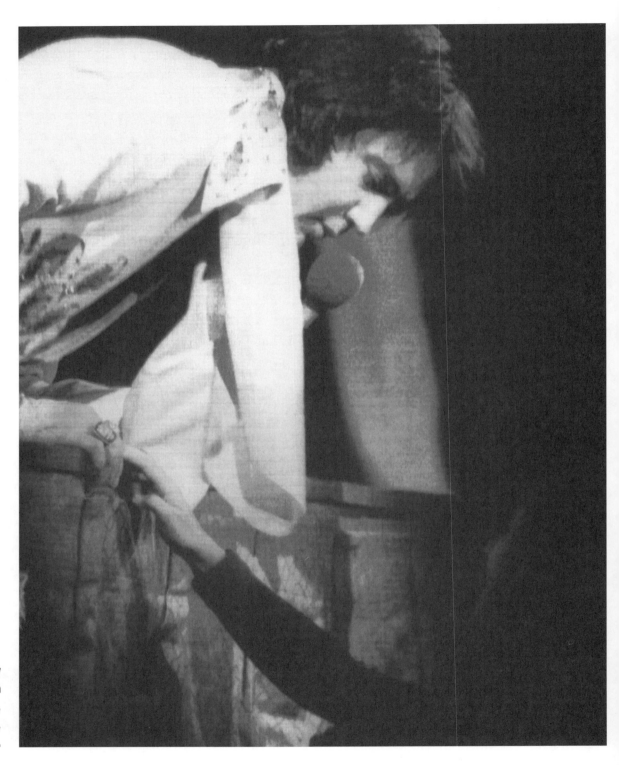

Leaning way
over to kiss a
ringside fan,
Las Vegas,
1974.

because I like 'em and they actually hold up better. This was a gift from a cousin of mine…she had it made for me. I promised her that I'd try to wear it on stage. I hoped it wouldn't tear. I had it reinforced.

The rings. This thing here I wore on the *Aloha from Hawaii* special. A lot of people thought it was one big solid diamond, but it's…it's a big diamond alright. The one in the middle is eleven and one-half carats, I think, the biggest I ever seen. A guy suckered me into buyin' it. Naw, I told him I needed some gifts for my grandmother [Minnie Presley] and my father and my daughter, and some friends of mine. So the guy brought it out to the house, opened his case and this thing accidentally fell out. "Accidentally" fell out! I said, "I told you, I don't want anything."

"That's not supposed to be there," he said. So anyway, I had to buy it. Sixteen carats.

This thing here I had designed for the stage. It's got all different shapes: pear shapes, fruitcake shapes, round, whatever. Just for the stage.

This one…I lost one on stage the other night…I had this big gold one I lost on stage. "Boom," it bounced and it went somewhere, I don't know. So anyway, I got nineteen tapes on my fingers to keep 'em on. This is my last night and [I don't want] to replace it.

The reason I'm tellin' you this is because… you helped pay for 'em.

AUGUST 30, 1974

LOCATION: *Las Vegas Hilton (late show).*
SOURCE: Night Fever in Vegas *(CD).*

About J. D. Sumner

[After "Amen."] Now I have to say something, really. He's the world's lowest bass singer, but he's been very sick. He has had bronchitis, and everything, brewsitis, Jack Daniel's and everything else. But anyway, he's the lowest bass singer in the world and he can do better than that. He's the original Deep Throat…artist…singer! So just listen to him this time. He goes off of the piano keyboard. He can go off the scale. Then we pick him up and set him back on the piano. No, but he can go off the piano keyboard when he's right. I don't know if he's right (laughs)…he don't sound too good.

My Name Is…

Thank you very much, ladies and gentlemen. Good evening. My name is Tom Jones. You went to the wrong place!

About Sickness

I had a cold one night this week, and I was sick. I had to quit. I had to miss two shows. No, that's all, I missed two shows. Missed one night. I had a temperature, they wouldn't let me go on. 'Cause with a temperature you lose your equilibrium and your balance and so forth. But in the whole nineteen years, I've only missed about six or seven shows out of illness, which I'm glad of.

I'm sorry, if you see me spit up every once in a while it's because this cold is breakin' loose in me, and it has to come out. I'd rather do that than…I'm sweating and…no, I don't have anything, I don't think unless I got… [fan screams "Elvis."]…honey, would you repeat that again, back there, and again? No, do it just the way you did it. No, honey, do it the way you did it. Call me the way you did before. [Fan again screams "Elvis."] Honey, you can have anything I got. You want the jacket? I have to keep the pants, otherwise I'll be lined up [playing] at the Hacienda or something like that.

You ain't [beginning "Hound Dog"]…I don't know if this suit will take it or not but I'm gonna give it one hell of a try, ummmm. Gimmie something…anything…towel, scarf, rug. I don't care…hoof and mouth (laughs)…hoof and mouth, open mouth, insert foot, right Charlie. Give me some Gatorade. That's right, you know, Gatorade is good for the…gator I guess, I don't know. And you gotta chase it with water 'cause it tastes like the devil. I mean it tastes like panther…breath (laughs). Ahhhhhgh! Now don't go and get me strangled with that water, I have troubles as it is. Ahhhhhgh!

About "Elvie"

[Fan shouts "Elvie."] Elvie? Don't call me [Elvie]…[it's] Elvis, come on now. Twenty years, man, and Elvie?

About Dean Nichopoulos

There's a guy in the audience that requested this…we'll do "Help Me" later, okay? I'll get to 'em, just give me time. I can't do 'em all at once, honey. Split my tongue. Anyway, there's a guy in the audience who's a friend of mine from Memphis, and his father is my doctor back in Memphis, Dr. George Nichopoulos, and it's his son…what's his name, Dean? No, no, Dean taught me to play hand, racquetball, you know, racquetball. So he asked me to do this song, so I committed him. I made him commit himself. If I would do the song, when we get back to Memphis, he would come to our karate school, and put on a little white suit and come out there and go…workin' out every day…and let me see him do that.

About Showroom Internationalé

I never liked the way this showroom is decorated. It's difficult for a performer to work this room because of its width. See how wide it is.

Introducing Bill Baize

Way over there, about the highest tenor in the gospel business, is Bill Baize. I don't mean singin'…I mean just [high] (laughs).

Just for the show tonight, ladies and gen-tlemen, every one of 'em, everybody employed with me got a card: "This is to certify that, with their name [reading Bill Baize's], is a member of the Elvis Presley Show," and the "E.P.S.," and it has little musical notes, and it has the lightning bolt "T.C.B." and it has the name of the group they're with [i.e., The Stamps, etc.]. Anyway, they all got that stuff, no big deal.

About Deodorant

I use Stay Free pads. Not Stay Free pads, Five Day Deodorant pads.

Introducing Voice

These fellows here that opened the show, they've been with me one year today, and I found them in Nashville, Tennessee, workin' in an upholstery shop. Swear to goodness, they were just forming a group, and I knew some of the guys from years back [Donnie Sumner] and I heard they were forming a group and I brought them to Las Vegas. I call them Voice.

About Karate

I'm gonna do something a little different for you, if you don't mind. I'm gonna…there are a lot of people who know that I have been involved in the art of karate for some time, but nobody knows to what degree, or whatever. So what I would like to do, am about to do, and I hope you take it in the right way, is do a, what's called a "kata," which is a series of movements representing blocks, kicks, punches, things that you see on Kung Fu and karate. Kung Fu and karate are the same thing. There's no difference, just the Chinese terminology uses kung-fu and the Japanese uses karate. The word karate, "kara" means "open hand"…I mean "open," "te" means "hand," karate. So just give me a second and I'll do a little bit for you, okay. You don't mind, do you? [Kata done to the music of "If You Talk in Your Sleep."]

Honey, I wasn't gonna hit you, goddamn (laughs). Wouldn't hit you, I just came close, you know. Right here, but we don't hit.

I'd like to tell you a little bit about this thing [karate belt] before I take it off. Now about the belt, see I've been doing this for sixteen years. I started it when I was in the Army, in 1959, and I've been doing it every day of my life ever since, for at least two to three to six hours a day. And it's been tremendous for me as far as body conditioning, mind control, weight control, breathing techniques. It involves yoga. It involves meditation. There's a lot to it.

It's not just breaking bricks and fighting. I mean, how many times is a brick gonna come out and attack you (laughs)? See these guys goin' "yeeoo!" and break a board. How many times is a board gonna come out and attack you? So it's not for that reason. It's a much deeper meaning.

It evolved in the Buddhist monks, they had no way to protect themselves from robbers, and they were forbidden to carry weapons, so they had to developed a way by which to keep themselves from being killed, beaten, or robbed. So they studied different animals.

They studied the tiger. The tiger fights on his back. "Screeagh!" Like this. In fact all the cat family does. Your housecat does. They roll up in a ball and they fight on the back, and you can't get near them because they got their claws…they protect the stomach with this, their paws…they got their mouths, "whaacht!" You can't get near them.

The cobra snake. A cobra snake will get in front of its victim and move around very slowly like this…Strike! Mesmerize you, hypnotize you.

And the eagle. The eagle is the highest flying of all animals, er, birds. So he comes down out of the sky, he sees his prey, food or his prey, his talons are very powerful. He can crush (laughs)…whatever! If they want to they can (laughs). Trying to be serious and I'm just laughin' my career away. Anyway, they come out of the sky to get their food and they go "sccrachtt!" with those powerful talons and they break the bones of their victims, prey.

Okay, they devised a system, over hundreds and hundreds of years, where human beings could do it. Using the hands, feet, legs, elbows, the outside of the hand, the inside of the hand, this part of the elbow, this part of the elbow, that part of the elbow, the back part of the hand, the front part of the fingers, one finger, two fingers, three fingers, sword…a shot like this. The side of the foot, kick, knife edge, front kick, ball of the foot, the heel, kick back, etc., and so on.

So anyway, I've been doing it for sixteen years, and practicing it, and I've never had to use it in my life in a violent way. And it's not for that reason, you see. On the contrary, it gives you a little more self-confidence. It makes you a little better citizen in your daily life.

There's no age limit in this. Half of the classes around the country nowadays are children and women, and older men and ladies. Because they realize that it doesn't require tremendous physical strength. It improves your balance, and it'll even take the weight off of you and increase your looks, actually, in that it will take a lot of excess away from you, at any age.

There was a man came into one of my instructor's schools in L.A. He was fifty-four years old. He said: "I guess it's too late for me to get a black belt." He watched the class and my instructor, a guy named Ed Parker who teaches the Kenpo system, in Los Angeles. He said: "I guess it's too late for me to get a black belt," and my instructor said: "Well, how bad do you want it?" He said: "Pretty bad" and so on. The guy's been coming out for three years and he's now a black belt. He's a businessman in Beverly Hills. It's true. He's fifty-seven, fifty-eight years old. He comes out every day on his lunch hour and he works out.

So you see, what I'm telling you is, it's not to harm. It's to protect life, and then help to make it better, you know. Now that's a little bit about the history. Now let me tell you about the belts:

You go through seven degrees before you get to the black belt category. You gotta go through degrees of white, yellow, blue, green, purple, orange, and brown…how many's that…before you even get to the seventh. And you test for each one of those. Now that takes approximately, according to the individual effort, it takes approximately a year and a half to two years. It took me a year and a half because I did it every day, from three to six. It's according to how much time you put into it.

[The correct Kenpo belt system differs slightly from that described by Elvis here. During the September 1 show, Elvis gets it right.]

So anyway, I got my first black belt in 1960. I tested five hours for it. I had to fight two guys, one a fourth-degree black and one a black, had to fight 'em both at once, and then separately (laughs). And they just beat the daylights outta me, I mean. But, it was a part of the training.

Anyway, this big part of the belt, the red part…see, the highest degree in karate is the red belt. A lot of people don't know that. The eighth-, ninth-, and tenth-degree red belt. You saw the red with black tabs on it. So this represents five degrees of black, this part, this big part here. This carries the title of…this carries the title of Professor of the Art. The sixth-degree carries the title of Associate Professor. This one, this tab, is Associate Master of the Art. The eighth…there's only ten, remember…this I got about three days ago, this carries the title of Master of the Art (applause). Thank you very much. I hope I didn't bore you at all. I didn't mean to do that (applause). Thank you very much.

Now you're probably wondering…you may be asking…what's next? Okay, you go to Senior Master of the Art, ninth. And then tenth is Grandmaster of the Art. So that's how far that I have to go and that'll take me a little while. I gotta work at that, you know. So that's the belt and the history of that.

This over here is Chinese writing saying my name, and my rank, and my title in the school is "Tiger." Everybody's got a name. Everybody's either a cobra or a snake or something. Mine happens to be Tiger. Look at the size of the belt. Look at that big dude. It takes four guys to tie it back there.

Anyway, this is a style of karate that's taught around the country, by various people, owned by Mr. Parker. It's called the Kenpo style of karate. You see this insignia right here? The one in the back is called the PaSaRyu system, is taught by a fellow from Memphis. He came [from] Korea to Memphis to teach karate. He's here with me tonight, I'd just like you to meet him. He's a very nice gentleman and he's a friend of mine. He's an eighth [degree]…he has three institutes in Memphis. When he came there he had nothing. He taught for nothing, he didn't charge. Now he has three institutes. I'd like you to meet Mr. Kang Rhee. And that word, "PaSaRyu," it means all systems under *one, which means you take the best of all the different systems and break 'em into one.*

A Surprise for Lisa Marie

This thing [lei, a gift from a fan] here is cute, honey. My little daughter is comin' in this weekend. She's six years old, just turned six, and if you don't mind, I'll give this to her, okay? She would love that. What'd you do? Did you come into the first show and see the thing, then have it made? You made it? You're a decorator. That's beautiful, it really is. And the girl made this too, she said, right? You made this, honey? That's beautiful man. Really. And people wonder why I wouldn't want to miss a show…no-no, I love it out here. I know people come from everywhere, and different things. Oh yes sir, you better believe it. We know that people come from all over…they fly and the drive here…and there's not anybody on this stage…I mean anybody…that wouldn't rather be here than anywhere else in the world.

You're from Where?

You're from France? I was in France once, but I was in the Army. I was in a tank so I don't remember it.

About Movie Magazines

Cool it, 'cause you know how those movie magazines and things are, you know. That stuff is junk, if I may [say]. If I did one tenth of the stuff that they said I did, and acted the way they say, my karate instructors would not allow me to wear that belt. I would not. [It's not] who I am. I could not perform on this stage. I could not face my father and my six-year-old daughter. Nothing!

About Planning the Show

Now, that wasn't planned. The girl happened to have that lei down here. Swear to God, we don't plan nothing. We plan nothing down here. No, no, we plan nothing. Everything that happens here is strictly spontaneous. We don't know anything [in advance].

Look at her. She's tryin' to fly. Give me something to give this woman over here (laughs), shut up, Charlie. I didn't ask for your personal advice.

AUGUST 31, 1974

LOCATION: *Las Vegas Hilton (late show).*
SOURCE: It's Midnight in Vegas *(CD).*

Joining Tom Jones during his show, Las Vegas, 1974.

Devil Woman

I must have recorded four hundred songs that started out with "Wel-l-l-l." So it's easy to do the wrong one...the same's true with women, ya know (laughs).

[Woman reaches for scarf.] Whoa! I'm not done yet, but take it. You know that thing about Hell hath no fury like a woman scorned [a line used in the film Follow That Dream*], that's so true. I mean, they got the power of the devil himself. Oh Lord, I love 'em...you can't live without 'em.*

My Name Is...

Good evening, ladies and gentlemen, I'm Tom Jones. You went to the wrong place. I hope you have a good time. We're gonna walk around, sing a lot of songs: old ones, new ones, and try to make you happy. Make you forget about Watergate and all that jazz.

Introducing John Bassett

The World Football League in Memphis had all their players stop at Graceland. Those guys are doing pretty good. I went to a couple of games and they are doing good, and next year they'll be gettin' better. So they're doin' real well, and the owner is here, ladies and gentlemen. His name is John Bassett. John, stand up and let 'em see you. Don't worry, they won't bite.

I went up there in his [private] booth... now listen to what happened. He's thirty-five years old, he's got the Memphis Southmen [football team], he's got a hockey team, he's got all kind of stuff. Anyway, I went to a football game in Memphis, I'm in his box, right. And they gave me a closed circuit television for instant replays...not him (laughs). He says to me, "How come you got a television for instant replays and I own the club and I haven't got one?" I said, "It's who you know, John."

I'm glad you're here, John. He came all the way from Memphis just to see the show.

LOCATION: *Las Vegas Hilton.*

SOURCE: *Audiotape.*

My Name Is...

Good evening, my name is Tom Jones. You went to the wrong hotel. We're gonna do a lot of songs: old ones, new ones, middle-age ones. Walk around, shake hands, kiss the girls, take gifts.

About the Fat Hand

I did this movie, G.I. Blues, *and we would work out [karate] between takes. We would do board breaking, and tiles and bricks and stuff...just demonstrating. Or showing off. I blocked a kick the wrong way, against my fingers, which is wrong.*

This happened in the middle of a movie with Juliet Prowse. I did a love scene, with a guitar, and here was this big fat hand. Nothing I could do. They tried to put makeup on it, but...it looked like it belonged to another person. The other hand was normal and here this hand was, except it was worse. It was a black hand. It came out on the album. Look at the album G.I. Blues, *and look at that hand. It looks like somebody blew it up.*

About Karate

The art of karate, and kung fu...there's no difference in the art, just a difference in the name. The [television] series Kung Fu *is a good series, but it doesn't give a clear-cut picture of the art. Because they're the same thing. Kung fu is a Chinese word meaning "karate"—"kara," which is open, "te," which is hand. Open hand...insert foot. Kung fu is a little more flowing motion.*

The best kung fu masters in the country recently went down to Thailand to compete with those Thailand [kick]boxers. You ever seen those guys on TV, the Wide World of Sports*? The kung fu guys went down to* challenge 'em. Those Thailand guys beat 'em all the way back to where they come from. Those Thailand boxers just beat the kung out of the fu.

On the other hand...is a wart. Naw, on the other hand (laughs). Don't get me started laughing, I'll never finish this. I'm afraid they'll come out here with a hook and pull me off the stage. It's good for body control, mind control, self-confidence. I've been doing it for sixteen years now and it's really helped me in a lot of ways in my life, even with stage work.

I wanna tell you about the belts. There are ten degrees of black belts. There's seven degrees before you reach the black belt. You start with the white, the yellow, orange, purple, blue, green, brown. Seven degrees, and they have a test for each one.

I do mine [workout] for two, three, to six hours, every day of my life. And I teach. We have a class upstairs in our suite. Ronnie [Tutt] is a member, Sonny [West] is taking it, and Red [West] is teaching, and we have a couple other people in our group here that study. We meet every day at six o'clock. We have about an hour-and-a-half class.

In 1960, I tested for the first-degree black belt. I'd been through the others when I was in the army. I was nervous. I had to fight these two guys, one was a fourth-degree black, one was a first degree. I had to fight 'em one at a time, then both at once. They beat the daylights outta me, I'll tell you. This one guy had a smile on his face all the time. For five hours this went on, from seven to twelve. I was so sore the next morning I couldn't get a comb to my head. Swear to God, 'bout broke my arm. Like to beat my muscles into the ground.

In sixty-three, I made second degree. I skipped the third degree. Mr. Parker made me

fourth degree, which carries the title of Associate Professor of the Art. I made the fifth degree [in 1972], which carries the title of Professor of the Art. So that's five degrees of black right there. Then I tested again and got the sixth degree, which is Senior Professor. The seventh degree, which is Senior Master of the Art. Then, three days ago and tonight, I got the eighth degree, which carries Associate Master of the Art.

We're starting our own style of karate, called the American Karate Institute, which is gonna be an Americanization of the art, which doesn't mean anything against the other people. It's just that we feel there's a need for an Americanized version. Like the words. Instead of using foreign languages, we're using [English].

The Gift of Gibson

I'd like to do one thing. There's a fellow down in front here...where are you from...Pennsylvania...he made a guitar for me, one of the most beautiful guitars...do we have it up here, Charlie [Hodge]?

[C.H.] No, it's upstairs.

That's a good place for it, upstairs. Anyway, the Gibson people did the guitar. He did the engraving on it, hand work. It took him six months...he worked on it. And I wanna thank you.

SEPTEMBER 2, 1974

LOCATION: Las Vegas Hilton.
SOURCE: Audiotape and Desert Storm (CD).

About a Tight Suit

I liked to never got in this suit, I mean like to never got in it. A guy made it for me and brought it down and they had to pour me in it, or pour it on me, or whatever. Paint it. I can't move, my breath is gone. You know, nothing. So that's why I'm sorry, folks, down here in the front. I'm sorry that the guitar is *flashing, but I have no control over nothing down here (laughs). Nah, the guitar flashing around down here. Nah, I don't mean to embarrass you, I'm just playing. It's just a sense of humor.*

About Microphone Position

Who fixed this microphone this way? Who fixed this microphone? Does [comedian] Jackie Ka-hoon do that? Whatever his name is…Jerky Ka-hoon. Na, who does this? No look, I'm six-one and a half and this son-of-a-bitch [microphone] is six-three and a half. I gotta have it down like this.

My Name Is…

Good evening, ladies and gentlemen. My name is Bill Cosby. Elvis closed last night. I'm a little lighter-skinned than you thought I was. And I don't have a natural [hairdo] like I do on my TV show. Me and old Harold, I mean, not Harold, what's his name…Albert…Fat Albert.

About Karate Promotion

Hey look, look, look. Somebody gave me this thing here. Yeah, it really is, somebody gave it to me. I just got an eighth-degree black belt in karate. After sixteen years of doing this art every day, for sixteen years, I was awarded the eighth degree, which carries—let me see, eighth degree, there's only ten degrees of black—so the eighth degree, I just got this week, the ninth degree carries Senior Master of the Art, the next one, and the tenth is Senior Grandmaster of the Art. So that's where I gotta strive to go to, which takes quite awhile you know.

About "You Gave Me a Mountain" and Priscilla

I want to make one thing clear. Let me make something clear. I've been singing that song for a long, just a minute here, I've been singing that song for a long time, and a lot of people kind of got it associated with me because they think it's a personal need. It is not. It's a beautiful song, written by Marty Robbins. And I heard Frankie Laine do it, I think it was, and I just love the song. And it has nothing to do with me personally, or my ex-wife, Priscilla. She's right here. Honey, stand up. Come out, honey. Come out. C'mon out. Turn around. Let 'em see you. Let 'em see you. Boy, she is a beautiful chick. I'll tell you for sure. Boy, I knows 'em when I picks 'em, I think. Hot damn. Now, show my little daughter, Lisa, she's six years old. Look at her jump up. Pull your dress down, Lisa! You pull your dress down before you jump up like that again, young lady!

And then at the same booth is my girl-friend Sheila [Ryan]. Stand up, Sheila. Turn around, turn around, completely around. Sheila, straight up…hold the ring up…hold the ring up…the ring…your right hand. Look at that son-of-a-bitch (laughs).

Nah, the thing I'm trying to get across is we're the very best of friends and we always have been. Our divorce came about not because of another man or another woman, but because of the circumstances involving my career. I was traveling too much, I was gone too much. And it was just an agreement, that I didn't think it was fair to her 'cause I was gone so much and everything. So, I therefore, as decently as you can do that type of thing…we just made an agreement to always be friends, and be close and care, 'cause we have a daughter to raise. And for her to have whatever she wanted as a settlement. After the settlement, it came out [in the news] about two million dollars…blah, blah, blah.

Well, after that I got her a mink coat— I know it. I'm talkin' about the mink coat…you hang loose over there—the XKE Jag, after the settlement I just gave it to her.

She got me—listen to this—tonight, a forty-two-thousand-dollar white Rolls-Royce.

That's the type of relationship that we have, you know. And it's not a bad setup, is it, fellows (laughs). You know, I got part of it back anyway, didn't I? I wasn't hurtin' too bad but I did get part of it back. You know, she bought the car just out of a gesture of love and I...and she liked this Stutz that I have. It's not a car, it's a Stutz. Nah, whew! God help me. No, it's called a stud...a Stutz. And she likes a stud (laughs) she likes the Stutz. Mike Stone ain't no stud, so forget it. She liked the Stutz, and so I'm gonna give her the Stutz, and she gave me the Rolls. Stone better wish he was a stud. He's a...nice guy.

About "Softly, As I Leave You"

I'd like to do a song here, ladies and gentlemen, that is one of the prettiest goddamn love songs I've ever heard in my life, man, I'll tell you. No, it is. It's just one of the prettiest songs I've ever heard in my life. I've never sung it. I've never recorded it. I never liked the damn thing until I found out—damn I got a toothache—until I found out the story behind why it was written...and then I really didn't like it because I don't like that type stuff. So the next song...nah...no, this is a true story of a song that's been around for a long time...Charlie [Hodge], take this belt off, really. It's gonna cut me...castrate me...do somethin'...really, I can't do that. I got things to do and places you know, places to go...and other tours and things, seeing cities and chicks and all that jazz, you know. Look I just caught...be careful, be careful, son, careful. Don't get it caught in the cord, I'll die out here...electrocute my ass—excuse me, folks, I just mumble...Ooooooo! Damn, is that tight! You cut off my air, man, I can't sing. You know I sing from down in the gut, the shoe soles. It'll never get up here.

I want to tell you a story, if you don't mind, before I do this.

See this young lady right here? Her name is Judy Spreckles. And let me tell you a story about her. When I came to Hollywood, I was twenty years old, to do "Love Me Tender," her family was the Spreckles Sugar family—you've heard of those, haven't you? Yeah, well I guess everybody has 'cause it's a big company—she gave me a four blackstar sapphire ring that I kept up until Priscilla and I were married. And Priscilla used it as an engagement ring. This lady right here did, twenty years ago...Judy Spreckles.

I don't know where she's been. She's been married, off in the hills, flying in the jets, climbing trees and all kinds of stuff, ridin' horses. She's a wild woman, but she did that and she comes around here once in a while to check on me.

So anyway, let me tell you about this song. All kidding aside.

It's the story of a man who's dying in the hospital. And his wife had been sitting by his bedside for three days and three nights. Somewhere on the third night, between midnight and day, she laid down beside him and dozed off to sleep—softly Glen [Hardin]—lay down beside him and dozed off to sleep. Well he felt her when she dozed off to sleep—and I hope you'd quit rattling glasses until I tell the story, please—he was dying and he felt her when she lay down beside him, and he didn't want her to see him pass away. So he took his note pad from beside the bed, and he very quietly wrote "Softly, As I Leave You."

About Audience Reaction

I couldn't a got a better audience if I'd sat outside and paid everybody twenty dollars to come in here. I really couldn't have. You are outta sight.

Introducing James Burton

On lead guitar, one of the funkiest, chicken-pickin' son-of-a-guns you've ever met in your life. From down in Shreveport, Louisiana, James Burton. Just pick a little somethin'…just listen to this dude.

Rolls Rules in Beverly Hills

Jerry Lewis…you know what he did one time. This is the truth. When I first got out of the Army in 1960, I bought a Rolls-Royce. I was driving it in Beverly Hills one day and Jerry Lewis pulled up beside me. He looked over at my car, and I did the same thing. He called my manager [Col. Tom Parker] that same day to say: "Tell Elvis not to drive a Rolls-Royce without a tie." Swear to God! Well, I'll give you a couple of guesses as to the message I sent back. The next day I was driving it naked as a jaybird.

About Sickness

There's a guy in the audience…I got sick one night last week and I had a temperature of about 102°. Wait a minute, don't applaud about a 102° temperature. No, I had a temperature, there was a flu goin' around in this town and all my employees were droppin' like flies and I was…they were in the room with me, getting me dressed and everything, breathing in my face. So I caught the flu and I missed one night, which I don't like to do. I've only missed about six or seven nights in nineteen years, from illness. Because, to me, a germ is an enemy and I hate that son-of-a-bitch and I'll fight it. That's why…I went into the hospital once in my life [sings a line from "For Once in My Life"] and then it was only for three days, because I had a little bronchitis, bronchial trouble in the tubes, and you know how they do in the hospital, they check you for everything in the world, man. I mean…liver, they'll find somethin' wrong with you…they'll create something if you

ain't got it. That guy took a liver biopsy. Do you know what a liver test is? You know what a liver…you know what they do? The doctor comes in and says, "Don't look at me." Turns your head, takes a needle this long and it goes errrgh, right between your ribs and pulls out a piece of your liver. I swear to God, that's it. John [O'Grady], you know what I'm talkin' about. So I said "ummph!" He said, "Now don't move for twenty-four hours…here I was like this. Damn, what'd he do to me. I was okay. I was gettin' well and he comes in and stabbed me. I swear to God—I saw him out the corner of my eye. I can't help it, I'm trained that way—he looked like a samuri warrior. He said "shedazz!" with that needle, man. Fastest son-of-a-bitch I ever seen in my life boy.

Anyway, when I got sick a fellow that volunteered his services to come in and fill in for me…he was way up north somewhere workin' or getting a TV show…he does so much. He volunteered to come in and work the show for me. And now that he's been here ever since, he'll open here tomorrow night. I'd like to thank him—Bill Cosby.

Introducing Vikki Carr

There's a lady in the audience I'd like to introduce you to…she's been in to see my show twice before. The reason we have a mutual respect is because the only way we know how to sing is from the gut out…both of us. You know who I'm talkin' about, her name is Vikki Carr.

Introducing John O'Grady

There's another fellow in the audience—let me see that book—that's a friend of mine. His name is John O'Grady. He's written a book. He was head of the narco squad in Holly/Las Vegas [Hollywood] for twenty-six years. And on the 166th page he's got about three pages about me and my ex-wife,

Priscilla, and about our friendship, and about that maternity [paternity] suit. It turned out to be a complete conspiracy and hoax, man. You know, just no way. I had a picture made with that chick and that's all. I mean she got pregnant by the camera…Polaroid or something. But anyway, it's all in this book. (Laughs.) Better watch them Polaroid cameras, boy (laughs). But you know what she did, where she goofed up? She named the night, and the night that she named, my wife was with me in the audience. And that's the night she said. Ain't no way I gonna fool around with her out there, are you kiddin' me?

So, anyway, let me tell you something. If you like things like The French Connection *the Chinese Connection, the British Connection, the knee connection to the hump/jump bone, the hump bone connected to the rump bone, the dingle bone connected to the…if you like that type stuff, buy this book. It's called* O'Grady [The Life and Times of Hollywood's Number One Private Eye]. *It'll be in print when, John? September twenty-seventh. It will fascinate you. It's about twenty-six years of a hard line policeman working in the narco squad out of Hollywood, so you can imagine what it's like. Buy this book, it's called* O'Grady.

John just came back from New York, where he had a meeting of this. I have been a member of this organization for five years: International Narcotics Enforcement Officers Association.

[Reading plaque.] In recognition of the outstanding loyalty and contributing support of narcotic law enforcement, this award and special honor is bestowed upon Elvis Presley, in testimony…so and so…lifetime member International Narcotics Enforcement Officers Association.

About "Strung Out" Rumors

I don't pay any attention to rumors. I don't pay any attention to movie magazines. I don't read 'em because they're all junk!

No, I don't mean to put anybody's job down. I'm talking about…they have a job to do and they gotta write something. So if they don't know anything they make it up. In my case, they make it up.

When I hear rumors flying around…I got sick in the hospital…well I was…in this day and time you can't even get sick. You are strung out!

Well by God I'll tell you somethin' friend. I have never been strung out in my life— except on music.

When I got sick, here in the hotel. I got sick here that one night, had a 102° temperature, they wouldn't let me perform. And from three different sources I heard I was strung out on heroin. I swear to God. Hotel employees, Jack, bellboys, freaks that carry your luggage up to the room, people working around, you know, talkin' maids. And I was sick, you know, had a doctor, had the flu, got over it one day. But all across this town, I was strung out.

So I told them earlier, and don't you get offended, ladies and gentlemen, I'm talkin' to somebody else, if I find or hear the individual that has said that about me I'm gonna break your goddamn neck you son-of-a-bitch!!

That is dangerous. That is damaging to myself, to my little daughter, to my father, to my friends, my doctor, to everybody, my relationship with you, my relationship up here on the stage.

I will pull your goddamn tongue out by the roots!!

Thank you very much.

About Jewelry

Ladies and gentlemen, I wanna tell you a little bit about this jewelry that I got on.

(Laughs.) No I can't sing about the jewelry, hell, you know. These rocks. Nah, this thing I wore in the Aloha From Hawaii *show and people thought it was one big stone and it's not. It's an eleven and a half carat stone, which is pretty big, you know. It's the biggest I've ever seen. And, anyway, this, next to Elizabeth [Taylor], I think she's got the biggest ones...you're right...and the biggest diamond too. You're fast, you're good, boy. This thing here I had designed for the stage. It's got all different shapes of diamonds, pear shaped, square shaped, screwball, whatever. You know, it's for the stage. This I got tonight for you. Really. I got it, just got it tonight, just like I got the suit, for closing. And the reason I'm telling you this, because I think you ought to know it—you helped pay for 'em (laughs). Good night!*

SEPTEMBER 28, 1974

LOCATION: *College Park, Maryland.*
SOURCE: A Profile—The King on Stage, Vol. 2 *(CD).*

A Fantastic Audience

Thank you very much, ladies and gentlemen. Thank you. You're a fantastic audience, I can tell you right away. Thank you. I've played before many a people...many a person...many an audience, whatever. But you're fantastic, really. J.D. [Sumner], tell 'em that they're fantastic.

[J.D. Sumner] You're fantastic!

That's the voice of the Lord talkin' over there.

About Show Bidness

Oh honey! Honey, if you give me a chance, I will make the rounds. I will turn completely around. I will turn around. I will go to every section of this big, big building. And it is a big building, but, anyway, just give me a lit-tle chance. I'll have to do a couple of songs and then I'll make the rounds and I'll come

back there, I'll go back there, I'll even go up there. But first of all I gotta do a song or two. You see, folks, I love what I do. I love show bidness...bidness...business. No, I do man. I dig it, see. A lot of people go out there and they breeze through it...[using funny voice] "well, I gotta work tonight." Not me! Hot damn, I love it! I ain't kiddin' ya.

My Name Is...

Thank you very much, ladies and gentlemen. Good evening. You think I'm Elvis Presley... I'm Wayne Newton, see. You went to the wrong place.

Don't Call It a Paunch

I'd like to say something right here. Those of you who saw the morning paper, er, the evening paper, whatever it was, they gave...they gave me a fantastic...they gave us a fantastic write-up. No, they did. Except they said I had a paunch here, and I want to tell you something...I got their damn paunch. I wore a bulletproof vest on stage. True. You know, in case some fool decides to take a .22 and blow my...belly button off. That's the truth. I got his paunch...son-of-a-bitch. Now where'd this fat son-of-a-bitch come from here? I'll tell you what, the guy that wrote the article gave me this. He thinks it's me, see. That, son, is a paunch, any way you look at it. This way, that way, up here, it doesn't matter. You know, silly lookin' fool. Nah, it's nice, who gave me this? Who gave me this, honey? Who gave me this foot[ball]...did you give it to me? Okay, bring her here. Might as well get it on, you know. They ain't gonna pick you up, I'll tell you. You want a scarf? Charlie [Hodge], get me a scarf. Now you wait a minute, see, 'cause I have to use it. It may have a slight perspiration odor, but, you know. You're very welcome. Oh, thank you. Who do you think I am, the Pope? Ladies and gentlemen, my first

Pope…nah…nah. My first…honey, I will be back there. If you don't leave me alone, I'm gonna walk off the stage and go back to the dressing room and play with my foot[ball] (laughs)…paunch, hell.

About the Broken Finger

I want to tell you somethin', ladies and gentlemen. You may or may not know that I practice the art of karate. Well, three weeks ago I was given the eighth-degree black belt…I been doing it for sixteen years (applause). Thank you. The reason I'm tellin' you is [fan asks "what style?"] ah, all the styles…it's Tae Kwon-Do, Kenpo, Shotokan…it's all rolled into one. I've had five different instructors in five different styles. So anyway…let me tell you what happened to ol' show-off here. You know, I got policemen up on my floor, so I was hittin' the wall, showing 'em how to hit. Right? I didn't hit it just once, I hit it about fifteen times. I hit it with that little finger…and broke it! *I mean, I broke that little finger, so [crowd says "awwwww"]. Awwww! I didn't break it, I'm lying, y'all are awwwing for nothing. Now wait a minute, where'd this come from? Hey wait a minute, that's cute. I shall take this and give it to my little daughter, really. It says on here: "We've come a long way, baby." We sure have, but I sure…who gave me this? Tell me. Now look, don't fake out on me, tell me who did it. Way back in the back? Run like a som'bitch, hon, run! Get up here! Honey, come on up here. You know, whenever somebody gives me a gift, I like to compensate. Honey. That's her. Okay, just come on up and I'll hum eighteen bars of "Blue Hawaii," or something. Mmmm mmm mmm mmm mmm. That's it. That's eighteen bars. Hope I don't fool around and fall off the stage. Honey, did you give me this? Did you give me this? Hey fellows…hey fellows, just*

play something. Honey, let 'em hold you up here and I will plant one on you, by God. Just a minute, folks, this is gotta be right. I mean, this chick is pretty fair lookin'…you know what I mean? [Kiss.] That's the end of the show…should go backstage for a few minutes and we'll be back…nah.

Introducing Voice

The fellows that opened our show tonight…– shouldn't have. No, no, I'm only kidding…I'm only kidding. Don't start throwing anything at me.

Introducing the Sweet Inspirations

The young ladies that opened…that was second in our show tonight, they think they're somethin'…they're really great. I call them the Sweet Inspirations. No, no, don't give 'em too much applause…damn, they'll ask for a raise. Ah, you remember them, folks, they used to be called the Crew-Cuts in the sixties. Don't get no black power jazz on me, man, I mean…I mean I got enough as it is…and besides, I know Neroy Lebenathy. Well, okay, Leroy…whatever the son-of-a-gun's name is…Abernathy, okay.

About Movie Magazines

Let me say something…for a moment please. For an audience, I will sing my can off, jack. In fact, I have! You're a fantastic audience. I'd like to pass on a bit of information for ya…to ya. Things that are written in movie magazines about me are trash! *Rumors that you hear about me are* trash! *I'm an eighth-degree black belt in karate. I am a Federal Narotics Agent. I am. Swear to God. No, you can do whatever you want to do, I'm just sayin' that I am. They don't give you that if you're strung out…if you done this…[blabbers like a junkie]. No, no, no, no, no, no. On the contrary, I have to be straight as an arrow because I'm around people all the time. I don't like to get out of it in either way. I* don't drink booze. I don't take any of this 'n that. [Applause.] No, no, now wait a minute. [Someone says "boo."] By God, don't say "boo," son, I'll whip your ass. I mean, don't say "boo" to me when I tell you that, because I'm tellin' you the God's truth. And that's not to cover anything. It's just to tell you the truth about the matter. You can take my word or you can take the goddamn movie magazines, you know. [Applause.]

Traveling First Class

Also, when we go on tour, we have three airplanes flying. We have a Viscount, a four-engine Viscount, our regular passenger plane for my band, and all the equipment, and my sound engineers, and Joe Guercio's group, and these fellows here [singers], and then we have an advance plane that goes ahead of us and sets up all the hotel…[and] the security. Then I have a plane, which happens to be the Playboy Bunny Plane. Hugh Heffner's just got to be out of his gord, man, I'll tell you. That thing looks like…whooo, Lord have mercy, I can't tell you what it looks like. Honey, you want this scarf? Come down here and be quiet. Oh, are you a grandmother? You don't look it dear. You really don't look it. Some grandmothers are just dried up like a prune, but you look pretty. Anyway, what I'm saying…if you'd just leave me alone a minute…I'm gonna talk and I got the speaker and there ain't no which way you can talk louder than me…no, we carry our own sound equipment. We carry the best equipment that money can buy. We have the most expensive show on the road, but I do not care. I want the people to get the best!

SEPTEMBER 1974

ITEM: *Handwritten note written (aboard the* Lisa Marie *jet, en route from West Coast to Memphis) and signed by Elvis Presley.*

SOURCE: *Original document.*

[Exact date not known.]

The TCB Oath—
More self-respect, more respect for fellow man, respect for fellow students & instr. [instructors]. Respect for all styles and techniques. Body conditioning, mental conditioning, meditation for calming & stilling of the mind & body. Sharpen your skills, increase mental awareness [sic] for all those who might choose a new outlook and personal phylosophy [sic], freedom from constipation.

TCB

One and all techniques into one.
Elvis Presley 8th [degree black belt, or "dan"]
Applying all techniques into one.

OCTOBER 1974

LOCATION: *Sahara Tahoe, Stateline, Nevada.*
SOURCE: *Audiotape.*

[Exact date not known.]

My Name Is…

Thank you very much. Good evening. My name is Pat Boone.

1974

ITEM: *Page of hand-printed notes of Elvis' thoughts about the martial arts. Made in conjunction with his involvement in a never-completed karate film project, then with the working title* The New Gladiators.

[Exact date not known.]

What is more ferericous [sic] than a raging typhoon? Or than a drop of water from a tidal wave. This is the objective & purpose behind all true martial artists. Never to use that which is learned except in extreme emergencies. To protect myself my friends my loved ones and if seeing a fellow karateka [karate student] using his skill to harm, to make afraid to cripple or maime [sic], to do all that is in my power to restrain with whatever force necessary. To report him to a board of regents comprised of 36 high ranking black belts where he is subject to immediate dismissal—stripped of all of his honors turned over to the authorities, never to regain status in this Assc. This is one of the purposes of karate, to protect the weak, helpless, and the oppressed of all classes, regardless of color, creed, or religion. To all true karateka this is the cata [kata] sworn never to use that which they have learned except in cases of extreme emergency. To this I pledge.

In concert, New York, 1975.

MARCH 18, 1975

LOCATION: *Las Vegas Hilton.*
SOURCE: Top Act in Vegas, Vol. 5 *(CD).*

Happy to Be Working Again

Thank you very much, ladies and gentlemen. Good evening. I can't see you but I know you're out there. I'd like to say that I'm happy to be back working. It's been five and a half months since I did anything, including work. You should have seen me about a month ago. I just got out of the hospital and, ah, I had come out in my robe like Mama Cass, you know.

Introducing David Briggs

This is a…he's not a newcomer…we got him out of Nashville, Tennessee. He works on all of my records. He arranges, he writes, he does a lot of things. You know, the guys that work for me, most of 'em have their "TCB" around their neck, he doesn't have one so he made one up. It says "I play with Elvis too, and I do screw." No, no, I can't say it up here. If I do, they'll close me down. "I play with Elvis too, and I do screw. Boom, boom, boom, do you?" David Briggs.

Introducing Glen Campbell

I'm gonna do something a little different. We got…whifff…somebody's smokin' a rope out there…I'd like to introduce you to a, a good friend of mine. He just closed here last night, and he should have. I'm only kiddin', ladies and gentlemen, he's one of the finest voices around, he plays a fair guitar, his hair never moves, jack, no matter what he does. Naw, he's a great friend, Glen Campbell.

MARCH 22, 1975

LOCATION: *Las Vegas Hilton.*
SOURCE: A Profile—The King on Stage, Vol. 2 *(CD).*

Introducing the Sweet Inspirations

The young ladies on my left…where're ya'll from?

[Sweets sing.] "In the Ghetto."

I wasn't gonna say anything about your hair [Estelle Brown], but don't say nothing about my feet (laughing)…nah, it's an inside joke. Every time I come over here, they say "what size shoe do you wear?" I wear a twelve, honey. I do, really, I can go skiing barefooted. I mean the Lord give me some built-in sleds, woman.

I want to tell you what you look like on television tonight, when they…in a close-up. First of all, you know somebody run over your head with a lawn mower, you know that. Man you got a close-up? You look like Stepin Fetchit, or somebody (laughs).

[Estelle Brown] Oooh, I hate you! I hate you! (Laughs.)

She looks like Flip Wilson, I'll tell ya.

MARCH 25, 1975

LOCATION: *Las Vegas Hilton.*
SOURCE: Top Act in Vegas, Vol. 1 *(CD).*

About *Cosmo*'s Nude Elvis centerfold:

You think I posed nude for a centerfold in Cosmopolitan? *Honey, I wouldn't do it for no amount of money in the world. No way, no way.*

APRIL 1, 1975

LOCATION: *Las Vegas Hilton.*
SOURCE: Rockin' with Elvis, April Fool's Day *(CD).*

My Name Is…

Good evening, ladies and gentlemen. My name is Wayne Newton. Hope you have a good time. We're gonna do our best to entertain you. We're gonna do a lot of songs, give you a lot of scarfs, and look up in the balcony a lot. Oh yeah, the second half of the show's been canceled tonight, so…April Fool!

Introducing Roy Clark

There's a gentleman in the audience I'd like you

to say hello to and have you meet. He's one of the finest entertainers in the country, and if you don't believe it just ask him. No, he's one of the best guitar players around, and he's a fine entertainer and a very nice fellow…say hello to Roy Clark. I hope you're out there, Roy. (Singing.) "Oh-oh-oh yes I'm the great preten-ender." I didn't know where you were. This room is so big, it takes a week to find somebody.

Introducing the Hiltons

And in the audience tonight, I think for the first time at one of our shows, is the owner of this whole thing. I met this gentleman about ten years ago. I was coming out of a doctor's office and he was going in. The doctor said, "This is Elvis Presley and this is Conrad Hilton." He said, "Elvis who?" Mr. Conrad Hilton and his son Baron Hilton, and they're opening the new wing today. I want to con-gratulate you and I want to thank you for being so nice to me. Thank you.

APRIL 24, 1975

LOCATION: *Macon, Georgia.*
SOURCE: From Vegas to Macon *(CD).*
My Name Is…

Good evening, ladies and gentlemen. My name's Johnny Cash. I'd like to say it's a pleasure to be back here in Atlanta, er, Macon. (Laughs.) It's a little mistake, just a little mistake.

APRIL 25, 1975

LOCATION: *Jacksonville, Florida.*
SOURCE: A Damn Fine Show *(CD).*
My Name Is…

Good evening, ladies and gentlemen. My name is Wayne Newton. I'd like to tell you it's a pleasure to be here in Tampa. Oh, in Jacksonville. I'm only kiddin'…really.

APRIL 26, 1975

LOCATION: *Tampa, Florida.*

SOURCE: The King Rocks On *(CD).*
My Name Is…

Thank you very much, ladies and gentlemen. My name is Wayne Newton. And we hope you have a good time. It's a pleasure to be back in Jacksonville…I mean…I know, I'm only kidding.

Introducing the Renaldis

I'd like to tell you something if you don't mind. There's a gentleman here in Tampa that's been making our posters and our scarves and advertising materials for the last eighteen years, ever since I was a mere child. I'd like to introduce Mr. and Mrs. Renaldi.

MAY 4, 1975

LOCATION: *Lake Charles, Louisiana.*
SOURCE: A Profile—The King on Stage *(CD).*
My Name Is…

Good evening, ladies and gentlemen. My name is Wayne Newton.

JUNE 3, 1975

LOCATION: *Tuscaloosa, Alabama.*
SOURCE: Deep Down South *(CD).*
My Name Is…

Good evening, ladies and gentlemen. My name is Johnny Cash.

"Hawaiian Wedding Song" Ending Translated

Ko-oh-lo…I know I like-a-nookie.

JUNE 9, 1975

LOCATION: *Jackson, Mississippi.*
SOURCE: Cut 'Em Down to Size *(CD).*
To Overbearing Security Staff

Don't be so rough on the people when they come down here. They just come down to get scarves. Don't treat 'em like they're going to jail, goddamnit.

LOCATION: *Memphis, Tennessee.*
SOURCE: Let Me Take You Home *(CD).*

Another Ripped Suit

Well, well. What'dya mean "over here"? Well, well, well, well, well, well, well, well, well, well, well, well. You thought you were gonna see a show. That's all I'm gonna do is sing…is sing: well, well, well, well, well, well, well, well.

Thank you, that's it!

I gotta confess somethin' to you, folks. When I bent over earlier, I ripped the seat out of this suit. It's not that bad, is it? Is it? Okay, I'll just stand like this for the whole night.

I hope you have a good time this evening. We're gonna do a lot of songs, and walk around…and kiss people. You know, it's funny because those [people using] binoculars look like frogs to me. [To a screaming girl in the audience.] You don't want a scarf, you just want a kiss? Honey, if I can get my lips that far out there I'll have to…be a Ubangi. You gotta come up closer. Of all the times and places to rip my pants, man.

The young ladies that you met earlier on the show—they're really fantastic—the Sweet Inspirations. Well, they're not fantastic, but pretty good.

Recently my father had a very serious heart attack, and he was very ill, but he's doing fantastic and I'm glad to see that he's up and about and he's here tonight. Dad [stand up].

In fact, his doctor is here tonight, Dr. Nick. Stand up, Dr. Nick, it's time, you know. I want you to watch something. There he is right there, see that little gray-headed guy. He looks like a shorter version of my daddy.

LOCATION: *Las Vegas Hilton.*
SOURCE: *Audiotape and* The Request Box Shows *(CD).*

Bathroom Humor

Good evening. You'll never guess where I was when the intro came on. You talk about some fast movement…I'm in the bathroom. That's the first time that's ever happened to me. I wouldn't do anything like that. That's what this lady said 'bout me the other day. I was at a football game…listen to this…went to the football game, and a lady said, she asked a friend of mine, she said: "I hear that Elvis Presley's here at the football game." My friend said: "Yeah." She said: "I hear he's staying in the press box." "Yes." She said: "I hear he's in the bathroom." He said, "Yeah?" The lady said, very seriously: "I didn't think he did that."

You know, I had a comedian by the name of Mort Sahl tell me that he has worked this town [Las Vegas] for fifteen years and he said that "Elvis Presley was truly one of the nicest people in the world." And I wish I could agree with him.

Introducing the Righteous Brothers

These fellows have been tremendous entertainers for a long, long time, Bobby Hatfield and Bill Medley, the Righteous Brothers. Are you out there? They never fail to come in and see me and I really appreciate it, fellows, really. I think you're really outta sight. They've had some of the best records since Fats Domino.

LOCATION: *Las Vegas Hilton.*
SOURCE: Neon City Nights *(CD).*

A Song for Rex

This next song is a gospel song that we do, ladies and gentlemen, that we have a lot of requests for. There's a gentleman in the audience that I'm sure you've heard or seen on television. He has a program called The Church of Tomorrow *and his name is Rex Humbard, Reverend Rex Humbard, I'd like to do this song for you, "How Great Thou Art."*

DECEMBER 13, 1975

LOCATION: *Las Vegas Hilton.*

SOURCE: Just Pretend *(CD) and Audiotape.*

My Name Is…

Good evening, ladies and gentlemen. You know who you are…and you think you know who I am.

Sometimes, All You Have to Do Is Ask

Thank you, ladies and gentlemen. You've been a fantastic audience, ladies and gentlemen. And if we don't see you again soon, I'd like to wish you a Merry Christmas and a Happy New Year.

Anyway, until we see you…

[Fan screams] "Blue Christmas!"

What? "Blue Christmas"? Let me tell you what's happening. The people in the casino, and the people waiting in line, and the maître d's can do better things than throw baseballs at me when I'm on the stage longer than fifty minutes. I've been on for an hour and five minutes.

So…you wanna hear "Blue Christmas"? [Sings "Blue Christmas."]

DECEMBER 14, 1975

LOCATION: *Las Vegas Hilton.*

SOURCE: The King of Entertainment *(CD).*

Cause for Concern?

The little girl that gave me this picture there said to read the thing at the bottom, so, she's got: "Excedrin headache number seventeen." Then down below it, she has in parentheses: "Did she or didn't she remember to take the pill?"

DECEMBER 15, 1975

LOCATION: *Las Vegas Hilton.*

SOURCE: *Audiotape.*

My Name Is…

Good evening, ladies and gentlemen. Welcome to the show. You know who you

are…and I think you know who I am…Tom Jones, you're right.

DECEMBER 31, 1975

LOCATION: *Pontiac, Michigan.*

SOURCE: *Audiotape.*

Gonna Rip It Up

Good evening, ladies and gentlemen. Guess what? I just ripped the seat outta my pants. Do you believe that? I'd like to tell you that…what are you laughin' at? It could have happened to you, you know that, don't ya? I'd like to tell you that it's a pleasure to be here and if I appear nervous, it's because I am. This is the largest [live] audience that we've ever played to…and I had to go and rip my pants. While I go and change pants, I'd like for the Stamps to sing "Sweet, Sweet Spirit."

Thank You! Thank You!

Thank you, fellas. You didn't know I was a quick change artist, did you? Of course it took ten people to get me into this thing.

There's a few people I'd like to thank for making the show possible…but I ain't got time for that. I'd like to thank all of you ladies and gentlemen for coming out. All kidding aside, I was very nervous when I came out here, and you've made it a real pleasure. For that, we thank you very much. And this is the largest live audience that we've ever performed for.

I've got news for you, ladies and gentlemen. This is the best evening that I've ever had. Happy New Year!

1975

ITEM: *Handwritten note from Elvis to "Rodney."*

SOURCE: *Document photocopy.*

[Exact date not known.]
To Rodney,
Thanks—hope to see you again.
Your friend
Elvis Presley
Las Vegas "75"

LATE JANUARY 1976

ITEM: *Typewritten form letter: Sent in response to inquiries from fans.*
SOURCE: *Document photocopy.*
   [Exact date not known.]

   Dear Friend:
Elvis sends his personal thanks for your very nice letter and your question about his forthcoming performances in 1976.
But first he wants you to know how much his growing family of fans means to him. This past year of 1975 was a most happy one and the warm welcome he received on his tours was a great inspiration to him. The thoughtful gestures, the friendly messages, the flowers back stage, the handshakes, the hello's [sic] from the balconies, the painted signs, the children, the stuffed dolls, the fun of being with you.
1975 was a happy, exciting year for Elvis because he was able to visit so many cities and meet so many warm and friendly people. Elvis feels his audiences—they give him something of themselves and he tries to return this in his songs.
Many letters have been received about 1976. At this point his immediate plans are to record. In fact, RCA has two special new releases—a special television album "Elvis in Hollywood" featuring title songs of his motion pictures and including a four color photo album and at your record dealers the second volume of "A Legendary Performer."
Personal appearances have not as yet been announced through [though] currently they are in the planning stages. But Elvis and all of us are looking ahead to when he can walk out on the stage and be with you all again. Until then he wishes you happiness and all good things.

   Sincerely,
   The Elvis Presley Show

[Handwritten note, by a member of the Presley Show staff, at bottom of page reads] Best wishes to all of the French fans from Elvis.

[This particular item was sent to the French "Treat Me Nice" Fan Club. It is likely that other copies of this letter, to different fans, have a similar handwritten note at bottom.]

MARCH 17, 1976

LOCATION: *Johnson City, Tennessee.*
SOURCE: Southbound *(CD).*
Introducing "Tryin' to Get to You"
Is there any way that we can turn the stage monitors so I can hear myself a little better? Is that possible? It's not that I like to hear myself, but you understand. It's just that it helps…This next song is a song that we've been doin' a lot recently. It's one o' my first records and we've been doing it a lot lately because we've had no requests for it…we've had a lot of requests for it. It's called "Tryin' to Get to You."

MARCH 20, 1976

LOCATION: *Charlotte, North Carolina.*
SOURCE: Running for President *(CD).*
Introducing David Briggs
And this fellow over here with the beard, that looks like a Viking, he's probably the weirdest guy on the whole stage, other than J.D. and Ed Enoch over there. Anyway, he plays the electric hairnet, er, clairinet [clavinet], David Briggs.

APRIL 25, 1976

LOCATION: *Long Beach, California.*
SOURCE: *Audiotape.*
My Name Is…
Good evening, ladies and gentlemen. My name is Wayne Newton.

LOCATION: *Seattle, Washington.*

SOURCE: *Audio tape.*

He's Come Undone

Well, let's see. My guitar strap's come undone. My shirt's comin' undone. That's about all I can afford to undo. Good evening ladies and gentlemen, we hope you enjoy the show. The announcement that the guy [Ed Hill] makes, "Just stay in your seats and sit there, blah, blah, blah," damn, you can relax and enjoy yourselves. That's all there is to it.

[Fan screams] I love you Elvis!

I love you too, dear, but I can't do anything about it right now. In case you're wondering why my fingers are taped up, it's to keep people from stealing my rings when I shake [hands] with them. I have to make an announcement. If you act right and if you appreciate us just right, everybody gets a Cadillac when the show's over.

Midnight in Michigan

On January the first of this year, we played at Pontiac, Michigan, at a place [Silverdome] that holds sixty-four thousand people. It's the largest number of people I've ever played to. I never was so scared in my life. People ask me if I get nervous before I go on stage . . . you better believe it boy. I mean, just before I go on stage, you could walk up to me and say "Hey, your hair's on fire," and I'd say, "yeah, yeah." Well anyway, the fourth song into the show, my pants ripped. Happy New Year everybody! I was up on a pedestal and I had everybody all around me. Luckily they had another suit off stage, so I went off stage, changed clothes, came back on. Charlie [Hodge] forgot what song was up next, we cut the show short. It got to be twenty seconds until midnight, I was supposed to do the countdown with everybody. Anyway, they had a huge clock, right, and I couldn't see it

because the spotlight was in my eyes. Finally, just five seconds before midnight, they turned the lights off so I could see the clock, so I started counting with them. Everybody started singing "Old Lang Syne." Well, I didn't know the words to it, so I started singing "May old acquaintance, umm-ummm, and let the audience sing it. So they ended the first verse, and I thought, "well, that's it." No! There's a second verse to it. So I go back to Charlie, and say "What song is up next?" He said, "Let's take it on home." We'd only been on stage for thirty minutes. They woulda killed us. Then on top of that, other than that, I supposedly got married last week to somebody. I just read it in the paper. I find out more stuff about myself in the paper than anywhere else. I just thought I'd relate a couple of stories to you, because they're real funny to me.

LOCATION: *Sahara Tahoe, Stateline, Nevada.*

SOURCE: Live at the Lakeside *(CD).*

Tough Way to Make a Living

There's something that was bothering me all night. I was listening to the Stamps [Quartet] last night, and each one of those guys do one song. Therefore, they can put all they got into it, 'cause they're only doin' one. Well I've gotta do twenty-five or thirty. No wonder you could do "You'll Never Walk Alone," you smart...

LOCATION: *Sahara Tahoe, Stateline, Nevada.*

SOURCE: A Crazy Show at Lake Tahoe *(CD).*

Won't You Wear My Ring

I'd like to ask how many people saw the show last night? Only two. Naw, I wanna tell you something about this ring. Can I talk for just a minute? First off, we got a lot of songs to go. We're doing one show tonight and unless you get bored, you know, we'll stay here as long as you want us to. Well okay, I'll do all the songs, you know, but I gotta explain to you about this ring…I hate it. I'll tell you why. It's so heavy…I mean, it looks good for the stage, but as soon as I get finished with the show it goes into a drawer or closet somewhere, really. It's heavy, it turns over, it cuts my fingers. That's why I had to use Band-Aids on it. See these Band-Aids? Now don't feel sorry for me, I've been cut before.

[Fan shouts.] Throw it over here, I'll take it.

I can't get it off right now. Maybe later in the show…if you act right. Now this is a medley of songs in which we do some of the older songs we recorded back when Charlie [Hodge] was copying me. You like that, uh?

[Fan] "That's All Right Mama."

"That's All Right Mama"? Man, that was the very first.

[Fan] I know, I bought it.

You got it?

[Fan] I got it.

I'll bet you got it. We'll get to it.

[Group] Elvis is king!

Thank you. That's very kind of you, but see kings don't get sick and go in the hospital, you know…and rip their pants on stage. And more important…see that? That's a guitar pick. You want this instead of the ring? He's laughing at me. Have you ever heard J.D. [Sumner] laugh? Ho-ho-ho-ho-ho. You'd think it was Christmas, you know. Okay, let's do "I'll Remember You." Now I'd like to tell 'em about, you know, something. How to raise gardens. No, this is a song from the Aloha from Hawaii *special that we did, the satellite show. The kid that wrote that song was very, very sick and we did a benefit*

[tribute] to him and it's called "I'll Remember You."

Introduction of Guests

I'd like to introduce you to somebody in the audience that's a fantastic actress. And I know you've seen her in a lot of things. Her name is Samantha Eggar. Would you please stand up and let 'em take a look at you? And at the same table—you know you've seen these cars on television catch on fire, and guys jumpin' off buildings and hangin' from ropes—there's a stunt man by the name of Dig Ziker. Okay folks…wait a minute. I want you to see…I want you to meet my…my comedian, you know. I want you to see him when he's not working…Jackie Kahane.

Ladies and gentlemen, I'd like to tell you that you know, since the last time I was in Lake Tahoe I was in the hospital a couple times. Nothing serious, I just…I shook too much and jarred some things loose. But I'd like you to meet my father. He's…Daddy, are you out there? Dad? He's back there.

About Running Long

I've been on stage for about an hour and fifteen minutes, and they don't like me to stay any more than an hour, but…heck with what they like.

LOCATION: *Sahara Tahoe, Stateline, Nevada.*
SOURCE: *Audiotape.*

My Name Is…

Good evening, ladies and gentlemen. My name is Flip Wilson. And we're gonna do something that you like, if I have to stay here all night.

You see, Jackie Kahane, when he's out here, he leaves the microphone way too short. And J.D. [Sumner] has it way too tall. And Charlie [Hodge], he just stares into the face of

God. Tonight we just start out slow and then taper off.

Bob Dylan Slept Here?

You know what happens to ya when you breathe this [recirculated] oxygen? It dries your mouth out. It feels like Bob Dylan slept in my mouth.

Anyway, there's only one show tonight, so we're gonna do all the songs you want to hear tonight. We got a list here of four hundred songs...and we can only do a hundred and twenty-seven of 'em.

MAY 7, 1976

LOCATION: *Sahara Tahoe, Stateline, Nevada.*
SOURCE: *Audiotape.*

Introductions

I have a couple of friends in the audience I'd like this song ["Hurt"] to. Jerry Kennedy and Ron Pietrafeso. Also, my karate instructor, Ed Parker.

MAY 9, 1976

LOCATION: *Sahara Tahoe, Stateline, Nevada.*
SOURCE: And Then the Lights Went Down (CD).

Mama Liked the Roses

Everybody [at the show tonight] was supposed to get roses from me. I don't know if they delivered them.

[Fan screams.] We got 'em!

Movie Memories

Somebody asked for "Hawaiian Wedding Song." I have got to tell the audience what happened, the ones that saw that movie. Did you see the movie Blue Hawaii? *There's a funny thing that happened. My co-star is Joan Blackman and she had on this short-sleeve purple dress and white lei of flowers. I was dressed in white and had a red [wrap]...anyway, we were moving down*

With *Blue Hawaii* co-star Joan Blackman, 1961.

this moat and people were throwing flowers and people were singing the "Hawaiian Wedding Song." The first time we did it, see, they had guys underneath the water pulling a cable, and the first time we did it they hit the side of the bank too hard and the boat crashed right into it. Pow! It took me three hours to get re-made-up and get ready to do it again. So we got married twice in the same day! Or did we?

One other time, in Viva Las Vegas *with Ann-Margret, we got married. It took us a week to film that wedding scene. It is so real, until you think you're married. It took us two years to figure out we weren't.*

Easy Money

In Las Vegas, one time the head maitre 'd [Emilio Muscelli] in tips in one month [during our engagement], made four million dollars! Swear to God. And [he] retired after that!

JUNE 5, 1976

LOCATION: *Atlanta, Georgia*
SOURCE: One Night at the Omni (CD).

My Name Is...

Good evening, ladies and gentlemen. I'm

*Jimmy Carter's smarter brother. All kidding
aside, the audiences we have down here in
Georgia are some of the finest that we have
anywhere in the nation. And we were all
really looking forward to coming here because
we were down in—where were we—in
Rathole, Texas? Manhole, Texas? In fact,
that was the name of the hotel we stayed in.*

*[Recent Texas dates were El Paso, June 2, and
Fort Worth, June 3.]*

*Now this is a song that was recorded by
Olivia Newton's John!*

    *You see, I did that in Pontiac, Michigan,
on New Year's Eve, and ripped my pants
from here to here. Had nowhere to go. It's one
big suit and it's hard to get out. So I was
gonna put on a diaper and come in as the
New Year baby.*

Can't Take It Off

*I put the suit on wrong, folks, and it's tight,
God o'mighty.*

[Fan screams.] Take it off!

*Take it off? Are you kidding? It took me two
hours to get into it…and two years to get out
of jail if I take it off. I was in such a hurry to
get over here tonight that I didn't drink any
water, put the suit on wrong, and I got two
left shoes on, and I can't turn around every
time you tell me to. I'd be spinning like a top.
It took me an hour and forty-five minutes to
comb my hair and three seconds to whoosh
[mess it up].*

JUNE 25, 1976

LOCATION: *Buffalo, New York*
SOURCE: One Helluva Night *(CD).*

My Name Is…

*Good evening, ladies and gentlemen. My
name is Wayne Newton. I Got a Wayne
Newton haircut. I hope you enjoy the show, I
get very nervous on opening night.*

JUNE 28, 1976

LOCATION: *Philadelphia, Pennsylvania.*
SOURCE: *Audiotape.*

Attire for a Hot Night

*Our conductor is from Las Vegas [Nevada],
his name is Joseph Guercio. Nice girl.*

    *And before I go any further, I'd like to
know where the band's uniform is.*

[Someone says.] They got 'em on.

*They got 'em on? Is that it? God, we're get-
ting cheaper in this outfit, you know that. I
mean I'm spending twenty-five hundred dollars for a suit and they're spending a dollar
and a quarter. Really. Anybody can get a T-
shirt with little beads around the neck. The
fantastic Joe Guercio Cheapies, play something. Who's that motley group? That's out of
sight, Cheapies.*

JULY 5, 1976

LOCATION: *Memphis, Tennessee.*
SOURCE: Goodbye Memphis *(CD).*

About James Burton's Guitar Playing

*James can play the guitar in the back of his
head, you know, better than I can in front.*

An Unforgettable Album

*I'd like to do a song that we recorded about
two years ago, called, uh, it was from an
album called* Elvis in the Gutter. *The song
is called "Help Me."*

About Hospitalization

*I'd like to tell you, ladies and gentlemen, since
I was here last time, I was in the hospital
[for] a couple of things…nothing really serious. And I'm over that and I'm out working,
and I'm glad to be back working again.*

Teasing the Team

*I'd like to thank all you guys on the stage. You
know these musicians are all hand-picked
from the bottom of the barrel. Nah, nah, I'm
only kiddin'…just a little.*

LOCATION: *Tuscaloosa, Alabama.*
SOURCE: Old Times They Are Not Forgotten *(CD).*

About Wiggling

Good Lord! I can't help this, folks, and you're laughing at me. Nah, I'm just tryin' to wake everything up, that's all. Feel like a chicken with his head cut off. That's enough of that.

LOCATION: *Macon, Georgia.*
SOURCE: Southbound *(CD).*

Somewhere in Georgia

Thank you very much, ladies and gentlemen. Thank you. I'd like to say it's a pleasure to be back in Atlanta…naw, I'm only kidding. It's just my warped sense of humor. Well we hope you enjoy the show. Honey, what is that? It's not alive, is it? I mean, you don't stick pins in it every night or nothin' like that, do you? Well that's beautiful. Very nice. What? What do you want?…Honey, the only thing I have is…is a guitar pick. What? You can't have the ring, I'm sorry. That's out. It belongs to J.D. [Sumner] anyway. I just borrowed it.

EVENT: *Phone call between Elvis in Memphis, Tennessee, and Red West in Los Angeles, California.*
SOURCE: *Audiotape.*
[Exact date not known.]

[Red West] This is Red West. You're about to hear a telephone conversation between Elvis Presley and myself that I recorded sometime in October 1976, while I was in Los Angeles writing the book *Elvis What Happened*, along with my cousin Sonny West and Dave Hebler. It was no secret that we were writing the book, and knowing Elvis as I did, I knew he would try to contact us. I also knew we would be called liars, Judases, traitors, and any other expletives by fans and even some people around him who we had been close to up until this time. I knew that he would reveal in this conversation enough information that would substantiate what we said in the book. It was even more than I had expected…and more than I wanted to hear. By this I mean I heard a sad and lonely man, a man I'd grown up with, and watched rise from near-poverty to become the greatest entertainer this world will ever see. A boy in a man's body who could not handle the celebrity that he had now become. I had a sinking feeling that I would never see my best friend again…and I didn't.

[Audiotape does not begin at the start of their conversation, so we are not certain of the preceding talk. One account and purported transcription appears in the book Elvis What Happened; *however, since the remainder of that transcription varies significantly from the actual conversation, we do not trust that account of the beginning of their talk. A comparison of the actual conversation, as transcribed here, with the version in the book, reveals many edits, omissions, and worse yet, additions of things Elvis does not say. To illustrate how a few altered words can completely change a meaning, on page 326 of* Elvis What Happened, *the third paragraph ends with Red West saying: "You have problems." In the actual conversation, West says: "It's like you say, you had problems." One is accusatory, the other sympathetic. Throughout the book's transcription are examples of omitting portions of the conversation that either cast Elvis in a more favorable light or demonstrated agreement or understanding on West's part. You can see why we choose to present only that text which is verifiable.*

Also, since much of the conversation focuses on the failed Presley Center Courts project, some background on that may be helpful. Providing that summary is Marti Martin, a Presley Center Courts associate:

"Presley Center Courts, formed in April 1976 and headquartered in Memphis, Tennessee, was the first commercial venture for which Elvis authorized the use of his name and served as chairman of the board. Presley Center Courts of Memphis was the first of a chain of racquetball court facilities [planned] to be built across the country. Elvis borrowed $1.3 million from the National Bank of Commerce, putting up Graceland as collateral to finance this venture. Dr. George Nichopoulos, Joe Esposito, and Michael McMahon were Elvis' business partners. Before the end of the year 1976, Elvis left the company. Elvis was asked to invest more money and Dr. Nichopoulos and Joe Esposito later sued Elvis for $150,000.

Michael McMahon, vice president and general manager of Presley Center Courts, employed my services to design promotional merchandise to be sold in the racquetball pro shops."]

[R.W.] Where were we?

My damn voice is so low, I make J. D. Sumner sound like a tenor.

[R.W.] (Laughs.) Ah…

It sounds like I got stuffed with a Martin [guitar].

[R.W.] (Laughs.) Yeah.

But my damn fingers are blistered. I'll tell ya.

[R.W.] Yeah, that's the way mine used to get when I'd sit up and try to write songs. My three…first finger just too big…I mean, just have big blisters on the ends of 'em. But aw shit, I wish I could get my mind cleared…just wakin' up, but talk about…oh yeah.

I'm not operating on but one cylinder either.

[R.W.] (Laughs.) Well, like I said, I've got

*a…that show's doin' pretty good [*Black Sheep Squadron*] and I got a regular, runnin' part [as Sgt. Andy Micklin] in it…it starts in the next three or four weeks, I think. And I think I'm just gonna hang with that.*

Well, you know that thing that happened was a combination of a whole lot of things building up. It wasn't necessarily personal or even the goddamn lawsuits, you know. It was like a fuse burning, because of a lot of things that piled up on me.

[R.W.] Yeah, well.

And maybe I did lose sight of…especially you, your family and everything.

[R.W.] Yeah, it was cold, El.

'Cause I love Pat [West, Red's wife] and your family and everything.

[R.W.] Well I have a lot of time to think 'bout, I mean, I could sit here and people would say all that old shit, but it did cross my mind. And all I ever done is try to, maybe sometimes over-protect you. And that's the God's truth.

Yeah.

[R.W.] And, ah…

Oh, I know that.

[R.W.] Man, here I was and. But that…hell just like you say, you had problems.

Well, you know what it is. It's [like the] old guy said in Cool Hand Luke, *a failure to communicate.*

[R.W.] Yeah. Well that's the God's truth. We sure didn't communicate in the last year or so.

That's it…just like I said, it was just a series of things. If I could lay them out to you one by one, I could show you the reasons why the separatism. Lack of communication.

[R.W.] Right.

My daddy was sick. You know he was nearly dead. My family is strung all over the face of the United States and, ah. It's just the goddamn lawyers and lawsuits, they're making a moun-tain out of the molehill.

[R.W.] Yeah. Yeah, I know that was some rough times goin' through that. Just some, you know. One lawsuit came along and then every-body else saw a chance to jump on it. Yet it mushroomed and then boy everybody and his cousin was after our ass, you know.

Yeah, that's what I mean. One gets away with it or thinks they do and what they try to do is establish a pattern of insanity and violence.

[R.W.] Yeah.

Like in bed…me shootin' that lamp.

[R.W.] What was that?

Hilton Hotel…a .22 target pistol.

[R.W.] Oh yeah, well, we were known as the Wild Bunch (laughs).

Yeah, that's for sure.

[R.W.] But, ah.

But, you know the good old days are still a fact.

[R.W.] Yeah, they're definitely a fact and always will be, I mean, what's done was done. We had a lot o' good times, man, there for a while…and it got…like you said, everything got real serious. And a lot of problems came up. I don't know, we just lost sight of lot o' things, a lot o' the good things and, I don't know, just…the fun left.

The fun ceased to exist, that's the thing.

[R.W.] Yeah.

I couldn't pinpoint it, just couldn't quite figure it out…boil it down.

[R.W.] But, ah.

Goddamn racquetball courts.

[R.W.] Yeah, I passed by there the other day…for a while while ya'll were gone. It was still Presley's Center Court, and then just before I came…

They're gonna take that down.

[R.W.] Huh?

They're gonna take that down.

[R.W.] They already have. Yeah, I was gonna say, just before I came out here, I didn't see that sign anymore.

Oh well, last I heard it was still up. But I got conned by evidence buyin' it there, then they got these builders and they got themselves bound to a contract.

[R.W.] Uh-huh.

Two [racquetball] courts there for a half a mil-lion dollars each.

[R.W.] That's too expensive.

What the fuck, man. Poor old Joe [Esposito] had his mother to hock her house…get a loan on her house to get the money.

[R.W.] I can tell you about goin' in business with sharpees. They don't care…if you hock your mother's ass.

That's what he had to do.

[R.W.] Did Joe get out of it?

Huh?

[R.W.] Is Joe out of it, or is…?

Well he's in the process of tryin' to get out of it.

[R.W.] Yeah.

You know the builders that were contracted to build the damn thing are the ones that hold up the ballgame because I pulled out of it.

[R.W.] Yes.

I had to 'cause it was souring. It was a con job, squeaky deal, you know.

[R.W.] Well, I didn't know if it was or not. I just had a feeling it was.

It started out kinda innocent. I was told one thing.

[R.W.] Yeah.

Like I wouldn't have to put up a dime. Wouldn't be no money or nothin'.

[R.W.] Yeah.

Well, that was the contract that I signed. Right, talked to Daddy about it just after he came out of the hospital. And said we talked over a period of time. You know, if it'll help Joe and Nick…

[R.W.] Yeah.

…they could use my name so…

[R.W.] Well I…

Because I couldn't benefit nothing from it.

[R.W.] Right. It was just somethin' to help to help them out. I don't think Nick knew the guy that well.

I don't think he did either.

[R.W.] No he just got sucked in. He saw the chance to make some money, and Joe did too. But this other guy's the one I was a little leery of.

Oh, that son-of-a-bitch, he ain't no good.

[R.W.] Ah.

I talked to my attorneys yesterday about the racquetball thing. You know Mr. Davis died?

[R.W.] Yeah, I know. I saw that in the paper just before I left.

And the guy that's takin' his place…what started happening would be they would start hitting me for ten thousand, twenty thousand.

[R.W.] Start hittin' you up for it?
Yeah.

[R.W.] Aw, yeah. Yeah, well…there's a pattern.
So I thought, well, you guys putting up that kind of money here? Ah, yeah.

[R.W.] Yeah (laughs), I remember he was on one of the tours with us.

On the tour, pretending being interested in the numerology books. It all falls into place. But was smart enough to do that. Then, it amounted they needed eighty thousand dollars. I said okay, for what? For a secretary.

[R.W.] (Laughs.) Goddamn! Boy, damn secretaries…they got a union or something?

That's exactly what I said. Wonderin' a-how a secretary is gonna cost eighty thousand dollars.

[R.W.] Shit. No, it was time to get the hell outta that shit.
I tried to hang on in there with them.

[R.W.] Yeah.
I didn't wanna crush their enthusiasm…their dreams or whatever they got.

[R.W.] Just crush their secretary (laughs).
Yeah, your eighty-thousand-dollar secretary.

[R.W.] God almighty. What'd the president of the board make?
Well, they had all these cards and shit printed up chairman of the board. It, hell started off Presley Center Courts and they changed that to Elvis Presley Center Courts without ever even asking me one thing about it.

[R.W.] Uh-huh damn.
They had all these cards and shit made up… president and vice-president. Still, didn't even come to me to ask me.

[R.W.] Aw hell, once they got your name on there…what's this Mike [McMahon], the guy that got your name on there, he. I heard it, he went to Nashville and everywhere just sayin' I represent Mr. Elvis Presley in this racquetball venture. Just on your name alone, he just got what the hell he wanted. I don't know what I'm tryin' to say…we gotta get back to my problem. Man, I've never done that. I just…ol' Red… tryin' to do a job, man.
No, I wasn't using an example. I was just telling you.

[R.W.] I know it. I just…we're talkin' about somethin'…don't know about is that racquetball court. I just know about my problems.
What started out just a friendship and favor and everything just turned it into a million-three-hundred-thousand-dollar project.

[R.W.] Yeah.

And you realize how long it would take to realize a profit? (Laughs.)

[R.W.] Yeah.

After puttin' that money into it.

[R.W.] Yeah, I'm afraid so. It'd take awhile.

You'd be so old until they'd change the racquet and hand you a fuckin' banjo.

[R.W.] (Laughs.)

(Laughs.) Where do you hit it…I'm tryin' to play it.

[R.W.] (Laughs.) Plaster fallin' off the walls. Awww shit. Yeah, poor old Nick [Dr. George Nichopoulos], man he…everybody's tryin' to make a buck but that Nick's Chips he went into, man that was a flop. He had everything figured but the damn truck that hauled the whole [thing] off. That fell through.

(Laughs.) I didn't even know…I was in the hospital.

[R.W.] (Laughs.)

Goddamn, I had mixed emotions. I hit the floor, first thing, just rolled there. Nick's Chips my ass. The first thing I could conjure up in my mind was a gambler decidin' to eat or raise. And Nick the Greek, you know, as the gambler. That's how crazy my mind is. Nick's Chips, shit, he obviously just don't know.

[R.W.] Yeah.

And these fuckin' contractors up there are just cold-hearted businessmen.

[R.W.] Aw sure. Look. You start messin' with 'em…a guy like that, I mean…dollars talk and that's it.

Yeah, but the way it was goin', they led the calf to slaughter.

[R.W.] Yeah, well, you got out of it…you're out of it then, right?

I'm in the process of getting out.

[R.W.] I don't blame you, 'cause it's a…

Well…

[R.W.] You start goin' in business with a bunch o' people…if you do it yourself, then you know what's happening, but if you got two or three other guys…

My signature…they all must of just went stark ravin' mad.

[R.W.] Sure it did. I know that Mike did.

The lawyer read to me the contract where it said that if anything happened I would stand good for the whole thing.

[R.W.] Yeah, well see there. They didn't tell you…

Now you know damn good I don't even care that much about racquetball.

[R.W.] Yeah. Right.

I would stand good for it. For the whole thing. So that was news to me.

[R.W.] Yeah.

I just found out yesterday that this guy Mike had set him up a management fee was fifty thousand dollars a year extra. Ah, Joe didn't know anything about it. Nick didn't know a damn thing about it. But yet the lawyers had it right there.

[R.W.] That's what I figured; this Mike conned Nick and everybody else into it. They ain't gettin' well on it you know.

Yeah.

[R.W.] That's a shame, man, Nick's always, man…I thought he was smart and I thought Joe was smart, but…

Not when it comes to business.

[R.W.] I think we're on a party line or somethin'.

And my whole thing, see, I could never possibly realize any kind of a profit out of it. I did it just as a friendship thing.

[R.W.] Yeah.

You know I didn't pay anything. It was no harm. Helping this idea go. A couple racquetball clubs, one here and one in Nashville, named after me.

[R.W.] Yeah.
I didn't see anything wrong with that.

[R.W.] No, not…
You see, the paper that I signed had nothing of that mentioned.

[R.W.] Yeah.
So, the lawyer figures that this shit was put in there after I signed it. You know what I mean?

[R.W.] Yeah.
Because, you know damn good and well I wouldn't sign as much as I'd stand to lose for a couple of fuckin' racquet…half-a-million-dollar racquetball courts.

[R.W.] Yeah.
That is part of what surprised me too. Half a million dollars for a racquetball [court]? Why, hell, I can get Earl in with a hammer, Albert right here

[R.W.] (Laughs.) Aw, shit (laughs).
…to put up one. As long as we keep the wood-peckers off of it.

[R.W.] (Laughs.) Build it for $39.98.
(Laughs.)

[R.W.] Well they must have gone in for the saunas…the whole health club bit, or somethin'. You'd have to, it don't cost that much to build no damn two racquetball courts.
No, I think it was gonna be ten courts in each half.

[R.W.] Oh.
I mean, yeah, ten places to play like out at Memphis State.

[R.W.] Well that's…
But still, you take that and you take a men's and women's showers, it can't add up to no half million dollars.

[R.W.] That's a lot o' money.
Why shit. I got one built here in…in the back-yard…you know where here.

[R.W.] Yeah.
That sombitch was only eighty thousand. You know how plush it is.

[R.W.] You're damn right.
These people just, like you said, they saw my signature and went stark ravin' mad.

[R.W.] Yes sir. Everybody was taken in after they got your signature. Plus…when was this damn guy's salary supposed to start, already? Mike and the secretary and all that shit.
Yeah.

[R.W.] Um-mmm. And you supposed to pay for that, uh?
Yeah.

[R.W.] Yeah. Bullshit.
Ah.

[R.W.] Bullshit. You should get the hell out.
Merchandise things: little cards, little pam-phlets, little advertisements, this 'n' that. And all without my knowledge, without con-sultin'…without askin' me about it, you know.

[R.W.] Well.
So it just built up into a fuckin' monster, [that's] all there is to it.

[R.W.] You're damn right it did. Tryin' to take advantage of ya. And I don't blame you…tryin' to get the hell out of it. But then I guess all that pressure and everything—lawsuits and every-thing—led up to our demise, whatever. But it was a shock to all of us. Old Dave [Hebler] was out here. He was flat-ass broke. Well, we're all broke. 'Course I had some property and stuff. I had…I sold every[thing]…I sold my house. I hated to do that, but when you gotta do some-thin', you gotta do it.
You sold your house?

[R.W.] Oh, yeah, I sold my house, both cars and everything. And Hebler, he's flat-ass broke, and Sonny [West] was just in…down to the…well, you know, it was just a bad…bad time by all, I'll tell ya.

Hell, I guess there was never any real good time.

[R.W.] No.

It was bad for me, too.

[R.W.] Yeah.

I hadn't been out of the hospital long enough to start rolling.

[R.W.] Yeah. But, ah.

My daddy…I almost lost him. He's my daddy, regardless of anything else.

[R.W.] Oh yeah. Listen, I can understand. But yeah, we just…hell, we were in shock there for awhile. What…what did we do, you know? But, then we thought about it, all the pressure and everything, and said well, I guess he's got his point too. Ya just…it's just…I wish, you know…we've always been able to talk. A lot of…most of the time. There's been some times we couldn't, but if I'd just heard from you, it would [have] been…it would have been easier to take.

Well in doing business and things of that nature, I don't…I don't do that.

[R.W.] Oh, you mean about firing us and everything?

Yeah.

[R.W.] Well.

I had to go to Palm Springs, analyze and weigh [the] goddamn racquetball courts.

[R.W.] Yeah.

I'm still seeing little fuzzy balls.

[R.W.] (Laughs.) Well.

But, ah, Charlie [Hodge] was telling…Charlie talked to you and you thought I was on the line.

[R.W.] Uh-huh. Well I thought…I heard, you know, I heard…

I was over at my daddy's house going through these figures.

[R.W.] Yeah.

You know…if I wanted to hear somethin', I wouldn't do that. I'd go another way.

[R.W.] Boy, you know how paranoid everybody gets after somethin' like that.

Aw sure.

[R.W.] I just…I don't know why…

Oh, sure, like looking over your shoulder and not knowing who the hell it is.

[R.W.] Yeah.

Regardless of what.

[R.W.] Yeah. But anyways, you know, it's all done and…that's it I guess now, you know, 'cause, ah.

How's Pat and the kids and things?

[R.W.] They all fine. Just hangin' on 'til I get somethin' goin'.

Well.

[R.W.] But just been kind of rough.

Yeah, I was very disillusioned with Hebler. He faked me off something terrible. You know, I thought he was…misunderstood.

[R.W.] (Laughs.) Well, what…what did he do?

Huh?

[R.W.] What did he do…on that?

Well, he just…he'd say little things to me…who he hated.

[R.W.] (Laughs.) Who he hated?

Yeah.

[R.W.] Damn.

You know, this went on over a period of two years.

[R.W.] Yeah.

It just…and Ed Parker told me when I hired

him…he said keep him at arm's length. And I still didn't catch on…dumb ass me.

[R.W.] Yeah. Well I…I really don't know what you're talking about, ah.

Well, it's hard to explain. I don't think that he liked anybody in this group, except maybe Dean [Nichopoulos].

[R.W.] Yeah. Well I…

I think that I'd become a dollar sign to him, Red, I think that…in the process he lost sight of Elvis…first. That can easily happen.

[R.W.] Oh, I guess…yeah, I guess so. Ah.

And, you know…well it happened, man. I'd become an object, not a person.

[R.W.] Yeah.

But you know, I'm not that sign, I mean that [Elvis Presley Boulevard] road sign down there. I'm not that image that's built up, I'm myself.

[R.W.] Yeah. Well that's the way I always, like, you know, tried to think of it.

And you're so wrong on one thing now, and listen, don't get paranoid on me, because I'm just a-talking to you as a friend now, we're on a private line and [there] isn't a fuckin' soul left.

[R.W.] Right.

I am not fucked-up by no means. On the contrary, I've never been [in] any better condition in my life.

[R.W.] Well, what I was talkin' about then…you had been pretty fucked-up…what I was talking about.

Well, you know; I went through a divorce. You know, you were there.

[R.W.] Yeah. What I'm saying.

That wedding thing, you know…that wedding thing [not including Red in his and Priscilla's wedding ceremony], I had nothing to do with that. That was railroaded through. I didn't even know who was there, we's all in a little old

room 'bout size of a bathroom with a [Nevada] Supreme Court Justice [David Zenoff]. It was in there, over and done with so quick so I didn't realize I was married at all.

[R.W.] Oh yeah, you're talkin' about your wedding. Yeah.

Yeah.

[R.W.] Right. Well you know, like you don't think about these things at the time it…it… once again that…ah, it's the old…like I been with you and all o' sudden I was held back and told when I was supposed to come in.

I could see it back then, you know. I could see it back then. But see, that wasn't my doing.

[R.W.] Right.

It wasn't my doing.

[R.W.] You know I figured that was the Colonel and…

It was a ramrod-type thing. I had nothing to do with it. All of a sudden I was gettin' married.

[R.W.] Yeah.

And you know.

[R.W.] Ahh.

When you go through that, you keep your mind on one thing.

[R.W.] Yeah.

(Laughs.)

[R.W.] Yeah right. Well I can understand that. That was a long time ago. It…that was just a point I was bringin' up with Charlie and, but let's get back to the last couple, three years. Let's face it, man, you haven't enjoyed yourself. You just been…you do your work, you go work and then, ah…

I enjoy my work.

[R.W.] Yeah, I know that. That's the only time we really see you…I…I really see you anymore. The rest of the time we just…it was just I don't know.

We had a pretty good time in Vail.

[R.W.] Oh yeah, we had a ball in Vail. That was a…man, that was a one time out of the last few years that we really got back to it…back to the…whatever…knowin' how to enjoy ourselves. And I mean everybody just had a ball.
I know I did.

[R.W.] I know I did too. So that…that was somethin' we'd all been wantin' to do just to get out away from it all.
Yeah…what…no, that's okay because they just want me to have a house up there.

[R.W.] Yeah.
And…and everything, so these real estate guys get a hold of that.

[R.W.] Right. No, I don't blame ya. Hey, you can always go up there and rent something.
Yeah, exactly.

[R.W.] But, ah…ahhh, I don't know what…I don't wanna get real serious, you know, it's been so long since I talked to ya, I'm gonna get real serious on the conversation but…
That's up…

[R.W.] We were all…we were worried about you. I always been worried about you, 'bout, you know, taking quite a few things. I thought that would, you know…
You worried about me so much that you turned around and tried to hurt me. But see, I know what that is.

[R.W.] Well, that's after you hurt me. You'd already hurt me. You hurt my…me and my family very bad, you know, left us out in the cold, so let's don't talk about me tryin' to hurt you.
Well, things went on that you didn't know about.

[R.W.] Yeah, well all I know is I was out in the cold, and couldn't understand why.

All I know there was friction was created in the group. The vibes so bad, people were scared to move and everything.

[R.W.] Yeah, well that's true too.
So who knows what the hell they were hearing and being told. I just know it was…it just got to be very, very tense situation whereas it should have been fun and a relaxed kinda thing.

[R.W.] Yeah.
Somethin' went wrong.

[R.W.] Yeah.
And that on top of the racquetball thing, everythin' else and all the personal shit. It was a fact that we did have to cut down on expenses.

[R.W.] You did. Well.
I had the feelin'…

[R.W.] Whatever you had to do…I told your daddy, you know, I'm…you gotta do what you gotta do. If you gotta cut down on expenses by firing me you know, it's a little weird to me. Seemed like you could…could have cut somewhere else. I thought I was important to the organization, and I'm glad I found out now that I wasn't. Then I…I still got a little life left and I'm goin'…I'm goin' to enjoy that. And I can…and I'm still young enough I can find somethin' else, you know.
Oh yeah.

[R.W.] But that was just…cuttin' down on expenses…I just couldn't understand that. All the other…a lot of other guys…man I thought I…that I was more important to the organization than they were, but I guess I wasn't. But I'm glad I found that out. So?
Well, it's just an unfortunate situation. It's just now startin' to get back on its feet. My daddy lost [weight]…down to a hundred sixty-five pounds.

[R.W.] You mean now?
I heard he's up to one [hundred] seventy-eight. That just shocked, scared me to death. Because

you know how I feel, you know how you felt about your daddy.

[R.W.] Yeah. That's right.

Well, suspicion was cast on this group. I couldn't figure out the source of it. Suspicion. Just like in that song that we did, "we can't go on together with Suspicious Minds."

[R.W.] Yeah.

So maybe I did act abruptly—first one to admit it—without thinking.

[R.W.] Yeah. Well it…

You know Sonny was never around, right?

[R.W.] Yeah.

You know we talked about that.

[R.W.] Yeah.

I ain't got nothing against Sonny. Hebler tried to bully his way, you know, through every-thing…

[R.W.] Uh-huh.

…with scare…scare tactics…

[R.W.] Yeah.

…with some of these young guys.

[R.W.] Well.

They would ask questions like names and that, and they never did…could get a straight answer, they were just…they were turned down at every corner.

[R.W.] Yeah.

That's all I needed to find out. You know, I think back, I know when I was twenty-one years old, shit, my mind was just scattered to the four winds.

[R.W.] Yeah. I know.

Without some kind of guidance, some things just weren't bein' done. You know, just little things just weren't bein' done. You know how they train people in the service—regimentation—doin' the same thing every day, and we knew, by God, there you did…in the service…anybody

ask if they really served legitimately…that, by God, at seven o'clock we had to do this, at three we had to do that, you know.

[R.W.] Yeah.

And they do that by repetition.

[R.W.] Sure.

That's how they train.

[R.W.] Yeah.

And all that energy of their youth, without proper guidance (whistles) is wasted.

[R.W.] Yeah.

So the only reason…I just felt that I should talk to you and let you see my side of it.

[R.W.] Yeah. Well I appreciate that, you know. That's…that's what I wish we'd a done at the very first, you know. Maybe I could have understood it a little…little bit better. But it's, you know, what's done is done. And have to go on from there. I mean, I just, believe me when I tell ya, I wish you all the luck, I hope you go right, you know, just stay right where, right on top, forty more…forty more years, man. Really do. I mean that with all my heart.

Well I'm working on it.

[R.W.] But I would like to see you get help there, E. And you hadn't been healthy in quite a while.

Oh yes I am.

[R.W.] No you're not.

Yes I am.

[R.W.] Well okay, you say that, but…

I just had an absolute physical, head to toe, in the last three weeks.

[R.W.] Okay. Well I'm glad to hear you're healthy. And ah…

Hold on a second. It was required by Lloyd's of London insurance office.

[R.W.] Well, then that's…then I don't have to worry about it then.

Yeah. That thing I had, that lower intestinal blockage, corrected itself.

[R.W.] Thank God. Good.

I just went on a weird liquid diet.

[R.W.] Yeah.

That big intestine down there has to have bulk.

[R.W.] Yeah. Yeah, that's what we discussed.

I went on a diet, twenty days of liquid, and I heard that was another mistake (laughs). Turns out that that large intestine had nothing to work with, so as a result it stopped working. And I keep hearing this shit about [being] fat and middle-aged.

[R.W.] No, no. Well I knew…we…I knew that…what…I knew you weren't…well, lets (laughs). You ate a lot, but you weren't…you weren't fat like people that are fat.

Yeah, well I burn it up…I burn it up.

[R.W.] You could tell there was something else wrong. And that's what I mean, you wasn't healthy. That's how you…somethin' was wrong inside. That's what I been tryin'…when I tried to talk to you about it you'd get mad, just like you kinda…awhile ago. No, you wouldn't listen to it. That's what I'm talkin' about, man. You were…something was wrong inside of ya. We didn't know what it…we were worried about it, we didn't know what it was. We knew it wasn't fat though. It was somethin' else. And you just…

Well that, I thought that I told y'all…I thought I told ya it was that lower intestine. Remember how I supposed to undergo surgery…

[R.W.] Yeah.

…and take part of it out.

[R.W.] Yeah. Right. Yeah, I was there. I remember when they were gonna do it. I was just sayin' I…

That was psyching me out because I didn't know what it was.

[R.W.] Well, I'm glad it's all straightened out. I really am.

It's been straightened out a long time. It just was just a failure to communicate, wasn't it?

[R.W.] Yeah. Well.

What we have is failure to communicate.

[R.W.] (Laughs.) Yeah. I…

You know that song Roy Hamilton did, "Understanding Solves All Problems."

> [It may have slipped Elvis' mind that this exact line, "understanding solves all problems," is in his own recording "One Sided Love Affair."]

[R.W.] Yeah. That's right.

That was a difficult song.

[R.W.] We didn't have much understanding there for a long time.

Well I don't know whether it was you and I as much as the thing coming from somebody else. You know, negative vibes.

[R.W.] Right. Well that could very well be too. I'm…I'm not really into the psychic thing.

Well I'm not either, but I do know that we constantly sending and receiving.

[R.W.] Yeah.

All the time.

[R.W.] Right.

Positive and negative.

[R.W.] Yeah, we've talked…we discussed that. Minds, if you can put a picture through air I guess you can put a thought wave through the air too. So…

So that's why I was feeling the negative things, and I couldn't exactly pinpoint what.

[R.W.] Yeah.

So I just reached a boiling point, hoped that you'd understand it. It was just a temporary thing.

[R.W.] Uh-huh. Well…

That was what it was, I didn't feel I could communicate with anybody.

[R.W.] Yeah.

I felt terribly alone. You know like that number eight?

[R.W.] Yeah.

The thing that says they are intensely lonely at heart. For this reason they feel they're lonely but in reality they have warm hearts toward the oppressed.

[R.W.] Yeah.

But they hide their feelings in life and do just what they please.

[R.W.] Right.

Well, I'm a number eight person and so are you.

[R.W.] Yeah, that's true. And it's been lonely (laughs). It's been lonely, man, I tell ya. It's been downright scary.

Well, I can see it.

[R.W.] But that's somethin' just…ah, I just…I'm old enough, I just chalk it up to life, man. That's another my…another step down that road, you know. And I just a…have to learn to cope with it, and go on try to do somethin'. But what can I say, I don't want, you know, feel sorry for myself. I'm a grown man, I can…I can do somethin' else…there's other things. But like you say, there was a failure to communicate there at the last, 'cause maybe I wasn't around the room enough when you wanted to talk to somebody, or whatever.

Well, yeah, maybe all that. Maybe that's how I been. Maybe I was absent and was listening too fast.

[R.W.] Uh.

But it just kinda bugged, you said after the show [I was]…fat, or whatever, to Charlie.

[R.W.] I can't hear you, E, I'm sorry.

You fucked up.

[R.W.] Yeah, well…

Because I'm not. I've got a daughter and a life.

[R.W.] Yeah.

You know.

[R.W.] Yeah.

What profiteth a man if he gains the world and loses his own soul?

[R.W.] Yeah.

I love to sing.

[R.W.] Yeah.

That's been my thing, since two years old.

[R.W.] Yeah. I know.

You know, we were sittin' here playing the guitars and everything, singing old songs: "Love Is a Many-Splendored Thing." And, you know, me and Charlie talked about that harmony part, missing that harmony part (laughs).

[R.W.] Yeah. Well, what can I say, I miss singing it (laughs), you know. That's the way the ball bounces.

(Laughs.) Well look, you take care of yourself and your family, and if you need me for anything, I'd be more than happy to help out.

[R.W.] I appreciate that. I appreciate it.

I mean it. Don't need that goddamn article for publication, none of that shit that I've heard. I've just heard bits and pieces. I don't know what…I was on tour and everything. I've just heard bits. 'Course I have never really sat down with anybody and had it laid out to me. I don't even know. I just know that you as a person, and Pat, and if there is anything I can do, any way of getting a job or anything else, let me know. I'm still here, son.

[R.W.] Well, I appreciate that and I'll tell Pat what you said that'll make her feel better. She was hurt, you know, she couldn't understand it, my kids, my kids, really, especially…I didn't realize.

You see, all of us were hurt.

[R.W.] Huh?

All of us were hurt.

[R.W.] Yeah.

In different ways. It's like that song "Desiderata." "Listen to the dull and the ignorant for they too have their story."

[R.W.] Yeah.

And then Hank Williams wrote: "You never walked in that man's shoes and saw things through his eyes."

[R.W.] Right. That's true.

So, you know, after analyzing the blamed thing, I can see it. I can see it clearly. That's why I saying, anything I can do at all.

[R.W.] Yeah.

I'll be more than happy.

[R.W.] Okay, I real…I appreciate it. And ah…

You take care of yourself.

[R.W.] Okay. And if…let me say one more thing before you hang up. If everybody's worried about the book, tell 'em not to, man, because…

Oh they aren't…

[R.W.] I mean…I mean includin' yourself…ah, we're writin' the good stuff, Elvis…people…

Worried about the book…I don't…I don't think so.

[R.W.] Okay.

Not…not on my part.

[R.W.] Okay, good. 'Cause I was out. I was broke. I was made an offer to write the book. I said, I'll write the book if I can [include] all that, from day one, the good…the good days.

Yeah.

[R.W.] He said alright, whatever. So…

You do whatever you have to do.

[R.W.] Okey-doke.

I just want to let you and Pat to know I'm still here.

[R.W.] Okay. I appreciate that. And you take care of yourself.

With Roy Hamilton, Memphis, 1969.

Okay. You too.

[R.W.] Okay, bye-bye.

NOVEMBER 29, 1976

LOCATION: *San Francisco, California.*
SOURCE: The Nation's Only Atomic Powered Singer *(CD).*

About Losing It

Hold up. If I get tickled, you know, I lose it. I really do.

DECEMBER 3, 1976

LOCATION: *Las Vegas Hilton.*
SOURCE: *Audiotape.*

My Name Is…

Thank you very much, ladies and gentlemen. My name's Wayne Newton.

DECEMBER 4, 1976

LOCATION: *Las Vegas Hilton.*
SOURCE: What Now My Love *(CD).*

Such a Deal

This guy [in the audience] said "I'll kiss you for your ring!" (Laughs.) I'd have to put a three-dollar bill with that ring. My brain's only working on four cylinders.

About Kids, Animals, and America

First of all, I know you've heard so many about the bicentennial, you're probably tired of all that stuff. But I'd like to do our version of "America, the Beautiful." I didn't say I was gonna do it…said I liked to.

Hey, a child just came here out of nowhere. Honey, now wait a minute. Aww, you're sweet. Oh, you're beautiful. I'll tell you what, you don't have a chance with kids and animals. No, you don't. This is a strange thing to do just before doing "America, the Beautiful."

Introducing Engelbert Humperdinck

There's a couple people in the audience I'd like for you to meet. I know you'd like to see them. They're some of the finest singers in the world. So that's one of the reasons I have to be good. I'm being judged, not only by you and the people on stage, but by them. You remember the song "Please Release Me, Let Me Go"? Well, nobody every sung it like Engelbert Humperdinck.

Introducing Roy Orbison

And next to him, ladies and gentlemen, another one of the finest singers of all time—Roy Orbison.

Introducing Daddy and Daughter

I'd like you to meet certain members of my family. My father's in the audience. Dad, stand up. And my little daughter, Lisa. Stand up. That's enough, sit down, Lisa.

DECEMBER 5, 1976

LOCATION: *Las Vegas Hilton.*
SOURCE: Elvis Presley at the Hilton *(CD).*

Might Look Like Chester

Thank you very much. First of all, let me apologize for being late, but I did twist an ankle today. Swear to God. Naw, really, in my bedroom there is a step down to go to the bathroom. So, it was dark, so I stepped off and BOOM! There went the ankle. So, if you see me [looking] like Chester on Gunsmoke…thank you…it's gonna be just slow love songs tonight…I'm glad that you're understanding. It can happen to anybody, really. It's just that I do so much stuff in the show, you know, physical movements…so if you'll just bear with me we'll…we'll do our best to do a good show, to entertain you and we're here to please you.

The Black Diamond Story

I wanna tell you about something. My birth…see I was born January eighth [1935], and since that time I have studied numerology and astrology, and so forth. In numerology it says that, according to my birthdate my lucky stone is supposed to be the dark-toned sapphire, a black pearl or a black diamond. I have never seen or heard of a black diamond in my life. So two weeks ago, some police office found this from a collector [in Denver, Colorado], not at a jewelry store. So it's about three and a half black diamonds. Yeah, it looks like a piece of coal. So it took me fourteen years to find one, 'cause I don't think they're in big demand, really. They don't shine, they don't do anything. They're just there. They're like Charlie [Hodge].

DECEMBER 7, 1976

LOCATION: *Las Vegas Hilton.*
SOURCE: Run On *(CD).*

It's a Traveling Pain

First of all, I'd like to apologize to you, about being late. Those of you that have been here [recently] will know, I've got a pinched nerve in my right foot. And between last night and today it [pain] has traveled. It has gone up the back of my right calf, into the thigh, and that's all I'm gonna tell you.

Nothing makes much sense tonight, except you people showing up, and that's fantastic. I would have come out here, if I'd had to do it from a wheelchair. Swear to God.

I really think you're fantastic for sitting here waiting for us. I'm sorry that I had a pinched nerve in my ankle and everything, but I hope it'll get better by tomorrow or the next day. You just have to give these things time, you know.

DECEMBER 7, 1976

LOCATION: *Handwritten note. Written by Elvis Presley in his Las Vegas Hilton suite.*
SOURCE: *Document photocopy.*

I feel so alone sometimes
The night is quiet for me
I would love to be able to sleep
I'm glad everyone is gone now
I will probably not rest tonight
I have no need for all of this
Help me Lord

DECEMBER 11, 1976

LOCATION: *Las Vegas Hilton.*
SOURCE: Vegas Remembering *(CD).*

Watch That Zipper

You talk about gettin' dressed fast, Lord have mercy. I drove my daddy back, out of the hospital today and he's fine. It's hard to get into a one-piece suit that quickly (laughs) without hurting yourself.

DECEMBER 11, 1976

LOCATION: *Las Vegas Hilton.*
SOURCE: *Audiotape.*

Suiting Up Takes Time

Thank you very much, ladies and gentlemen. Before I do anything in the world, I'd like to apologize about being a few minutes late. I had some personal problems that came up…it takes a while to get into this suit. It takes five people to get me into this thing. There was a girl the other night that said "take it off!" I said, "No, I had a hard enough time gettin' it on!"

An Odd Mix of Cultures

Sherrill Nielsen is gonna do the Italian version [of "O Solo Mio"] and I'm gonna do the ancient Hindu version.

Introducing Kay Stevens and Lola Falana

There's a couple of people in the audience that I'd like to acknowledge. I know you've seen one of them on television quite a bit, and you've seen the other one on the Johnny Carson show. So I'd like to introduce one of our fine actresses, Miss Kay Stevens [starred in The Interns*]. And this other lady is one of the finest singers and performers, you've seen her on the Johnny Carson show, Lola Falana.*

Closing Comments

I'd like to say a couple things, if I could, about how good it is to be back working again and to have you people come out to see the show.

With Engelbert Humperdinck, Las Vegas, 1972.

And we'll be working quite a bit next year.
We may come to your hometown, or wherever
you are.

I'd like to thank my sound man, Mr. Bill
Porter, who handles all the sound up here.
And Felton Jarvis, he's helping with the
sound. And he's my record producer.

This has really been a fantastic engagement, one of the best we've had. And if we
don't see you, have a Merry Christmas and a
Happy New Year. Be careful driving home
and may God bless you. Adios!

DECEMBER 12, 1976

LOCATION: *Las Vegas Hilton.*
SOURCE: *Audiotape.*

Helping Hearts

*I don't know if you know this or not, but
with Colonel Parker, my manager, we started
a [souvenir sales] booth when we came here,
for the Heart Fund—American Heart
Association—and they gave me this…they
made me a member of the American Heart
Association today.*

My Name Is…

*Thank you very much, ladies and gentlemen.
Good evening. My name is John Davidson.*

A Moist Souvenir

**[Fan screams.] Elvis, can I have a drop of
your sweat over here?**

Honey, you can have it all if you want.

DECEMBER 28, 1976

LOCATION: *Dallas, Texas.*
SOURCE: A Hot Winter Night in Dallas
(CD).

Having Fun on Stage

*If I died tonight, it would take a year to get
the smile off of my face. And if I ever get the
show started, we got it made.*

DECEMBER 29, 1976

LOCATION: *Birmingham, Alabama.*
SOURCE: Burning in Birmingham *(CD).*

My Name Is…

*Good evening, ladies and gentlemen, my
name is Glen Campbell. I'd like to say welcome to the show and…we've never been to
Birmingham. We've never played here, this is
the first time.*

DECEMBER 1976

LOCATION: *Handwritten note. Written by
Elvis Presley in his Las Vegas Hilton suite.*
SOURCE: *Document photocopy.*

[Exact date not known.]
*I will be glad when this engagement [December
2–12] is over. I need some rest from all of this.
But I can't stop. Won't stop. Maybe I will take
everyone to Hawaii for awhile.*

DECEMBER 1976

LOCATION: *Handwritten note. Written by
Elvis Presley in his Las Vegas Hilton suite.*
SOURCE: *Document photocopy.*

[Exact date not known.]
*I don't know who I can talk to anymore. Nor to
turn to. I only have myself and the Lord. Help
me Lord to know the right thing.*

DECEMBER 1976

LOCATION: *Handwritten note. Written by
Elvis Presley in his Las Vegas Hilton suite.*
SOURCE: *Document photocopy.*

[Exact date not known.]
*I wish there was someone who I could trust and
talk to. Prayer is my only salvation now. I feel
lost sometimes*
*Be still and <u>know I am God.</u> Feel me within,
before you know <u>I am there.</u>*

LOCATION: *Montgomery, Alabama.*
SOURCE: Moody Blue and Other Great Performances *(CD).*

At the Piano

Ladies and gentlemen, I'd like to do a song that I've never done on stage before in my life. We have never rehearsed it, never done it. I have never sung it with the group. And it's a gospel song called "Where No One Stands Alone." I have to play the piano because I know the chord changes. Fellows, "Where No One Stands Alone." This is gonna be the Stamps and Sherrill Nielsen. Alright!

You don't mind me sittin' back here playing [piano]…I mean, I know you can't see me but I's here, I's here. Damn this piano's loud. Can we turn it down a little bit? Okay.

LOCATION: *Charlotte, North Carolina.*
SOURCE: Moody Blue and Other Great Performances *(CD).*

A Complete Mental Block

*[Singing.] "Are you lonesome tonight
Do you miss me tonight
Are you sorry we drifted apart
Do the chairs in your parlour…no, wait a minute, wait a minute, wait a minute, wait a minute!. Good grief, what's the words to that song?*

[Estelle Brown] Does your memory stray…Does your memory stray to a bright summer day.
I can't hear you honey.

[E.B.] Does your memory stray…
Does yours?

```
MAILGRAM SERVICE CENTER
MIDDLETOWN, VA, 22645

western union   Mailgram   UNITED STATES POSTAL SERVICE
                           U.S.MAIL


COLONEL TOM PARKER MANAGER OF ELVIS PRESLEY
CARE OF RCA RECORD TOURS
6363 SUNSET BLVD
HOLLYWOOD CA 90028


DEAR COLONEL:

I AM LOOKING FORWARD TO DOING THE SPECIAL FOR CBS TELEVISION DURING OUR
JUNE TOUR THIS SUMMER, AS I UNDERSTAND WE WILL HAVE COMPLETE CONTROL
UNDER YOUR DIRECTION AS TO FORMAT AND TOTAL PRODUCTIONS, I WILL OF
COURSE COOPERATE TO THE FULLEST TO MAKE THIS ONE OF OUR BEST SPECIALS
EVER, I UNDERSTAND THAT CBS TELEVISION IS TO HANDLE THE NEGOTIATIONS OF
THE USE OF ALL THE TALENT ON MY SHOW WHEN NEEDED FOR THE SPECIAL WITH
FELTON JARVIS MY RECORD PRODUCER FOR ME THANKS FOR EVERYTHING SEE YOU
ON TOUR


ELVIS

23:16 EST

MGMCOMP MGM
```

Telegram to Col. Parker, 1977.

[E.B.] No...yours did!

Cute. Cute, Estelle. Can you believe that? I mean just a complete mental block. I've only sung it about nine...try it again.

MARCH 1977

ITEM: *Telegram from Elvis Presley (Memphis, Tennessee) to Col. Tom Parker (Hollywood, California).*

SOURCE: *Document photocopy.*

[Exact date not known.]

Dear Colonel:

I am looking forward to doing the Special for CBS Television during our June tour this summer. As I understand we will have complete control, under your direction, as to format and total productions. I will of course cooperate to the fullest to make this one of our best specials ever. I understand that CBS Television is to handle the negotiations of the use of all the talent on my show when needed for the special, with Felton Jarvis, my record producer, for me.

Thanks for everything, see you on tour.

Elvis

APRIL 23, 1977

LOCATION: *Toledo, Ohio.*

SOURCE: Goodbye Memphis *(CD).*

With Rosemary and Ginger Alden, Hawaii, 1977.

About Being Late

We were a little slow getting here, and everything, but I hope you enjoyed the show. And we're gonna be here, around here somewhere for the next couple nights so if you get the chance, come in and see us. Till we meet you again, God bless you.

APRIL 25, 1977

LOCATION: *Saginaw, Michigan.*

SOURCE: Greetings from Saginaw *(CD).*

My Name Is...

Thank you very much, ladies and gentlemen. My name is Glen Campbell, and I don't know how we got here, but we came by bus. We did!

APRIL 28, 1977

LOCATION: *Green Bay, Wisconsin.*

SOURCE: *Audiotape.*

Not imitating Chester

Thank you very much, ladies and gentlemen. It's a pleasure to be here. And hope you enjoy the show. Last night, I gotta tell you, I'm going on stage and the spotlights blind me, so, I twisted an ankle, I mean jack I turned into an acrobat, you see, I about turned myself inside out. And so, if you see me hobbling around I'm not doing an imitation of Chester on Gunsmoke.

MAY 22, 1977

LOCATION: *Largo, Maryland.*

SOURCE: Elvis Presley Tonight *(CD).*

Sound System Goes on the Fritz

On our last tour, when we were playing up in...where were we? Saginaw, the entire sound system blew. I mean, everything went out. We have two separate sound systems. [Fan screams "turn around."] I'll turn around, honey, but let's get ready first. In other words, what you're hearing out there is different than what we are hearing up here on stage, and it's a big, big technical problem. But we'll work it out. He'll figure it out...I'd like to tell you that you've been a fantastic audience and anytime you want us back here, we'll be back. And next time, we'll have our sound system right. Until we meet you again, be careful, may God bless you.

JUNE 19, 1977

EVENT: *Random comments recorded on tour and included in the video* The CBS Tapes.
LOCATION: *Omaha, Nebraska.*
SOURCE: The CBS Tapes *(Video).*

Thank you very much. You're all on Candid Camera. You know that, don't ya? Well now, what is this, Roller Derby?

I got to tell you something, really. All kidding aside, I never wear makeup on stage. But this is being televised and I have to wear makeup. And if you think I'm nervous, you're right.

Anyway, I talk kind of soft. So when I'm talking, bring it up [microphone volume] a little bit. Just when I talk, okay? I ain't supposed to sweat either.

They got me all made up. I don't really look like this. I look more like Cochise.

Sherrill [Nielsen], I'll ask you a question, son. Would you look at this suit. Why is it prettier than mine?

We had a technical problem in our sound department, and it'll take just a second. So I'll just walk around and act like I know what I'm doing.

The [Stamps Quartet] baritone singer, he's the guy that does all the talking and announcing just before I come out, and tells you to sit in your seat and don't move and spit, and don't chew gum and all that stuff. I'm only kidding you. You're just doin' your job. He's from Nashville and his name is Ed Hill.

Their lead singer, the blond-haired guy over here with the wild look in his eyes. He looks like he's been up for forty-eight hours straight, I'm tellin' ya. But he's...he's got one of the most powerful voices in gospel music...providing: he's got some rest, he hasn't chased every girl he's seen around the hallway of the motel, [he's had] rest and fruit juice, stuff like that. His name is Ed Enoch.

Their tenor singer, he's got a name that's a little...well, I don't know. It's a little weirder than mine. I never thought I'd meet anybody [with a name] any stranger than Elvis Presley. But, he's got a beautiful voice. His name is Buck Buckles.

Thank you, ladies and gentlemen. I'd like to say something to you if I could. You know we're working under very hard circumstances, and everything. But you've...you've really been a great audience for us, and you've really helped us, and everybody on stage has really worked hard. And we've enjoyed it. And any time you want us back, just call us and we'll come back up here any time, you know. I'd like to thank everybody on stage. Thank you for the show. I'd like to thank my sound engineers, my record producer, Felton Jarvis, my sound [man], Bruce Goose. What's your name? Bruce...Bruce Jackson. What's your name, yeah [other sound man]? Jerry. And the guy that handles the sound out in the lobby, Bill Porter. So, what I'm trying to say to you is that...this thing's gonna be on television and so you're gonna be in it, so watch yourself. 'Til we meet you again, may God bless you. Adios.

JUNE 21, 1977

EVENT: *Random comments recorded on tour and included in the video* The CBS Tapes.
LOCATION: *Rapid City, South Dakota.*
SOURCE: The CBS Tapes *(Video).*

[Gary] Monique, you come right in here, sweetheart, that's it. You face that way. Turn right around that way.
How are you, sweetheart?

[Monique Brave] Fine.
Hi.

[Gary] Okay, in one second we're ready to roll. One second.
Isn't she pretty.

[Tom Hulett] Beautiful.

[Gary] Okay. Go ahead, Tom.

[Tom Hulett] Elvis, I'd like to introduce you to Monique Brave, from the Sioux Indian Tribe here in Rapid City, and Mayor Lacroix, who's got a presentation for you also.

[Mayor Lacroix] Elvis, on behalf of the citizens of Rapid City and the community, welcome to Rapid City, and we appreciate you being our first concert in our new [Rushmore Plaza Civic Center] auditorium.
Thank you, sir.

[M.L.] And this says so on our plaque. It's for your grand opening concert here.
That's fantastic. Thank you. Thank you. Very nice.

[M.L.] And Monique.
Isn't she pretty. Hi, Monique.

[M.B.] Hi. This is a medallion of life, for you Elvis, from the Sioux Nation.
Oh, that's lovely. Thank you, sweetheart. Thank you.

[Joe Esposito] We've gotta get ready for the show.
Do you have a scarf or something I can give to her?

[M.L.] Good luck to you, Elvis.

JUNE 21, 1977

LOCATION: *Rapid City, South Dakota.*
SOURCE: The CBS Tapes *(Video).*

My Name Is…

Thank you very much. Thank you, ladies and gentlemen. Good evening, ladies and gentlemen. My name is Wayne Newton. Naw, I'd like to say that it's a pleasure to be here. Somebody told me that it's a new building or something, that I was the first person to perform here. Is that true? [Applause.] Yeah, I'll see y'all later. We're gonna do a lot of songs, old ones, new ones, and hope we do something that you like. And we're here to entertain you and make you happy. So just enjoy yourself and leave the driving to us. That's our job. Boy it's hot. You know, I'm on television, and I got on makeup stuff, [which] I usually don't. So if you see it start streaking, well don't worry about it. We'll just edit, cut it, x-rate it.

Film Scene Quite Realistic

We did a movie called Blue Hawaii, *and in the movie there was a song called the "Hawaiian Wedding Song." And it was so real, it took me two years before I realized it was just a movie. I thought I was married to the chick. Anyway, I'd like to sing it.*

JUNE 25, 1977

LOCATION: *Cincinnati, Ohio.*
SOURCE: *Audiotape.*

Battling Dead Mouth Syndrome

Thank you, ladies and gentlemen. Thank you very much. Thank you. I'd like to apologize for being a little bit late tonight but I had to go to the dentist. We had to solve a problem, and my…part of my mouth was dead with Novocain, you know. You can see me doing this [makes funny face].

LOCATION: *Indianapolis, Indiana.*
SOURCE: Adios! The Final Performance *(CD).*

Polish Folk Songs?

We're gonna do a lot of songs: old ones, new ones, some that you've never heard…Polish folk songs. Our job is to entertain you, so just have a good time and leave the driving to the drummer, 'cause I guarantee he'll drive ya.

The Story of Our Lives

This next song is kinda the story of our lives…it's called "Fairytale."

The Impossible Dream

Most of all I'd like to thank you and I like to say this is the last day of our tour. And we couldn't have asked for a better audience. You've really made it worthwhile. If you want us back just let us know and we'll come back.

JULY 19, 1977

ITEM: *Typewritten letter to David Ferrari (Phoenix, Arizona) signed by Elvis (Memphis, Tennessee).*
SOURCE: *Document photocopy.*

Dear David:

Congratulations on winning the talent competition you were in and good luck on the show this Friday!

I really do appreciate you as a fan … and mimcry [sic] is a sincere form of being a fan. Do develop your own *special talents and abilities though, David.*

This is a great compliment to me that you would work so hard on this act like mine but never neglect your own special abilities to be yourself also.

Best wishes in the future and God bless you.

Sincerely,
Elvis Presley

Elvis Presley
3764 Elvis Presley Blvd. • Memphis, Tenn. 38116

July 19,'77

Dear David:

Congratulations on winning the talent competition
you were in and good luck on the show this Friday!

I really do appreciate you as a fan....and mimcry
is a sincere form of being a fan. Do develop your
own special talents and abilities though, David.
This is a great compliment to me that you would
work so hard on this act like mine but never neglect
your own special abilities to be yourself also.

Best wishes in the future and God bless you.

Sincerely,

Elvis Presley

Congratulatory letter to an Elvis impersonator, 1977.

AUGUST 5, 1977

ITEM: *Typewritten Hallmark thank-you card: Signed by Elvis, in Memphis, Tennessee, sent to Naomi Frisby, Milpitas, California.*
SOURCE: *Document photocopy.*

[Card is dated August 5, though envelope has an August 8 postmark.]

Dear Naomi,
*Thank you very much for your concern and loyal support as such a dedicated fan of long standing. I really do appreciate your attitude about this gossip put out as a book [*Elvis, What Happened?*]. It was so thoughtful of you to write. Best wishes always & may God bless you.*

Sincerely,
Elvis Presley

August 5, '77

Dear Naomi:

Thank you very much for your concern
and loyal support as such a dedicated
fan of long standing. I really do appreciate your attitude about this gossip
put out as a book. It was so thoughtful
of you to write. Best wishes always &
may God bless you.

Sincerely,

A thank-you
card to a fan.

AUGUST 15, 1977

ITEM: *Handwritten letter from Elvis, in
Memphis, Tennessee, to "Liz," in Germany.*
SOURCE: *Document photocopy.*

Dear Liz,
*You have been so nice about writing and
sending packages, and I have been somewhat
negligent about it. Anyway, I appreciate
hearing from you and getting your calls and
look forward to your visit in December on
the 21th [sic]. I will see you in a few weeks
and be "Willkommen" [Welcome]. It is very
hot here. Today is the first rain we have had
here since the 20th of July.*
*Of course you know by now that American
football is a big thing in this house. I
played in high school and in the army and
have always been a big follower of the
game. Ricky [Stanley] has done better
than some of us expected but he has*

*worked awfully hard to get where he is. I
took Friday [August 12] off from "work"
and Ginger and I went up to a small
town in the middle of the state of
Tennessee. They were having a football
game and the best players from the high
school[s] of Tennessee were playing. The
best players of the West Tennessee played
the best players of the East of Tennessee. It
is what they call an All Star game. They
played Friday night in Murfreesboro, TN,
and our West beat the East 21–14. The
regular football season starts today.*
*I was pleased to receive a letter from a little
German girl [Brigitte Dietman]. She sent
me a drawing. I'm giving you her address
to let her know that I was very pleased
[Address given].*
*Looking forward to seeing you again and
hope you enjoy your stay once again and
[we] will enjoy having you.*
Until then, have a good trip. See you soon.
Elvis Presley

1977

ITEM: *Handwritten letter page by Elvis, on
"The History of the United States Flag" cover.
Signed to Tommy Kilpatrick.*
SOURCE: *Document photocopy.*
[Exact date not known.]

For Tommy Kilpatrick,
*This was given to me by a dear friend. Please
take care of it for me Tommy. Live and be
happy. Love this land of ours, defend her
name and be proud [of] her achievements.
She is ours under God and thru liberty
and freedom only as long as we fight for,
respect and keep her free.*

Love,
Elvis Presley '77

LOCATION: *Various concert appearances.*
SOURCE: Havin' Fun with Elvis on Stage *(LP).*

[Exact dates not known.]

You Ain't Nothin' but a...

You ain't nothin' but a...you don't know what I'm gonna do yet, you just think you do. I'll do just about anything. You ain't nothin' but an aardvark...bush hog...wart hog...cricket...frog...bush baby...anything, forget it.

Down to a Low Flat

I'd like you to listen to our bass singer [J. D. Sumner], on the very last line, listen to him. He goes down...he goes down to a...an "E" below low flat—whatever that is. Low flat? I never heard of that. You ever heard of that, Ronnie [Tutt]? It's on your drum. Low flat...it's a Chinese guy.

How I Got on TV

I'm sorry folks, I have those occasionally [bouts of wiggling], I can't help it. That's actually how I got in show business...by turning around. No wait a minute! No, I just did that one day. My Fruit of the Loom was too tight. And that's all there was to it. They said, "Put him on TV, hot damn."

He's Joking, of Course

On the piano is Colonel Parker.

Not Trying to Be Sexy

See people have thought for a long time that was a thing I do to be sexy and all [shake]. I'm just tryin' to stand up, that's all...brace myself.

ITEM: *Handwritten annotation on the page of a book.*
SOURCE: *Original document.*

[Exact date not known.]

God loves you, but he loves you best when you sing.

ITEM: *One handwritten page, on Las Vegas Hilton letterhead, of thoughts by Elvis.*
SOURCE: *Document photocopy.*

[Exact date not known.]

From The Infinite Way.
There is a way when we are able to rid ourselves of some sin, sickness, poverty and the results of wars and economic changes. This way is the exchanging of our material sense of existence for the understanding and consciousness of life and spiritual illumination. Illumination first brings peace then confidence and assurance. It brings rest from the world's contests and then all good flows to us

Patriotic note to a fan.

THE HISTORY OF THE
UNITED STATES FLAG

Introspective thoughts.

LAS VEGAS HILTON

LAS VEGAS, NEVADA 89114

From the Infinite Way

"There is a way whereby we are able to rid ourselves of some sin, sickness, poverty and the results of wars and economic changes. This way is the exchanging of our material sense of existence for the understanding and consciousness of life and spiritual Illumination — Illumination first brings peace, then confidence and assurance, it brings rest from the world's contests and then all good flows to us through grace. We see now that we do not live by acquiring, gaining or achieving. We live by grace. We possess all as the gift of God. We do not get our good because we already have all good — Elvis Presley

through grace. We see now that we do not
live by acquiring, gaining or achieving.
We live by grace. We possess all as the gift
of God. We do not get our good because we
already have all good.

Elvis Presley

ITEM: *Typewritten generic thank-you letter
from Elvis Presley (Memphis, Tennessee),
signed by a member of the Presley staff.*
SOURCE: *Original document.*
[Exact date not known.]

*Dear [Name of Recipient]
I would like to thank you for the
thoughtfulness you expressed in your 'Get
Well' message to me. I deeply appreciate
your concern and I can assure you that I
am doing everything I can to get well.*

Hopefully, I will be performing for my
fans in the very near future. Please accept
this short note of thanks. I just wanted you
to know that I received your message and
appreciate it more than I can express. May
God's richest blessings be bestowed upon
you and yours.

*Sincerely,
Elvis Presley*

ITEM: *Typewritten generic thank-you letter
from Elvis Presley and Col. Tom Parker (Las
Vegas, Nevada).*
SOURCE: *Original document.*
[Exact date not known.]

*Thanks for helping make this another great
Elvis Summer Festival*

Index

E

Earth News, 33
Earthquake, 97, 235
Easter, 179, 203, 234
Eastwood, Clint, 213
"Easy Part's Over," 239
Eckstine, Billy, 274
Eddy Arnold, 12
Edwards, Jim, 46, 47
Edwards, Tommy, 129
Egan, Richard, 85, 237
Eggar, Samantha, 302
El Paso, Texas, 304
Electrifying, 221
Ellington, Ann, 177, 178
Ellington, Gov. Buford, 175, 177, 178
Elliott, Mama Cass, 268, 296
Ellis Auditorium, 174
Elvie, 282
Elvis (LP), 87, 88, 96
Elvis (Speaks to You), 222
Elvis A Legendary Performer, Vol. 2, 300
Elvis A Legendary Performer, Vol. 4, 48, 49
Elvis Answers Back (magazine), 65
Elvis Answers Back, Vol. 1, 2
Elvis Answers Back, Vol. 2, 27
Elvis Army Interviews, 148, 153, 156
Elvis Aron Presley, 25, 179
Elvis As Recorded in Stereo '57, Vol. 2, 97
Elvis At Full Blast, 260
Elvis Exclusive Interview, 29
Elvis in Days Gone By, Vol. 1, 216
Elvis in Hollywood, 300
Elvis in Memphis, 221
Elvis in the Gutter, 304
Elvis Is Back, 166
Elvis On Tour, 246, 247, 248, 256, 265, 268
Elvis Presley (EP), 29
Elvis Presley (LP), 13, 27, 48, 61, 64
Elvis Presley at the Hilton, 318
Elvis Presley Boulevard, 312
Elvis Presley Enterprises, 15
Elvis Presley Fan Club, 8, 9, 86, 91
Elvis Presley Interview Record, 134
Elvis Presley Interview Record—An Audio Self-Portrait, 49, 83
Elvis Presley Mystery, 198, 199
Elvis Presley Record Player, 90
Elvis Presley Story, 91
Elvis Presley Tonight, 322
Elvis Presley Youth Center, 174
Elvis Sails, 123, 124, 125, 135
Elvis Tapes, 103
Elvis What Happened?, 305, 317

Elvis, Exclusive Live Press Conference, 168
England, 199, 200, 202, 205, 209, 210, 212, 214
Enoch, Ed, 242, 243, 300, 323
Epstein, Brian, 201
Esposito, Joe, 177, 186, 211, 226, 236, 242, 243, 244, 245, 248, 250, 251, 252, 253, 254, 276, 306, 307, 308, 309, 324
Essential '70s Masters, 226
Eternal Elvis, 3
Europe, 118, 119, 120, 126, 136, 140, 149, 160, 212, 257, 258, 262, 264
European Tour, 152
Exchange Program, 150
Exercise, 19
Eye Color, 76

F

Fabares, Shelley, 220
Face to Face with Elvis, 183
Fadal, Eddie, 116, 117
"Fairytale," 325
Falana, Lola, 319
"Fame and Fortune," 161
Fantastic Weirdos, 277
Far East, 258
Fastest Guitar Alive, 202
Favorite Color, 64
Favorite Foods, 15
Federal Narcotics Agent, 293
Ferrari, David, 325
Fetchit, Stepin, 296
"Fever," 142
Fike, Lamar, 236, 242, 249, 250, 252, 254
Finlator, John, 234
Finske, L.J., 181
Fire in Vegas, 269
Firearm Registration, 230
Firestone Orchestra, 159
"First Time Ever I Saw Your Face," 276
Fisher, Bill, 169
Flaming Star, 166, 169, 213
Flamingo, 221
Florida, 2, 46, 182
Florida State Theaters, 181
Florida Theater, 250
Foley, Red, 12, 27
Folk Music, 1
Folk Songs, 264
Follow That Dream, 181, 182, 286
Fontainbleau Hotel, 161
Fontana, D.J., 27, 39, 180, 206, 207
"Fool Such As I," 137
Football, 15, 28, 59, 113, 145, 166, 185, 326

"For Once in My Life," 290
"For the Good Times," 253
Ford, Tennessee Ernie, 176
Fort Dix, New Jersey, 158
Fort Hood, Texas, 116, 119, 121, 122, 123, 131
Fort Worth, Texas, 304
Fortas, Alan, 131, 177, 186, 206
Four Aces, 222
Fox Trot, 51
France, 244, 285
Francis, Connie, 117
Frankie and Johnny, 202
Fremont Hotel, 239
French Connection, 291
Friars Club, 143
Friedberg, Germany, 126, 129, 131, 134, 139, 148, 153
Frisby, Naomi, 325
Frizzell, Lefty, 12
From Burbank to Vegas, 209
From Introduction to Demob, 41, 153
From Sunset Blvd. to Paradise Road, 276
From the Bottom of My Heart, 143, 261
From Vegas to Macon, 229, 297
Frontier Hotel, 271
Fruit of the Loom, 327
Fun in Acapulco, 193
Funky Angels, 214
Funny Side of Elvis Presley, 270

G

G.I. Blues (film), 146, 149, 152, 154, 164, 165, 166, 215, 218, 286
G.I. Blues (LP), 166, 286
Gable, Clark, 184
Galaxy of Stars, 94, 95
Gambrell, Jerry, 55
Gardner, Hy, 41
Gargiulo, Jean-Marc, 239
Garland, Hank, 180
Garland, Judy, 50
Gator Bowl, 251
Gatorade, 228, 229, 282
Gentry, Bobbie, 271
Georgia, 251, 304
German, 119, 120
Germany, 118, 119, 120, 121, 125, 126, 127, 129, 131, 133, 134, 136, 137, 138, 139, 143, 145, 146, 147, 149, 156, 158, 159, 160, 174, 179, 214, 220
Gettysburg Address, 69
Ghanem, Dr. Elias, 279

Tupelo, Mississippi, 14, 21, 37, 67, 75, 83, 84, 174, 176, 216, 277
Turner, Major Elbert, 116
Turtle, 221
Tuscaloosa, Alabama, 297, 305
Tutt, Ronnie, 219, 253, 275, 279, 287, 327
"Tutti Frutti," 48, 90
TV Guide, 49, 51
TV Guide Presents Elvis, 41
Twentieth Century-Fox, 65, 71, 74, 81, 83, 88, 89, 138, 146, 149, 154
"Twenty Days and Twenty Nights," 228
Tyson, Lottie, 271

U

U.C.L.A., 269
U.S. Air Force, 97, 98, 158
U.S. Army, 98, 99, 107, 112, 116, 118, 119, 120, 121, 122, 123, 125, 126, 133, 134, 136, 137, 139, 140, 145, 146, 149, 150, 152, 153, 154, 155, 157, 159, 160, 161, 163, 169, 170, 172, 174, 184, 185, 186, 191, 215, 218, 220, 229, 257, 283, 285
U.S. Army Reserves, 157
U.S. Army-Air Force Postal Service, 141
U.S. Department of Justice, 234
U.S. Marines, 97, 98
U.S. Navy, 97, 98
U.S.S. Arizona, 171, 180, 266
U.S.S. Potomac, 194, 195, 196, 197, 198
U.S.S. Randall, 118, 125
Ubangi, 298
Uggams, Leslie, 272
Uncensored, 49
Union Station (Los Angeles, California), 96
Union Station (Portland, Oregon), 115
United Artists, 202
United Nations, 186
United States, 101, 138

V

Vail, Colorado, 313
Vancouver, Canada, 103, 104, 225
Vaughn, Billy, and His Orchestra, 145
Vegas Birthday Show, 276

Vegas Remembering, 319
Vegas Throat, 214
Vehicles
  '32 Roadster, 84
  Bugatti, 84
  Cadillac, 8, 41, 42, 64, 75, 84, 85, 100, 105, 120, 174, 187, 252, 301
  Chrysler, 187
  Dodge Motor Home, 187
  Dodge Truck, 11
  Lincoln, 37, 60, 75, 84, 96, 100, 120, 187
  Messerschmitt, 37, 75, 85
  Model T, 84
  Motorcycle, 11, 28, 37, 57
  Packard, 84
  Rolls Royce, 187
  Volkswagen, 187
Velvet, Jimmy, 271
Veteran's Memorial Coliseum, 250
Vincent, Gene, 47, 48
Viscount Plane, 294
Vitamin E, 256
Viva Las Vegas, 268, 303
Voice (group), 282, 293
"Volare," 122
Vulgar, 51, 101

W

Wagner, Ellery, 46
Waldorf Hotel, 32
"Walk a Mile in My Shoes," 221, 226
Walker, Charlie, 23, 25
Wallace, Don, 40
Wallace, Sgt., 131
Wallis, Hal, 18, 28, 61, 69, 75, 95, 103, 138, 154, 157, 193, 232, 233
War Protesters, 257
Ward, Billy, and Dominoes, 90
WARL, 137
Warwick Hotel, 10, 41
Washington D.C., 180, 240
Washington Hotel, 240
Water Skiing, 28
WBPM, 145
Weight, 76, 155
Weight Gain, 15
Welcome Home Elvis, 163
Welcome in Germany, 126
Wembley Empire Stadium, 214
West Texas, 2

West, Pat, 306, 311, 316, 317
West, Red, 236, 249, 250, 251, 252, 253, 254, 274, 276, 277, 278, 279, 287, 305, 306, 307, 308, 309, 310, 311, 312, 313, 314, 315, 316, 317
West, Sonny, 177, 236, 240, 250, 251, 278, 279, 287, 305, 311, 314
Western Music, 108
Westmoreland, Kathy, 268, 269, 275, 277
"What Now My Love," 317
WHBQ-TV, 34
When All Was Kool, 62, 99
"Where No One Stands Alone," 321
White Niggers, 278
White, Alan, 97
Wichita Falls, Texas, 22
Wide World of Sports, 287
Widmark, Richard, 29
Wild in the Country, 169, 178
Wild, Wild West, 269
Wildflecken, Germany, 141
Wilkinson, John, 222, 273
Williams, Bill, 88, 89
Williams, Gunter, 276
Williams, Hank, 227, 317
Wilshire Boulevard, 172
Wilson, Flip, 296, 302
Wilson, Jackie, 91
Wiman, Al, 198, 199
Witchcraft, 163
WJBK, 49
WJBS, 65
WMPS, 3, 8
WNOE, 44, 46
Wood, Anita, 109, 115, 116, 117, 123, 127, 129, 131, 141, 172
World Football League, 286
WRCA-TV, 41

Y

Yoga, 283
"You Gave Me a Mountain," 255, 288
"You'll Never Walk Alone," 120, 301
"Young Love," 12
Young, Faron, 91

Z

Zenoff, David, Justice, 312
Ziker, Dig, 302

About the Author

Aside from being an avid collector of Elvis Presley records and memorabilia for more than forty years, Jerry Osborne has also been writing and producing Elvis books since 1975. Of his seventy-five published music books, sixteen have been Elvis titles. Jerry has also published numerous Elvis periodicals and has, since 1965, been a regular contributor of Presley features in countless music publications, making him one of the longest standing in the field.

Worldwide sales of the fifteen previous Elvis titles by Osborne have exceeded 1.5 million, firmly establishing Jerry's credentials and expertise in many aspects of the impact of Elvis Presley.

In 1965, the International Elvis Presley Appreciation Society made Jerry an honorary lifetime member.

Elvis and Jerry met and became friends in 1967, a time when both men lived in Memphis, Tennessee. Jerry had been a deejay since 1962 and had already established a reputation as one of the most pro-Presley disc

jockeys in the country. He has received several plaques and awards for his efforts to advance Presley's career.

The photo of Elvis and Jerry shown above was snapped in Phoenix, Arizona, on April 22, 1973, just after Jerry presented Elvis with the Key to the City, compliments of the Phoenix mayor.

During one of Elvis' performances in Las Vegas—February 21, 1971—the King paused right in the middle of a song to introduce Jerry to the audience, then swapped scarves with him.

In August 1973, Elvis rewarded Jerry's imperishable support by personally placing one of his gold "TCB" necklaces around his neck, while ceremoniously proclaiming: "This makes it official!" Though the two exchanged other gifts and shared several visits over the years, it is this hot night in Las Vegas that is Jerry's favorite Elvis memory.

For more than two decades, when a person calls Graceland asking about Elvis collectibles, they routinely refer such calls to Jerry Osborne and to his series of Presley reference books.

Jean-Marc Gargiulo (pictured on the right in above photo) founded the Treat Me Nice Fan Club, also known as *Les Amis d'Elvis* (The Friends of Elvis), in Paris, in early 1965.

Though Gargiulo discovered Elvis Presley in July 1960, when he first heard "King Creole," he could not have known that, because of this singer, his entire life would follow a completely different course.

During the early years of the fan club, Jean-Marc kept in touch with Elvis and Colonel Parker by mail. Then came August of '69 and his first trip to America and the Las Vegas International Hotel. While there, he met Elvis backstage between shows and visited for about fifteen minutes.

Another thrilling experience that month for Jean-Marc was his being able to sit in on an afternoon rehearsal session. For about twenty minutes he watched and listened to a half-awake Elvis experimenting with some unusual songs, such as "This Is the Story" and "Without Love."

After experiencing Elvis' warm hospitality and having such an exciting time in Las Vegas, Jean-Marc and members of his club vowed to return to America. And so they have, every August since, as well as for many other Elvis concerts and, after 1977, the tribute events. Since 1978, the Fan Club has represented France at each year's I.E.T.W. in Memphis.

Over the years, Gargiulo took in more than eighty Elvis shows, the last being in Lakeland, Florida, on September 4, 1976. He even got to meet Elvis backstage again in Las Vegas, in 1971 and in '73.

Traveling so often to the States, Jean-Marc became close friends with many in the Elvis world. Among his closest are Kathy Westmoreland, D. J. Fontana, and Jerry Osborne.

The Fan Club holds a fun-filled meeting every Saturday in Paris and publishes a six-page newsletter (in French) eight times a year.

Fan Club membership is just $20 per year. For more information, contact:

Jean-Marc Gargiulo
P.O. Box 69
75961 Paris Cedex 20, France.
Phone or fax: 33 1 43 64 23 64.
(From U.S.A. dial 011 first)
e-mail: amisELVIS@wanadoo.fr
Home Page: http://perso.wanadoo.fr/elvispresley